"... and when th' moon is full and th' fog settles in th' valley, if yew lissen real clost, yew kin hear th' little ol' train a-puffin', jist like it usta, whenever it crossed th' crick and started up th' fir side of th' mountain, a-carryin' all th' folks yew usta know . . . Kindly makes a feller wonder . . ."

"Lissen! I kin hear it now . . . Cain't yew?"

The little Climax locomotive and the stubby wooden coach with the single amenity characterized the essential services of the narrow gauge Licking River Railroad in transporting passengers to and from the junction with the standard gauge Chesapeake & Ohio Railway at Salt Lick. The long pause at Yale enabled the erstwhile patrons to enjoy a spot of mountain-style socializing, while the boys and dogs of the Licking River region found the steam trains a matter of mixed awe and admiration.
                    Painting by Norman C. Miller, Jr.

ACKNOWLEDGEMENTS

More than one hundred railroaders, retired railroaders, buffs, passengers who rode the ghost routes, local historians, collectors, newspaper editors and reporters gave the author valued help. He is deeply grateful for this assistance.

Aid far beyond the traditional call of duty was rendered by the late Kincaid Herr and W. E. Quinn of the Louisville & Nashville Railroad; the late John S. Horine and L. E. Nollau of the University of Kentucky College of Engineering; and Miss Laura Armitage, Charles E. Fisher, S. P. Guthrie, C. G. Massoth, George H. Yater, and B. E. Young.

May "high green" always be with you.

Ghost Railroads of Kentucky

Elmer G. Sulzer

Indiana University Press
Bloomington and Indianapolis

This book is a publication of

Indiana University Press
601 North Morton Street
Bloomington, IN 47404-3797 USA

http://www.indiana.edu/~iupress

Telephone orders 800-842-6796
Fax orders 812-855-7931
Orders by e-mail iuporder@indiana.edu

Originally published in 1967 by Vane A. Jones Company, Publishers, Indianapolis, with a second printing, revised, in 1968; first reprinted by Indiana University Press in 1998

© 1967, 1968 by Elmer G. Sulzer

All rights reserved

No part of this book may be reproduced or utilized
in any form or by any means, electronic or mechanical,
including photocopying and recording, or by any information storage
and retrieval system, without permission in writing from the publisher.
The Association of American University Presses' Resolution on Permissions
constitutes the only exception to this prohibition.

The paper used in this publication meets the minimum
requirements of American National Standard for Information
Sciences—Permanence of Paper for Printed Library
Materials, ANSI Z39.48-1984.

Manufactured in Hong Kong

Cataloging information for this book is available from the Library of Congress.

ISBN 0-253-33484-5 (cloth)

1 2 3 4 5   03 02 01 00 99 98

TABLE OF CONTENTS

	Introduction	10
Chapter 1 —	"The Late and Early"	13
	North Winchester to Maloney (Louisville & Nashville Railroad)	
Chapter 2 —	"The Dinky"	27
	Campton Junction to Campton (Mountain Central Railway)	
Chapter 3 —	"The Riney-B"	33
	Millville to Irvine (Louisville & Nashville Railroad)	
	Heidelberg to Ida May (Louisville & Nashville Railroad)	
Chapter 4 —	"Cannel Carrier"	43
	O&K Junction to Licking River (Ohio & Kentucky Railway)	
Chapter 5 —	"Four Lumber Carriers"	51
	A. Kings Mountain to Yosemite (Cincinnati & Green River Railway)	
	B. KN Junction to Simcoe (Kentucky Northern Railroad)	
	C. Caryton to Turkey Foot (Kentucky, Rockcastle & Cumberland Railroad)	
	D. Lombard or Nada to Big Woods (Big Woods, Red River & Lombard Railroad)	
Chapter 6 —	"Two Southern Segments"	57
	A. Versailles to Georgetown (Southern Railway System)	
	B. Burgin Junction to Burgin (Southern Railway System)	
Chapter 7 —	"Back in the Menifee Hills"	63
	A. Mt. Sterling to Rothwell (Chesapeake & Ohio Railway)	
	B. Rothwell to McCausey and Apperson (Red River Valley Railroad)	
Chapter 8 —	"The Route of 'Old Henry'"	71
	Lancaster to Fort Estill (Louisville & Nashville Railroad)	

Chapter 9 — "One Track — Two Railroads" 73
    A. Salt Lick to Blackwater (LICKING RIVER RAILROAD)
    B. Olympia to Owingsville (OWINGSVILLE & OLYMPIA RAILROAD)

Chapter 10 — "Two Northern Kentucky Abandonments" . . 81
    A. Brooksville to Wellsburg (BROOKSVILLE & OHIO RIVER RAILROAD)
    B. Hillsboro to Flemingsburg Junction (CINCINNATI, FLEMINGSBURG & SOUTHEASTERN RAILROAD; AND FLEMINGSBURG & NORTHERN RAILROAD)

Chapter 11 — "The 'Kinney' Branch" 89
    Garrison to Gesling (CHESAPEAKE & OHIO RAILWAY)

Chapter 12 — "Commuters' Narrow Gauge" . . . 93
    Water Works to Prospect (LOUISVILLE & INTERURBAN RAILROAD)

Chapter 13 — "Up North Fork Way" 101
    A. Clack Mountain Tunnel to Redwine (MOREHEAD & NORTH FORK RAILROAD)
    B. Redwine to Rush Branch (LENOX RAILROAD)
    C. Five Shorties:
        i. Lawton Junction to Brinegar (PORTSMOUTH & TYGERT VALLEY RAILROAD)
        ii. Rodburn to Pine Springs (KENTUCKY NORTHERN RAILROAD)
        iii. Limestone to timber (PANTHER GAP RAILROAD)
        iv. Rodburn to timber (TRIPLETT & BIG SANDY RAILROAD)
        v. Rodburn to clay mines ("CHRISTY CREEK RAILROAD")

Chapter 14 — "In the Pennyrile" 113
    A. Russellville to Adairville (LOUISVILLE & NASHVILLE RAILROAD)
    B. Gracey to Princeton Junction (LOUISVILLE & NASHVILLE RAILROAD)
    C. Elkton to Guthrie (ELKTON & GUTHRIE RAILROAD)

Chapter 15 — "Phantom Rails of Southeastern Kentucky" . 123
    A. Rockcastle Route:
        i. Altamont and East Bernstadt to Viva (LOUISVILLE & NASHVILLE RAILROAD)
        ii. Viva to McKee (ROCKCASTLE RIVER RAILWAY, AND BOND-FOLEY LUMBER COMPANY RAILROAD)
    B. Short Shifts:
        i. Burnside Junction to Burnside Landing (CINCINNATI, BURNSIDE & CUMBERLAND RIVER RAILWAY)
        ii. Jellico to Halsey (JELLICO, BIRDEYE & NORTHERN RAILWAY)
        iii. Greenwood to Beaver mine (GREENWOOD RAILWAY & COAL COMPANY)
        iv. Honorable Mentions

Chapter 16 — "In Breckinridge, Ohio, and Hancock" . . . 133
    A. Irvington to Hartford (LOUISVILLE & NASHVILLE RAILROAD)
    B. Cloverport to Victoria (BRECKINRIDGE COAL ROAD)

Chapter 17 — "Memory Routes of Eastern Kentucky" . . 139
    A. Riverton to Webbville (EASTERN KENTUCKY RAILWAY)
    B. Walbridge to Richardson via Peach Orchard (CHESAPEAKE & OHIO RAILWAY)
    C. "Streaks of Rust"

Chapter 18 — "Western Coal Field Lines of the Past" . . . *149*
    A. Clay to Morganfield (LOUISVILLE & NASHVILLE RAILROAD)
    B. Clay to Dixon (ILLINOIS CENTRAL RAILROAD)
    C. Henderson to McClain (ILLINOIS CENTRAL RAILROAD)
    D. "Work Extras"

Chapter 19 — "Three Jackson Purchase Odyssies" . . . *157*
    A. Mississippi Odyssey (RAILROADS OF COLUMBUS)
    B. Obion Odyssey—Hickman to Union City (NASHVILLE, CHATTANOOGA & ST. LOUIS RAILWAY)
    C. Bayou Odyssey—Barlow to East Cairo (ILLINOIS CENTRAL RAILROAD)

Chapter 20 — "A Thoroughbred, A Workhorse and Two Old Sires" . . . *167*
    A. The Death of a Thoroughbred—Chicle to Paris (LOUISVILLE & NASHVILLE RAILROAD)
    B. A Workhorse Expires—Shelbyville to Bloomfield (LOUISVILLE & NASHVILLE RAILROAD)
    C. Mention of Two Old Sires
    D. And a Patriarch Breathes its Last—LaGrange to Eminence (LOUISVILLE & NASHVILLE RAILROAD)

Chapter 21 — "Gay 'Nineties Rendezvous" . . . *195*
    Glasgow Junction to Mammoth Cave (MAMMOTH CAVE RAILROAD)

Chapter 22 — "Black Diamond Routes in Knox and McCreary" . *203*
    A. Artemus to Wheeler and Anchor (ARTEMUS-JELLICO RAILROAD)
    B. White Oak Junction to Bell Farm and Oz to Co-Operative (KENTUCKY & TENNESSEE RAILWAY)

Chapter 23 — "The Whiskey Route" . . . *225*
    Georgetown to Paris (FRANKFORT & CINCINNATI RAILROAD)

"Kentucky's Modern Railroads for the Future" . . . *233*

Bibliography . . . *242*

Appendix 1 — Locomotive Rosters of the Ghost Lines . . . *244*

Appendix 2 — Chronology and Mileage Table of Abandonments . *250*

Appendix 3 — Abandoned Railroads by Counties . . . *252*

Appendix 4 — Kentucky's Abandoned Narrow Gauge Railroads . *253*

Appendix 5 — Abandoned Mileages by Trunk-Line Systems . . *253*

Appendix 6 — Index and Cross-References of Abandoned Line Names . *254*

INTRODUCTION

THE BACKGROUND OF STEAM RAILROAD ABANDONMENTS IN KENTUCKY

Four reasons are generally presented to explain the causes of railroad abandonments. They are (a) the exhaustion of natural resources, (b) relocation or cessation of industries, (c) highway competition, and (d) the "rationalization of the railroad plant."

In Kentucky, in fact in many parts of the Ohio and Mississippi River valleys, another reason might be presented, namely the decline of the rivers as important arteries of commerce. And this decline, brought about by the superior capabilities of the railroad, actually led to abandonment of many early trackages.

Without exception, the first Kentucky railroads were constructed as auxiliaries to the traffic troughs of the Ohio and Mississippi rivers. The pioneer Lexington & Ohio Railroad started its sinuous course to Louisville to intercept and benefit by the river traffic centering on that town. The main stem of the L&N RR was built from Louisville south for similar reasons. The Mobile & Ohio was planned to extend north from Mobile, Alabama, to some point on the Mississippi or Ohio rivers in the vicinity of Cairo, Illinois, to divert the river traffic flowing into the port of New Orleans; and Columbus, Kentucky, became the northern terminal.

Numerous Kentucky short lines, conceived before connections with a railroad network were possible, were built to the rivers to take and deliver traffic from and to the water carriers. Such lines included the Ashland Coal and Iron Railway, the Eastern Kentucky Railway, the Breckinridge Coal Road, the DeKoven Coal Road, and the Hickman & Obion Railroad.

Today, all of these pioneer railroads built as tributaries to the river traffic have suffered one of two fates: they have either been incorporated into longer lines of main track, or they have been abandoned. The Ashland Coal and Iron Railway is now part of the Lexington-Ashland line of the C&O Railway. The Lexington & Ohio constitutes one of the crookedest portions of the Louisville-Lexington section of the L&N, and the original line of the Louisville & Nashville running between the cities so-named is a part of that system's main stem.

Columbus, Kentucky, was later by-passed by the Mobile & Ohio, now the GM&O RR, in favor of a more direct route to Cairo and St. Louis, and eventually the short stub track into Columbus, itself, was abandoned. The line of the Hickman & Obion, later to become part of the main line (in name only) of the NC&StL Ry, was abandoned from the river port of Hickman back to Union City, Tennessee. And the other short lines to the river—the Eastern Kentucky, the Breckinridge Coal Road, and the DeKoven Coal Road—are all phantoms of the past.

Generally speaking, however, three of the more conventional reasons account for virtually all of Kentucky's railroad abandonments. They are (a) exhaustion of natural resources, (b) highway competition, and (c) rationalization of railroad plant. In some cases, a combination of these factors has been present. A fourth reason, relocation or cessation of industry, prominent as a reason for abandonments in some parts of the United States, has been a minor factor in Kentucky abandonments, if we classify a few apparent cases as due to the exhaustion of natural resources on which such industries were built. For example, many of Kentucky's old timber railroads served lumber mills, but these mills were always predicated on the timber resources of the surrounding regions. Hence, the abandonment of such railroads is classified herein as due to exhaustion of natural resources, rather than relocation or cessation of industry.

Kentucky abandonments, chargeable to exhaustion of natural resources, include lines built primarily to bring logs into a lumber mill and then move the milled lumber to the outside world, such as the Licking River Railroad; lines constructed to tap cannel coal deposits, for example, the Ohio & Kentucky Railway; railroads built to bring out deposits of clay, such as the Portsmouth & Tygert Valley Railroad; and trackage laid down to transport bituminous coal, exemplified by the Artemus-Jellico Railroad. In recent years, abandonments of lines serving bituminous mines have not always been due to the exhaustion of natural resources. The depressed state of the coal industry has made coal mining so unprofitable in some cases that mines have closed before their deposits were exhausted; then the railroads, depending entirely on such operations, had to go. An example is the abandonment of the Kentucky & Tennessee Railway's line to Co-Operative, where a large mine with sizable coal deposits still in the ground was forced to close for economic reasons.

In a few cases, the poor quality of a natural resource has doomed a rail line. The Eastern Kentucky Railway, originally built to exploit the iron resources in the Kentucky portion of the "Hanging Rock" area, became unprofitable almost from the start as the substandard qualities of the Carter County ore deposits became evident.

The competition of highway vehicles, making its first inroads in the early 20's, became a compelling factor during the 30's. Most of the trackage rendered unprofitable by the age of gasoline were branch lines serving relatively small communities, whose construction was justified at one time, but whose utility became later a matter of serious question. Both parts of trunk line systems and short independent lines became ghost trackage for these reasons. The Shelbyville-Bloomfield line of the L&N and the Versailles-Georgetown segment of the Southern were quite as hopeless from this point of view as the Brooksville & Ohio River Railroad and the famous Mammoth Cave Railroad traversed by the dummy locomotive "Hercules."

An important reason for abandonment, the rationalization of the railroad plant, constitutes a factor frequently not appreciated in the abandonment picture. In Kentucky, this has accounted for many miles of abandonment. The L&N Railroad, in its desire to have a heavy duty, low grade line to the Hazard coal fields, was compelled to construct its own trackage from Winchester to Irvine. Upon the completion of this segment, duplicate but light duty main lines, heading in the same direction between North Winchester and Maloney, and between Frankfort and Irvine, became superfluous and their respective dooms were sealed as their value for main line movements vanished. Similarly, when L&N passenger service between Lexington and Cincinnati, Ohio, became a thing of the past, the utility of the Chicle-Paris line for freight became negligible, as a duplicate although slightly longer, route existed by way of Winchester.

It is probably a gratuitous comment to make today, but there were a few miles of Kentucky railroad that were so poorly constructed, so inadequately financed, and so uneconomically situated, that they should never have been built. A typical example was the short-lived, narrow gauge Owingsville & Olympia.

As an optimistic note, it should be stated that as yet there have been no abandonments of basic trunk line trackage in Kentucky. In a few cases, however, important through routes have been severed. Examples are the breaking of the L&N's Cincinnati-Lexington route by the Chicle-Paris abandonment, already referred to; or the breaking of the Illinois Central's Paducah-Cairo line by the Barlow-East Cairo abandonment.

In summary, 1,088.16 miles of main line trackage have been abandoned. On the basis of decades, Kentucky's maximum mileage was 4,055 in 1930. To obtain Kentucky's all-time mileage there should be added to this figure 416.72 miles abandoned before 1930 as well as somewhat less than 200 miles built since 1930.

Rounding off these various figures then, approximately 1,000 miles of the all-time high of 4,600 miles have been abandoned, or, to put it another way, almost 22%. Eleven Kentucky county seats and eight Kentucky counties, formerly having railroads, are now completely without such facilities.

Kentucky abandonments by years and decades, follow:

Years	Abandoned in Year	Decade	Years	Abandoned in Year	Decade	Years	Abandoned in Year	Decade
1848	6.00	6.00	1912	32.30		1940	16.74	356.07
1856	3.00	3.00	1914	4.34		1941	80.53	
1890	2.00	2.00	1916	14.85		1942	47.55	
1891	4.75		1918	7.75	74.24	1943	9.03	
1892	12.30		1923	73.13		1944	1.00	
1893	24.50		1926	23.01		1945	2.70	
1894	5.00		1927	7.70		1946	12.00	
1895	8.00		1928	15.41		1947	8.56	
1896	13.00		1929	4.11		1948	15.52	
1897	12.08		1930	3.00	126.36	1950	4.33	181.22
1898	8.50		1931	52.89		1951	23.18	
1899	2.50		1932	87.56		1952	38.80	
1900	9.00	99.63	1933	99.53		1953	2.41	
1901	4.50		1934	30.95		1954	2.16	
1907	14.50		1935	18.68		1955	5.60	
1908	23.25		1936	10.40		1957	10.95	
1909	61.75		1937	2.08		1960	11.85	94.95
1910	4.49	108.49	1938	16.57		1964	19.50	19.50
1911	15.00		1939	20.65		1967	16.70	36.20

Total Mileage Abandoned 1,088.16

SCOPE OF VOLUME

Detailed or brief notices are presented on—
  (1) standard and/or narrow gauge railroads which maintained common carrier service, with or without the blessing of the Interstate Commerce Commission, and
  (2) all Kentucky abandonments coming to the attention of the ICC since that body was empowered to pass on applications for abandonments.

Not included are—
  (1) electric lines never having a history of steam operation in their pasts,
  (2) abandonments due to track relocations within the same segments, and
  (3) short industrial spurs.

CHAPTER 1
"The Late and Early"
North Winchester to Maloney
(Louisville & Nashville Railroad)

The Kentucky Union Railway was incorporated in 1872, primarily to reach coal and timber resources in southeastern Kentucky. Construction started in 1886 and during the same year the 14.7 miles between Kentucky Union (now L&E) Junction and Clay City were completed. The line was extended west to Lexington in 1890, east to Jackson in 1891, for a total of 92 miles.

The KU Railway was placed in receivership in 1891. On October 16, 1894, it was reorganized as the Lexington & Eastern Railway. In November, 1910, the Louisville & Nashville Railroad purchased the entire capital stock of the L&E and proceeded with its plans to extend the line approximately 100 miles from Dumont (near Jackson) to McRoberts at the headwaters of the North Fork of the Kentucky River and close to the Virginia state line. This was to be the L&N's route to the promising coal fields of southeastern Kentucky.

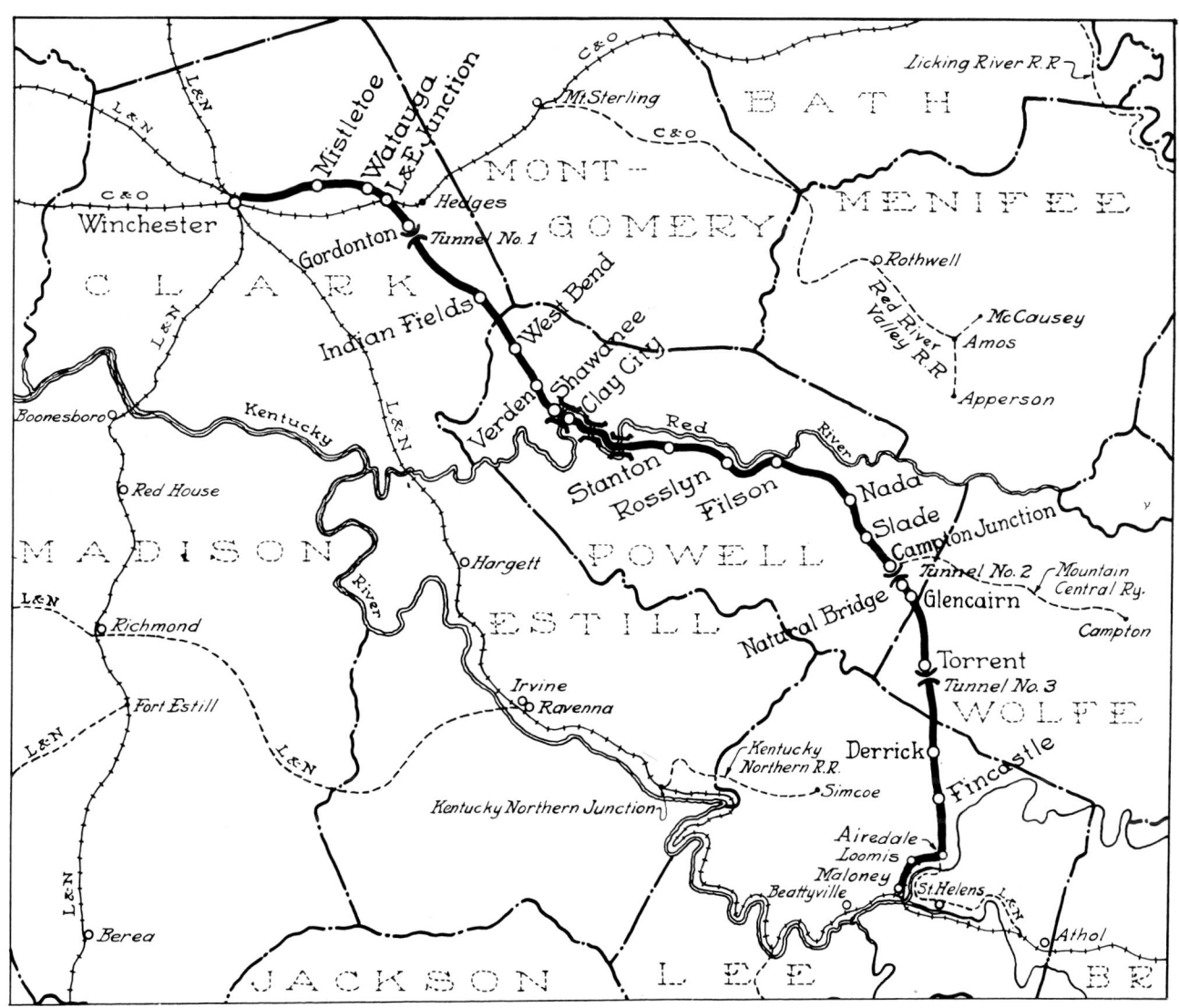

However, the grades and tunnels between Winchester and Maloney made the use of this segment as a heavy hauling coal line impractical. A new route was completed in 1916 between Winchester and Irvine. Traffic between Winchester and Maloney became less and less, and losses for the L&N mounted. In 1942 the 46.6 mile portion between North Winchester and Fincastle was abandoned; in the latter part of 1947, permission was given by the Interstate Commerce Commission to abandon the final six miles between Fincastle and Maloney.

Kentucky Union Railway's No. 10, a 2-6-0 (Baldwin 10410) built in 1889. After this locomotive became L&N's No. 459 it was used for a number of years in passenger transfer service between Latonia, Kentucky, and the old Central Union Depot in Cincinnati, Ohio. In the background are the Clay City engine house and shops.   L&N RR.

Rolling stock on the Kentucky Union included 7 locomotives, 5 passenger cars, 2 baggage cars, an officers' car, 130 box cars (100 of them leased), 65 gondolas, 24 construction cars, 2 boarding cars, and several cabooses.   Richard Hardin

The Lexington & Eastern owned eight Baldwin-built consols. Here is No. 24 with a north-bound freight at the Jackson station.   Ray Alford

In the picture at the right L&E No. 26 is pulling the first solid train of cannel coal to pass over the railroad. Lulbegrud Creek. Time about 1905.   L&N RR.

Opposite Page—Examples of wooden freight rolling stock of the Lexington & Eastern. All three pictures from Richard Hardin.

It is interesting to note that the passenger tariff below lists not only points on the L&ERY but also includes the rates to points on the connecting Ohio & Kentucky Railway.   Ray Alford

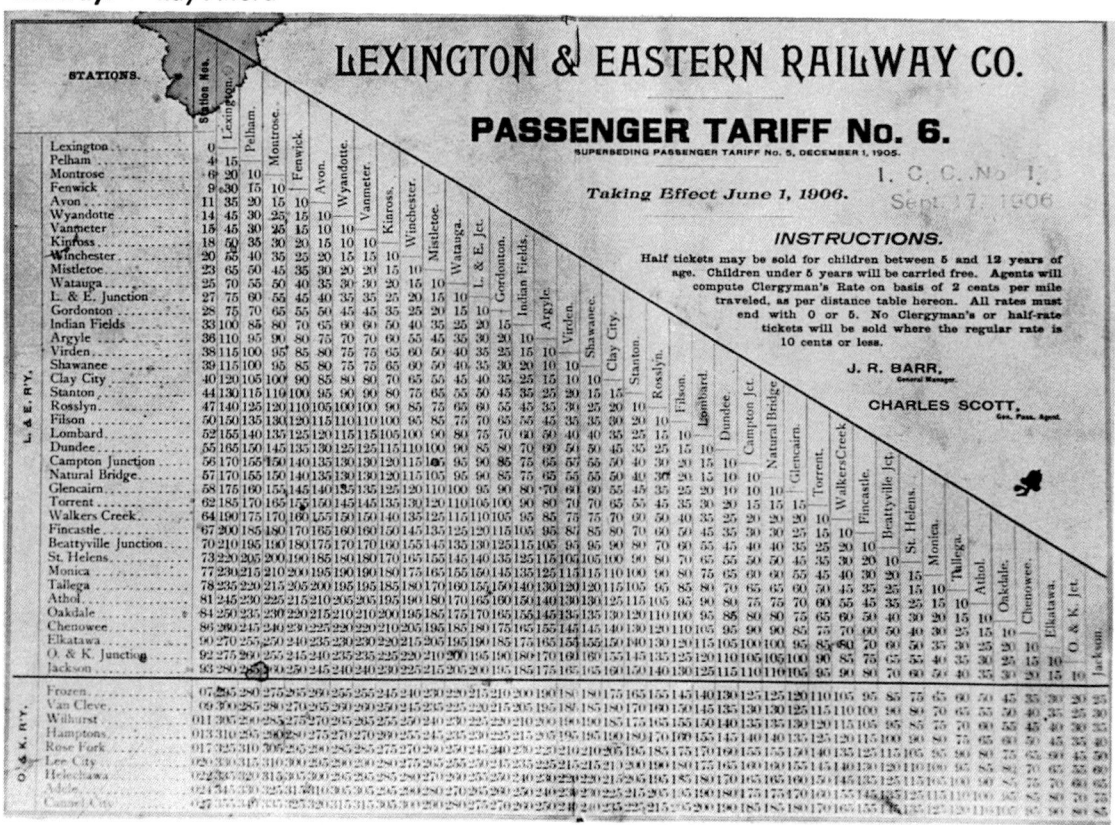

During the early part of the century, much of the important business of the L&E originated with feeder lines. The Ohio & Kentucky Railway (See Chapter 4) made a junction with the L&E 1.37 miles west of Jackson. It was completed in 1901 and operated by the L&E under contract until July 1, 1904. Solid trains of cannel coal from this source were hauled to Winchester or Lexington. In 1920 almost 175,000 tons of this commodity moved from the O&K to the L&E.

Two narrow gauge railroads whose principal business was the transportation of timber and lumber, added their bit. The Mountain Central Railway (See Chapter 2) joined the L&E at Campton Junction, and the Big Woods, Red River & Lombard's rails met those of the L&E at Nada. At Maloney logs of hemlock and pine, rafted down the Kentucky River, were loaded in flat cars and moved to a lumber mill at Clay City.

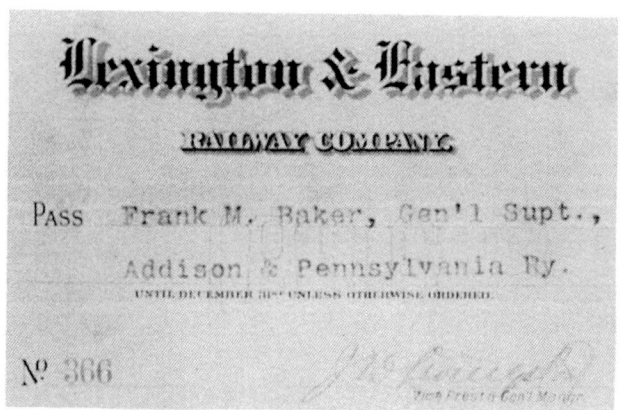

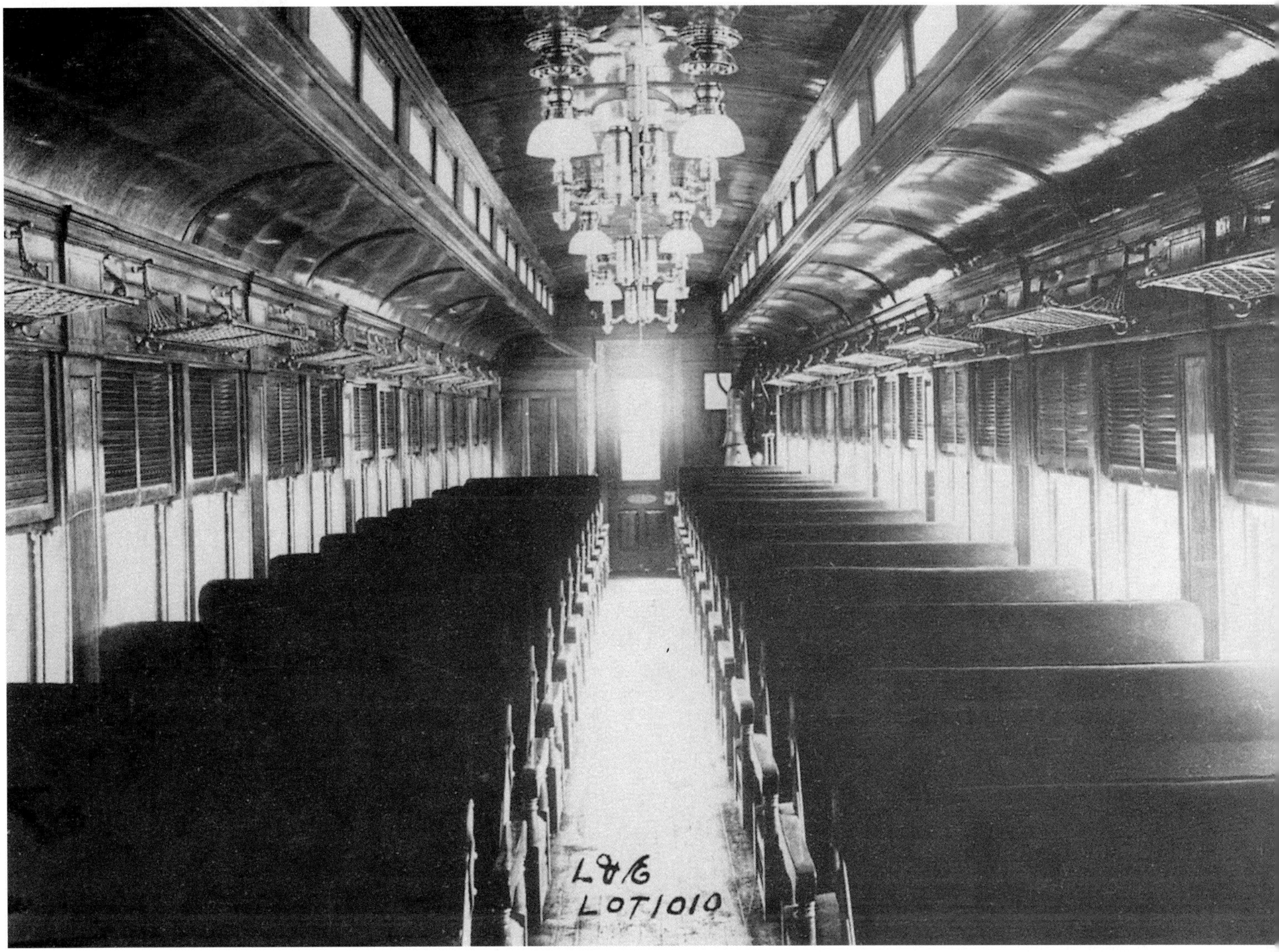

Passenger service was an important function of the Lexington & Eastern Railway. Roads in the foothills of the Kentucky mountains served by the L&E were primitive or nonexistent. Automobiles were scarce. Prior to the coming of the railroad, principal travel was on muleback for both humans and mail.

But the Kentucky Union and its successor, the Lexington & Eastern, changed all this. Now, Lexington and other flatland cities were only hours away. And the wooden coaches with their plush seats, pintsch gas illumination, wooden blinds, and indoor plumbing were the last word in luxury.

At least two passenger trains daily ran the length of the line. Working mail cars were attached to these trains, and Adams Express provided an additional service.

All four pictures from Richard Hardin.

The 725' tunnel just to the north of Natural Bridge Station was one of three on the North Winchester-Maloney segment, the others being located at Gordonton (250') and Torrent (1,110'). Roof heights of these bores ranged from 16'10" to 18'3", thus creating permanent bottlenecks for high loads. S. P. Guthrie

Natural Bridge was an outstanding scenic attraction of Eastern Kentucky long before the days of highway travel. Inherited from the Lexington & Eastern Railway, the Louisville & Nashville developed an extensive Sunday excursion business to the Park. Although the popularity of such trains reached its heydey around 1915, they were operated until 1925 or '26.

Every Sunday during the summer, excursion movements of ten to fourteen cars were run to Natural Bridge from Cincinnati. Other specials came from Hazard. Extra cars were added to regular trains from Lexington and other points.

In those days there were no hotel accommodations at Natural Bridge, and travelers wishing to spend the night were advised to go on five miles more to Torrent where almost a hundred guests could be accommodated.

Opposite Page—Natural Bridge Station, 1925 or '26. L&N RR.

SPECIAL SUNDAY ROUND-TRIP FARES
Lexington to Natural Bridge, Ky., and Return.

DATES OF SALE
Sundays—
July 23, 1916
August 6 and 20, 1916
September 3 and 17, 1916
October 1 and 15, 1916
Round-Trip Fare $1.00

DATES OF SALE
Sundays—
July 30, 1916
August 13 and 27, 1916
Sept. 10 and 24, 1916
Oct. 8, 22 and 29, 1916
Round-Trip Fare $1.25

On week days, until September 30, 1916, round-trip rate of $1.00 per capita for parties of 50, or more, will be made.

Special train will be operated for parties of 100, or more.

Go to Natural Bridge, one of the prettiest spots in Kentucky.

For tickets or other information, apply at City Ticket Office, Louisville & Nashville R. R., 129 East Main Street.

B. S. YENT, City Ticket Agent   F. B. CARR, General Agent
E. J. TEED, Depot Ticket Agent   W. H. HARRISON, Trav. Pass. Agent

Ray Alford

Track scene at the north end of Campton Junction. S. P. Guthrie

Four views of L&N No. 7 (southbound) and No. 8 (northbound), 1941. This mixed train constituted the last remnant of service on the once busy trackage. Scene at left is at Natural Bridge Station. Below, No. 7 is turning on the wye at Maloney. L&N RR

Top, No. 8 is halted at Clay City. Below, a passenger has just left the mixed train near Nada, a picturesque spot in the Kentucky foothills.   L&N RR.

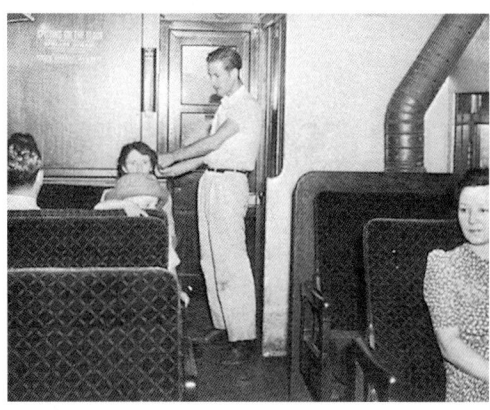

The conductor and brakeman, uninhibited by uniform, diligently attended to the wants of their passengers. Some of the younger mothers made it a practice to seat their entire families (minus husbands) in a single seat. The conductor would arrange for lunches at Clay City to satisfy the wants of hungry passengers. And a white flag hung out the coach window was the signal to the engineer to stop at the next likely point.

All photos L&N RR

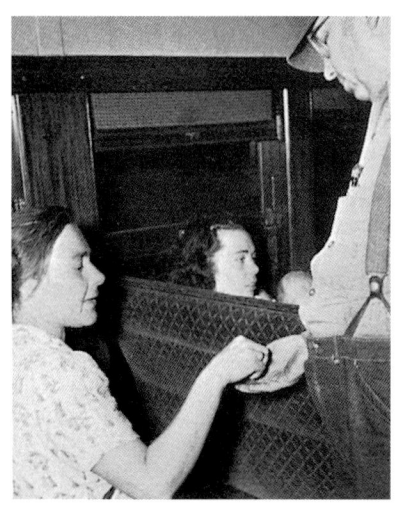

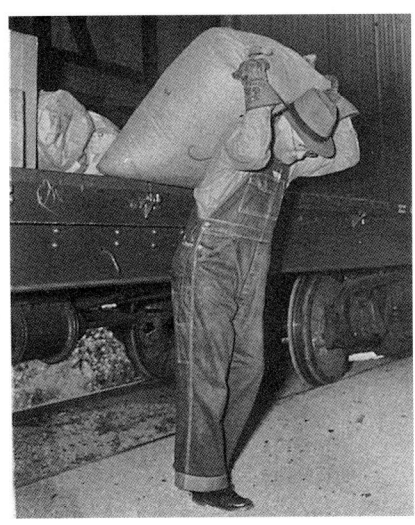  

The mixed runs, Nos. 7 and 8, required crews that combined muscles with native intelligence. An average trip required the toting of feed sacks, wrestling with milk cans and bottled gas, and distributing other LCL items at points unmarked by timetable. The latter-day schedules permitted ample time for the engine crews to douse the running gear with oil and make light running repairs far removed from a terminal.

All photos L&N RR

Kentucky Union Railway Company.

No. 6. TIME TABLE. No. 6.

Taking Effect at 5:30 A. M., September 22d, 1889.   Trains Run on [90th Meridian] Standard Time.

For the Guidance and Information of Employes Only.

EAST BOUND TRAINS					TIME TABLE NO. 6.	WEST BOUND TRAINS				
SECOND CLASS	FIRST CLASS					FIRST CLASS			SECOND CLASS	
NO. 9 Local Freight	NO. 7 Passenger	NO. 5 Passenger	NO. 3 Passenger	NO. 1 Passenger	STATIONS	NO. 2 Passenger	NO. 4 Passenger	NO. 6 Passenger	NO. 8 Passenger	NO. 10 Local Freight
Daily ex Sunday	Sunday Only	Sunday Only	Daily ex Sunday	Daily ex Sunday		Daily ex Sunday	Daily ex Sunday	Sunday Only	Sunday Only	Daily ex Sunday
LEAVE 2 00 pm	LEAVE 1 30 pm	LEAVE 3 30 pm	LEAVE 8 30 am		WINCHESTER (W T)	ARRIVE 3 00 pm	ARRIVE 7 00 am	ARRIVE 9 50 am		ARRIVE 11 55 am
2 14 pm	1 37 pm	3 36 pm	8 36 am	2.8	ECTON (F)	2 53 pm	6 52 am	9 43 am		11 40 am
2 22 pm	1 42 pm	3 42 pm	8 42 am	5.4	CLARION (F)	2 45 pm	6 45 am	9 38 am		11 27 am
Ar 2 30 pm Lv 3 15 pm	1 45 pm	3 45 pm	8 45 am	6.4	DODGE (S T)	2 40 pm	6 40 am	9 32 am		Lv 11 20 am Ar 10 40 am
3 45 pm	2 05 pm	4 05 pm	9 05 am	12.4	INDIAN FIELDS (S)	2 15 pm	6 17 am	9 14 am		10 10 am
4 15 pm	2 20 pm	4 21 pm	9 21 am	17.7	VERDEN (F)	2 06 pm	6 07 am	8 57 am		9 30 am
Ar 4 45 pm Lv 5 00 pm	LEAVE 2 27 pm	4 30 pm	9 30 am	20.0	CLAY CITY (S W T)	Lv 2 00 pm Ar 1 45 pm	Lv 6 00 am Ar 6 20 pm	8 50 am	ARRIVE 4 30 pm	Lv 9 30 am Ar 8 30 am
6 10 pm	2 37 pm	4 40 pm	9 36 am	23.8	STANTON (S T)	1 00 pm	6 10 pm	8 37 am	4 17 pm	8 10 am
6 25 pm	2 44 pm	4 47 pm	9 46 am	26.4	CAT CREEK (F)	12 47 pm	5 59 am	8 29 am	4 05 pm	7 55 am
6 37 pm	2 55 pm	4 58 pm	10 10 am	29.3	BOWEN (S F)	12 35 pm	5 52 am	8 15 am	3 50 pm	7 30 am
6 50 pm ARRIVE	3 10 pm ARRIVE	5 08 pm ARRIVE	10 30 am ARRIVE	34.2	SLADE (T)	12 15 pm	5 30 am	8 00 am	3 45 pm LEAVE	7 15 am LEAVE

SPECIAL INSTRUCTIONS.

All regular East Bound trains have the right of track over trains of the same or inferior class moving in the opposite direction when running in accordance with General Rule No. 84. In case of doubt take the safe side.
A train of inferior class must in all cases keep out of the way of a train of superior class.

GEORGE DOLE WADLEY, Gen. Manager. T. B. SLADE, Superintendent. W. F. PACKARD, Master of Transportation.

BETWEEN NORTH CABIN AND MALONEY

SOUTH BOUND					TIME TABLE No. 57						NORTH BOUND
SECOND CLASS	FIRST CLASS				In Effect Sunday, October 5, 1930, at 12:01 a.m.			FIRST CLASS			SECOND CLASS
181 Mixed Daily ex. Sunday	307 Passenger Sunday only	7 Passenger Daily ex. Sunday			STATIONS			8 Passenger Daily ex. Sunday	308 Passenger Sunday only		182 Mixed Daily ex. Sunday
7.04 am	8.50 am	7.40 am			NORTH CABIN			6.05 pm	6.05 pm		10.45 am
7.08	8.51	7.42			NORTH WINCHESTER			6.01	6.01		10.35
7.25	8.57	7.48			MISTLETOE			5.58	5.58		10.20
7.55	9.05	7.55			L. & E. JUNCTION			5.45	5.45		10.05
8.50	9.31	8.10			INDIAN FIELDS			5.29	5.29		10.00
9.15	9.55	8.36			CLAY CITY			5.11	5.11		9.15
9.30	9.47	8.38			STANTON			5.01	5.01		9.00
9.40	9.54	8.46			ROSSLYN			4.55	4.55		8.40
10.00	9.59	8.48			FILSON			4.40	4.40		8.20
10.20	10.12	9.01			SLADE			4.37	4.37		8.00
10.52	10.18	9.06			CAMPTON JUNCTION			4.33	4.33		7.50
10.57	10.20	9.07			NATURAL BRIDGE			4.28	4.28		7.45
11.05	10.32	9.09			GLENCAIRN			4.20	4.20		7.40
11.15	10.38	9.17			TORRENT			4.21	4.21		7.35
11.45	10.47	9.29			FINCASTLE			4.06	4.06		7.20
12.12 pm	11.05 am	9.42 am			MALONEY			3.50 pm	3.50 pm		6.40 am
Daily ex. Sunday 181	Sunday only 307	Daily ex. Sunday 7						Daily ex. Sunday 8	Sunday only 308		Daily ex. Sunday 182

NORTH CABIN AND MALONEY

Southward				WINCHESTER AND MALONEY BRANCH			Northward
FIRST CLASS				TIME TABLE No. 91. Takes effect Saturday, May 2, 1942, at 12:01 p.m.			FIRST CLASS
	7 Mixed Daily ex. Sunday A.M.	Distance from Lexington		STATIONS	Car Capacity of Passing Sidings based on 42 feet per car	8 Mixed Daily ex. Sunday P.M.	
	11.20	21.2	L	NORTH CABIN E A	35	5.13	
	s11.23	21.8		0.6 NORTH WINCHESTER	63	f 5.11	
	f11.33	24.7		2.9 MISTLETOE		f 5.02	
	f11.43	28.3		3.6 L. & E. JUNCTION	8	f 4.52	
	f12.03	34.8		6.5 INDIAN FIELDS		f 4.34	
	s12.23	41.8		7.0 CLAY CITY	24	f 4.14	
	s12.39	45.9		4.1 STANTON	8	f 4.02	
	f12.49	48.2		2.3 ROSSLYN	40	f 3.56	
	f12.59	51.4		3.2 FILSON	10	f 3.48	
	f 1.14	56.6		5.2 SLADE E	10	f 3.33	
	f 1.24	58.8		2.2 NATURAL BRIDGE E	14	f 3.27	
	f 1.27	59.8		1.0 GLENCAIRN E		f 3.24	
	f 1.39	63.5		3.7 TORRENT E	32	f 3.12	
	f 1.55	68.7		5.2 FINCASTLE N C E	8	f 2.52	
	s 2.20	74.5	A	5.8 MALONEY E L		s 2.35	
	P.M. Daily ex. Sunday 7					P.M. Daily ex. Sunday 8	

Regular southward trains are superior to trains of the same class moving in the opposite direction.

Employees' timetables for 1889, 1930 and 1942.   L&N RR

CHAPTER 2
"The Dinky"
Campton Junction to Campton
(Mountain Central Railway)

It was a memorable day in Campton, the fall of 1907. Word had been passed around that the first train was due to arrive, and from far and near, coming by horseback, muleback, wagon and foot, a large crowd of people had collected. Many had never seen a train, and they were on hand hours before the scheduled arrival of the "express." A dinner and speeches of welcome had been arranged by Floyd Day, the builder and owner of the railroad, for the coming of the iron horse was to mean great things to Campton and her people. It meant a means of egress to the outside world, heretofore denied them during the winter months. It meant the availability of luxuries that they had never been able to enjoy before. It even meant receiving the mail on time *and daily*.

One old lady who had never seen a train and who had ridden miles on an old yellow mule to see "Floyd Day's train" was among the spectators. At last, when the train arrived, she could scarcely restrain her surprise, and immediately asked "Did it come all the way from Campton Junction this marnin' pullin' them cars?" When informed that it had, she sympathetically patted the engine and exclaimed "Poor thing, I know its tard."

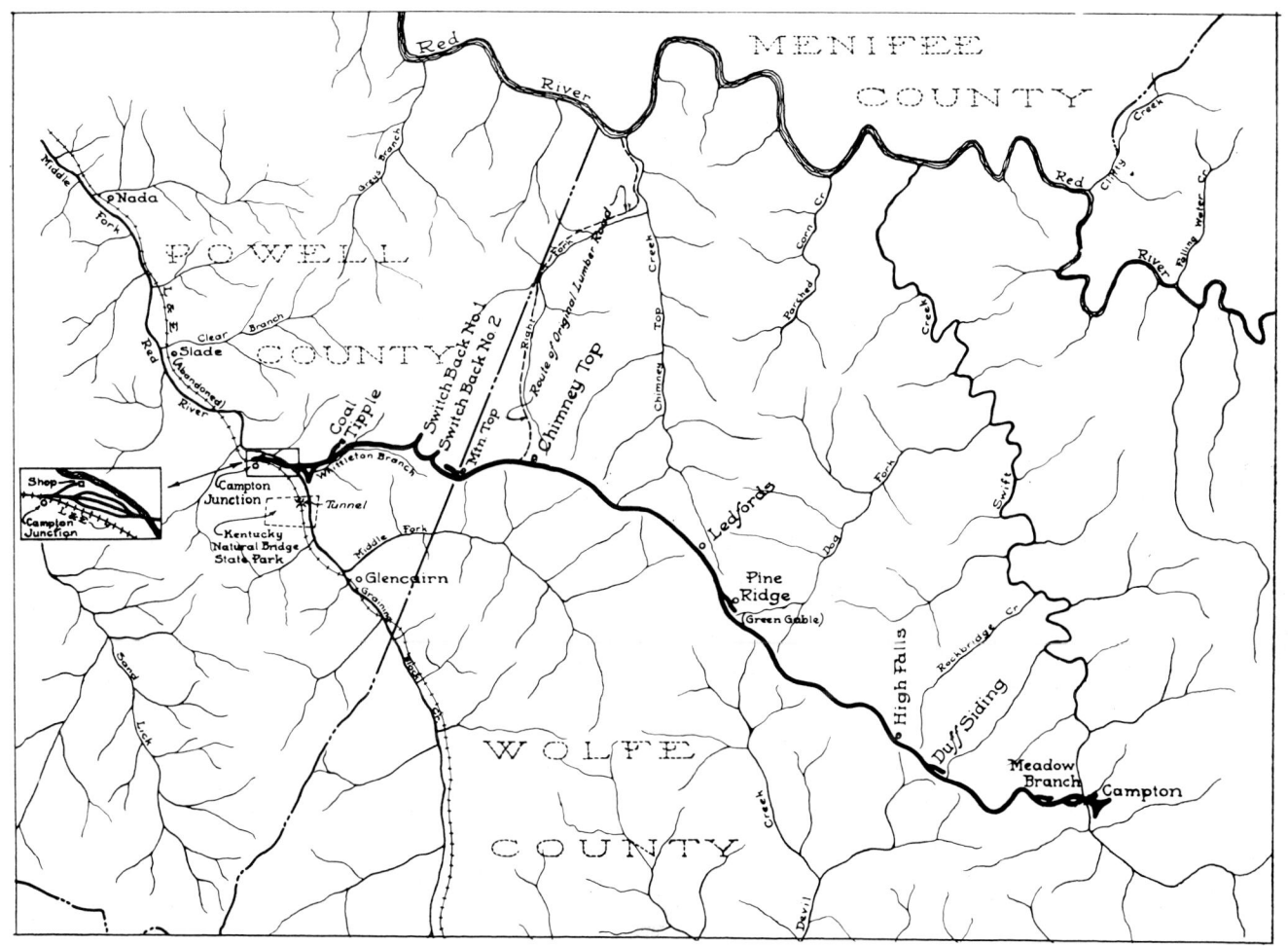

One of the two precarious switchbacks in the ascent to Mountain Top.   S. P. Guthrie

The 12 mile, narrow gauge (36") Mountain Central Railway was the creation of the Swan-Day Lumber Company which owned a large sawmill at Clay City on the Lexington & Eastern. Originally a logging road, it ascended the mountain top east of the Junction by a series of switchbacks, then descended Chimney Top Creek to Red River.

As the Red River forests were worked out, a new line was built along Pine Ridge from the mountain top to Campton, the county seat of Wolfe County, and then practically inaccessible in winter. The rails reached Pine Ridge in the spring of 1906, and freight and passenger service commenced. In the fall of 1907, the little Climax locomotives entered Campton and the entire line was placed in operation.

A scenic view along the 40' rail in the ascent to Mountain Top.
S. P. Guthrie

The Mountain Central abounded in fearsome trestle work and "angular turns." Another view in the climb to Mountain Top. S. P. Guthrie

Locomotive No. 4 and Combine No. 4 at Campton Junction. The station was joint with the L&E (later L&N). The MCRY had a small shop at the Junction. S. P. Guthrie

Another view of the same locomotive and combine. Train has just arrived from Campton and will wait for passengers, mail, and perhaps freight, from the big, standard gauge connecting line. S. P. Guthrie

A close-up view of MC No. 3, a single geared Climax. This engine formerly ran on the impressively named Big Woods, Red River, and Lombard, a logging carrier.
S. P. Guthrie

Combine No. 4, the passenger end apparently packed with passengers, is about to depart for Campton from Campton Junction, 1920.   S. P. Guthrie

At the right, the passenger train is about to negotiate the turnout at the switchback. The switchtender is a barefoot lad.   S. P. Guthrie

Below, mixed train nearing Campton. Climax locomotive is either No. 1 or No. 2.   Mrs. Taylor Booth

The ride between the terminals of the Mountain Central Railway was uniquely picturesque. Winding through the Whittleton hollow, then climbing the mile-long hill, one could thrill at the wild beauty, the high cliffs that proudly raised their heads—the hillsides, no more beautiful in the summertime with their wealth of flowers and ferns than in the winter with their barren and somber rocks. At one point in the ascent of the hill, a passenger could look directly through the famous Natural Bridge.

The little Mountain Central was never a great money maker, but by making ties from its own timber and by mining its own coal, expenses were kept at a minimum. Freight shipments were heaviest in the fall and early spring because in the fall merchants were anxious to procure their supplies in order that they could be distributed before the roads became impassable, and they needed their spring items in advance of the farming season.

Business on the railway began to dwindle when the first state road reached Campton in 1924. In 1928 operations on the Mountain Central ceased. The physical structure was left intact until 1930 when dismantling of the line commenced, a chore that was completed in 1931.

Whittleton drop-in track, about a mile east of Campton Junction. S. P. Guthrie

Track of the Mountain Central near Pine Ridge, 1920. A small oil boom took place in this area during that period. S. P. Guthrie

The Mountain Central Railway as finally constructed was 12.31 miles long. Rail was all steel, 40' for the first five miles from Campton Junction, 20' for the next three, and 40' again for the remainder.

Campton Junction was the headquarters for the MCRY. Here was located the railroad's shop which included a 200-ton wheel press, band saws, lathes, drills, and other equipment. Ten or twelve houses for employees, a commissary, and post office were maintained nearby at McCormick (now Natural Bridge).

A single station at Campton Junction served both the Lexington & Eastern, and the Mountain Central, the agent there being paid by both parties. Trains of the Mountain Central reached the station by means of a third rail laid in the L&E passing track. Besides the joint track, the MC had a shop track, three other tracks, and a wye.

Leaving the Junction, there was the Whittleton drop-in track, used largely for storage purposes, and named after the creek that the Mountain Central crossed 26 times in its first mile or two. One and a quarter miles further at the foot of the hill there were two switch tracks leading, respectively, to a rock crusher development, and to a coal bank owned by the Mountain Central and from which its locomotives fueled. About two-thirds of the way up the hill was the first of two switch-backs, and a short distance on was the second one. The leg of each was approximately 300' long, thus limiting operations to trains of that length. At the top of the hill was a spur, and a few miles further was Green Garrett siding located at Pine Ridge. Then followed High Falls station with its 200' double deck trestle, Duff siding, Meadow Branch siding, and Campton, the end of the line. Campton had a wye, a 20 car sidetrack, three employees dwellings, and a station building that had been constructed at Clay City and hauled by train to the terminus.

The four water tanks on the line were located at Campton Junction (gravity fed from springs), two-thirds of the way up the hill (also gravity fed from springs), High Falls (pumped), and Campton (pumped). The railroad had its own telephone system which consisted of a single pair of wires with phones at Campton Junction, Pine Ridge, and Campton, plus two homes of employees along the line. In addition the coaches on the passenger trains carried their own phones, wired to long poles which could effect a connection at any point.

For most of the life of the Mountain Central, regular service consisted of two passenger round trips daily, making connections at the Junction with trains of the L&E. The 12 mile trip took one hour and 20 minutes. Although there were no published speed restrictions, the geared locomotives could not operate at speeds in excess of 15 miles per hour. Freight trains ran on no definite schedule, and the practice was to add freight cars to the passenger trains unless business justified solid freight runs. No operating timecards were published, but, as one of the old MC engineers said, "They weren't necessary because we knew where every train was anyway."

The passenger fare was 75c from Campton Junction to Campton, and other fares were in proportion. While the passenger trains would stop practically any place to take on or let off the fares, there were a number of regular stops:

   Campton Junction
   At the Switchbacks
   Top of Mountain
   Chimney Top
   Ledfords
   Pine Ridge
   High Falls
   Duff Siding
   Meadow Branch
   Campton

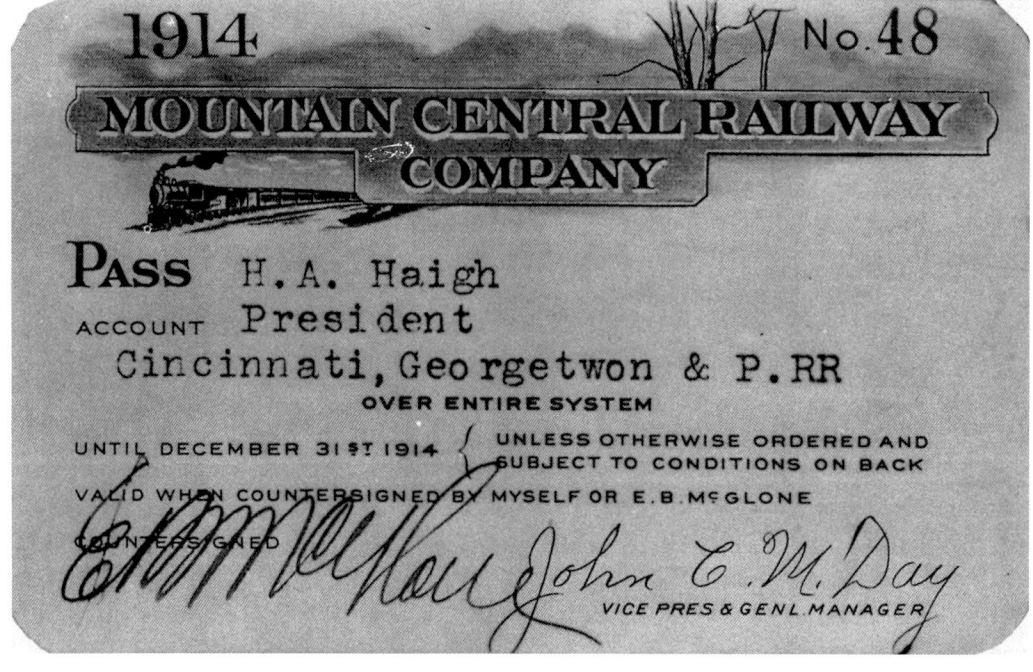

S. P. Guthrie

CHAPTER 3
"The Riney-B"
Millville to Irvine -- Heidelberg to Ida May
(Louisville & Nashville Railroad)

It was a tense evening at Irvine. Rumors of this and that were rampant, while little knots of men started gathering, groups that were destined to be part of a mob. In jail was one Alex Richardson who the previous night had been arrested and charged with brutally clubbing a woman to death at Rice Station.

Soon the mob welded itself together and, when it gained sufficient strength, assaulted the portals of the jail and removed Richardson. Despite the latter's pleas of innocence and his stout denials to the last, he was taken to the new railroad bridge and hanged from that structure until dead.

Soon after this event, the husband of the murdered woman, a Mr. White, moved to Indiana where he died a few years later. Just before his death he made a confession in which he stated that he and not Richardson had committed the crime. Unfortunately, such delayed timing could be of little help to Richardson.

Thus, in 1895, was informally dedicated a $170,000 structure, spanning the Kentucky River at West Irvine, that, for forty years, was to serve the railroad successively operated by the R.N.I.&B. (Riney-B), Louisville & Atlantic, and Louisville & Nashville.

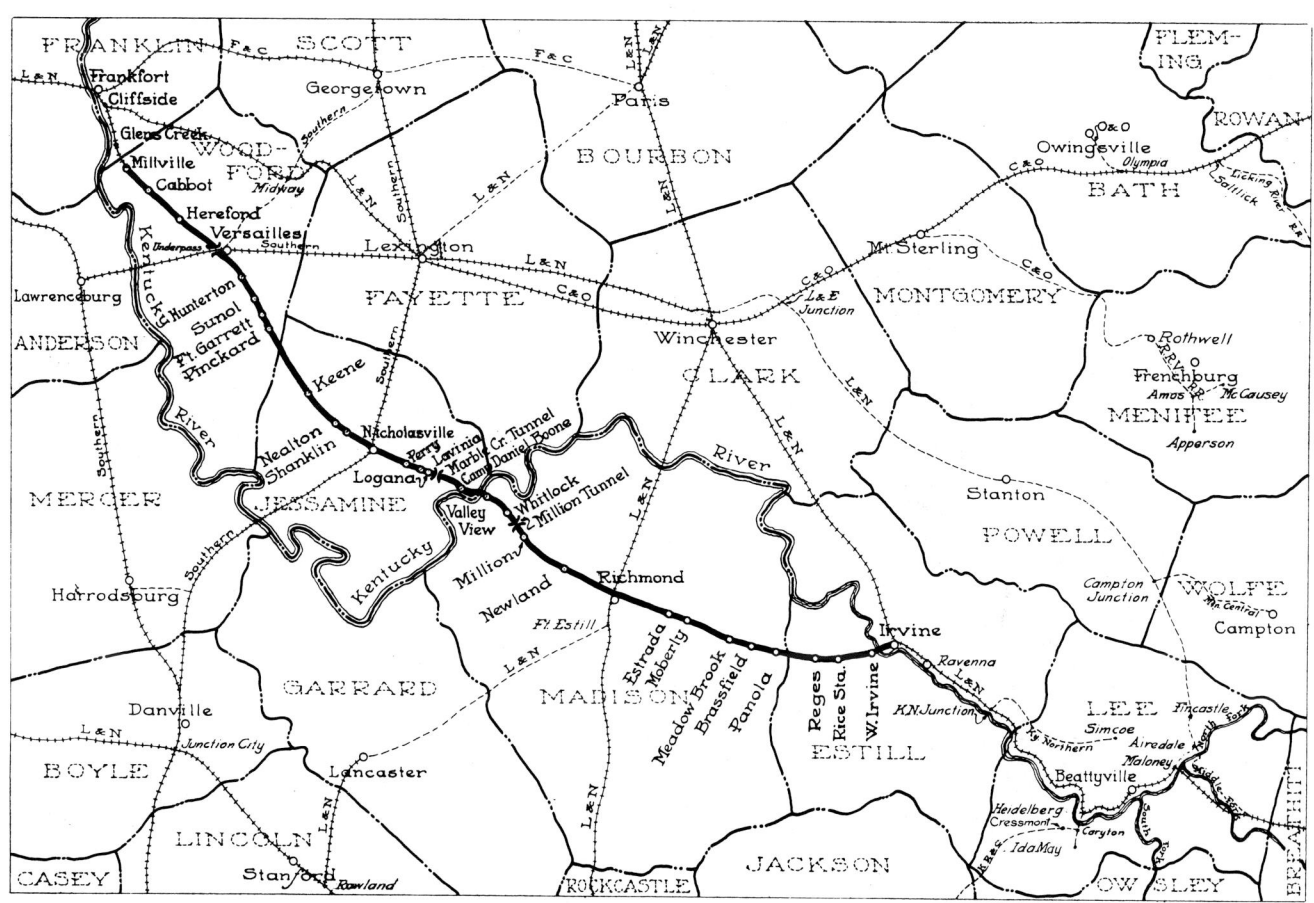

L&A work train with engine No. 7 at Cow Creek bridge just south of West Irvine. C. B. Hendren

2-6-0 No. 11 of the Louisville & Atlantic with a freight drag, photographed in November, 1906. B. B. Ballard

The Richmond, Nicholasville, Irvine & Beattyville Railroad Company completed the 60.76 miles between Versailles and Irvine in 1890. Two daily passenger trains were scheduled in each direction, connecting at Versailles with the tracks of the Louisville Southern. One or more freight trains daily traversed the line in each direction.

The Riney-B went into the hands of a receiver on December 2, 1891. It was sold under foreclosure in 1897, and after a series of minor maneuvers was conveyed on August 19, 1899, to the Louisville & Atlantic Railroad, which had been incorporated for the purpose of taking over the Riney-B.

L&A No. 4 (2-6-0) with freight train. No. 4 was renumbered 550 when the L&A was taken over by the L&N. L&N RR.

The 34.74 mile segment between Irvine and Beattyville was completed by the L&A in November, 1902, which, with the purchase of the 5.6 mile Beattyville & Cumberland Gap Railroad which ran from Beattyville east to Airedale on the Lexington & Eastern, gave the Louisville & Atlantic Railroad a continuous route of 101.10 miles extending from Versailles to Airedale (Beattyville Junction).

The first engine and train to go through Yellow Rock tunnel on the newly completed Irvine-Beattyville segment. L&N RR.

LOUISVILLE & ATLANTIC RAILROAD COMPANY
1330
Aug 15th 1907.
PASS B B Ballard & wife
FROM Versailles
TO Richmond
GOOD IN ONE DIRECTION ONLY, UNLESS ACCOMPANIED BY A COUPON
GOOD FOR ONE TRIP ONLY, UNTIL Sept 15th 1907.
COUNTERSIGNATURE.
R N Hudson
GENERAL MANAGER
ACCEPTED SUBJECT TO CONDITIONS ON BACK HEREOF
VOID AFTER DECEMBER 31, 1907.

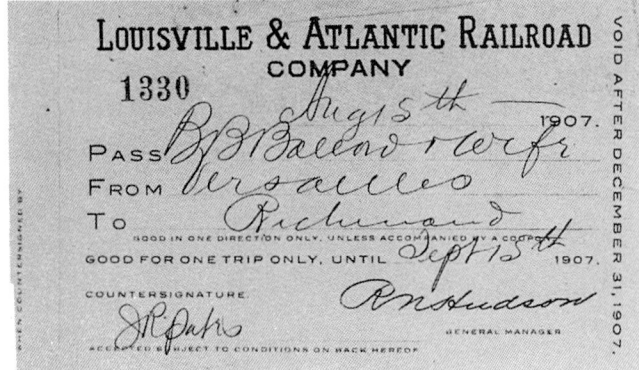

B. B. Ballard

Looking towards a possible route into the coal fields of Southeastern Kentucky, the Louisville & Nashville Railroad acquired the stocks and bonds of the L&A as of July 1, 1909. However, the L&N also acquired the Lexington & Eastern in November, 1910 (See Chapter 1). Neither of these routes provided the low-grade line needed by the "Old Reliable." It was decided eventually to build a new line from Winchester to Irvine, using as a main route only that part of the L&A between Irvine and Beattyville.

A train on the L&A at Gamble's Curve, leaving Irvine in 1904. B. B. Ballard

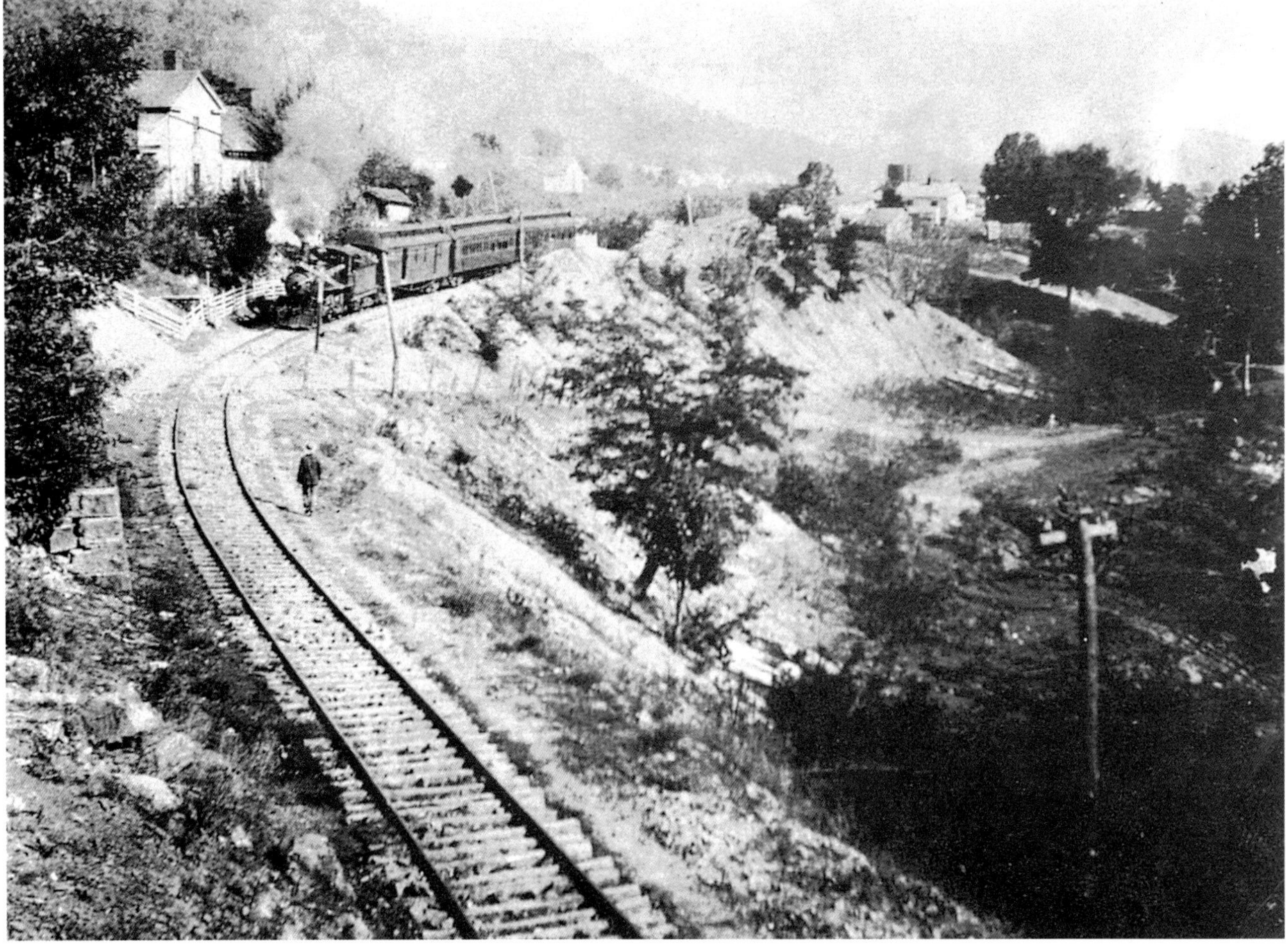

The Kentucky Highlands Railroad Company commenced the construction of a line between Frankfort and Millville in April, 1907, to serve important distilleries south of Frankfort. The 6.46 mile track was completed in April, 1908. The following year the L&NRR acquired the Kentucky Highlands Railroad and started the construction of a 9.42 mile extension from Millville to Versailles, which was completed and placed in operation May 1, 1911. From then on this track was operated in conjunction with the Riney-B line, the trains now scheduled to run through from Beattyville to Frankfort.

KENTUCKY HIGHLANDS RAILROAD COMPANY.
1911
PASS Mr. H. W. Conard
of Colorado Midland Ry. Co.
UNTIL DECEMBER 31ST, 1911 UNLESS REVOKED.
No. 41
PRESIDENT

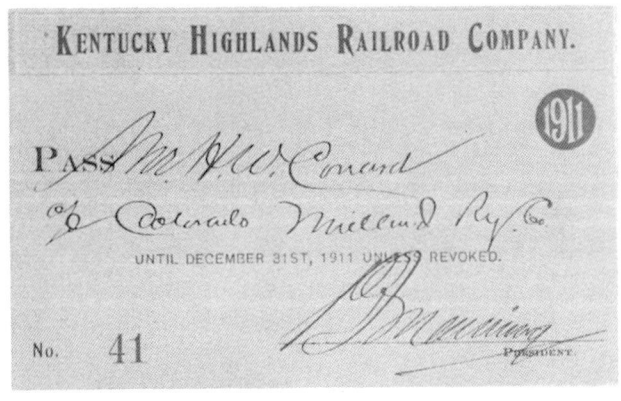

S. P. Guthrie

The Riney-B east of Nicholasville was replete with grades up to 1.7 percent, a 253' tunnel, two trestles of 570' and 770' lengths, respectively, and numerous curves. The grade at Hell Creek was typical of the operating conditions.
J. Wade Sellers

Less than carload freight was carried on the combination way car-cabooses of the L&A.   L&N RR.

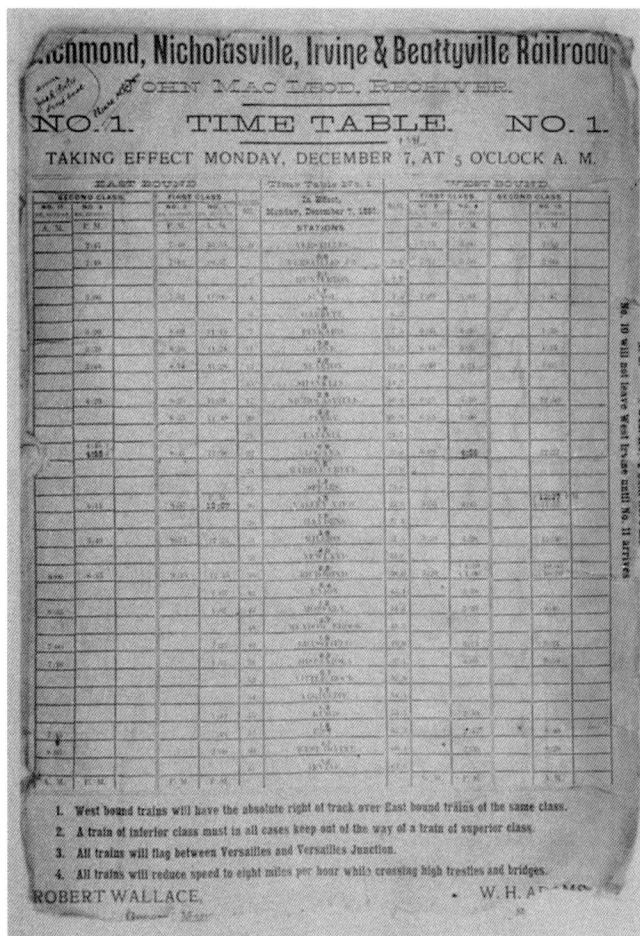

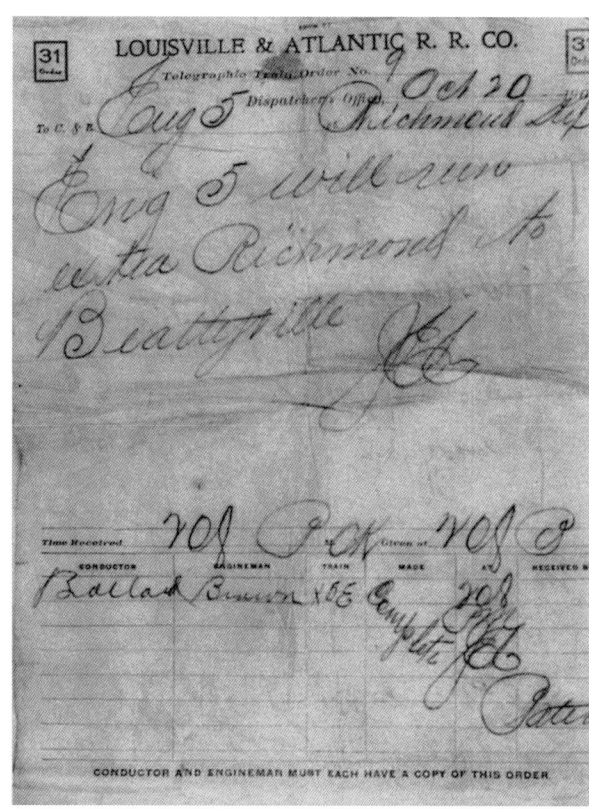

The first and one of the last. Employees' timetable No. 1 of the Riney-B, effective December 7, 1891; and the L&N timetable No. 57, in effect October 5, 1930. L&N RR. L&A train order of October 20, 1907. B. B. Ballard

BETWEEN FRANKFORT AND RAVENNA

SOUTH BOUND / **NORTH BOUND**

TIME TABLE No. 57 In Effect Sunday, October 5, 1930, at 12:01 a.m.

SECOND CLASS	FIRST CLASS				Station Numbers	Distance from Track	STATIONS	Distance between Stations	Capacity of Sidings	Minimum Time between Stations	FIRST CLASS			SECOND CLASS
21 Mixed Daily ex. Sunday	11 Passenger Daily	3 Passenger Daily	1 Passenger Daily								12 Passenger Daily	4 Passenger Daily	2 Passenger Daily	22 Mixed Daily ex. Sunday
7.30AM	4.40PM				V65	.0	L.. FRANKFORT (L. C. L. Division) .. N.. A	0.9	6	3	3.20PM			1.25PM
7.35	4.45				V866	0.9	CLIFFSIDE .. E	4.3	Yard	10	3.15			1.20
7.58	4.55				71	5.2	GLENS CREEK	1.0	3		3.02			1.05
8.03	4.57				72	6.2	TAYLORTON	1.0	3		3.00			1.00
8.06	4.59				73	7.2	MILLVILLE	4.9	61	3	2.57			12.55
8.35	5.10				77	12.1	HEREFORD	4.1	55	12	2.45			12.40
8.54	5.20				82	16.2	VERSAILLES .. N C	5.5	44	14	2.35			12.25
9.13	5.32				87	21.7	FORT GARRETT	1.2	2	3	2.21			12.05PM
9.25	5.35				88	22.9	PINCKARD	3.8	29	10	2.18			11.59AM
9.41	5.44				92	26.7	KEENE	1.9	19	3	2.09			11.42
9.48	5.48				94	28.6	NEALTON	3.7	10	10	2.04			11.25
10.04	5.56				98a	32.3	NICHOLASVILLE JUNCTION	0.2		3	1.56			11.08
10.05	5.57				98	32.5	NICHOLASVILLE .. N C	5.2	19	13	1.55			11.02
10.18	6.09				103	37.7	LOGANA	3.7	12	12	1.42			10.48
10.25	6.17				107	41.4	VALLEY VIEW	5.6	14	10	1.33			10.25
11.00	6.31				112	47.0	MILLION	6.4	20	14	1.20			10.00
11.20	6.45				119	53.4	RICHMOND SHOPS	0.7	27	4	1.07			9.25
11.25	6.50				120	54.1	L. & A. JUNCTION	0.7	19		1.00			9.20
11.30 11.40	7.05 7.15				f229	54.3	RICHMOND .. N				12.55 12.40			9.15 8.45
11.45AM	7.20				f120	54.1	L. & A. JUNCTION	5.9	19	15	12.34			8.40
12.20PM	7.31				125	60.0	MOBERLEY .. N C	5.3	35	15	12.20			8.15
12.35	7.42				131	65.3	BRASSFIELD	2.1	16	5	12.08			8.00
12.50	7.47				133	67.4	PANOLA	3.5	22	9	12.03PM			7.50
1.05	7.55				136	70.9	REGES	1.8	10	5	11.55AM			7.40
1.15	7.59				138	72.7	RICE STATION .. N C	3.1	23	8	11.50			7.30
1.30	8.06				141	75.8	WEST IRVINE	1.6	20	5	11.43			7.15
1.45	8.15	1.17PM	1.58AM		143	77.4	IRVINE	1.2	15	5	11.35	11.49AM	10.25AM	7.05
1.55PM	8.20PM	1.25PM	2.03AM		144	78.6	A .. RAVENNA .. N		Yard		11.30AM	11.45AM	10.22AM	7.00AM
Daily ex. Sunday 21	Daily 11	Daily 3	Daily 1								Daily 12	Daily 4	Daily 2	Daily ex. Sunday 22

Regular South-bound trains are superior to trains of the same class moving in the opposite direction.

New cars for the RNI&B are shown in these builders photos from the collection of Richard Hardin. Note the builders photos throughout this book usually show a picket fence in the background, indicating the favorite photo-taking spot at the American Car & Foundry Company's Ohio Falls Plant at Jeffersonville, Indiana, which built many freight and passenger cars for railroad as well as interurban lines.

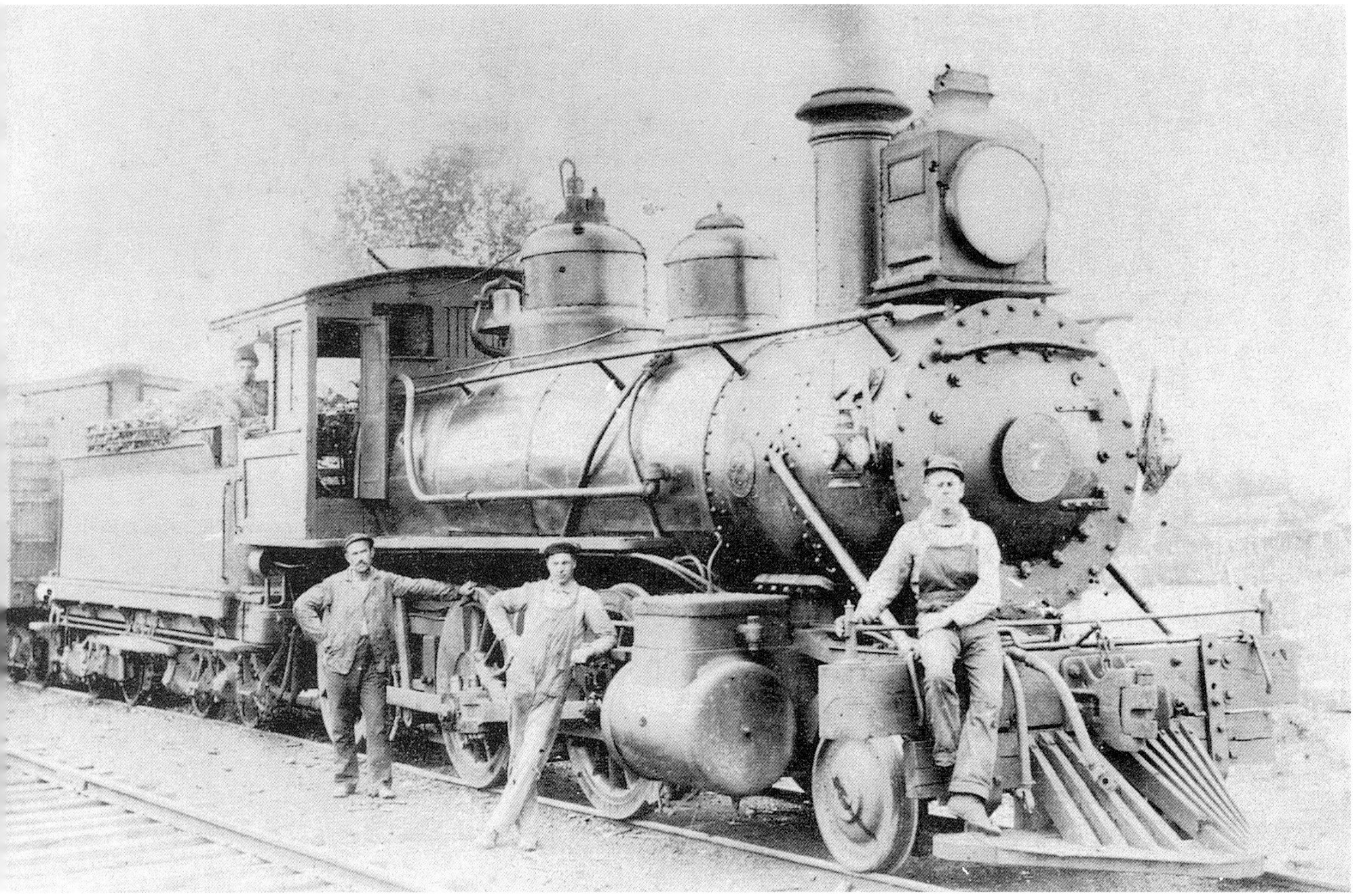

Louisville & Atlantic 2-6-0 No. 7. L&N RR.

RICHMOND, NICHOLASVILLE, IRVINE AND BEATTYVILLE RAILROAD COMPANY

No 65

SHARES.

This is to certify that

entitled to Shares of the Capital Stock of the Richmond, Nicholasville, Irvine and Beattyville Railroad Company, transferable only on the books of the Company in person or by Attorney, upon surrender of this Certificate.

In Witness whereof, the signatures of the President and Secretary are hereunto affixed this day of 18

SECRETARY. PRESIDENT

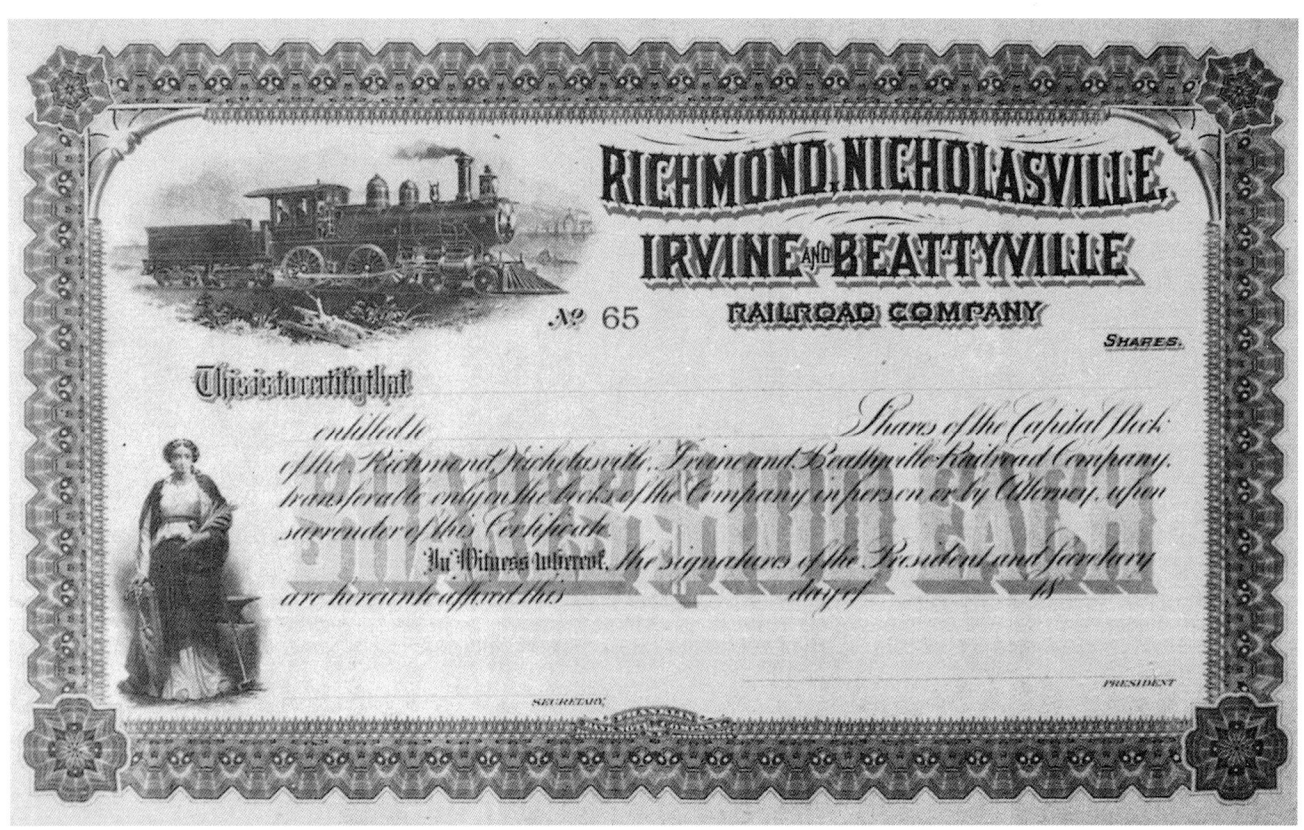

Stock Certificate from the collection of E. G. Baker.

After the L&N's low grade line from Winchester to Irvine was completed in 1916, the segment between Frankfort and Irvine became devoid of most of its former traffic and the lack of business became more acute as good roads and more automobiles invaded the area. Permission to abandon this section was granted by the I.C.C., and on September 30, 1932, the last scheduled run was made. About 5½ miles of track between Cliffside (just south of Frankfort) and Millville remain to provide switching service to a distillery.

The Riney-B never lost a passenger in an accident, and never had any serious wrecks. The most disastrous occurred around 1904 when an engine overturned on Foster's Curve between Million and Richmond. The triple circumstances of a 10 degree curve, an engineer who was making his third trip, and a cow on the track proved the locomotive's undoing, and it went over the end of a trestle.

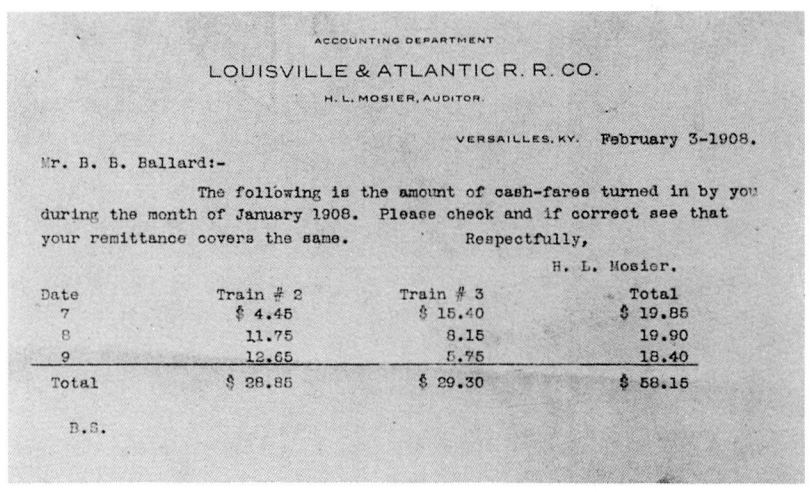

Considering the number of open agencies on the Louisville & Atlantic, cash fares collected on the local passenger trains weren't bad, amounting to almost $20 a day for numbers 2 and 3.   B. B. Ballard

The Riney-B bridge over the Kentucky River at Irvine remained almost intact after abandonment until the demands of the scrap drive during World War II made its salvaging desirable. On November 17, 1942, an army engineer battalion from Fort Knox set off a dynamite blast that effectively spelled its doom.   L&N RR.

After the L&A reached Beattyville, a line of railroad was built up Sturgeon Creek from Heidelberg to Ida May, 2.98 miles, by the Kentucky Coal Development Company. Construction started in March, 1907, and was completed in January, 1908. On November 1, 1909, it was taken over by the Louisville & Atlantic, then passed into the possession of the L&N when it acquired the L&A. The branch was abandoned April 13, 1935, but for a time was an important traffic producer because of its connection at Caryton with the Kentucky, Rockcastle & Cumberland. (See Chapter 5.)

Scheduled service on the Sturgeon Creek Branch consisted of a mixed daily except Sunday round trip that originated and terminated at Beattyville, operated on the main line to Heidelberg, then on the Branch.
L&N RR.

BETWEEN HEIDELBERG AND IDAMAY
(STURGEON CREEK BRANCH)

TIME TABLE No. 57 — In Effect Sunday, October 5, 1930, at 12:01 a.m.

South Bound Mixed 23 Daily ex. Sunday	Distance from Lexing-ton	Stations	Distance between Sta-tions	North Bound Mixed 24 Daily ex. Sunday
8.00 AM	74.0	L...HEIDELBERG...N..A	1.0	8.32 AM
8.05	75.0	CARYTON	2.0	8.28
8.15 AM	77.0	A...IDAMAY...L		8.20 AM

Regular South-bound trains are superior to trains of the same class moving in the opposite direction.

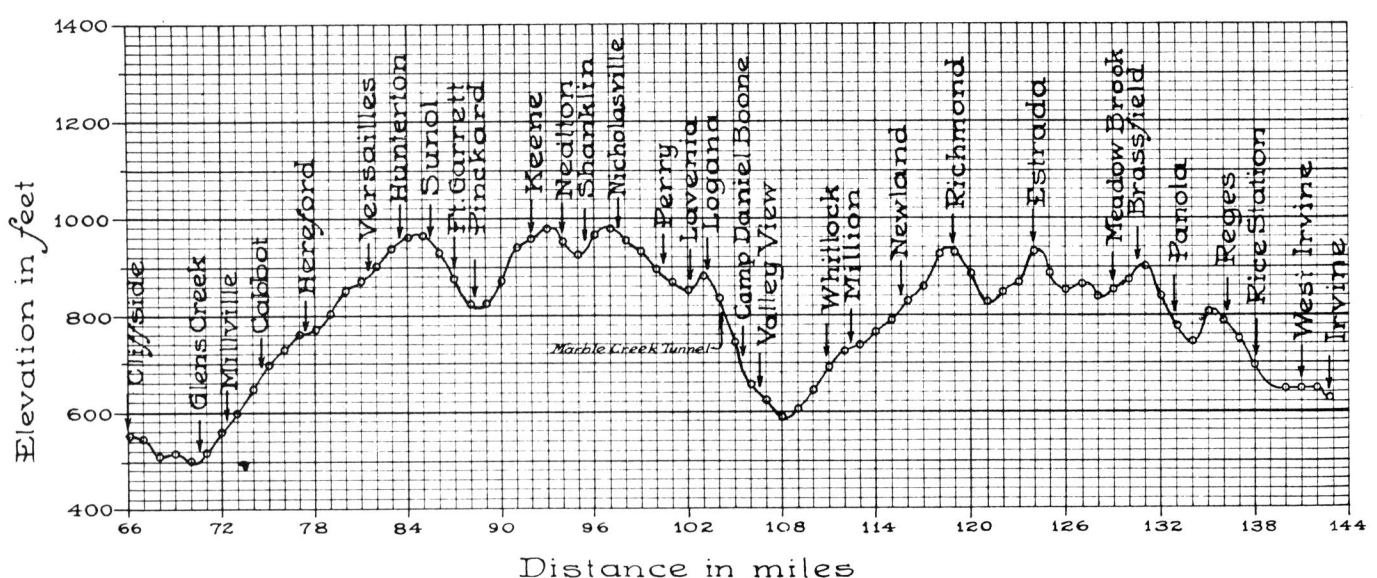

Profile of the torturous Riney-B.
J. S. Horine

Ohio & Kentucky Railway Co.
1923   No. 71
PASS   Mr. Charles E. Graham,
ACCOUNT Treasurer and Traffic Mgr.,
        Central Railroad of Oregon,
BETWEEN All Stations.
UNTIL DECEMBER 31ST, 1923, UNLESS OTHERWISE ORDERED AND SUBJECT TO CONDITIONS ON BACK

GENERAL MANAGER   PRESIDENT

W. E. Bach

CHAPTER 4
"Cannel Carrier"
O&K Junction to Licking River
(Ohio & Kentucky Railway)

The Ohio & Kentucky Railway was the creation of the Kentucky Block Cannel Coal Company, a corporation that had taken under lease about 5,400 acres of cannel coal land adjacent to what was formerly known as Walnut Grove, later Caney, in Morgan County. A leading spirit in the enterprise was W. DeL. Walbridge, president of the coal company, who was to become the railroad's first chief executive.

Construction of the railroad started in October, 1899, at O&K Junction, a point on the Lexington & Eastern Railway 1.37 miles west of Jackson. The 26 miles to Cannel City were completed on June 10, 1901, and trains started running. From that date until July 1, 1904, the O&K was operated under contract by the L&E, the latter road furnishing all equipment. During these three years all trains of the O&K operated through to Jackson. But when the contract with the L&E expired and the O&K took over its own operation, only its passenger trains ran into Jackson via trackage rights over the L&E. Freight trains on the O&K terminated at O&K Junction and mixed trains headed for Jackson dropped their freight cars at the Junction to be picked up by the L&E.

Since additional coal deposits down Caney Valley seemed worthy of development, and at Licking River a lumber industry was in process of expansion, it seemed desirable to extend the Ohio & Kentucky Railway for 12.80 miles down Caney Creek to Licking River. For this purpose a new corporation wholly owned by the O&K, the Caney Valley Railway, was incorporated. Construction of the extension was started in 1910 and completed in 1911, resulting in a railroad with a total length of almost 40 miles.

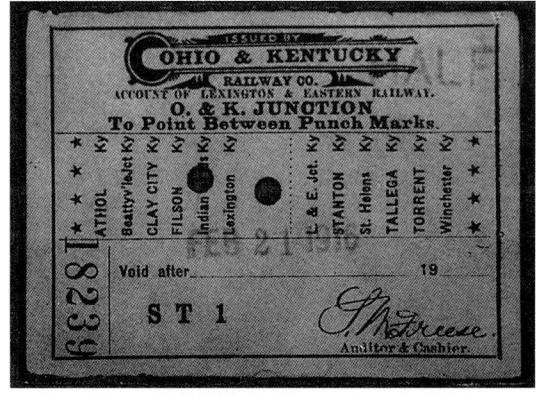

S. P. Guthrie

View of Cannel City showing mines, railroad wye, and shops.   W. J. Urfer

To natives of the Cannel City area the coal and the railroad opened a new world. The easterners who formed the Kentucky Block Cannel Coal Company and promoted the Ohio & Kentucky Railway brought with them new music, new fashions, and new speech. Their culture mingled with the culture of the hill people and the walls of their homes and the Cannel City hotel often rang with the Blue Danube played on the violin, or Turkey in the Straw masterfully done on a fiddle. The polished shoes of the New Yorkers soon were dulled with dust from mountaineers' boots as their owners attempted the intricacies of the square dance.

Headquarters of the railroad were located at Cannel City. Here a well equipped set of shops did all of the road's boiler, blacksmith, planing, painting, and wheel-press work. The dispatcher's office gave train orders by telegraph but the O&K also maintained a telephone line for messages and emergencies, of which there seemed to be an abundance.

Coal for the O&K was produced by the railroad's own mine at Cannel City, and ties were furnished by farmers along the right-of-way.

January 19, 1910, on a curve about one mile south of Frozen Station, mixed train No. 34, southbound, consisting of five cars of coal, three of ties, two of lumber, combine No. 1002, and coach 1010 had difficulties. All freight cars of the train passed over the spot where the trouble occurred, but the rear trucks of the combine left the rails resulting in the overturning of both the combine and the coach. One passenger was killed and five were injured. No other passenger mortality ever took place on the O&K.

The O&K had no big hook and when wrecks of this nature happened human ingenuity aided by blocks and tackle took its place.

The station at Neola post office was named Helechawa after the daughter of the president of the Ohio & Kentucky — HELEn CHAse WAlbridge. Picture at right.

W. E. Bach

O&K train No. 21 at Jackson Station. Locomotive is No. 14, a 2-6-0 Pittsburgh of 1904 birth. The middle set of drivers were blind, so converted because of frequent derailment due to an extremely crooked track. W. E. Bach

Among the operating challenges of the O&K were two tunnels. The 300' timbered bore at the head of Frozen Creek was approached on each end by curves of 10 and 12 degrees respectively. The second (Claney) tunnel bridged the Red River and the Licking River watersheds, and northbound trains emerging from this tunnel immediately dropped down a 3 percent grade for 4,200'. This was the maximum grade on the O&K and obviously the ruling one.

Builder's photo of O&K No. 16. This mogul was a product of the American Locomotive Company. Cylinders had a diameter of 18". Weight of locomotive was 55 tons. J. H. Lynch.

A view of the No. 18, photographed in the familiar yards of the Southern Iron & Equipment Company, Atlanta, Ga., just prior to its trip to Kentucky. W. J. Urfer

Abandonment came to the Ohio & Kentucky as the cannel coal resources played out, the forest resources of the Licking River region became exhausted, and passable roads made their appearance in Breathitt and Wolfe Counties. On November 1, 1933, the last whistle of the little eight wheelers echoed through Frozen Valley, then operations ceased and the line was scrapped.

Another view of venerable No. 18, this time flying the white flags of an extra. Rules of the Louisville & Nashville Railroad were used and O&K employees took their examinations with L&N trainmen. W. J. Urfer

47

The O&K owned two cabooses, 900 and 901, one being this four wheel "bobber," of which we present builder's exterior and interior photographs.

Both pictures—Richard Hardin

Shortly after the Ohio & Kentucky reached Cannel City, a 3½ mile feeder line, the Caney & West Liberty Railroad was built. This was a standard gauge line that ran from Cannel City to Caney, up Spring Branch to its head which it crossed by a tortuous switch back, then descended into the head of White Oak Creek where it served the newly constructed mines of the White Oak Cannel Coal Company at Piedmont. After bankruptcy the C&WL emerged as the Caney, Piedmont & Morehead Railroad. In December, 1907, operations permanently ceased.

Geared Shay and Climax locomotives were used on the line, the Shay being a 20-ton machine built by Lima, 11/04, c/n 959, and carrying Road Number 3. Natives were reluctant to ride the east portion of this little line because of the switchbacks and the resulting dangers. The bottom picture on the opposite page shows why. Both pictures on opposite page—Helen Price Stacy

REFRESHMENTS EN ROUTE

Although it was a late summer afternoon, the midday heat had not been dissipated. At O&K Junction, the little 8-wheeler locomotive, motionless but panting spasmodically, seemed to echo the general lassitude of the surroundings, and one could hardly suspect that within a short time the engine would be energetically pulling the wooden combine and coach up Frozen Creek Valley as if impatient to get to Cannel City and tie up for the night.

Scheduled as Number 33, the train waited at the junction each day until Number 3, the eastbound passenger from Lexington, arrived with its quota of passengers to be transferred.

On the day in question No. 3 finally hove into view and rapidly ground to a stop. The usual coterie of people disembarked, but one passenger particularly gained the attention of the O&K train crew. She was a woman of perhaps thirty years, and she was carrying a six months old baby who was crying the wail of a hungry infant. A discreet inquiry from a member of the train crew brought forth the explanation. The mother and baby had been traveling all day from a point up in Ohio. The milk which the mother had prepared for the trip, had gone sour due to the summer heat, and the child would have none of it.

Hardly a problem for a railroad which was the country's leading cannel coal carrier, you say? Guess again, for at O&K junction was stationed one Charlie White as car inspector, and Charlie owned a farm scarcely a mile down the road. As an employee who must have been a pioneer in the "service above self" philosophy, he quickly made some arrangements with the conductor, and then took one of the mother's empty milk bottles and hied himself down the track to his farm.

Meanwhile O&K 33 had loaded its passengers, baggage and mail, and was ready to start, but for some reason conductor Everett Bach failed to give the signal. In fact, he spent some valuable time inspecting the storing of the baggage and then he hit the ground and meticulously checked all of the trucks for hot boxes. Next he went up to the front of the train and satisfied himself that the tender did contain both water and coal.

After taking these wise precautions he gave the go-ahead signal and the 8-wheeler got under way; but a mile down the road the engineer got a stop signal, which he quickly obeyed. Coincidently, the coach stopped directly in front of the home of Charlie White, and that samaritan climbed aboard proudly displaying the baby's bottle of milk, still warm from the jersey cow he had milked while the train was doing its "business" at the junction. Needless to say the gratefulness of the mother was matched only by that of the other passengers who had pictured a tearful child for the entire trip to Cannel City.

Thus the little O&K set an example of service which even yet hasn't been approached by the big roads. For instance, who ever heard of the Congressional Limited stopping so a trainman could milk a cow for a passenger?

O. & K. BRANCH.

WEST BOUND.

No. 33. Daily, ex. Sunday.	Miles.	STATIONS.	Miles.	No. 21. Daily, ex. Sunday.
3 30	0	......Jackson......	0	11 20
3 35	6	.O & K Junction	6	11 26
4 17	11	.....Wilburst.....	11	11 52
4 30	13	.....Hampton.....	13	11 55
5 10	20	.....Lee City.....	20	12 22
5 18	22	.....Helechawa.....	22	12 28
5 45	27	...Cannel City...	27	12 45
P.M. ARR.				P.M. ARR.

EAST BOUND.

No. 34. Daily, ex. Sunday.	Miles.	STATIONS.	Miles.	No. 22. Daily, ex Sunday.
A.M. LVE.	27		6	P. M. ARR
7 15	21	...Cannel City...	6	1 05
7 41	19	.....Helechawa.....	11	1 22
7 50	13	.....Lee City.....	13	1 28
8 30	10	.....Hampton.....	20	1 52
8 43	1	.....Wilburst.....	22	1 58
9 25	0	.O & K Junction.	27	2 30
9 30		......Jackson......		2 35

Nos. 3 and 4 make close connection for Cannel City and points on Ohio and Kentucky Railway Division, daily except Sunday.

Nos. 1 and 2 connect at L. & E. Junction with Chesapeake and Ohio for Mt. Sterling and local points.

Nos. 1 and 2 connect at Beattyville Junction with L. & A. for Beattyville, daily except Sunday.

J. R. BARR, Gen'l Manager.
CHAS. SCOTT, Gen. Pass. Agent.

FEUDIN' LAWYER RUNS AMUCK

Since he may still be living, we will have to dispense with his name, but a lawyer living near Frozen station, and commuting to Jackson each day on the O&K was well in the Callahan-Hargis trials "up to his neck." While No. 33 was standing at the Jackson station one afternoon about ready to pull out, our barrister friend rushed breathlessly up to the engineer and requested the ride back to Frozen in the locomotive cab, declaring that one of the opposing clan was out to kill him, and had entered his office by the front door but a few minutes previously. (The lawyer had made his exit by the back door.)

Standing on the regulation against unauthorized persons riding in the cab, plus perhaps an understandable doubt regarding his personal safety, engineer Urfer allowed him to secrete himself in a box car of the mixed train, and there he rode to Frozen and temporary security. Temporary it was, for a few days later, after he had gained enough confidence to ride the cushions again, the lawyer disembarked at Frozen in the evening and was immediately covered by a neighborhood bad man, who, in full view of the train crew and passengers, stuck a gun in the ribs of the lawyer. The latter slowly backed away across the porch and into the doors of the general store, the pistol wielder maintaining his close contact. Suddenly, the lawyer made a grab for an old long-muzzle rifle, reposing in the corner of the store, aimed it at his assailant and fired. The pistol toter died immediately, and once more the lawyer had gained temporary safety from the ministrations of the opposing faction. However, he must have figured that two narrow escapes were enough in any man's life, for shortly after this last episode, the lawyer washed his hands of the Callahan-Hargis matter and moved away from Kentucky, bag and baggage, never to return.

CHAPTER 5

"Four Lumber Carriers"
Kings Mountain to Yosemite
(Cincinnati & Green River Railway)
KN Junction to Simcoe
(Kentucky Northern Railroad)
Caryton to Turkey Foot
Kentucky, Rockcastle & Cumberland Railroad)
Lombard/Nada to Big Woods
(Big Woods, Red River & Lombard Railroad)

The little eight-wheeler chugged merrily as it started its backward trip away from Kings Mountain, pushing four loaded box cars and the red combination coach, which, being placed on the end of the train, was actually in the lead. The journey to Yosemite was apparently going to be made without incident, which, after all, was the customary order of things. Events were not quite right, however, because Engineer Matt Horton thought he detected a faint odor of burning material, a smell that didn't quite jibe with the burning bitumens in the firebox. It was not until the train was between McKee's and Duncan, that he noticed a slight haze rising from one of the box cars, the one loaded with hay. Stopping the train he descended to investigate while Conductor Stan Petty came running up from the combination coach on a similar mission. Together they shoved open the box car door. Immediately they were greeted by a burst of flame that argued against any effort to subdue the fire.

There wasn't much time to go into a conference on the subject but Engineer Horton and Conductor Petty hastily arrived at a unanimity of opinion. Quickly pulling the train to a fill and disconnecting the cars on the other side of the flaming vehicle, the crew got out their frogs, dexterously set them under the burning car of hay, uncoupled the engine, and gave the car a slight push—just enough to send it

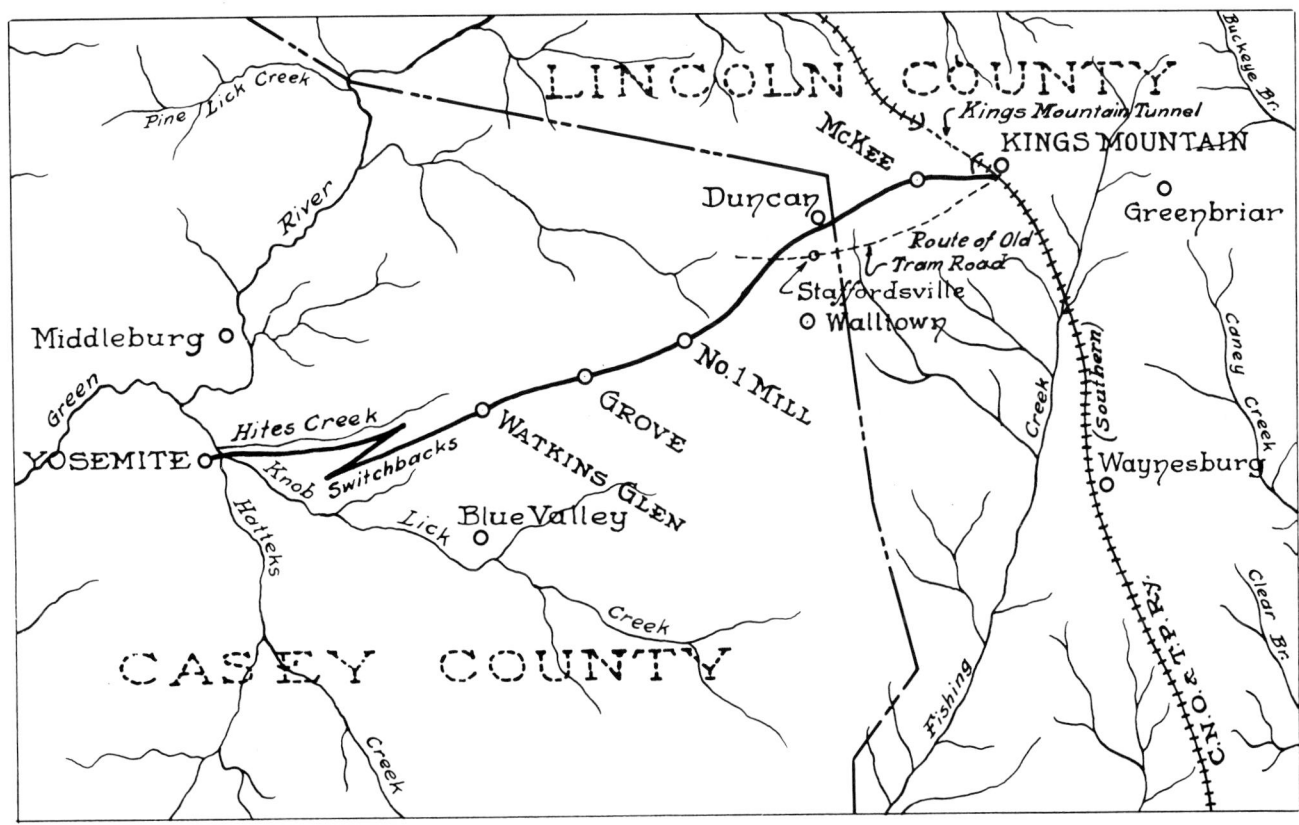

over the embankment.

A simple solution, but one which removed a menace from the right-of-way, saved the rest of the train, and permitted the remainder of the journey to Yosemite to be made with more peace of mind.

This was just one example of the ingenuity that dominated the history of the Cincinnati and Green River Railway, a colorful carrier of the late Nineteenth Century that included in its operations such diverse incidents as (a) one of its trains being stolen by a couple of swains who wanted to go a 'courtin'; and (b) a killin' when A. O. Watkins, an official of the Company, was forced to shoot a man as they rode from Kings Mountain on the train.

About 1882, a wooden railed tram road powered by oxen and mules, and running from Kings Mountain, a station on the CNO&TPRY (Southern) to Staffordsville in Casey County, was replaced by a 36" railroad which was extended to Grove. Passenger service was provided by a crude coach built on the bed of a flat car.

In 1883 the Green River Lumber Company was organized and a year later the Cincinnati & Green River Railway was incorporated, both new companies taking over the properties of the antecedent organization. The C&GR track was changed to the gauge of 5', corresponding to the Southern with which it connected, and during 1885-86 it was extended from Grove to Yosemite. During the latter year the Southern made its gauge change to 4'8½" and the C&GR did likewise.

The Cincinnati & Green River owned two locomotives Numbered 5 and 7, 4-4-0 coal burners, equipped with link and pin couplers and steam jam brakes. A wooden open vestibuled combine completed the rolling stock roster.

The road did well for a time, but with the exhaustion of the timber resources it went into bankruptcy, emerging on July 1, 1891, as the Cincinnati & Kentucky Southern Railway. Prosperity did not return, however, and on August 6, 1896, the 13 mile road was sold at a sheriff's sale, dismantled and junked.

The Kentucky Northern Railroad was a standard gauge line eight miles long. It made a junction with the old Eastern Kentucky Division of the Louisville & Nashville Railroad at a point to be known as KN Junction, a few miles south of Ravenna. It followed Miller's Creek from its mouth to its termination at Simcoe. From there the Simcoe Land Company built about five miles of 36" track on up to Bald Rock. From here the Miller Creek Logging Company built five more miles of narrow gauge track up Big Sinking Creek.

The KN owned a single locomotive, a 4-4-0 Baldwin, probably from the Northern Pacific at Fargo.

As the timber resources of the region became exhausted the need for the Kentucky Northern diminished. It was abandoned in 1909.

The Kentucky, Rockcastle & Cumberland Railroad was an 18 mile, standard gauge railroad owned by the Turkey Foot Lumber Company and running from Caryton, a junction on the Sturgeon Creek Branch of the L&N (See Chapter 3) to Turkey Foot in Jackson County, the seat of the Lumber Company's logging operations. An extensive saw mill was established at Cressmont, a few miles beyond Caryton. The railroad's shops and headquarters were also located here.

The KR&C was incorporated December 3, 1913, acquired some trackage that had been previously constructed and completed the route to Turkey Foot in 1914. Grades were fairly moderate with the exception of the climb up Wild Dog to Ridge which was about 6 percent, and the drop from Ridge into Hughes Fork which approached 8 percent! Locomotives of the KR&C included three Climax B's, a Shay, and a 2-6-2 Vulcan built in June 1915.

The KR&C was abandoned in sections, that from Turkey Foot to Wild Dog about 1923; Wild Dog for three miles north in 1930; and the remaining eight miles in 1935.

The Big Woods, Red River & Lombard Railroad was a narrow gauge line built around the turn of the century to penetrate the virgin forests of the Red River area. Originally it made a junction with the Lexington & Eastern Railway at Lombard. Later, to ease the grades over the ridge into the Red River Valley, a new junction was made at Nada, one-half mile east of Lombard. The ridge was penetrated by a tunnel which today is occupied by a narrow highway feasable for one-way traffic.

North of the ridge, the BWRR&L descended into Red River Valley and followed the main fork of that stream east to Big Woods in Menifee County.

S. P. Guthrie

Lee, Owsley, Estill, and Jackson Counties abounded in railroads, standard and narrow, built to serve logging operations during the early part of the century. Shown on the map are the standard gauge Kentucky Northern Railroad and the Kentucky, Rockcastle & Cumberland Railroad. At Simcoe, a nest of narrow gauge logging lines junctioned with the Kentucky Northern. At Turkey Foot, tracks of the Turkey Foot Lumber Company extended up War Fork, Steer Fork, and other streams. Other more temporary, logging lines were the English narrow gauge, and the Beattyville Southern, another 36" track.

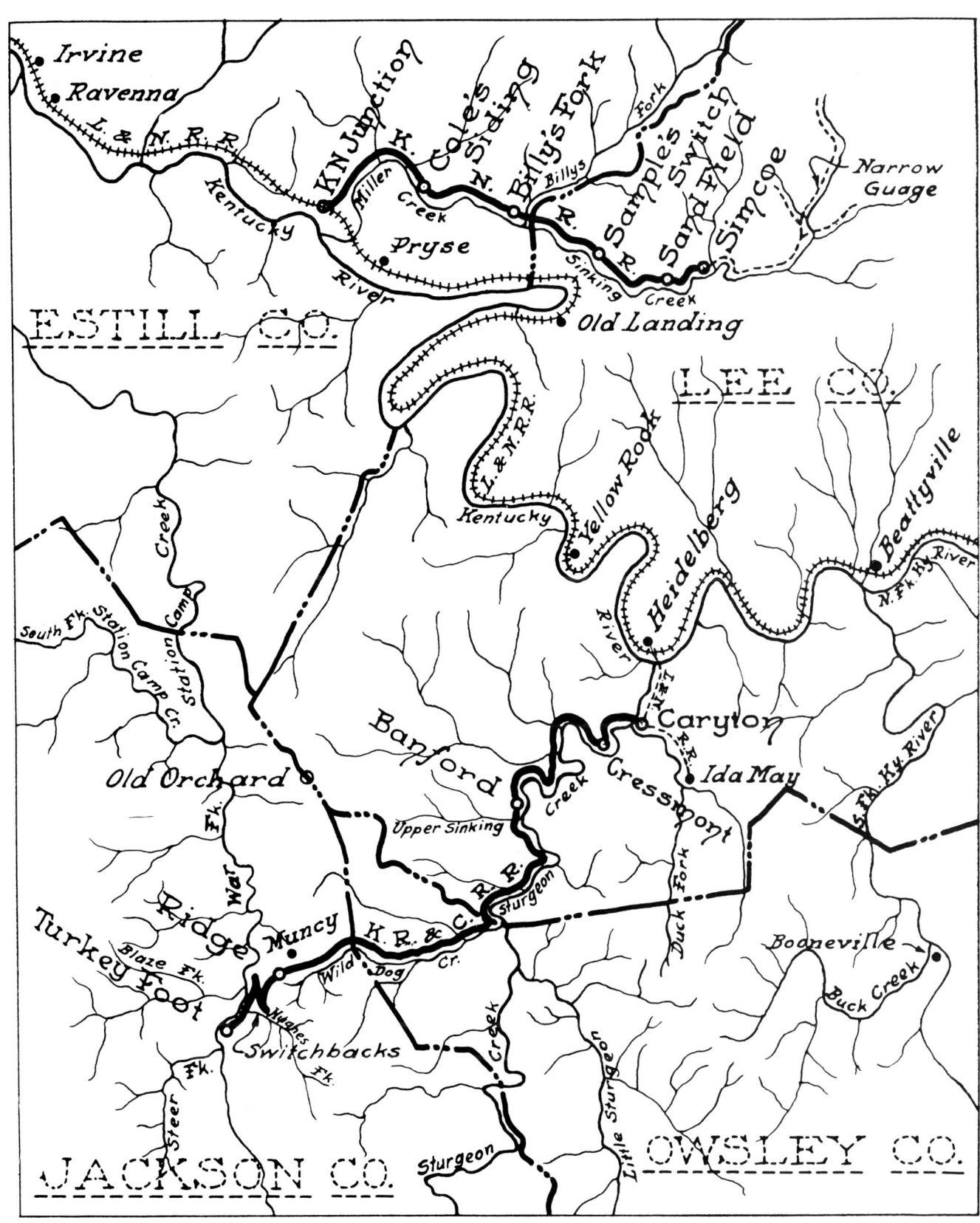

Locomotive No. 5 of the Cincinnati & Green River Railway at Yosemite. T. M. Horton

Locomotive No. 7 at Yosemite. T. M. Horton

Top picture—Climax Locomotive, c/n 177(?), road No. 2 of the Big Woods, Red River & Lombard, was built in 1897, and came to the BWRR&L from the Simcoe Land Company. It was a B-type, 25-ton model.   Hugh Boutell

Above—BWRR&L No. 2 participated in a run-away that wrecked a train and killed the engineer and fireman. No. 2 later became the Mountain Central Railway's No. 3.
Ray Alford

To the right—BWRR&L's narrow gauge train at Lombard, 1903.   C. W. Wittbeck

Lexington & Eastern 2-6-0 No. 11 on Sturgeon Creek Branch which formed a junction with the Kentucky, Rockcastle & Cumberland Railroad at Caryton.   L&N RR.

KR&C #4, "Edwin", a Shay built in 1916. Scene is at Cressmont.   Thomas Lawson, Jr.

Turkey Foot Lumber Company's #1, a 1913 Climax. Cressmont.   Thomas Lawson, Jr.

Climax Locomotive of the Turkey Foot Lumber Company, War Fork.   J. A. Heaton

O&K Station and tracks at Cannel City. Man on velocipede is Dr. J. D. Whitaker, company physician.   Leslie

CHAPTER 6
"Two Southern Segments"
Versailles to Georgetown
Burgin Junction to Burgin
(Southern Railway System)

The Versailles & Midway Railway Company was chartered in 1884 to build a line between the two bluegrass towns in its name. In November, 1885, the seven mile railroad was opened. In 1889, the ambitious Louisville Southern Railway, anticipating the early completion of its line between Lawrenceburg and Lexington, purchased the Versailles & Midway and extended it nine and one-half miles to Georgetown, making a junction with the CNO&TP division of the Southern about 1,000 feet south of the Georgetown station.

With the completion of the Versailles-Georgetown link as well as the line between Versailles and Louisville a round trip of a daily manifest freight between Louisville and Cincinnati was arranged, making use of the Louisville Southern between Louisville and Georgetown via Versailles, and the CNO&TP division of the Southern between Georgetown and Cincinnati. This route, however, was much longer than the competing line of the Louisville & Nashville, and it was discontinued after approximately one year. Thereafter business between Versailles and Georgetown was handled the great majority of the time by the one or two scheduled round trips of the mixed train.

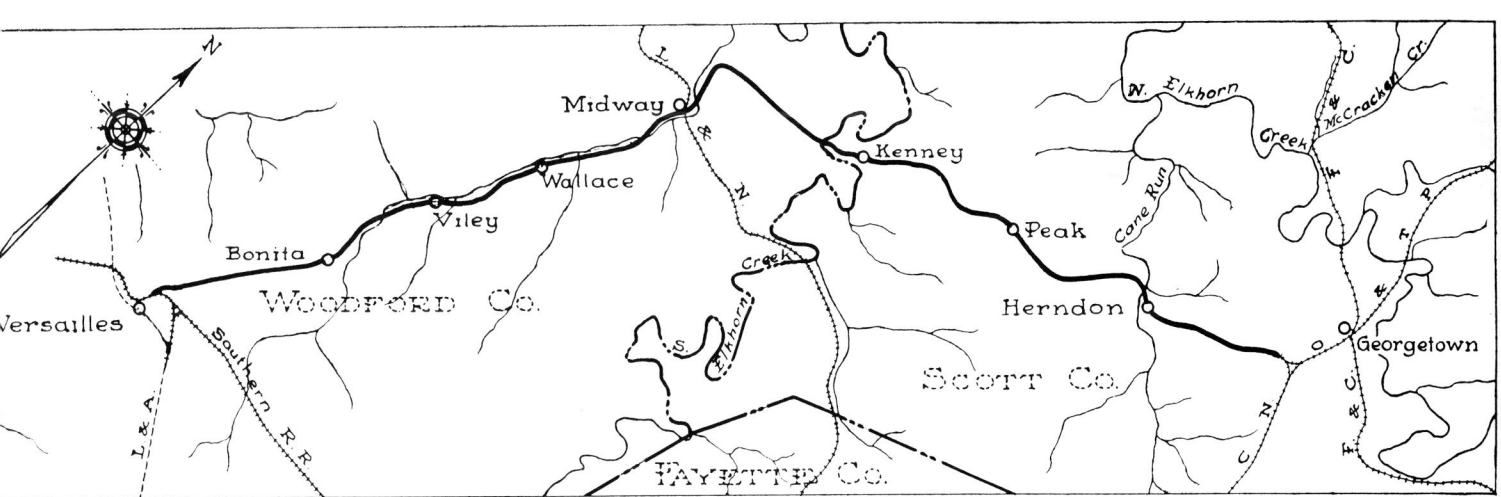

Map and Profile of the Southern's Versailles-Georgetown segment.

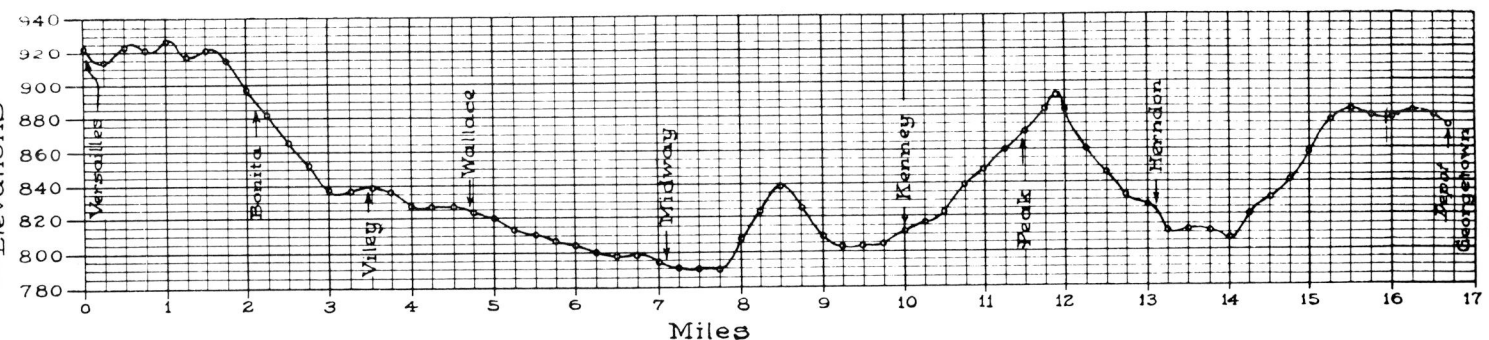

BETWEEN LAWRENCEBURG AND BURGIN.

Cap. of Siding in Cars.	EASTBOUND TRAINS.				Miles from Lawrenceburg.	Time Table No. 1. In Effect July 4, 1897. STATIONS	Sta'n Nos.	WESTBOUND TRAINS.				Min'm Time bet. Stations	
	Second Class.		First Class.					First Class.		Second Class.		Pass.	Frt.
	61 Ex. Sun.	31 Daily.	13 Daily.	11 Daily.				14 Daily.	12 Daily.	62 Ex. Sun.	32 Daily.		
	P.M.	A.M.	P.M.	A.M.				A.M.	P.M.	A.M.	P.M.		
95	1.45	1.35		6.40	0.0	Lv. Lawrenceburg N Ar.	63w	8.25	5.25	9.55	10.35		
					4.5							8	14
26	2.09	1.43	f 6.49	f 10.09	4.5	McBrayer	4x	f 8.12	f 5.14	9.25	10.20		
					2.0							3	6
1			f 6.54	f 10.12	6.5	Nevin	6x	f 8.06	f 5.09				
					1.9							3	6
40	2.30	1.59	s 6.58	s 10.16	8.4	W Salvisa D	8x	s 8.00	s 5.04	8.55	10.05		
					2.1							3	6
5			f 7.02	f 10.20	10.5	Vanarsdell	10x	f 7.55	f 4.59				
					2.9							5	9
50	2.57	2.20	f 7.09	f 10.27	13.4	McAfee	13x	f 7.45	f 4.51	8.20	9.45		
					2.8							5	9
4					16.2	Curry	17x						
					4.5							7	14
102	3.35	2.50	s 7.25	s 10.45	20.7	Harrodsburg D	21x	s 7.35	s 4.33	7.35	9.21		
					5.4							9	17
	4.05	3.15	7.40	10.58	26.1	W Burgin N Lv.	26x	7.25	4.20	6.40	9.00		
	P.M.	A.M.	P.M.	A.M.				A.M.	P.M.	A.M.	P.M.		
	Ex. Sun.	Daily.	Daily.	Daily.				Daily.	Daily.	Ex. Sun.	Daily.		
	61	31	13	11				14	12	62	32		

BETWEEN VERSAILLES AND GEORGETOWN.

Cap. of Siding in Cars.	EASTBOUND TRAINS.		Miles from Versailles	Time Table No. 1. In Effect July 4, 1897. STATIONS	Sta'n Nos.	WESTBOUND TRAINS.		Min'm Time bet. Stations	
	Second Class.	First Class.				First Class.	Second Class.	Pass.	Frt.
	67 Ex. Sun.	15 Daily.				16 Daily.	68 Ex. Sun.		
	A.M.	P.M.				A.M.	P.M.		
29	10.35	7.00	0.0	Lv. Versailles D Ar.	74w	8.05	4.15		
			2.2					4	8
4		f 7.06	2.2	Bonita	2y	f 7.58			
			2.8					4	8
15	11.00	f 7.13	5.0	Wallace	5y	f 7.50	3.48		
			2.1					4	7
31	11.20	s 7.20	7.1	Midway D	7y	s 7.45	3.38		
			2.9					5	9
19		f 7.28	10.0	Kenney	10y	f 7.35			
			2.2					4	8
		f 7.32	12.2	Peak	12y	f 7.28			
			1.3					3	7
22		f 7.39	13.5	Herndon	13y	f 7.25			
			3.2					6	11
	12.15	7.50	16.7	W Georgetown N Lv.	17y	7.15	3.00		
	P.M.	P.M.				A.M.	P.M.		
	Ex. Sun.	Daily.				Daily.	Ex. Sun.		
	67	15				16	68		

"F," Stop on Signal.   "S," Regular Stop.   "D," Day Telegraph Station.   "N," Night and Day Telegraph Station.

...eburg to Burgin and from Versailles to Georgetown have the right of track over trains of the same class moving in the opposite direction unless otherwise specified by train order.

Operating Timetable of the Southern Railway Company (in Kentucky) dated July 4, 1897, and showing scheduled services between Versailles-Georgetown and Harrodsburg-Burgin.   J. V. Yocum

EASTBOUND — VERSAILLES AND GEORGETOWN — WESTBOUND
(LOUISVILLE DIVISION)

		SECOND CLASS 111 Ex. Sun.	Capacity of Tracks in Cars		Station Nos.	Distance from Versailles	TIME TABLE No. 56 EFFECTIVE JANUARY 15, 1939 STATIONS	Minimum time in minutes between stations All Trains	SECOND CLASS 112 Ex. Sun.		
			Sidings	Other Tracks							
		A.M.					Lv. Ar.		A.M.		
		6 10	15	57	10 X	0.0	Y..VERSAILLES..D		8 15		
						2.2		7			
		6 17		1	2 Y	2.2	BONITA		8 07		
						2.8		9			
		6 26		10	5 Y	5.0	WALLACE		7 58		
						2.1		5			
		6 31	18	5	7 Y	7.1	MIDWAY		7 53		
						2.9		9			
		6 40		2	10 Y	10.0	KENNEY		7 41		
						6.7		21			
		7 10 112		75	17 Y	16.7	WY.GEORGETOWN Ar. Lv.		7 20 111		
		A.M.							A.M.		
		Ex. Sun. 111						All Trains	Ex. Sun. 112		

(St. L.-Lou.)

Operating Timetable No. 56, dated January 15, 1939, showing last scheduled service between Versailles and Georgetown.   Southern Railway System

Versailles-Georgetown passenger train at Versailles, 1900.   H. M. Jacobs

The 16.64 miles of track between Versailles and Georgetown traversed one of the most picturesque landscapes in America, crossing as it did the heart of the bluegrass region in Woodford and Scott Counties. Laid largely with 60' rail, mostly relay, the line had a maximum curvature of 8 degrees and a maximum grade of 1.52%. Curves through this rolling country were numerous and cuts were few. Trestles on the line had a combined length of 784', and deck plate girder bridges, 170'.

The CNO&TP division of the Southern Railway System was joined about 1,000' south of the Georgetown station by a wye, the north leg of which was an independent track to the station, thus obviating the necessity of Versailles-Georgetown trains fouling the main line. Water tanks were located 1¼ miles north of Versailles, and at Georgetown. At the latter point it was necessary for Versailles-Georgetown locomotives to cross over on the main CNO&TP track to take water. Dispatching was done from Harrodsburg by telegraph, with continuous offices at Versailles and Georgetown, and a day office at Midway. Telephones were never used on the Branch. Station buildings at Versailles and Georgetown were used jointly with other divisions of the Southern. A freight house was maintained at Midway.

Travel on the Branch was not expensive, the fare from Versailles to Midway being 21c, and from Versailles to Georgtown, 62c. Each day a distillery at Midway consumed two or three cars of grain and one of coal, and shipped its product out in carload lots. At Wallace a flourishing phosphate plant developed, sending out two or three cars of the material daily. Gradually, this business faded away. It is said that farmers in the vicinity of the plant kept raising the price for mining the phosphate from their land until a profitable undertaking became impossible.

As roads improved in Woodford and Scott Counties, prospects darkened for the Versailles-Georgetown line. The closing of a distillery at Midway in February, 1939, did not help matters. As business dwindled to a minimum, application for abandonment was filed with the I.C.C. The requisite permission was granted December 5, 1940. Dismantling of the line was completed April 10, 1941.

Burgin-Lawrenceburg train at Burgin headed south, circa 1902. 4-4-0 No. 2300 is on the point.
Forrest Cunningham

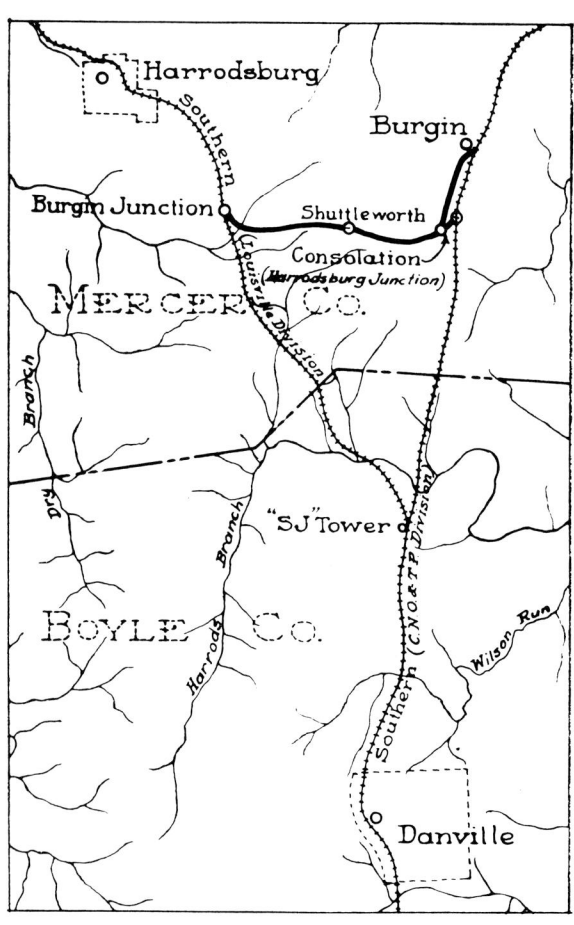

The Southwestern Railway, a four mile road between Harrodsburg and Harrodsburg Junction, was completed and placed in operation November 12, 1877. It was originally built to a gauge of 5' to conform to that of the Cincinnati Southern (CNO&TP) at the junction. In 1886 when the big road changed to 4'8½", the Southwestern did likewise. In 1888, the Louisville Southern gained control of the Southwestern, having completed the construction of its track from Harrodsburg to Lawrenceburg on its Louisville-Lexington route. It immediately extended the Southwestern's track north one mile from Harrodsburg Junction to Burgin to effect a better connection with the CNO&TP.

Both the Louisville Southern and the CNO&TPRy came under the hood of the Southern Railway System. The route from Louisville to the south via Harrodsburg and Danville became increasingly important. A more direct connection between the LS and the CNO&TP was effected in 1906 when a 5.1 mile segment between a point one mile from Harrodsburg on the Southwestern, and SJ Tower 3.1 miles north of Danville, was completed. Immediately, important traffic was diverted to the new trackage, and the Southwestern, with the exception of the one mile mentioned, was left with a skeleton schedule. Nevertheless, the old route remained in service a matter of 32 years until abandonment was authorized April 26, 1938. Some kind of speed record was set by wreckers as dismantlement was completed on May 27 of the same year.

Burgin Branch train at Lawrenceburg in 1896. Two car passenger train is headed by 4-4-0 No. 158. H. C. Daniel

Mixed train between Burgin and Harrodsburg, March 22, 1920. Passengers were carried in the caboose. A. S. Jensen

THE WRECKERS

It was a late summer afternoon in 1894. Engine 158, followed by a combination car and two coaches, was highballing it at a rate of between 30 to 40 miles per hour. The train had left Burgin around four p.m. and was comfortably filled with passengers bound for Harrodsburg, Lawrenceburg, and other points on to Louisville. Suddenly as the curve near Shuttleworth was rounded, there was a screechy whistling for brakes, and almost simultaneously the front of the engine raised up to a height of several feet and jolted forward for some distance until a stop could be made. As soon as engineer, A. M. Judd, and fireman Clay Daniel, could recover from their astonishment (and bruises), they dismounted from their cab and went forward to see what manner of accident would elevate the front of their locomotive to such a skyward position.

To their astonishment they saw that their engine had hit a healthy pile of ties and had climbed over the top of them. Attempts to back the locomotive off of the obstructions were futile as they merely succeeded in pulling the ties back with them. Finally, the jacks were gotten out and after several hours delay, No. 158 was free and ready to continue its journey.

This isn't the end of the story, however, as the detectives of the Louisville Southern went into action as railroad detectives do. The arrest of two negro boys living near the scene of the action followed, and the culprits readily admitted their guilt. Questioned as to why they put the ties on the track they made the noteworthy comment: "We wanted to see if the engine could knock them off."

HIGH POINTS OF THE TRACK

In order to secure a valuable right-of-way through Harrodsburg, the Louisville Southern had promised citizens of that city that an important terminal would be established there. Bennett H. Young of Louisville was said to have taken an important part in these negotiations. True to its promise, the Louisville Southern did establish machine shops, a round-house, and yard at Harrodsburg, facilities which were maintained for a number of years.

Eventually, however, most of this was moved back to Louisville, an act which so incensed citizens of Harrodsburg that some of them informed Young that he would be shot if he ever set a foot in Mercer county again.

There were no sidings between Harrodsburg and Burgin, but there was a yard at the former point and a six track yard at Burgin. There was a Wye at Harrodsburg, a turntable at Burgin, and pumped water tanks at both of these points. Stations and the approximate distances between them in miles were as follows:

Harrodsburg
    1.5
Burgin Junction (after completion of the cut-off)
    1.7
Shuttleworth
    1.1
Consolation
    1
Burgin

Agents and telegraphers were maintained at Burgin and Harrodsburg. The former office was continuous, and the latter varied, sometimes being continuous and at other times day only. The section was dispatched from Harrodsburg.

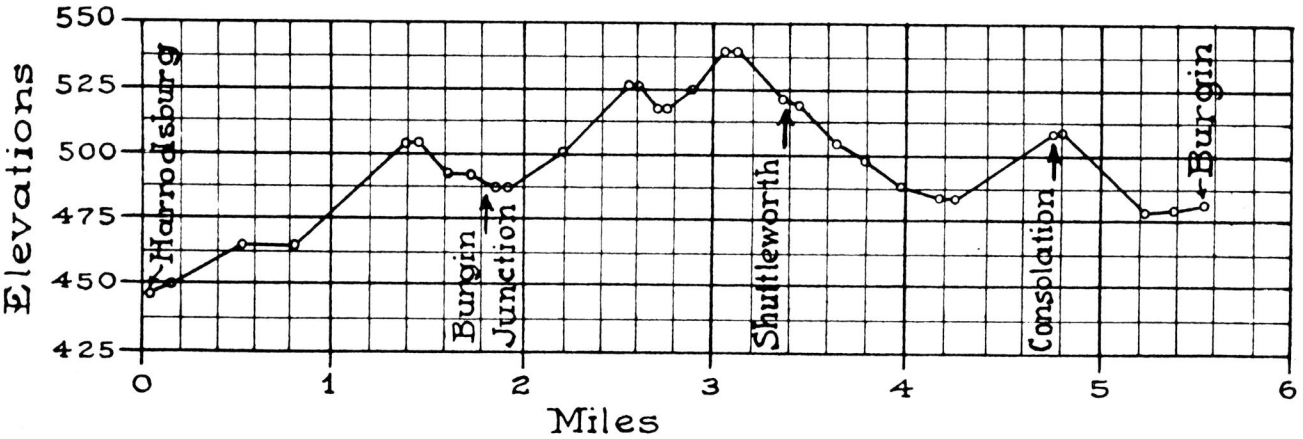

CHAPTER 7

"Back in the Menifee Hills"
Mt. Sterling to Rothwell
(Chesapeake & Ohio Railway)
Rothwell to McCausey and Apperson
(Red River Valley Railroad)

The original line from Mt. Sterling to Rothwell was built as a narrow gauge (36") railroad by the Mt. Sterling Coal Road, principally to bring its own coal and timber to market. It was opened in July, 1875. Originally it was constructed as a strap bar line with the iron bars laid on wooden stringers. Its total length was 19.54 miles, and it owned as rolling stock two 4-4-0 locomotives, 1 passenger coach, and 40 freight cars, mostly 4-wheel 10 ton vehicles for hauling coal.

The Mt. Sterling Coal Road defaulted on its bonds, and was reorganized in 1878 as the Coal Road Construction Company. The new organization replaced the strap rail

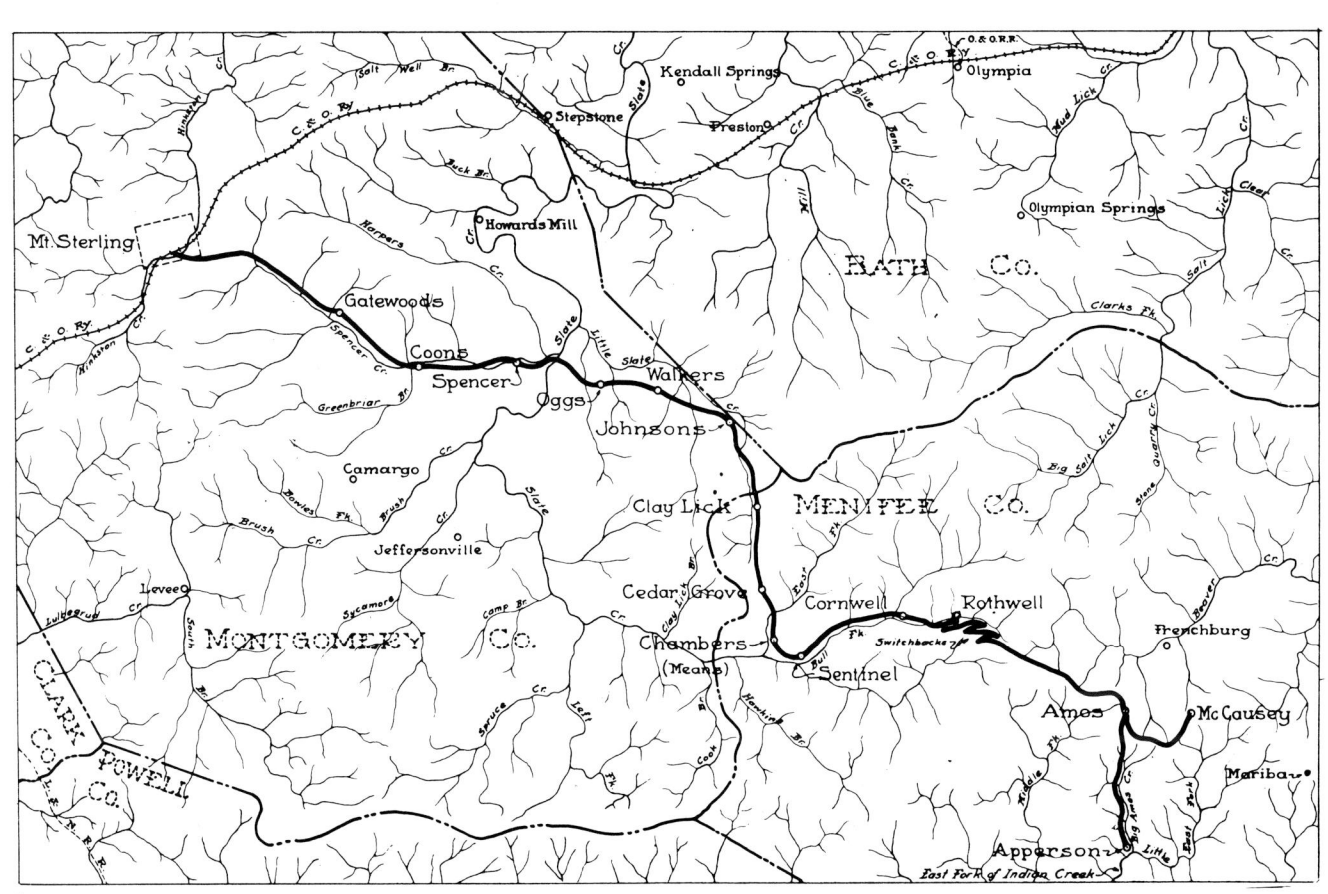

Slate Creek bridge and trestle looking west on the C&O's K&SA Branch.   C&O Ry

with 35' T rail and secured additional rolling stock. Under a special act of the Kentucky legislature approved January 14, 1882, and due to a change in ownership, the name of the line was changed to the Kentucky & South Atlantic Railway.

Business did not come up to expectations and a receiver was appointed December 15, 1885. A number of other transactions involving the line took place, culminating in the Chesapeake & Ohio Railway taking control of the road July 1, 1892. Plans were made to standard gauge the Branch and this was completed in August, 1895.

Although the Kentucky & South Atlantic was acquired by the Chesapeake & Ohio Railway in 1892, it was July 1, 1907, before the K&SA was formerly deeded to the C&O, two intermediate steps pointing to this merging having taken place in 1902 and 1904, respectively.

The termination of the K&SA at the unlikely community of Rothwell, 19½ miles from Mt. Sterling, did much to doom the line. The builders had ambitions of a railroad of much greater length, penetrating the heart of the eastern Kentucky coal field. Undoubtedly a shortage of funds accounted for the abrupt end of track. However, a small oil field developed in the vicinity of Rothwell in the twenties,

Mt. Sterling Coal Road waybill for six barrels and three boxes of eggs. March 11, 1879.   J. C. McNeal

Pass given S. S. Pinney, superintendent of the Red River Valley Railroad in 1903, by the Ferrocarril Oxaca a Ejutla (of Mexico), another narrow gauge "pike." S. S. Pinney

and carloads of drilling outfits and other machinery were shipped in. The oil field became exhausted in 1931, and the equipment was just as promptly shipped out.

The Branch had many feet of rather low trestle work that were susceptible to floods as well as occasional accidents. One of these occurred during the severe winter of 1917-18 on the Turkey Run trestle. The coach of the mixed train headed for Rothwell overturned bottom side up, injuring 18 or 20 people as well as the conductor. A stove set the car on fire which was quickly extinguished by the train crew. In spite of the zero weather, the injured were brought to Mt. Sterling and placed in private homes, as there was no hospital. It is said that the C&O claim agent settled all damages before the passengers could leave their improvised hospitals.

By the end of the twenties the fate of the Branch was obvious. Permission to abandon the line was granted on August 8, 1931, and trains on the Branch were cancelled effective midnight September 7. However, service was not completely suspended until September 20. The work of taking up the track was not started until March 1, 1933. It was completed April 22 of that year. When the old rails were removed it was noted that some of them were made in 1881 at the Krupp Works in Germany, and the Creusatt plant in France.

The K&SA Branch of the C&O for many years had a valuable feeder in the Red River Valley Railroad. Around 1892 or '93, a lumber company built a narrow gauge (36") railroad from Rothwell, a matter of two and one-half miles to the top of the ridge. The hill was ascended by four switch-backs. This venture was not a success, and the short line was purchased by the Union City Lumber Company of Union City, Michigan. This company had acquired large tracks of timber around Big Amos Creek and it was decided to extend the old narrow gauge line to these areas.

The Red River Valley Railroad was incorporated May 19, 1898. The old ascent of the hill, including the four switchbacks, was preserved, and the new construction ran along the ridge to a point south of Frenchburg which was promptly named McCausey after the president of the RRV. This location was reached in 1898 and the nine miles of the railroad were placed in operation. In 1899, a five mile branch line was constructed, which made a junction with the main line at a point about two miles west of McCausey named Amos, and ran in a southerly direction from Big Amos Creek to Apperson, for an additional five miles.

Rolling stock of the Red River Valley included three Climax locomotives of the B type, of which two were conventional and the other of the saddle-tank variety. The road owned about ten coal cars, 16 lumber flats, and for a time a small combine. Locomotive No. 1 was popularly known as "Old Jim."

As long as the lumber business flourished, so did the Red River Valley. The trans-loading of cars at Rothwell from narrow to standard gauge vehicles was a huge operation in itself. But when the important timber stands had been removed it was decided to scrap the railroad. This was done during the latter part of 1911. The three Climax locomotives were shipped to various points outside Kentucky.

"Old Jim", Red River Valley Railroad's No. 1, a B-type Climax. Note combine which closely resembles the more conventional way car.

Above—Siding and Station at Cornwell. Note loading platform.
Below—Chambers Station.   C&O Ry.

Upper—Spur and General Store at Johnsons.
Lower—Rothwell, the end of the line. C&O Ry.

Another view of the Slate Creek bridge and trestle.
C&O Ry.

Track scene between Walkers and Johnsons. C&O Ry.

Employees' Timetables of the Kentucky & South Atlantic Branch, dated May 19, 1895 and June 19, 1904, respectively.   C&O Ry.

KENTUCKY AND SOUTH ATLANTIC BRANCH.

WESTWARD — **EASTWARD**

SECOND CLASS 123 Lv. Daily ex. Sund'y	SECOND CLASS 121 Lv. Daily ex. Sund'y	Side Track—Capacity in Feet		STATIONS	Station Numbers	Distance from Mt. Sterling	SECOND CLASS 122 Arr. Daily ex. Sund'y	SECOND CLASS 124 Arr. Daily ex. Sund'y
4 15 pm	9 00 am	241		ROTHWELL	K 20	19.7	8 45 am	3 45 pm
				0.8				
f 4 20	f 9 05			Cornwell	K 19	18.9	f 8 40	f 3 40
				2.2				
f 4 29	f 9 09	200		Sentinel	K 17	16.7	f 8 33	f 3 30
				0.9				
f 4 33	f 9 13	350		Chambers	K 16	15.8	f 8 30	f 3 25
				0.9				
f 4 37	f 9 17	347		Cedar Grove	K 15	14.9	f 8 25	f 3 20
				1.1				
f 4 43	f 9 23			Clay Lick	K 13	13.8	f 8 20	f 3 15
				3.0				
f 4 50	f 9 32	313		Johnsons	K 11	10.8	f 8 05	f 3 05
				1.6				
f 4 57	f 9 40			Walkers	K 9	9.2	f 7 58	f 2 58
				1.2				
f 5 03	f 9 45			Oggs	K 8	8.0	f 7 52	f 2 52
				1.8				
f 5 10	f 9 54	100		W Spencer	K 6	6.2	f 7 45	f 2 44
				2.1				
f 5 20	f 10 03			Coons	K 4	4.1	f 7 35	f 2 34
				1.5				
f 5 30	f 10 10			Gatewoods	K 3	2.6	f 7 27	f 2 27
				2.6				
5 45 pm	10 30 am	310		W MT. STERLING	L 90		7 15 am	2 15 pm
Arr. Daily ex. Sund'y	Arr. Daily ex. Sund'y						Lv. Daily ex. Sund'y	Lv. Daily ex. Sund'y

s—Regular stop.   f—Stop on signal.   W—Water tank.

A.—Standard Clock and Bulletin Book located in telegraph office, Mount Sterling.
D.—Maximum speed 20 miles per hour.
K.—Train 121 has right to Mt. Sterling over train 124.

L. S. ROBERTSON,
Train Master.

E. H. EDSALL,
Chief Train Dispatcher.

KENTUCKY & SOUTH ATLANTIC BRANCH.

WESTWARD — **EASTWARD**

SECOND CLASS No. 123 Mixed Daily ex Sun P.M. Leave	SECOND CLASS No. 121 Mixed Daily ex Sun A.M. Leave	Side Track Capacity in Narrow Gauge Cars		STATIONS	Station Numbers	Distance from Mt. Sterling	SECOND CLASS No. 122 Mixed Daily ex Sun A.M. Arrive	SECOND CLASS No. 124 Mixed Daily ex Sun P.M. Arrive
3 15	8 00	11		Rothwell	K 20	19.7	7 30	3 00
				0.8				
s 3 20	s 8 05	14		Cornwell	K 19	18.9	s 7 25	s 2 55
				2.2				
f 3 30	f 8 15	4		Sentinel	K 17	16.7	f 7 15	f 2 45
				0.9				
f 3 35	f 8 20	10		W Chambers	K 16	15.8	f 7 10	f 2 40
				0.9				
f 3 40	f 8 25	12		Hedgers	K 15	14.9	f 7 05	f 2 35
				1.1				
f 3 45	f 8 30			Clay Lick	K 13	13.8	f 7 00	f 2 30
				3.0				
s 3 57	s 8 42	20		Johnson's	K 11	10.8	s 6 48	s 2 18
				1.6				
f 4 04	f 8 49			Walker's	K 9	9.2	f 6 41	f 2 11
				1.2				
f 4 10	f 8 55			Ogg's	K 8	8.0	f 6 35	f 2 05
				1.8				
f 4 18	s 9 03	10		Spencer	K 6	6.2	f 6 27	f 1 57
				2.1				
f 4 27	f 9 12			Coon's	K 4	4.1	f 6 18	f 1 48
				1.5				
f 4 33	f 9 18			Gatewood's	K 3	2.6	f 6 12	f 1 42
				2.6				
4 45	9 30	36		W Mt. Sterling	L 90		6 00	1 30
P.M. Arrive Daily except Sunday	A.M. Arrive Daily except Sunday						A.M. Leave Daily except Sunday	P.M. Leave Daily except Sunday

s Regular stop.   f Stop on signal.   w Water tank.

...y & South Atlantic regular trains of the same class will have right of track in either direction to terminals against...
...should not exceed 20 miles per hour under any circumstances.

S. STEWART,
Train Master and Chief Dispatcher.

H. C. BOUGHTON,
Assistant Superintendent.

CHAPTER 8
"The Route of 'Old Henry'"
Lancaster to Fort Estill
(Louisville & Nashville Railroad)

For many years a mixed train leisurely plod the 33 miles of the Louisville & Nashville Railroad's branch line between Richmond and Rowland. The engineer, a person familiar to everyone living within hearing distance of the locomotive's whistle, was one Henry Lammers. The sobriquet "Old Henry" came into use as the designation, first for the mixed train, and later for the entire Branch.

Construction of the Branch was started in July, 1867, and was completed November 8, 1868, the first run taking place on that date. Trains were scheduled to run through from Richmond to Louisville via the Branch.

When the Kentucky Central Railroad built south from Cincinnati and desired to extend its track beyond Richmond to a junction with the L&N north of Livingston, it decided to lease the entire Richmond-Rowland Branch of the L&N, partly to get control of the two miles between Fort Estill and Richmond for a portion of its main line. The lease was made effective June 1, 1882, and continued until the latter part of 1890. In December of that year the Louisville & Nashville gained control of the Kentucky Central, thus returning the Fort Estill-Rowland Branch to its fold. For a number of years thereafter the Branch enjoyed two round trips daily of passenger trains running to and from Louisville and Cincinnati, respectively, as well as a local making a round trip between Richmond and Stanford.

Below—Things were humming on the Branch in 1922 with three daily round trips.   L&N RR.

Table 51—ROWLAND BRANCH.							
25	27	71	M	Nov. 12, 1922.	26	28	70
P M	P M	A M	..	LVE.] [ARR.	A M	P M	P M
†8 10	*1 45	†7 00	0	+.Richmond.ᵟ	6 03	1 10	1 45
8 13	1 48	7 05	3	.Fort Estill.	5 57	1 03	1 25
8 19	1 53	7 11	6	. Duncannon .	5 48	12 54	12 54
8 34	2 09	7 29	10	Silver Creekᵟ	5 40	12 46	12 46
8 47	2 21	7 50	15	. Paint Lick .	5 27	12 33	12 05
9 02	2 36	8 15	21	Point Leavell	5 12	12 20	11 47
9 06	2 40	8 25	23	. Hyattsville .	5 07	12 15	11 40
9 15	2 50	8 40	26	+Lancasterᵟ	4 57	12 07	11 10
9 35	3 12	9 40	34	.Rowlandᵟ	†4 40	*11 50	†10 45
9 45	3 22	9 50	35	Stanford .	†4 30	*11 40	A M
P M	P M	A M	..	ARR.] [LVE.	A M	A M	.....

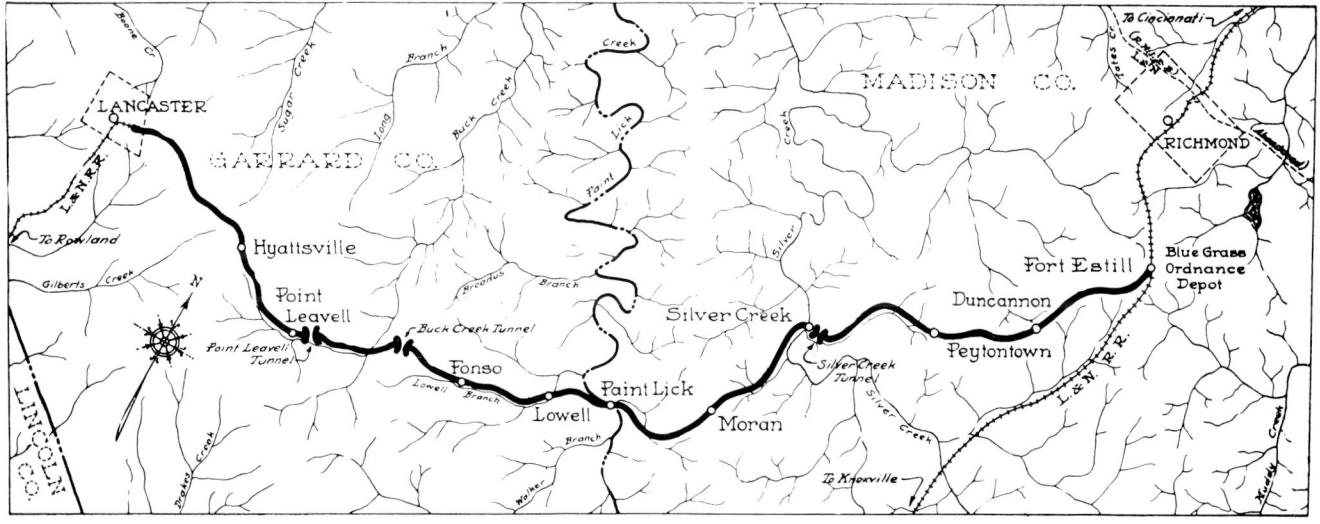

Above—Station Depot at Paint Lick.
J. Winston Coleman, Jr.
At left—Station Depot at Silver Creek.
J. Winston Coleman, Jr.
At Left Below—Piers of Water tank one-half mile west of Paint Lick.   J. Winston Coleman, Jr.

Most of the Fort Estill-Rowland segment suffered the same fate as other short country lines that rendered important services before the era of the automobile and truck. The 8 mile segment between Lancaster and Rowland was spared, however, so as to continue to provide for freight movements to and from Lancaster.

Washington approval for the abandonment of the 22.89 miles between Lancaster and Fort Estill was granted December 1, 1933. Service was discontinued January 15, 1934, and the segment was removed soon thereafter.

Schedule on the Richmond-Rowland Branch during the Eighties.
L&N RR.

RICHMOND TO ROWLAND.

	No. 17 EX. SUN.	Distance.	Trains do not stop at Stations where no time is shown.	No. 18 EX. SUN.	
. . . .	1 50 pm	.0	Lv . . Richmond . N Ar	10 15 am	. . . .
. . . .	2 02 "	2.6	. . . . Ft. Estill . . . D	10 06 "	. . . .
. . . .	2 17 "	5.9	. . . Duncannon . . .	9 50 "	. . . .
. . . .	2 55 "	10.0	. . . Silver Creek . . D	9 30 "	. . . .
. . . .	3 20 "	15.2	. . . Paint Lick . . D	8 45 "	. . . .
. . . .	3 33 "	16.3	. . . . Lowell	8 35 "	. . . .
. . . .	3 55 "	20.9	. . Point Leavell . . .	8 17 "	. . . .
. . . .	4 05 "	22.5	. . . Hyattsville . . .	8 07 "	. . . .
. . . .	4 45 "	25.8	. . . Lancaster . . D	7 50 "	. . . .
. . . .	5 00 "	29.2	. . . . Gilbert	7 17 "	. . . .
. . . .	5 20 pm	33.0	Ar . . Rowland . N Lv	7 00 am	. . . .

CHAPTER 9

"One Track—Two Railroads"
Salt Lick to Blackwater
(Licking River Railroad)
Olympia to Owingsville
(Owingsville & Olympia Railroad)

S. P. Guthrie

The 32 mile narrow (36") gauge Licking River Railroad started life as the Licking Valley Railway. Incorporated in 1896 as the creation of the Sterling Lumber Company. It made a junction with the Chesapeake & Ohio Railway at Salt Lick, then ran in a southeasterly direction, for twelve miles to Yale, where a lumber mill was erected. The route of the line largely followed the meanderings of the Licking River.

The Licking Valley Railway was sold at a receiver's sale, October 24, 1899, for $29,000. The name of the line was changed to Licking River Railroad. The new owners organized the Yale Lumber Company, built another large mill at Yale, and eventually were employing over 500 men between the mill, the railroad, and the timber gangs.

Plans were made to extend the railroad. By 1902 the track had been pushed on to Morgan, 14.5 miles from Yale, and 26.5 miles from Salt Lick.

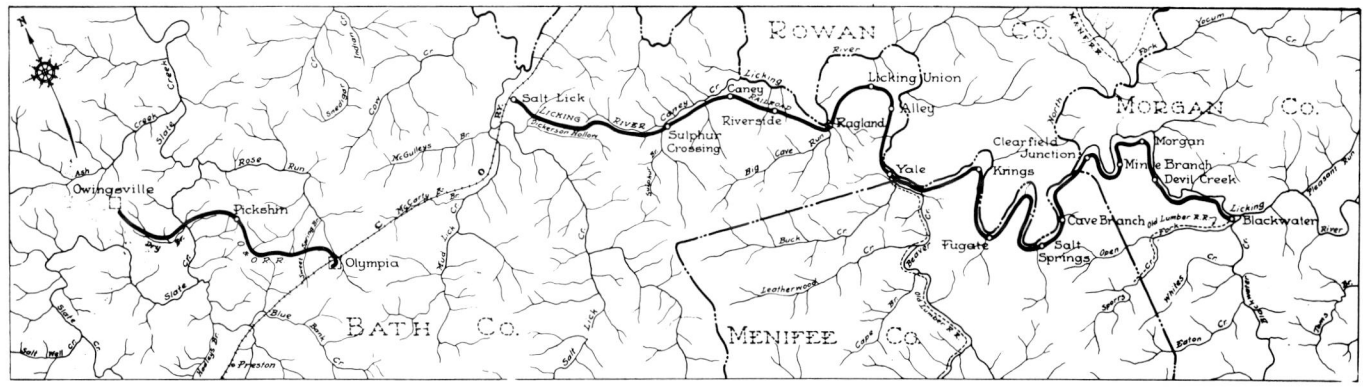

Passenger service on the Licking River consisted of a daily round trip the length of the line by a mixed train. Schedules were broken at Yale in such a way that two days were required for the in-bound trip from Salt Lick to Blackwater.

Licking River No. 9, a 4-4-0 Baldwin, said to have been purchased from the Cincinnati Equipment Company and formerly used on the narrow gauge Cincinnati, Georgetown & Portsmouth. J. L. Cassidy

In 1903, the Licking River Railroad was extended 3 miles to Devil Creek, and in 1905 a two and one-half mile addition brought it to the mouth of Blackwater, the point that formed the final terminal of the LR.

A typical mixed train on the Licking River. Locomotive No. 8, another 4-4-0 Baldwin was reported to have the same background as No. 9. J. L. Cassidy

Freight rolling stock on the Licking River included one wooden caboose, at least five homemade wooden box cars, approximately 25 flat cars equipped with side racks to handle staves, etc., about the same number of log cars, and one coal car.

Second No. 1, a B-type Climax purchased new. This machine weighed in at 20 tons, had 9x12" cylinders and 28" drivers.
J. A. Power

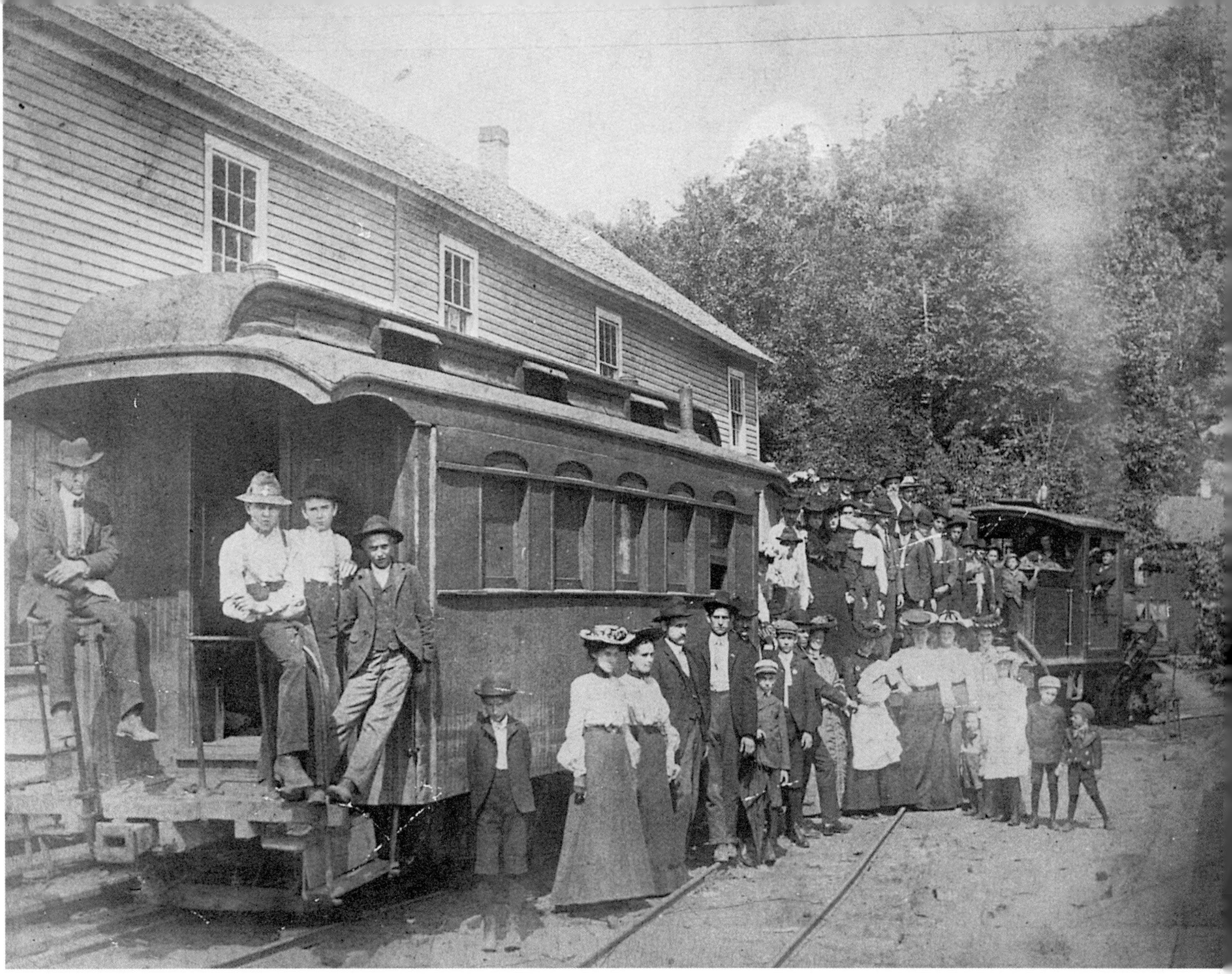

Licking River Railroad funeral train at Yale. Locomotive is Climax No. 2, the second LR locomotive to bear this number. Coach is probably No. 12.   Bud Hunt

The railroad at one time or another owned three wooden coaches, all containing single wash rooms and lit by kerosene lamps. No. 10, the longest, was obtained from the Cincinnati Equipment Company, and formerly ran on the CG&P. Numbers 11 and 12 were shorter than No. 10 and home-built.

A Licking River RR section crew photographed in 1908. Joe Stayton

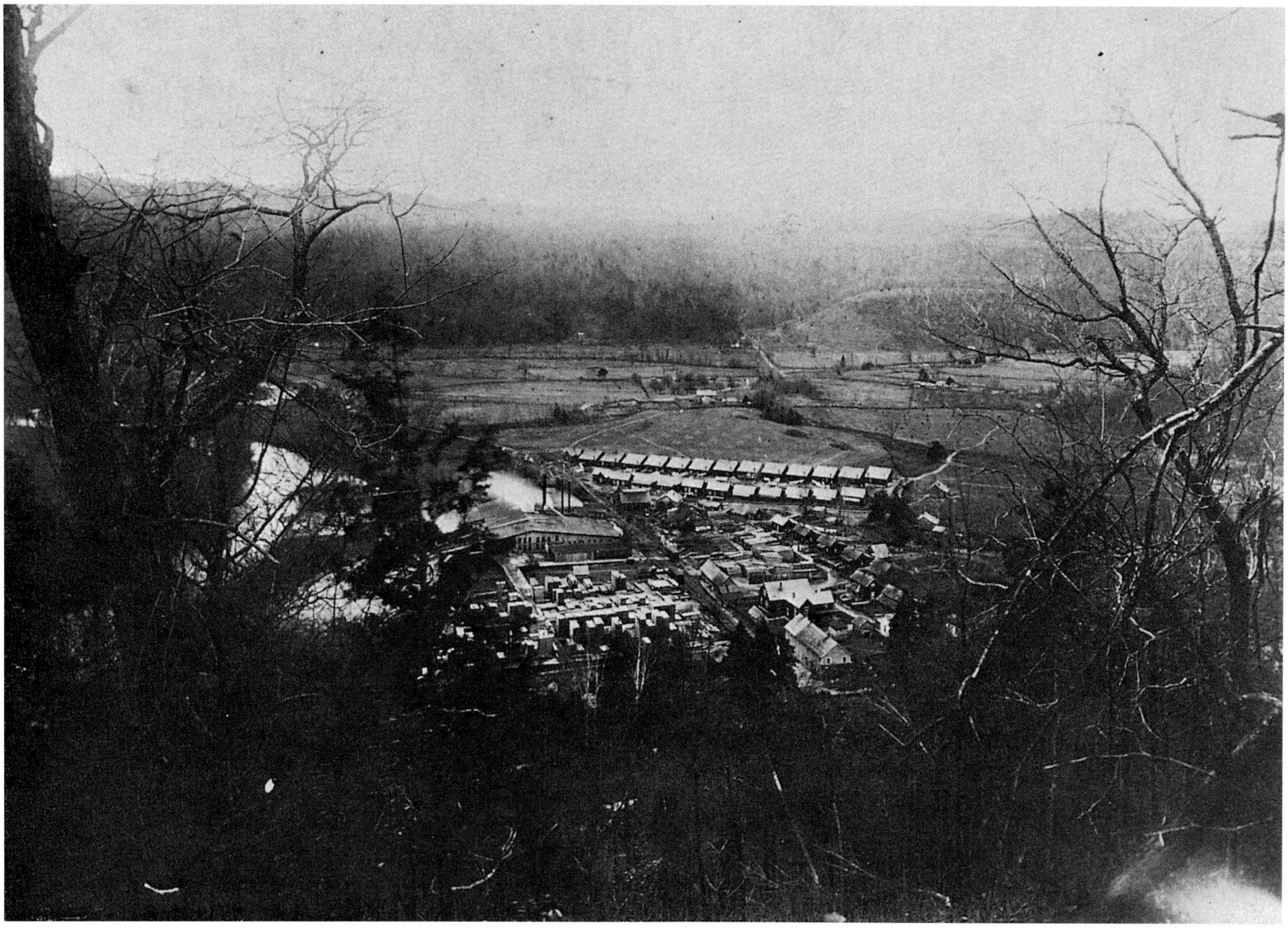

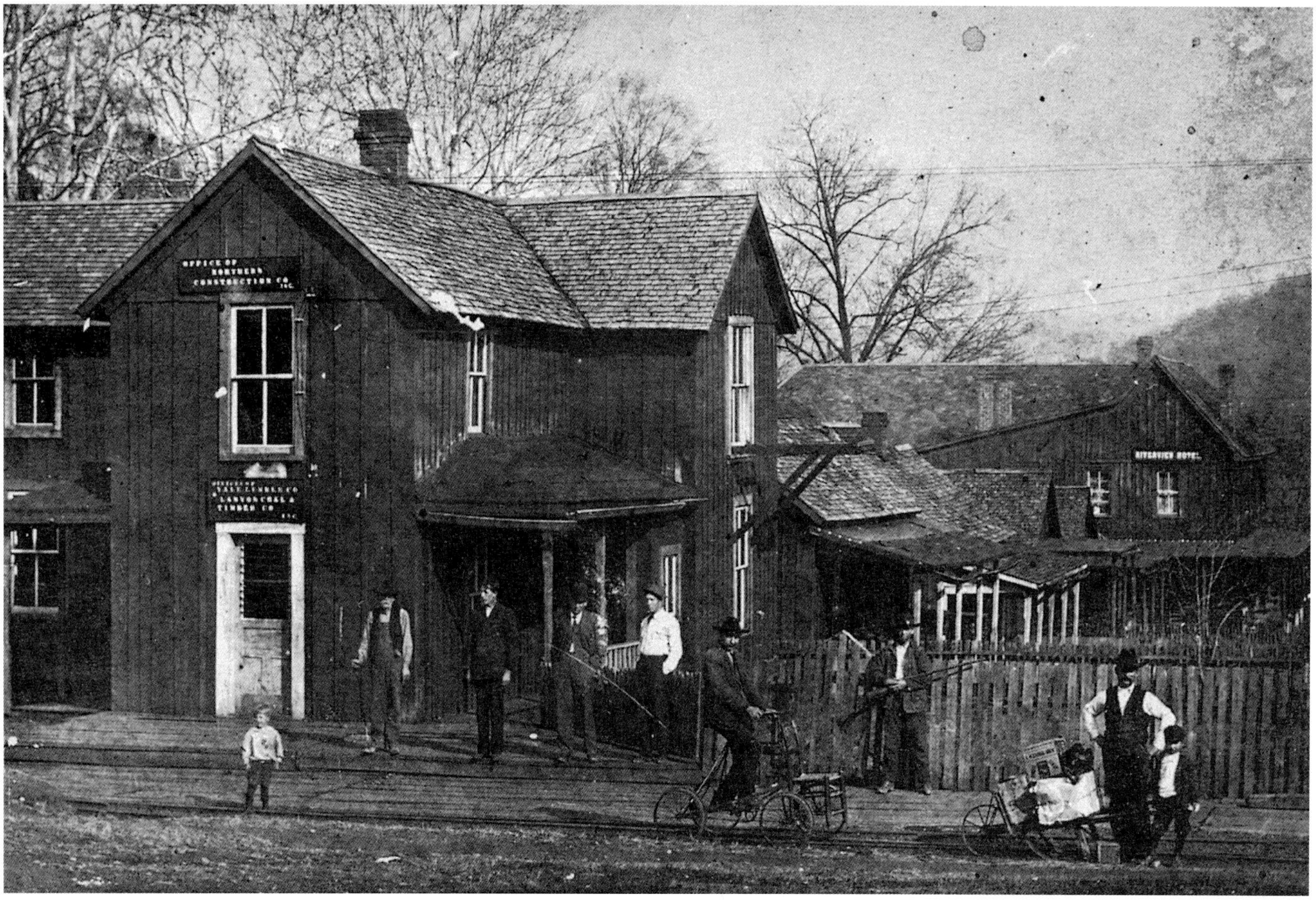
OFFICE OF
NORTHERN
CONSTRUCTION CO.
INC.

Left top—Yale, a matter of 12 miles from Salt Lick, was the headquarters of the railroad and the site of the Sterling Lumber Company's large mill. The railroad was opened to this point April 1, 1897. J. L. Cassidy

Left bottom — This building served as the railroad's depot at Yale, as the headquarters of the railroad, and contained the offices of at least two other companies.
J. L. Cassidy

Above—A rare picture of the first No. 3, an A-type Climax bought second-hand from a timber railroad in West Virginia. J. L. Cassidy

Below, one of the Licking River's Climax locomotives dozes in the LR yards at Salt Lick. Elevated horizontal tank supplied the locomotives with water. Tank cars in far right background are on a siding paralleling the main line of the C&O. J. L. Cassidy

Mixed train on the Licking River Railroad at the foot of Caney Mountain. The locomotive has cut off from the coach and box car and has gone ahead to assist a freight train over the grade, a customary operating procedure. A. J. Utterback

As the timber sources of the Licking River area began to play out, so did the fortunes of the railroad. Beginning in 1906, the line was constantly in the red, and the hue became more vivid in the ensuing years. In the summer of 1913 all operations ceased, the track was removed, and the Licking River Railroad was no more. Practically, however, the railroad did not completely die. While the LR was in process of abandonment, W. W. "Mother" Hubbard, its general manager, arranged to secure much of the rail, a locomotive, one coach, and some other rolling stock. The story of the Owingsville & Olympia which follows, carries on the tale of this "wandering railroad."

The Owingsville & Olympia Railroad enjoys the dubious distinction of being the shortest lived railroad in Kentucky. As the Licking River Railroad was gasping its last, "Mother Hubbard" approached the citizens of Owingsville and obtained their 'co-operation' in raising a sum variously estimated at $20,000 to $40,000 to build a six mile narrow gauge railroad connecting Olympia on the Chesapeake & Ohio Railway, with Owingsville, the county seat of Bath County.

Bringing with him the 30 and 40 pound rail from the Licking River as well as Locomotive No. 7, Coach No. 10, and Box Cars 48-52, the line was constructed so promptly that trains started running near the first of 1915.

Operation of the steam locomotive proved impractical, so it was disposed of and an internal combustion locomotive was purchased (on credit) to take its place. Then in October, 1915, this new locomotive broke loose when its brakes failed to hold, coasted to the first trestle south of Owingsville where it jumped the track and was wrecked. Although no injuries resulted, the public was apprehensive that another accident might occur with lethal results and, as a consequence, refused to ride the train. By 1916 there was no traffic whatever on the O&O. A reorganization changed the name of the line to the Olympia & Owingsville, but this did not generate the needed traffic. In 1918, the line was dismantled and the light rails were sold to a number of Kentucky coal mines.

Coach of the Cincinnati, Georgetown & Portsmouth Railroad being overhauled at the Cincinnati Equipment Company before being turned over to the Licking River as its No. 10. The coach was later used on the Owingsville & Olympia after the LR was abandoned.
Lad G. Arend

Washout on the Licking River Railroad. Joe Stayton

"SHOOTIN' ALONG THE LICKIN'"

William Cochran, engineer of the Licking River Railroad was called out one night to run an extra to Blackwater to return some raft hands that had been down the river. While oiling around the locomotive awaiting the time to start, an old man came up and demanded to ride in the cab. Telling him that it was against orders, Cochran turned his back on the stranger, considering the matter closed. An informal poke in the back caused him to turn around again, this time to face a six-shooter in the hands of the stranger. With the demand for the cab ride so reinforced, Cochran felt that the rules could be dispensed with this once and told the stranger so. Immediately, the latter was the soul of courtesy, put away his gun, and brought up a jug that had escaped Cochran's attention previously. Stowed away in the cab with this container, the stranger gave the crew no further trouble.

Other adventures of this sort, however, were less pleasant. One night a notorious neighborhood bad man boarded the passenger train at Salt Lick. It hadn't run far before his fellow passengers realized that he was dead drunk. To add to the color of the occasion, the man pulled out two huge pistols, and started to let bullets fly through the coach. Then

Licking Valley Railway's No. 1, a 0-4-0 Baldwin, buried in the earth after jumping the trestle.
J. L. Cassidy

he discovered the presence of Fred Pischel, an official of the company, and started after him with killing as his objective. By some means, the official evaded the bad man until Yale was reached. At this point Conductor Utterback removed the rest of the passengers and locked the coach. Then he called "the law," got himself a revolver and stood guard until the local constabulary arrived.

On another occasion, a drunken raft-hand boarded the train at Salt Lick and started shooting up the car on Caney Hill. This time Conductor Utterback took his gun away from him and put him off the train at Caney. The raft-hand walked the seven miles to Yale, arriving that night in a highly chastened condition. His gun was returned to him.

S. P. Guthrie

Owingsville & Olympia train over the newly constructed Slate Creek bridge.   J. L. Cassidy

Dismantling crew on the Licking River Railroad at Riverside, 1913.   J. L. Cassidy

CHAPTER 10
"Two Northern Kentucky Abandonments"
Brooksville to Wellsburg
(Brooksville & Ohio River Railroad)
Hillsboro to Flemingsburg Junction
(Cincinnati, Flemingsburg & Southeastern Railroad; and Flemingsburg & Northern Rd.)

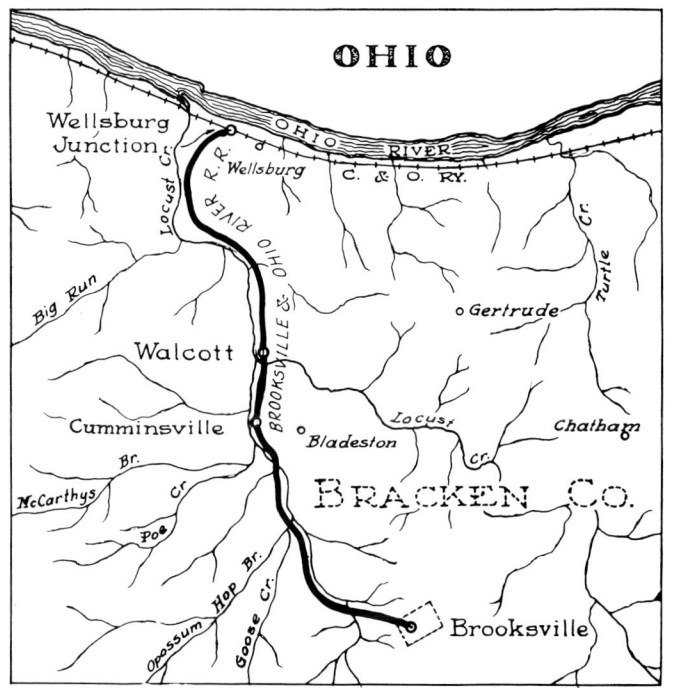

The latter part of the nineteenth century was a period of intense railroad construction, particularly as far as feeder lines were concerned. Almost every community demanded its railroad, and Brooksville, the county seat of Bracken County with a population of 500 was no exception.

The Brooksville Railroad was fathered largely by Younger Alexander of Lexington, who on August 8, 1895 organized the company with a capitalization of $32,000. The line was to run from a junction with the Chesapeake & Ohio Railway where it crossed Locust Creek, to Brooksville, a distance of 10 miles.

Construction started sometime in 1896 but proceeded slowly due to a scarcity of money. Nevertheless, during June 1897, the 9.89 mile railroad was completed and put into operation. Initially the new road was profitable. Several new industries sprang up along the line including a tobacco factory at Brooksville, whose building later became a distillery, and still later a lumber mill.

But this prosperity was short-lived. The nemesis of all short-line railroads, improved highways, were making their appearance. Passenger service was discontinued in 1918. A group of Brooksville business men bought the bankrupt Brooksville Railroad in 1919 and changed the name to the Brooksville & Ohio River Railroad.

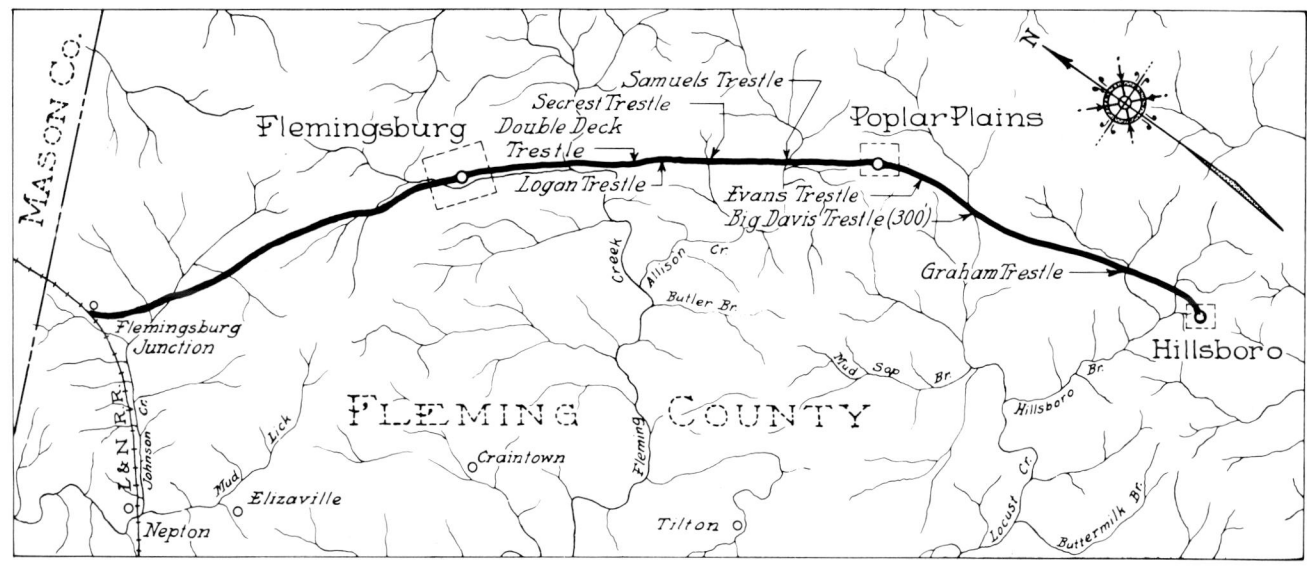

Above — The terminal of the Brooksville Railroad at Brooksville, showing Depot, Engine House, Locomotive and Combine.   W. G. Tilton

At right—Mail and a few reluctant passengers were carried on one of the Brooksville Railroad's motorized section cars after "formal" passenger service was discontinued in 1918.   W. T. Breeze

But the age of gasoline spelled the little line's doom. On April 11, 1931, the Interstate Commerce Commission gave the B&OR permission to abandon the railroad. At this time the track was virtually unusable and three foreign-line freight cars were stranded at Brooksville, one belonging to the C&ORY. A crew from that company sent a wrecker to Brooksville to get its car, and succeeded only after 21 derailments in the 10 miles. The other two vehicles—tank cars—were loaded on huge trucks and taken to Augusta where they could be re-railed.

The railroad owned one wooden passenger car painted maroon. It was purchased as a straight coach and rebuilt by the railroad into a combine. Lighted by gas, the car boasted of pug stoves at both ends, and a super-short ventilator pipe, since the one of conventional length was knocked off regularly by tree limbs encroaching on the right-of-way. The coach was eventually sold to a farmer near Wellsburg who converted it into a stripping room for tobacco.

Although the railroad made use of six locomotives during its existence, apparently not more than two were in its possession at one time. (See roster in Appendix 1)

Belles of the Wellsburg neighborhood "decorate" the railroad's No. 2 (Baldwin 4-4-0) while the engine rested at that junction point with the C&O.   S. P. Guthrie

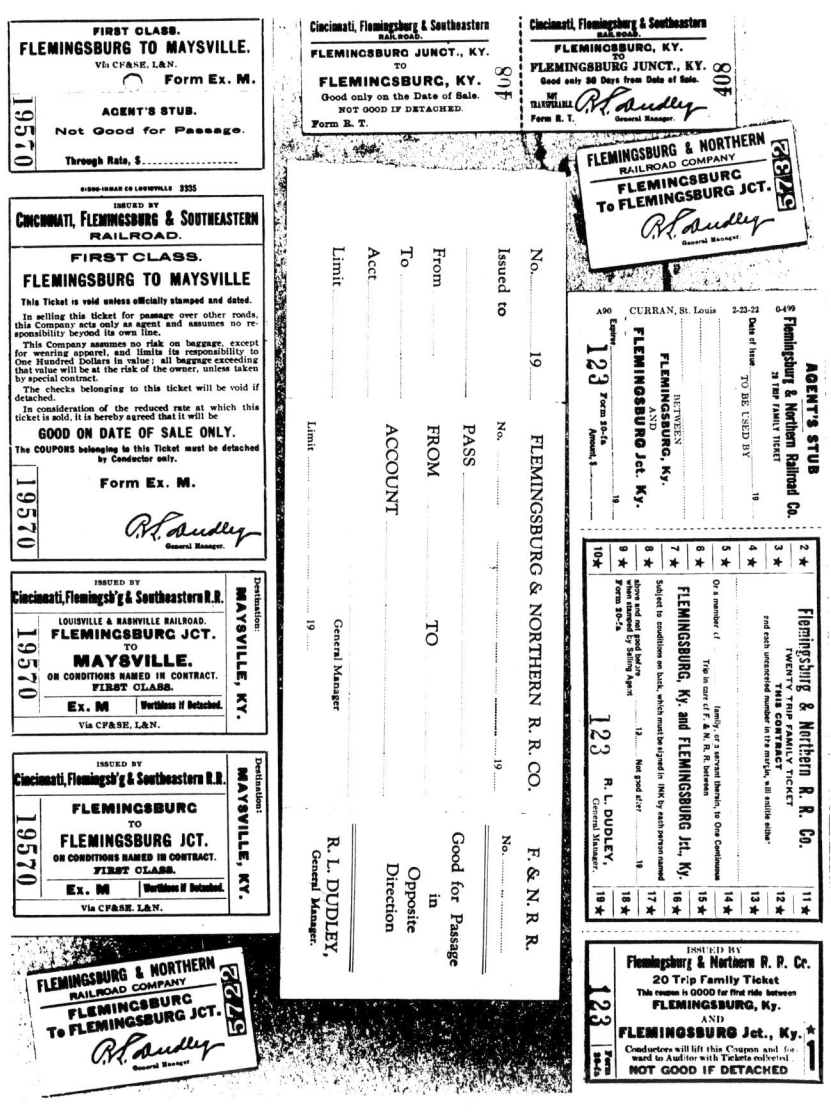

Seven different legal designations at one time or another were applied to the 17 mile railroad between Flemingsburg Junction (Johnsons) and Hillsboro. The line was chartered in 1876 as the Covington, Flemingsburg & Pound Gap Railway. Despite the geographical ambitions evident in its name, by the spring of 1877 trains were running between Johnsons and Flemingsburg. The following year the line was opened to Hillsboro.

The railroad was built as a narrow gauge (36") line. In 1879, the various contractors, understandably irked by unpaid bills, persuaded the Fleming County Circuit Court to force the sale of the railroad. The purchasers, on January 24, 1880, formed a new company, the Licking Valley Railway Company; but that name was shortlived and on September 11 of the same year the company was reorganized as the Covington, Flemingsburg & Southeastern. The year, 1880, was a busy one for the railroad, because before the advent of 1881 the railroad was again sold under Court decree and this time was acquired by the newly organized Cincinnati & Southeastern Railway, the fourth company to operate the line.

Financial troubles continued to plague the railroad and on May 7, 1887, the line was sold under foreclosure and reorganized as the Covington, Flemingsburg & Ashland Railway. The fifth reorganization (and the sixth name) occurred on May 24, 1905, resulting in the designation, Cincinnati, Flemingsburg & Southeastern Railroad. Then on Friday, May 10, 1907, the little narrow gauge line had its one wreck. It happened two miles southeast of Flemingsburg at a point known as Weaver's Ford where a double bent trestle, 38' above ground at its highest point spanned a ravine. The train consisted of locomotive No. 1, a box car and a coach. As the engine ran on the trestle the timbers gave way and the train crashed to the ground. Three passengers were killed and a score were injured.

Service on the segment between the Junction and Flemingsburg was resumed the next morning but the accident spelled the doom of the Flemingsburg-Hillsboro section and it was never again operated. Then on a single day in December, 1909, the six miles remaining in operation were widened to standard gauge despite a pouring rain that slowed the efforts of the 50 workers.

On January 1, 1920, the road adopted its seventh and

FLEMINGSBURG TIMES-DEMOCRAT.

"TIMES," Established 1879. A Democratic Journal, Devoted to the Interests of Kentuckians. "DEMOCRAT," Established 1867.

VOLUME XXIX. FLEMINGSBURG, KENTUCKY, FRIDAY MORNING, MAY 17, 1907. NUMBER 37.

TWO DEATHS RESULT

From the Horrible Accident on the C. F. & S. Railroad of Last Friday.

All Those Thought to Be Fatally Injured Are Now Better and It Is Believed Will Recover.

LATEST REPORTS FROM THE INJURED!

THE DEAD.

The terrible railroad accident of Friday evening, May 10, 1907, a hurried but full account of which appeared in our [illegible] of Saturday morning, May 11, resulted in two deaths:

HARRY THOMAS — barber, of 1901, Eastern avenue, Cincinnati, Ohio, who was killed instantly.

THOMAS A. FOWLES—a timber dealer at Hillsboro, who died in about two hours without regaining consciousness.

In the following pages will be found all the details of the sad occurrence, illustrated by the best views to be procured by liberal outlay.

THE INJURED.

Drs. Garr & Brice make the following report of condition of patients under their treatment up to Thursday forenoon:

CLARENCE E. BROWNING—Multiple fracture of left thigh; concussion of brain; scalds of neck, left ear and left hand; bruises over body; remained in an unconscious condition for 18 hours; permanent dress put on (plaster cast) Wednesday; condition still critical, but shows a gradual improvement. Nurse, Miss B. L. Martin. At home.

MISS ADDIE NEWMAN—Fracture, compound comminuted, of right femur. Limb has been adjusted in plaster cast. Having an external wound makes her case a serious one. If wound does not become septic recovery is assured, but will be slow. Bruises on body. Miss Boone, nurse, at C. J. Sutton's.

MRS. HARRY THOMAS—Severe injury to kidneys; cut on forehead, necessitating four stitches; general bruises over body; extremely nervous and suffering pain. Her progress is satisfactory. At the Merchants Hotel.

MATT. BRAMBLE—Comminuted fracture of right leg; cut on face; bruises over body; suffered profound shock; [illegible] injury to spine; is doing satisfactorily. J. D. Barnes, nurse, at home.

MRS. MYRTLE WHEELER—Suffering from punctured wound of left jaw and right ankle; bruises all over body. At Ryan's Hotel, doing satisfactorily, Miss Nellie Jones, nurse.

MRS. LIZZIE GRAHAM—Fractured rib and general bruises. At Ryan's Hotel, doing satisfactorily, Miss Nellie Jones, nurse.

MISS ETHEL RAWLINGS—Two scalp wounds, general bruises over body. Doing well. At J. M. Rawling's.

JOHN MOORE—Dislocation of right shoulder; punctured wounds of head and face; bruised over body. At home.

KIRBY MOORE—Severe bruises about shoulders and chest. Able to be out.

C. P. DULEY—Two incised wounds of scalp, and cut on left hand; general bruises over body. Able to be out.

BABY RANKINS—Cut on forehead and chin; nose bruised; punctured wound of hand. At C. M. Lee's. Out.

BABY THOMAS—son of Harry Thomas, was taken to Falmouth Tuesday by his aunt, Mrs. Held.

ORIE MANNING — Shaken up and dazed by the shock but has now about recovered. Taken to his home at Hillsboro Saturday.

Drs. Robertson & Vice make the following report of the condition of those under their care, up to Thursday forenoon:

MRS. AMELIA SNODGRASS—Suffering from a severe scalp wound and profound shock of the brain and spinal column. Is now semi-conscious, and shows signs of improvement. At the residence of J. W. [illegible].

MRS. C. B. RANKINS—Suffering from [illegible] fractures and dislocated shoulder of [illegible] arm and fracture of the left arm [illegible] above the wrist. Doing very well, sitting up some. At the residence of Mrs. Susan Fant.

C. B. RANKINS—Severe bruises all over his body and limbs. Has suffered severely, but is now able to go about. At the Merchants Hotel.

WILL. B. CAMPBELL—Suffering from severe shock and bruises in chest. Has spit some blood. He is now improving and able to go about. At the Merchants Hotel.

LAN. DONALDSON—of color, is minus one tooth but otherwise all right.

Grateful For Help.

We desire to extend our thanks to the medical profession of the neighboring towns of the county, who responded so promptly and rendered us such efficient aid. Flemingsburg Physicians.

Relief Mass Meeting.

A mass meeting in the interest of the sufferers was called and held at the Christian Church Sunday night and the large house was filled and appropriate talks made by Rev. A. H. Lindsay and Rev. J. T. Sharrard. At the close the latter announced that no collection would be taken, as Mr. Bush, General Manager of our railroad, had assumed for the company the expense of caring for the victims and paying all the expenses of restoring them to their homes when they should have sufficiently recovered to go home. Mr. Bush also requested that the money contributed Saturday be returned to the donors.

Bruce Allen's Good Luck.

Bruce S. Allen thinks there are such things as blessings in disguise. Some time ago he got a severe bruise on one of his legs which seemed to have affected the bone, [illegible] a great deal of trouble, and some three weeks ago he temporarily gave up his place as brakeman to Matt. Bramble to have his leg operated on. He is now able to be out, almost well, while his substitute has been down to death's door.

Thousands View The Wreck.

Saturday the crowds rolled into town early and spent the day. Great numbers had either acquaintances or kinspeople in the wreck and were anxious to know their condition. It is estimated that not less than 2,000 persons visited the scene of the wreck on Saturday and 3,000 to 4,000 on Sunday. Many of them carried away pieces of the wrecked trestle as souvenirs, and we heard of one man who prized them so highly that he put them under lock and key.

Clearing Away The Wreck.

Master Mechanic John F. Mills and a force of men have been at work this week clearing up the wreck and getting the engine ready to be pulled back on the track. They have it on its wheels on a temporary track laid up the side of the ravine and it will soon be pulled up by powerful tackle and put on the track to be brought to the shops here.

Engine No. 1.

The engine is No. 1, the original engine, built by the Baldwin Locomotive Works, Philadelphia, in January 1877. It has been almost continuously in use on the road since then. It does not seem to be badly wrecked, none of the axles being sprung and the boiler being intact so far as can be seen.

Train Service to Johnson.

Train service was resumed between here and Johnson Saturday morning with Fred. Singleton as engineer and Thos. H. Lee as conductor.

Help For The Injured.

The open-hearted manner in which the sufferers from the wreck were received by our people was a credit to our city. Not one was turned away from any house where taken and to the tender care and splendid attention given them in the first few hours after the wreck is to a large degree due the small mortality list. The stranger within our gates received just as assiduous attention as the loved ones of our homes. Nothing was omitted to be done that could be done to promote their comfort and hasten their recovery.

Telephone Service a Great Help.

As the news spread through the country, aided by the splendid service of our local telephone exchange by their efficient operators, Mrs. Bertie Kendall and Misses Elizabeth Kendall and Emma Lewis Hopper, the people began to flock into town from all parts of the county to learn the full measure of the disaster and to tender such aid as lay in their power. It is said there was not a single horse or conveyance left in Hillsboro which could be used to bring a man to town. Many of them remained in town over night or until a very late hour.

All-Night Electric Light Service.

An imperative demand was made for an all-night service of electric lights for both streets and dwellings and Mayor Reynolds called on Messrs. Henderson & O'Bannon and ordered the service. The night was a dark and gloomy one and the lights were much needed.

Trained Nurses Arrive.

The management of the road has done all it could to assist in mitigating the suffering caused by the wreck. On Saturday night five trained nurses were brought here and assigned for duty among the most desperate cases. The manager has also given orders to have everything done to promote the comfort of the sufferers and bring about their speedy recovery. These ladies have given most faithful service and unremitting attention to the helpless sufferers in their charge, ably assisted by local volunteer nurses.

Remains of Harry Thomas.

The remains of Harry Thomas were embalmed Friday night and shipped Saturday via Maysville to his home at 1901 Eastern avenue, Cincinnati, Ohio, for interment. Mr. Thomas conducted a barber shop at that place and was the support of his aged parents.

Sign of His Own Death.

The following dispatch from Cincinnati to Monday's Courier-Journal illustrates another pathetic feature of the disaster. It says:

"The sign, 'Closed On Account of Death,' which Harry Thomas, of Eastern avenue, placed on his place of business when he went to his father-in-law's funeral on Friday, hung there today as an announcement of his own death in the wreck of the funeral train at Flemingsburg, Ky."

Burial of Thos. A. Fowles.

Sunday morning Undertaker Obed Collins left with the remains of Thos. A. Fowles, who was to be taken to a point some miles this side of Morehead for interment. After arriving there the family decided to take him on to Morehead for burial, and Mr. Collins says an immense crowd attended the burial. Mr. Collins did not get back till Monday forenoon.

A pathetic incident was connected with the death of Mr. Fowles. Thos. S. Evans, of this city, was a cousin of Mr. Fowles and had known him for years. Mr. Evans was at the wreck and assisted in conveying his cousin up the steep hill from the wreck but owing to the crushed and bloody condition of Mr. Fowles' head he did not know who he was until the next day when he saw the Times-Democrat special edition with the list of dead and injured. He afterward accompanied the remains to Morehead, returning here Monday afternoon.

Fund To Aid Sufferers.

On Saturday a subscription paper was started to raise a fund to aid the sufferers, all of whom are in very moderate circumstances and some of them almost destitute, and nearly $900 was contributed.

A VIEW OF THE FATAL TRESTLE.--From Photograph furnished us by Mrs. Henry B. Dudley.

A GOOD VIEW OF THE WRECK.--From Photograph taken Day After the Accident.

SCENE AT THE WRECK.--From Photograph taken Half-Hour After Accident.

CAUSE OF THE WRECK.

Engineer Kirby Moore Gives a Graphic Description of the Acccident.

How The Trestle First Gave Way, and the Frightful Plunge of The Train Into The Ravine.

SAD SCENES FOLLOWING THE CRASH!

Engineer Moore's Account.

In an interview with Kirby Moore, engineer of the ill-fated train, he says that as the train ran on the trestle he was looking down to see an old dove which had made her nest and was brooding over her eggs on one of the lower timbers of the trestle, when he saw one of the timbers sink down under the weight of the engine. He at once realized that it meant disaster, and calling to the fireman, Clarence Browning, to jump, he started out on the running-board on his side. Seeing in an instant that the engine was careening slightly to his side he drew back and sat down on his seat with his feet outside the window leading to the running-board and was in that position when the engine struck the ground. Browning was still in the cab with his head almost against the boiler-head. After pulling him away from the boiler Mr. Moore then went to the coach and with his bare hands tore away the splintered end of it, giving him a view of the inside.

Right in the corner was Miss Addie Newman, apparently lifeless, while near her was the Thomas babe, which was crying. Mr. Moore says this was all the sign of life to be seen or heard in the wrecked coach at that time, Chas. P. Duley having gotten out on the other side and gone to the branch to wash the blood from his eyes.

Mr. Moore at once took Miss Addie Newman from the wreck and laid her out on the grass, thinking her dead.

He next took from the wreck the Thomas babe and as soon as it was outside it seemed to faint away and he thought it also dead.

The third person to be taken out by Mr. Moore was Thos. A. Fowles, who had a terrible gash on his head and was breathing with great difficulty. He laid the dying man on the grass and taking off his own coat placed it under Fowles' head.

About this time Chas. P. Duley, who had been up the track to call the section hands and who quickly responded, came down the hill and joined Mr. Moore.

They then went to see about Clarence Browning and found him sitting upon a big timber which had plunged through the cab. They took him out and laid him upon the grass, and then proceeded to the relief of the other unfortunates.

About this time Mr. Moore discovered that fire had started among the freight in the wrecked box car, which was between the engine and coach, the fire starting in the end of the car next the engine, caused by a case of matches having been ignited by the fall. He at once took the coal scoop and dipped water from the wrecked tank and subdued the fire, only to have it break out again in a short time, but the blaze was finally put out before it had done much damage.

By this time two colored section men arrived on the scene to aid in the work of rescue, an then in a short time, though it seemed ages, John F. Mills appeared on the bank above, the advance guard of the army of relief. Then in a few minutes they came by scores, but not until all living victims had been taken from the wreck.

Mr. Moore is most emphatic in his belief that the accident was not caused by rotten timbers. His theory, and a reasonable one, too, is that in lining up the mud-sills of the trestle that morning the section men had probably raised one of them too much, thus causing one or more of the upright timbers to be released from the springing up of the stringers when the weight of the engine struck it, thus causing the whole structure to buckle and give down. He also says that it did not fall rapidly at first but rather seemed to be eased down until within possibly ten or fifteen feet from the bottom when it appeared to let go and fall heavily.

One of the big timbers knocked off the whistle valve and soon emptied the boiler of steam, it being thrown up the valley and away from the wreck.

The above story as to the way the horrible accident occurred and the manner in which the work of relief was accomplished, was told us by Mr. Moore in his usual straightforward manner, and as he is a man who has never been known to lose his presence of mind during excitement, his version as to the way the trestle first began to fall can be relied on as being correct.

A Dismal Day.

The evening on which the accident occurred was a rainy, lowering one, and at the time of the accident it was raining a steady, slow rain, which continued until nearly all the victims had been removed. This rendered the work very difficult, as the steep bank of the ravine was so slippery that a footing was maintained with difficulty and in order to make the ascent with the helpless sufferers it was necessary to form a double human chain by linked hands to draw the bearers up.

The hills on all sides were so steep that it was impossible to get vehicles within 100 yards of the scene without danger of overturning, and then some of the vehicles had to be held down.

Some rolls of matting which were in the wrecked freight car, were cut open and used in lieu of cots or stretchers.

The Treacherous Trestle.

The fatal trestle which collapsed and hurled the passengers and train crew to death or injury, was located at the end of the ravine about three hundred feet beyond the bridge over Fleming creek, being about two miles southeast of Flemingsburg. The ravine [illegible] runs down in a northerly direction from the Poplar Plains pike near the old McIlvaine place, now occupied by Raleigh Saunders, and empties almost at right angles, just below the trestle, into the branch which comes down from the old Robert Armstrong place and empties into Fleming creek a hundred yards below. The hills on either side rise abruptly and the place is isolated and difficult of access from any public road. The old dirt road to Bell Grove Springs formerly crossed Fleming creek at what was then known as the Weaver ford, just above the present railroad bridge and at the mouth of the Armstrong branch, and wound its way up the branch past the mouth of the ravine and on through the Armstrong place. But this road has probably been closed 60 years.

The trestle was first built in the winter of 1878-9, the first regular trains being run over it in the spring of 1879. It was a "double-deck," the lower deck being 20 feet and the upper 16, which with the stringers and ties made the highest point about 38 feet. It has been rebuilt by renewing the timbers several times, new timbers being put in after every spring and fall inspection. It is true that many of the timbers were very much decayed, but they looked all right from the outside.

About 11 years ago this trestle was partly washed out by a cloudburst in the little valley which is drained by the ravine which is spanned by the trestle, the train which was on the Hillsboro end at the time making a hair-breadth escape from plunging into the abyss.

In late years, since timber has become so high, the maintenance of these heavy trestles has been quite an item in the expense account.

The Talk About Damages.

As to suits for damages for injuries sustained there are all sorts of rumors afloat, but we believe it is the purpose of the management to make as liberal settlement as possible with each individual sufferer. They are interested in maintaining the good will of the community and will do better by the sufferers than they could do by allowing an "ambulance chaser" lawyer to take the case on a basis of 50 per cent. of what he could get out of it. A rush of big damage suits would almost certainly cause the road to be thrown into the hands of a receiver, in which case the court costs, lawyers fees and the bonded debt of the road would take the cash and leave nothing for those who need it. But we think there is a disposition on the part of the friends of the victims to meet the management of the road on a fair basis of settlement.

last name, Flemingsburg & Northern Railroad. From then on the history of the line paralleled that of other local routes. Losses increased to the point where abandonment was inevitable. On December 6, 1955, the F&N made its last trip to the Junction, taking in tow the 13 freight cars remaining in Flemingsburg. Scrapping of the road commenced October 11, 1956, and was completed shortly thereafter.

Top Left—The wreck at Weaver's Ford trestle, two miles southeast of Flemingsburg. Narrow gauge locomotive No. 1 (Baldwin, 2-6-0) is on its side. George Faulkner, Jr.

Top Right — Construction scene during gauge widening between Johnsons and Flemingsburg.
George Faulkner, Jr.

Track facilities in Flemingsburg comprised a team track clear through the city, a 400' siding on the south end of the team track, a 350' siding in the depot yard, a 300' spur serving a coal yard, a 450' passing track at the state highway garage in the northern part of Flemingsburg, and a 650' spur off this siding serving the stockyard.

Above — A curiosity in railroad construction — a three-way stub switch south of the Flemingsburg depot. Paul Holton

At right—Coal dock and freight house, Flemingsburg. S. P. Guthrie

Opposite Page—The Tragedy of Friday, May 10, 1907, is reported in detail by the weekly Flemingsburg Times-Democrat.
George Faulkner, Jr.

Above—F&N Locomotive No. 549, ex-L&N same number. Leased from the Dixie Line in 1937, and purchased December 1, 1949. Scrapped early in 1956.   S. P. Guthrie

Center—Depot and freight house, Flemingsburg, looking north.
S. P. Guthrie
At right—Engine house, Flemingsburg.   S. P. Guthrie

Opposite Page top—No. 9, a 4-6-0 Baldwin, constructed June, 1913, and retired and scrapped by the Flemingsburg & Northern 1937.
S. P. Guthrie
Opposite Page bottom—The old covered station at Flemingsburg with narrow gauge locomotive No. 1 and flat car No. 7.
George Faulkner, Jr.

The top two photographs picture the trolley passenger car purchased in 1919 from the Richmond & Appomattox Railroad. The vehicle was actually a combine that seated about 20 passengers and had a compartment for baggage, mail, and package freight. For operation on the Flemingsburg line it was converted to gasoline-electric operation. One of its outstanding features was a big water tank perched over the front pilot to supplement the engine radiator.

After it went into service, the use of the steam-hauled passenger trains ceased except when the available business exceeded the capacity of the "Toonerville."

S. P. Guthrie

Above — F&N box car 97856 at Flemingsburg freight depot. This was purchased from the L&NRR where it bore the same number.
S. P. Guthrie

At right—F&N caboose. This vehicle was secured from the Louisville, Henderson & St. Louis Railway and remodeled to carry passengers and LCL freight. S. P. Guthrie

CHAPTER 11
The "Kinney" Branch
Garrison to Gesling
(Chesapeake & Ohio Railway)

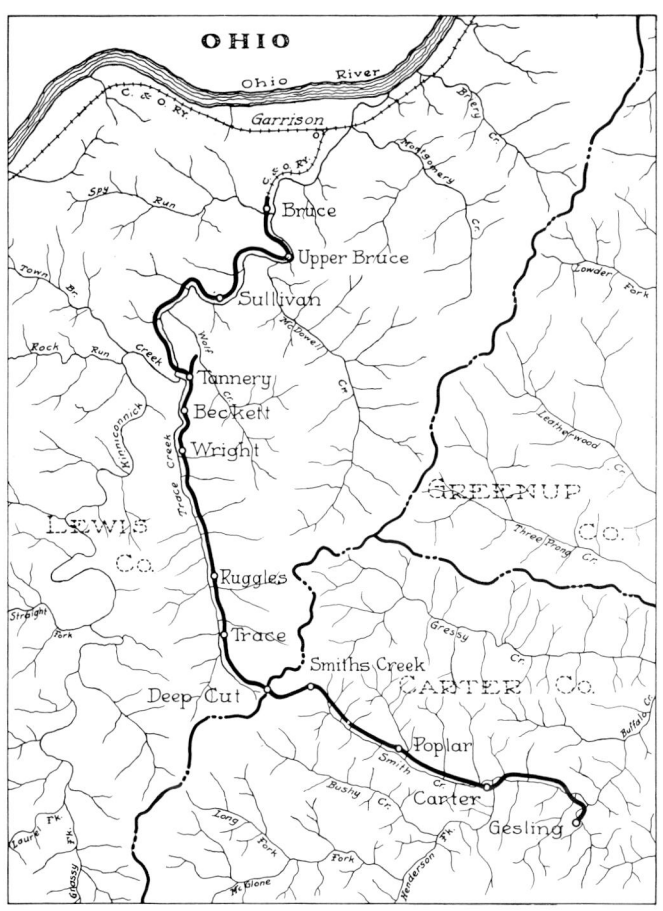

The Kinniconnick & Freestone Railroad was incorporated March 20, 1890, for the purpose of providing an outlet for the fine freestone at Tannery and Wolf Creek. In June, 1891, the road was completed from Stone City (later renamed Garrison) to Tannery, a total of 8.94 miles. In 1892 it was extended up Trace Creek .8 mile to Beckett's spur, and a few months later to a point then known as Blue House, now Wright. At both of these points stone quarries were opened.

CINCINNATI AND RUSSELL DIVISIONS
KINNICONNICK AND FREESTONE SUB-DIVISION

WESTWARD					EASTWARD	
Calls	Distance from Poplar	SECOND CLASS 127 Mixed Mon., Wed., Fri.	Supplement "B" to TIME TABLE No. 130. In Effect Sunday, Aug. 4, 1940. STATIONS.	SECOND CLASS 128 Mixed Mon., Wed., Fri.	Distance from Garrison	Side Track Capacity in Cars (41 ft.)
2 short	.0	L AM 10 55	POPLAR 1.1	A AM 10 25	17.4	o 53
--------	1.1	f10 59	W Smith's Creek 1.3	f10 10	16.3	o 4
7 short	2.4	f11 03	Deep Cut 1.3	f10 00	15.0	o 4
6 short	3.7	f11 07	Trace 1.4	f 9 40	13.7	o 9
4 short	5.1	f11 12	Ruggles 4.1	f 9 25	12.3	o 7
5 short	9.2	f11 25	Tannery 3.0	f 9 05	8.2	o 17
--------	12.2	f11 34	Sullivan 1.8	f 8 50	5.2	--------
--------	14.0	f11 40	Upper Bruce 3.4	f 8 45	3.4	o 4
1 long	17.4	11 50 A AM	Wy GARRISON	8 30 L AM	.0	o177
		127 Mixed Mon., Wed., Fri.		128 Mixed Mon., Wed., Fri.		

Employees' timecards of the Branch of 1940 and 1904.
C&O Ry.

KINNICONNICK BRANCH.

Westward.						Eastward.
SECOND CLASS.						SECOND CLASS.
No. 127. Daily ex. Sunday.	Station Numbers.	Distance from Carter.	STATIONS.	Side Track—Capacity in Cars.	Telegraph Offices, Full Fever, D. W. N. Light, Day only	No. 128. Daily ex. Sunday.
P. M. Leave.						P. M. Arrive.
1 00	H 19		Carter 1.8	O. 20		12 45
1 08	H 18	1.8	Poplar 1.9			12 25
1 15	H 16	3.7	W Smith Creek 2.4	O. 15		12 15
1 25	H 13	6.1	Trace 1.3	O. 5		12 05
1 35	H 12	7.4	Ruggles 4.3	O. 5		11 59
1 50	H 8	11.7	Tannery 3.6	O. 50		11 40
2 05	H 3	15.3	Upper Bruce 3.0	O. 3		11 30
2 15	H 1	18.3	Bruce 1.5	O. 10		11 20
2 30	563	19.8	W Stone City	O. 10 P. 56 KD		11 15
P. M. Arrive.						A. M. Leave.

J. W. HAYNES, Train Master.   C. M. FREEMAN, Chief Dispatcher.   GEO. W. LEWIS, Assistant Superintendent.

Above—Inspection train on the K&F about 1891. The 4-4-0 locomotive was C&O's No. 34.　　William Cox

At right—Locomotive No. 264 taking water at the spring fed tank on the east side of the Big Hill. This 2-8-0 was similar to No. 286.　　William Conway

A little later a 2.3 mile extension was built to Ruggles to furnish an outlet for the virgin timber in that vicinity. Still later the railroad was carried on up the 3.92% grade from the head of the creek to Deep Cut. This last extension was made at heavy expense as the 1.5 mile grade included five rather tortuous bridges.

At Deep Cut the grade sliced through the backbone of the mountain and descended the other side by a 3.56% grade into Smith Creek, reaching a place later to be known as Poplar where several saw mills were established. In June, 1893, the line reached Carter City, 19.77 miles from Stone City. In building the extension from Tannery to Carter City, the C&ORY advanced a sum estimated at $75,000 for which the company received the entire capital stock of the K&F as well as $100,000 in 6% bonds. On June 1, 1906, the K&F was merged into the C&O of Kentucky, which, in turn was deeded July 1, 1907 to the Chesapeake & Ohio Railway Company.

Snow scene on the wye track at Carter.
　　William Conway

Locomotive No. 286 (later renumbered 653) with typical mixed consist, descending grade between Deep Cut and Trace over one of five sizable trestles. No. 286 was originally 160, built April, 1883, by Cooke. The light Consolidation was C&O's Class G-1. It was scrapped in December, 1931. C&ORy

In 1926-27 the Louisville Fire Brick Works, Inc. and the North American Refractories Company built a 1.77 mile extension from Carter to Gesling to reach a deposit of fire clay the two companies had purchased. This line, costing the companies $85,887, was sold to the C&O for $30,000.

With this extension the "Kinney" Branch reached its maximum length of 21.54 miles.

C&O's No. 87 with spartan combine on the Branch's highest trestle.
William Conway

In the year 1896 the Oligunuk Caves were opened at Carter, and that summer the C&O started running excursions to the attraction from Cincinnati. The train would leave the Queen City at 7 a.m. and arrive at Garrison at 9:30 a.m. Here the train would split into sections of four coaches which was the limit the locomotives could handle over the Big Hill through Deep Cut.

At the caves there were separate grounds for city folks and country people. On those rare occasions when an excursionist wandered into the wrong area, a good fight would inevitably result.

As the stone, clay, and timber resources of the region became exhausted or in less demand, and as improved highways began to penetrate the region, the business of the Branch diminished. After a number of years of losses the C&O Railway received permission on November 30, 1940, to abandon the line. Operations continued, however, until February 1, 1941. On April 22 of that year the track was officially retired.

The wye at Garrison was left in, as well as 1.97 miles of the old railroad for use as a storage track.

Above—Distant view of the high trestle showing locomotive No. 264 with cars of ballast, and the combine. Note by comparison with earlier picture of this trestle how the round poles have been replaced with square timbers and 16' iron girders. This was part of a bridge strengthening program made necessary when the line started hauling stone ballast. Note also the steep descent, right to left. William Conway.

Load Track and Bins of the Poplar Ballast Company.
William Conway
Quarry of the Poplar Ballast Company. William Conway

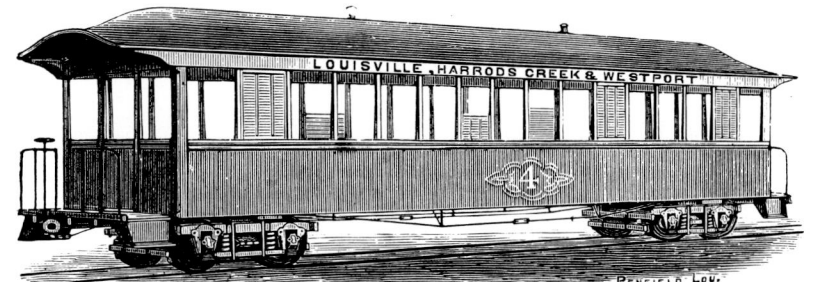

Coaches of the narrow gauge built by the Ohio Falls Car Company. No. 4 was used for special excursions.

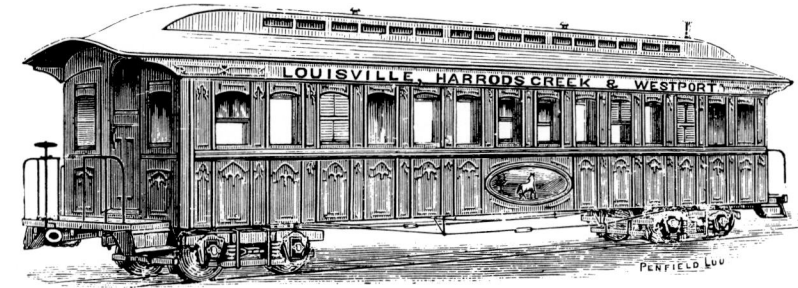

This ornate vehicle with the painted horse on the side was the "ladies coach". Note hand brakes and link and pin couplers.

Courtesy of George Yater.

CHAPTER 12
"Commuters' Narrow Gauge"
Water Works to Prospect
(Louisville & Interurban Railroad)

The Louisville, Harrods Creek & Westport Railway was organized by persons who were prominent in the business activities of Louisville and the upper river road region. The company was incorporated March 19, 1870.

By September, 1872, work was in progress on the Fulton Street fill, and President James Callahan was authorized to purchase the railroad's first locomotive and 21 steel dump cars. The engine secured, No. 1, was named the "James Callahan." In 1874 construction reached Goose Creek, 7.75 miles from the First Street terminal in Louisville. A second locomotive, No. 2, the "Glenview," was built for the road by the firm of Webster & Marks, Chattanooga. A baggage car, smoker, and ladies' coach were also purchased.

Little by little the little narrow gauge line was extended up the Ohio Valley, coming to an abrupt halt in the summer of 1877 at Sand Hill (now known as Prospect). Here the railroad terminated for all time. A third locomotive, the "Alex Duerson" was purchased in 1875; and pits and other accommodations for all three locomotives were located with the turntable at Brook and Fulton.

For many years the steam-hauled trains maintained a schedule of four round trips daily between Louisville and Prospect. Special trains were run for such diverse activities as beer parties, temperance meetings, prize fights, church picnics, theatre parties and conventions. Freight traffic on the LHC&W was never heavy but a track-side lime kiln, two quarries, a distillery, and miscellaneous agricultural activities provided some business.

In 1878 the narrow gauge line was reorganized and the *Railway* in its name was changed to *Railroad*. Then on June 23, 1880, the Louisville, Cincinnati & Lexington Railway purchased the LHC&W. This ownership was short-lived, however, for on June 1, 1881, the Louisville & Nashville Railroad acquired the LC&L.

During 1887-1888 the Louisville-Prospect line was widened to the L&N's standard gauge of 4'9". During the process, heavier rail was substituted for the old 30' iron, the 5.05 mile section beginning at Louisville receiving steel rail and the remainder getting new iron. In a matter of 10 years or so the L&N succumbed to the gauge of 4'8½" and presumably the track to Prospect shared in the half-inch reduction.

Around the turn of the century, electric interurban operation enjoyed a blooming development. The Louisville & Interurban Railroad Company, a wholly owned subsidiary of the Louisville Railway Company, cast its eyes over the L&N's line to Prospect and on April 22, 1904, it purchased the 7.7 miles of the old LHC&W from a point 841' east of Pipe Line Avenue to Prospect. The L&N agreed to provide steam-operated freight service at times it would not interfere with the interurban operations.

BETWEEN LOUISVILLE AND PROSPECT.

Distance.	All trains stop on signal at all Stations and Platforms.	EX. SUN	EX. SUN	EX. SUN	EX. SUN	SUN.	SUN.
.0	Lv. Louisville	6 00 am	8 00 am	2 10 pm	5 00 pm	....	8 00 am
1.6	..Ohio Street	6 10 "	8 09 "	2 22 "	5 10 "	....	8 09 "
3.3	..Water Works	6 15 "	8 13 "	2 30 "	5 14 "	....	8 13 "
4.6	..Bullitt	6 25 "	8 18 "	2 38 "	5 19 "	....	8 18 "
5.9	..Longview	6 29 "	8 22 "	2 43 "	5 23 "	....	8 22 "
6.8	..Glenview	6 32 "	8 25 "	2 48 "	5 26 "	....	8 25 "
8.4	..Harrods Creek	6 37 "	8 30 "	2 55 "	5 31 "	....	8 30 "
9.6	..Sherley	6 41 "	8 34 "	3 00 "	5 35 "	....	8 30 "
11.2	Ar. Prospect	6 45 am	8 38 am	3 10 pm	5 38 pm	....	8 38 am

BETWEEN PROSPECT AND LOUISVILLE.

Distance.	All trains stop on signal at all Stations and Platforms.	EX. SUN	EX. SUN	EX. SUN	EX. SUN	SUN.	SUN.
.0	Lv. Prospect	7 00 am	9 00 am	3 45 pm	5 40 pm	....	3 45 pm
1.6	..Sherley	7 03 "	9 10 "	3 48 "	5 43 "	....	3 48 "
2.8	..Harrods Creek	7 07 "	9 15 "	3 52 "	5 47 "	....	3 52 "
4.4	..Glenview	7 12 "	9 20 "	3 57 "	5 52 "	....	3 57 "
5.3	..Longview	7 15 "	9 24 "	4 00 "	5 55 "	....	4 00 "
6.6	..Bullitt	7 19 "	9 32 "	4 03 "	5 59 "	....	4 03 "
7.9	..Water Works	7 24 "	9 40 "	4 10 "	6 04 "	....	4 10 "
9.6	..Ohio Street	7 29 "	9 48 "	4 15 "	6 09 "	....	4 15 "
11.2	Ar. Louisville	7 38 am	10 00 am	4 25 pm	6 17 pm	....	4 25 pm

Schedule of the LHC&W while a Narrow Gauge Line.

BETWEEN LOUISVILLE AND PROSPECT.

Distance.	All trains stop on signal at all Stations and Platforms.	2 EX SUN	4 DAILY	6 DAILY	8 EX SUN		
.0	Lv. Louisville	6 20 AM	8 25 AM	2 10 PM	5 02 PM		
1.6	Ohio Street	6 30 AM	8 35 AM	2 20 PM	5 12 PM		
3.3	Water Works	6 35 AM	8 40 AM	2 24 PM	5 17 PM		
4.6	Bullitt	6 38 AM	8 45 AM	2 31 PM	5 20 PM		
5.9	Longview	6 42 AM	8 49 AM	2 36 PM	5 24 PM		
6.8	Glenview	6 45 AM	8 52 AM	2 41 PM	5 27 PM		
8.4	Harrods Creek	6 48 AM	9 07 AM	2 50 PM	5 30 PM		
9.6	Sherley	6 52 AM	9 11 AM	3 00 PM	5 34 PM		
11.2	Ar. Prospect	6 56 AM	9 15 AM	3 10 PM	5 38 PM		

BETWEEN PROSPECT AND LOUISVILLE.

Distance.	All trains stop on signal at all Stations and Platforms.	1 EX SUN	3 DAILY	5 DAILY	7 EX SUN		
.0	Lv. Prospect	7 10 AM	9 20 AM	3 55 PM	5 41 PM		
1.6	Sherley	7 14 AM	9 24 AM	3 59 PM	5 45 PM		
2.8	Harrods Creek	7 17 AM	9 28 AM	4 02 PM	5 48 PM		
4.4	Glenview	7 22 AM	9 39 AM	4 07 PM	5 52 PM		
5.3	Longview	7 25 AM	9 42 AM	4 10 PM	5 54 PM		
6.6	Bullitt	7 29 AM	9 50 AM	4 23 PM	5 58 PM		
7.9	Water Works	7 34 AM	9 55 AM	4 30 PM	6 02 PM		
9.6	Ohio Street	7 39 AM	10 00 AM	4 35 PM	6 06 PM		
11.2	Ar. Louisville	7 48 AM	10 10 AM	4 45 PM	6 15 PM		

Schedule of the LHC&W as of January 5, 1903.
Frank H. Miller

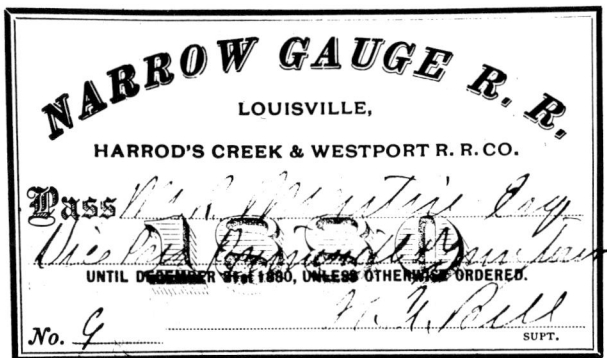

S. P. Guthrie

Opposite page top—L&N mogul No. 437 at East Louisville, July, 1895. This locomotive and similar sisters provided the motive power on the Prospect Branch in the Gay Nineties. Glore

Opposite page bottom—After the Prospect Line was electrified, the L&NRR maintained freight service at night using steam locomotives. Light switcher (0-6-0) No. 1023 was assigned to this job. In 1903 its number was changed to 2023. L&NRR

The route was electrified promptly and by October 15, 1904, interurban cars were operating from the intersection of Mellwood and Frankfort Avenues, to Prospect. On December 17 the route was extended west to the heart of Louisville. The L&I's Prospect line was unique in the sense that it was the only route of the company that was of standard gauge and didn't conform to the 5' gauge of the city street cars. For the exclusive use of this line four cars of the 900 series, Numbers 903, 907, 914, and 916, were fitted with standard gauge trucks. Additional interurban equipment for this route included passenger trailers Nos. 336-337, a wire car No. 4, and express car No. 200.

The steam-operated freight service of the L&N was discontinued in the early part of 1930; and the L&I discontinued the freight service it had taken over from the L&N May 15, 1934. The interurbans were suffering heavy losses as passenger carriers also, and on October 31, 1935, the last cars were run, ending 64 years of passenger service over the rails between Louisville and Prospect. Today the 3.46 mile segment of the old LHC&W remains in service east to the water works at Pipe Line (Zorn) Avenue for freight service, only.

Express car used in electric interurban operations to Prospect. This car, built by the Louisville & Eastern Railroad in 1902 and originally numbered 100, was later changed to L&I No. 200.

Opposite page—Interior of cars used on the Prospect Line after electric service replaced the steam trains. St. Louis Car Co.
Above—Exterior of Louisville & Interurban car 909, identical with the exception of track gauge, to those used on the Prospect Line. St. Louis Car Co.

LOUISVILLE TO PROSPECT

EAST BOUND TRAINS

STATIONS Read Down	Miles from Louisville	2 Daily A.M.	4 Daily Ex. Sun. A.M.	6 Daily A.M.	8 Daily A.M.	10 Daily Ex. Sun. A.M.	12 Daily A.M.	14 Daily A.M.	X 94 Daily Ex. Sun. A.M.	16 Daily A.M.	18 Daily A.M.	20 Daily A.M.	22 Daily P.M.	24 Daily P.M.	26 Daily P.M.	28 Daily P.M.	30 Daily P.M.	32 Daily Ex. Sun. P.M.	34 Daily P.M.	36 Daily Ex. Sun. P.M.	38 Daily P.M.	40 Daily P.M.	42 Daily P.M.	44 Daily P.M.	46 Daily P.M.	STATIONS Read Down
TERMINAL STATION	.0	5.22	6.08	6.08	7.08	7.34	8.08	9.08	9.08	10.08	11.08	12.08	1.08	2.08	3.08	4.08	4.08	5.08	5.38	6.08	7.08	8.08	9.08	10.08	11.22	TERMINAL STATION
DOUBLE TRACK 2.7					5	7					95					29	31		35							DOUBLE TRACK 2.7
FRANKFORT AVE. .3	2.7	5.39	6.24	6.24	7.24	7.50	8.24 9	9.24	9.24	10.24	11.24	12.24	1.24	2.24	3.24	4.24	4.24	5.24	5.54	6.24	7.24	8.24	9.24	10.24	11.38 45	FRANKFORT AVE. .3
CITY LIMITS SIDING 1.8	3.1	5.43	6.28	6.28	7.28	7.54	8.28	9.28	9.28	10.28	11.28	12.28	1.28	2.28	3.28	4.28	4.28	5.28	5.58	6.28	7.28	8.28	9.28	10.28	11.42	CITY LIMITS SIDING 1.8
CALLAHAN 1.4	4.9	5.46	6.31 3	6.31 7	7.31 11	7.57	8.31 13	9.31 13	9.31 15	10.31 17	11.31 19	12.31 21	1.31 23	2.31 25	3.31 27	4.31 27	4.31 31	5.31 33	6.01	6.31 37	7.31 39	8.31 41	9.31 43	10.31	11.45	CALLAHAN 1.4
BLANKENBAKERS .7	6.3	5.50	6.35	6.35	7.35	8.01	8.35	9.35	9.37	10.35	11.35	12.35	1.35	2.35	3.35	4.35	4.35	5.35	6.05	6.35	7.35	8.35	9.35	10.35	11.49	BLANKENBAKERS .7
LONGVIEW 1.0	7.0	5.51	6.36	6.36	7.36	8.02	8.36	9.36	9.38	10.36	11.36	12.36	1.36	2.36	3.36	4.36	4.36	5.36	6.06	6.36	7.36	8.36	9.36	10.36	11.50	LONGVIEW 1.0
GLENVIEW .3	8.0	5.55	6.40	6.40	7.40	8.06	8.40	9.40	9.50	10.40	11.40	12.40	1.40	2.40	3.10	4.40	4.40	5.40	6.10	6.40	7.40	8.40	9.40	10.40	11.54	GLENVIEW .3
FLORIDA HEIGHTS 1.2	8.3	5.56	6.41	6.41	7.41	8.07	8.41	9.41	9.52	10.41	11.41	12.41	1.41	2.41	3.11	4.41		5.41	6.11	6.41	7.41	8.41	9.41	10.41	11.56	FLORIDA HEIGHTS 1.2
HARRODS CREEK 1.6	9.5	6.00	6.46	6.46	7.46		8.46	9.46	10.00	10.46 95	11.46	12.46	1.46	2.16	3.46	4.46		5.46	6.16 33	6.46 35	7.46	8.46	9.46	10.46	12.00	HARRODS CREEK 1.6
BEECHLAND .4	11.1	6.04		6.50	7.50		8.50	9.50	10.12 15	10.50	11.50	12.50	1.50	2.50	3.50	4.50		5.50	6.20	6.50	7.50	8.50	9.50	10.50	12.04	BEECHLAND .4
BURFORD .8	11.5	6.05		6.51	7.51		8.51	9.51	10.13	10.51	11.51	12.51	1.51	2.51	3.51	4.51		5.51		6.51	7.51	8.51	9.51	10.51	12.05	BURFORD .8
PROSPECT	12.3	6.08		6.54	7.54		8.54	9.54	10.16	10.54	11.54	12.54	1.54	2.54	3.54	4.54		5.54		6.54	7.54	8.54	9.54	10.54	12.08	PROSPECT

NOTE—On Double Track small figures indicate the trains to be met, the time being omitted.

No. 30 will leave from Brook and Liberty Sts.
No. 28 will run ahead of 30 from Brook St.

LOUISVILLE & INTERURBAN R. R.

PROSPECT TO LOUISVILLE

WEST BOUND TRAINS

STATIONS Read Up	Miles from Prospect	3 Daily A.M.	5 Daily Ex. Sun. A.M.	7 Daily A.M.	9 Daily Ex. Sun. A.M.	11 Daily A.M.	13 Daily A.M.	15 Daily A.M.	X 95 Daily Ex. Sun. A.M.	17 Daily A.M.	19 Daily A.M.	21 Daily P.M.	23 Daily P.M.	25 Daily P.M.	27 Daily P.M.	29 Daily Ex. Sun. P.M.	31 Daily P.M.	33 Daily P.M.	35 Daily P.M.	37 Daily P.M.	39 Daily P.M.	41 Daily P.M.	43 Daily P.M.	45 Daily P.M.	47 Daily A.M.	STATIONS Read Up
TERMINAL STATION 2.7	12.3	6.54	7.34	7.54	8.42	8.54	9.54	10.54	11.30	11.54	12.54	1.54	2.54	3.54	4.54	5.24	5.54	6.54	7.24	7.54	8.54	9.54	10.54	11.54	12.54	TERMINAL STATION 2.7
DOUBLE TRACK			8		10				18							32		34		38						DOUBLE TRACK
FRANKFORT AVENUE .3	9.6	6.38	7.18	7.38	8.24 12	8.38	9.38	10.38	11.14	11.38	12.38	1.38	2.38	3.38	4.38	5.08	5.38	6.38	7.08	7.38	8.38	9.38	10.38	11.38 46	12.38	FRANKFORT AVENUE .3
CITY LIMITS SIDING 1.8	9.2	6.34	7.14	7.34	8.21	8.34	9.34	10.34	11.11	11.34	12.34	1.34	2.34	3.34	4.34	5.04	5.34	6.34	7.04	7.34	8.34	9.34	10.34	11.34	12.34	CITY LIMITS SIDING 1.8
CALLAHAN 1.4	7.4	6.31 4-6	7.11 8	7.31	8.18 12	8.31 14-94	9.31 16	10.31	11.08 18	11.31 20	12.31 22	1.31 24	2.31 26	3.31 28-30	4.31	5.01 32	5.31	6.31 36	7.01	7.31 38	8.31 40	9.31 42	10.31 44	11.31	12.31	CALLAHAN 1.4
BLANKENBAKERS .7	6.0	6.27	7.07	7.27	8.14	8.27	9.27	10.27	11.01	11.27	12.27	1.27	2.27	3.27	4.27	4.57	5.27	6.27	6.57	7.27	8.27	9.27	10.27	11.27	12.27	BLANKENBAKERS .7
LONGVIEW 1.0	5.3	6.26	7.06	7.26	8.13	8.26	9.26	10.26	11.00	11.26	12.26	1.26	2.26	3.26	4.26	4.56	5.26	6.26	6.56	7.26	8.26	9.26	10.26	11.26	12.26	LONGVIEW 1.0
GLENVIEW .3	4.3	6.22	7.02	7.22	8.10	8.22	9.22	10.22	10.53	11.22	12.22	1.22	2.22	3.22	4.22	4.52 28	5.22	6.22	6.52	7.22	8.22	9.22	10.22	11.22	12.22	GLENVIEW .3
FLORIDA HEIGHTS 1.2	4.0	6.21	7.01	7.21	8.09	8.21 10	9.21	10.21	10.52	11.21	12.21	1.21	2.21	3.21	4.21		5.21	6.21	6.51	7.21	8.21	9.21	10.21	11.21	12.21	FLORIDA HEIGHTS 1.2
HARRODS CREEK 1.6	2.8	6.16	6.56 6	7.16		8.16	9.16	10.16	10.46 16	11.16	12.16	1.16	2.16	3.16	4.16		5.16	6.16 34	6.46 36	7.16	8.16	9.16	10.16	11.16	12.16	HARRODS CREEK 1.6
BEECHLAND .4	1.2	6.12		7.12		8.12	9.12	10.12 94	10.40	11.12	12.12	1.12	2.12	3.12	4.12		5.12	6.12	6.42	7.12	8.12	9.12	10.12	11.12	12.12	BEECHLAND .4
BURFORD .8	.8	6.11		7.11		8.11	9.11	10.11	10.39	11.11	12.11	1.11	2.11	3.11	4.11		5.11	6.11	6.41	7.11	8.11	9.11	10.11	11.11	12.11	BURFORD .8
PROSPECT	.0	6.08		7.08		8.08	9.08	10.08	10.36	11.08	12.08	1.08	2.08	3.08	4.08		5.08	6.08	6.38	7.08	8.08	9.08	10.08	11.08	12.08	PROSPECT

NOTE—On Double Track small figures indicate the trains to be met, the time being omitted.
Bold figures Train 11 at Florida Heights are precautionary.
Bold figures Train 5 at Harrods Creek are precautionary.
Bold figures Train 29 at Glenview are precautionary.

Louisville & Interurban Employees' Timetable of the Prospect Line as of March 16, 1927. F. D. Childs

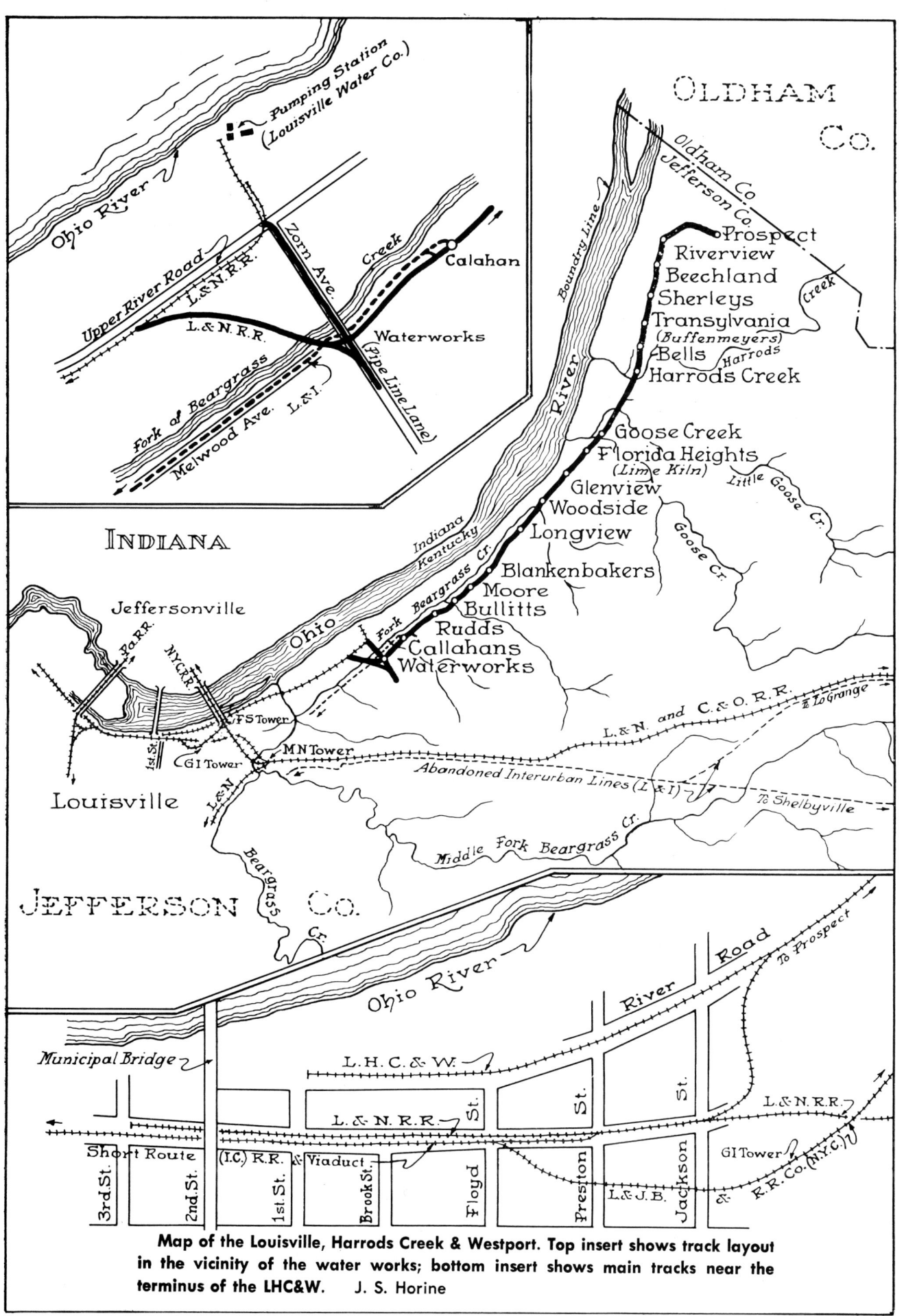

Map of the Louisville, Harrods Creek & Westport. Top insert shows track layout in the vicinity of the water works; bottom insert shows main tracks near the terminus of the LHC&W.   J. S. Horine

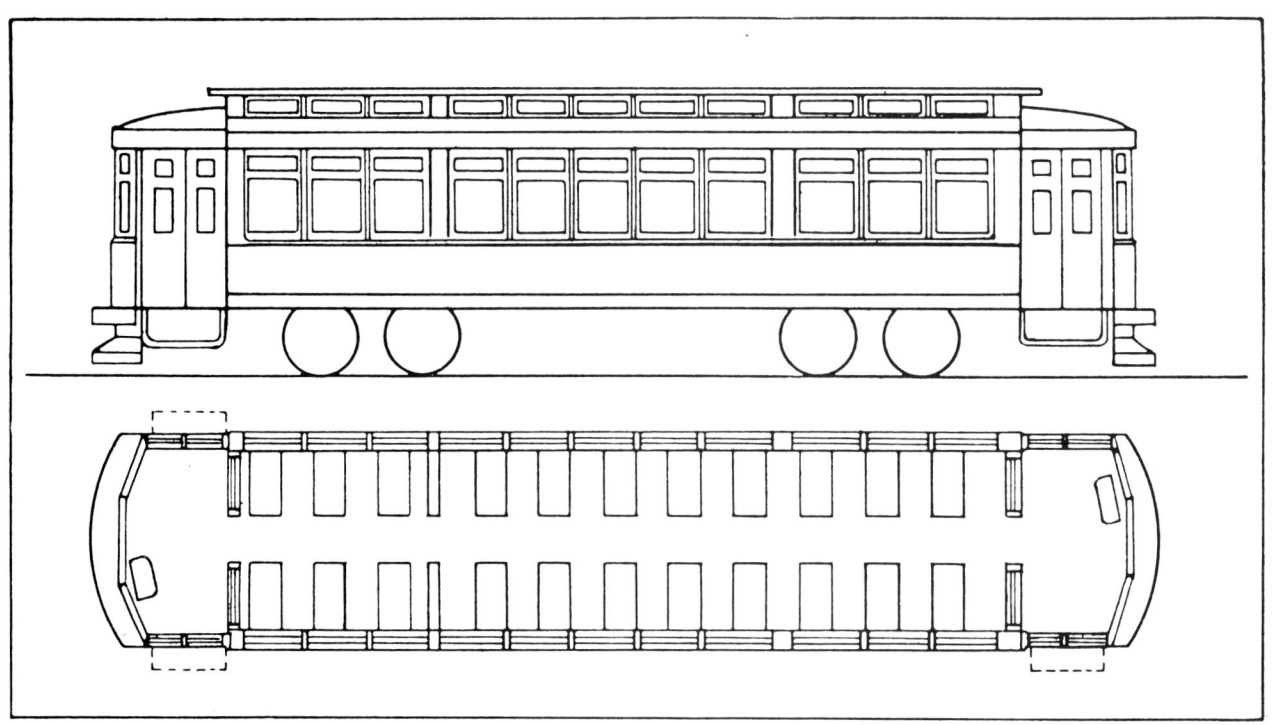

Plan of L&I electric cars which were assigned to the Louisville-Prospect service.
St. Louis Car Co.

Louisville & Interurban Railroad Station, Louisville. Since the Prospect line of the L&I was standard gauge and the other lines of the L&I were 5-foot gauge, it was necessary to have three-rail tracks into this station.   George Yater

CHAPTER 13
"Up North Fork Way"
Clack Mountain Tunnel to Redwine
(Morehead & North Fork Railroad)
Redwine to Rush Branch
(Lenox Railroad)

Shorties—
Lawton Junction to Brinegar
(Portsmouth & Tygert Valley Railroad)
Rodburn to Pine Springs (Kentucky Northern Railroad)
Limestone to timber (Panther Gap Railroad)
Rodburn to timber (Triplett & Big Sandy Railroad)
Rodburn to Clay Mines ("Christy Creek Railroad")

"ONE HORSE TUNNEL"

The day the Clack Mountain tunnel was opened for the first time, William W. Wrigley, then bookkeeper and general passenger agent of the new railroad, attempted to ride a black mare by the name of Maude through the bore. In the middle of the tunnel the animal was seized with fear to the extent that she could not be persuaded to complete the journey. Later, when tracks were laid through the tunnel, Wrigley piloted the first locomotive to pass through the hole, which appropriately enough, was No. 1.

Considering that the Morehead and North Fork Railroad was built before the days of shovels and bulldozers, the speed with which the line was constructed is worthy of note. Small, horse-drawn dump carts were used to distribute dirt, and a considerable number of gangs were used to expedite the work. The Poppin Rock tunnel at Paragon was built entirely by steel drills, driven by white and colored help who were experts in this line of work.

OPERATION DERAIL

It had been rainy for several days. In fact the weather was just plain nasty, and engineer L. C. McClellan as well as Superintendent M. C. Crosley were anxious to get the twelve-car train of coal and merchandise freight back to Clearfield as promptly as possible. In fact, the entire crew wanted to get home and hover over a warm fire.

Perhaps engineer McClellan was too anxious. Just two miles out of Redwine there was Adkins curve, a rather short turn in the track. As the train rounded this curve McClellan chanced to look back. The sight he saw was not reassuring. Five cars had gone off the tracks and were lying on their sides in grotesque positions. It was too late to do anything about the matter, so the remainder of the train was coupled up and started.

Things went well until the train reached Lost Point Cut, about a mile east of Blairs Mills in the section known as the "Winding Stairs." At this point engineeer McClellan looked back again. This time he saw four of his cars in process of leaving the track. These cars ceased their motion well off the main grade, and came to rest in a position that precluded any possibility of their rescue that day. So again the train departed, this time with three cars. Superintendent Crosley, however, decided to take over the throttle, feeling, perhaps, that a steadier hand on the controls would bring the remainder of the train, at least, into the terminal safely.

But luck was still against the train. At McClure's near Paragon, soft track was encountered and another car left the steel.

Needless to say, it was a very disgusted set of trainmen who brought the two-car train into Clearfield that evening. But still more disgusted were the section crews that had to go out the next morning and re-rail the ten cars.

This true tale of the train that had three wrecks is matched by the "story of the vanishing car." One day, the ten car southbound freight train had arrived at Wrigley and the conductor walked back to cut off the rear car. One can picture his surprise when the car could not be located, although his crew was certain that the train had left Clearfield with it.

However, the train continued on to its terminus at Redwine. On its return trip the crew sighted the missing car reposing in the waters of the North Fork at Cuba, another point in the "Winding Stairs" section. In some manner the car had become uncoupled and had left the track without any of the crew being the wiser. It was a long time before the other trainmen on the Morehead & North Fork Railroad stopped kidding the crew who had made that run.

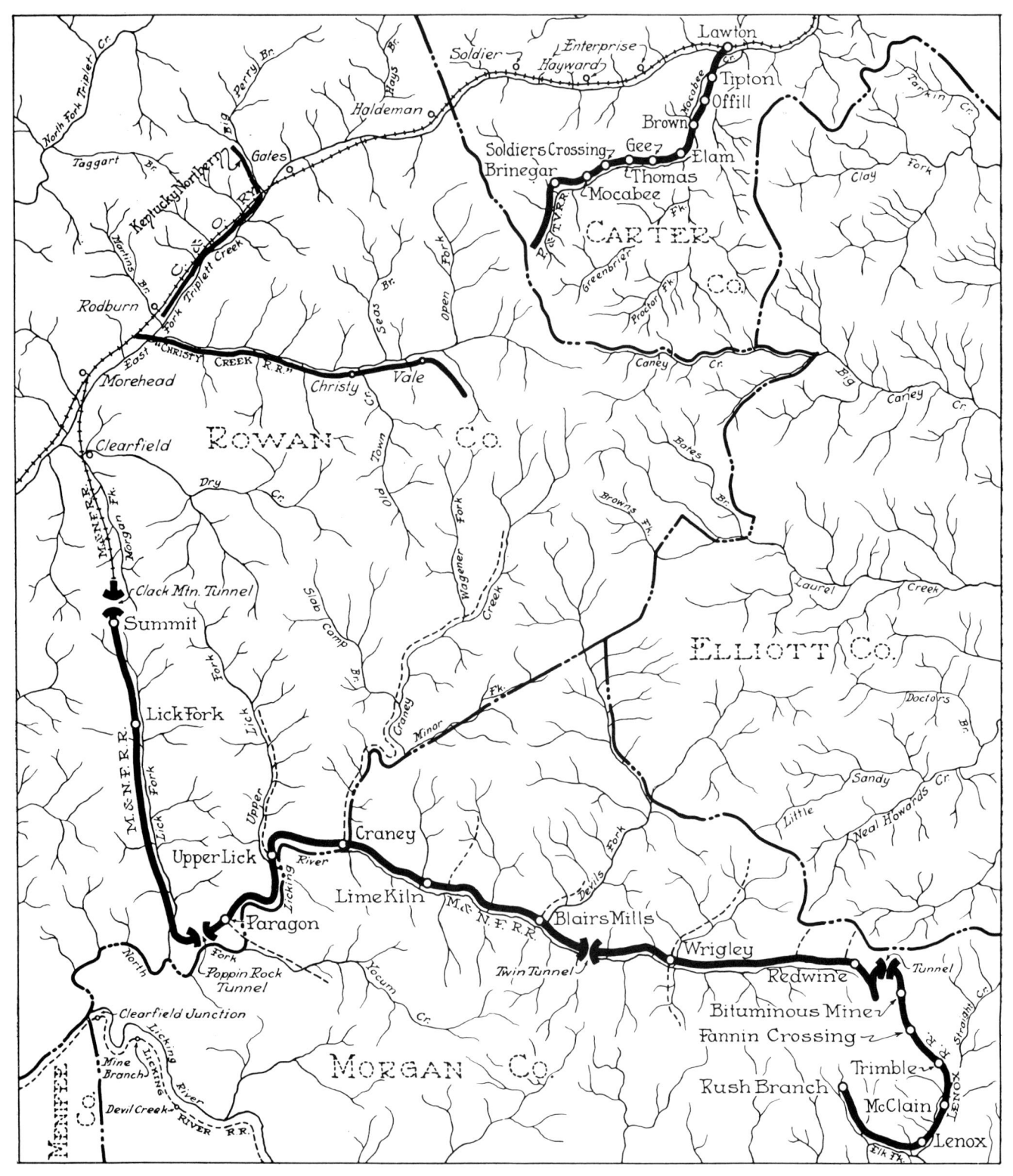

MAP
MOREHEAD AND NORTH FORK RAILROAD
LENOX RAILROAD
PORTSMOUTH AND TYGERT VALLEY RAILROAD
KENTUCKY NORTHERN RAILROAD
CHRISTY CREEK RAILROAD

The Morehead & North Fork Railroad Company was incorporated September 27, 1905, in the interests of the Clearfield Lumber Company, Clearfield, Pennsylvania, which had been accumulating large holdings of timber along the North Fork of the Licking River and its tributaries. The parent company had also acquired coal land under the corporate name of the Lee Coal Company.

Construction started the latter part of 1906, and on September 27, 1908, the entire 25 mile line to Redwine was completed and opened to traffic. Meanwhile, as the main line advanced, branch lines were thrown up the valleys and logs started moving to the saw mill at Clearfield, one and one-half miles from Morehead. Clearfield was set up as the railroad's headquarters and was named, obviously, for the parent's headquarter-location in Pennsylvania. Coal also quickly became an important traffic item and was hauled to Morehead for further movement on the Chesapeake & Ohio.

Locomotive No. 8 (Rogers 4-4-0) with No. 10 tender and coach.   C. E. Fisher

Another view of M&NF No. 8.   S. P. Guthrie

M&NF's Shay, No. 2 (Lima, blt 4/07) with log loader. Photographed 1918 at Redwine.   S. P. Guthrie

At Right Top—The M&NF flanged Ford Motor Car in Twin Tunnel.   William Wrigley

At Right Lower—Poppin Rock Tunnel as it looks today. After the abandonment of the major part of the M&NF, the county took over part of the former right-of-way (including the tunnel) for a highway.   John Sutterfield

At Left Top—The Morehead & North Fork had accidents occasionally. Here section men are attempting to upright a car east of Wrigley at the junction of a spur.
M. C. Crosley

At Left Lower—Similarly, the railroad's staff is pondering what to do about rerailing No. 4, off the high iron near Wrigley.   M. C. Crosley

During the maximum extent of the railroad, Clearfield had a shop for light repairs although some car-building also took place there, a water tank, track scales, storage tracks, and other appurtenances of a railroad terminal. Today it is still the headquarters of the four mile Morehead & North Fork Railroad.

The M&NF General Offices and Engine House, Clearfield.
S. P. Guthrie

Above—No. 5 at Wrigley Station. Wrigley was an important station for passengers and goods that were to be transported to points on the upper Licking River by horseback or wagon.   M. C. Crosley

Below—By 1926 the effect of the automobile on the railroad's passenger business had begun to be apparent. The steam train which was costing 59c a mile to operate was replaced by a new Edwards rail car which cost but 25.8c per mile to run. This steel vehicle, 43' long and seating 36, was placed in service July 22, 1926, and on August 9, a schedule of two daily round trips between Morehead and Redwine was adopted. The expected increase in passenger travel did not materialize and on November 22 of the same year the schedule of a single daily round trip was resumed.

General Foundry and Machine Company

MOREHEAD & NORTH FORK RAILROAD CO.

TIME TABLE No. 15
CANCELLING TIME TABLE No. 14
EFFECTIVE 6:00 A. M. OCTOBER 24, 1921

SOUTH BOUND First Class			Miles	STATIONS	Telephone Calls	NORTH BOUND First Class		
No. 1	No. 3	No. 5				No. 2	No. 4	No. 6
Leave Daily Except Sunday	Leave Daily Except Sunday	Leave Daily Except Sunday				Arrive Daily Except Sunday	Arrive Daily Except Sunday	Arrive Daily Except Sunday
s8:00 am	s1:20 pm	s3:35 pm	0.0	.. MOREHEAD ..	1Lg	s7:35 am	s12.45 pm	s3:15 pm
s8:05 am	s1:25 pm	s3:40 pm	1.5	. CLEARFIELD	2Lg	s7:30 am	s12:41 pm	s3:10 pm
f8:18 am				.... SUMMIT	1L 1s 1L		f12:27 pm	
f8:28 am			7.3	.. LICK FORK ..			f12:19 pm	
s8:39 am			10.5	... PARAGON ...	4Lg		s12:07 pm	
f8:49 am			13.0	. UPPER LICK .	3Lg		f11:54 am	
s8:53 am			15.0	... CRANEY ...	5Lg		s11:50 am	
f9:03 am				.. LIME KILN ..			f11:44 am	
f9:07 am				... BUCKET ...			f11:40 am	
f9:12 am			19.0	BLAIRS MILLS	1L 2S		f11:35 am	
s9:30 am			22.0	.. WRIGLEY ..	1L 1s		s11:23 am	
s9:40 am			25.0	.. REDWINE ..	1s 1L		s11:08 am	
Arrive Daily Except Sunday	Arrive Daily Except Sunday	Arrive Daily Except Sunday		"S" Regular Stop "F" Flag Stop		Leave Daily Except Sunday	Leave Daily Except Sunday	Leave Daily Except Sunday

Issued by GEO. H. GEARHART, General Manager,
MOREHEAD & NORTH FORK R. R. CO., Clearfield, Kentucky.

SPECIAL INSTRUCTIONS

Yard limits, Morehead to Dry Creek; Summit, Paragon, Big Branch to Walnut Siding; Wrigley and Redwine, designated by "yard limit" boards.

North bound trains are superior to south bound trains of the same class.

Maximum speed through yard, protected by "yard limit" boards; freight trains 8 miles per hour; passenger trains 12 miles per hour.

Maximum speed for extra trains, between Craney and Wrigley, 12 miles per hour, except through yard limits.

MOREHEAD & NORTH FORK RAILROAD CO.
MOREHEAD DIVISION
TIME TABLE No. 15
TO TAKE EFFECT 6:00 A. M. OCT. 24, 1921, CANCELLING TIME TABLE No. 14

GEO. H. GEARHART, General Manager.

At left—No. 3 at Clearfield. This Baldwin-built machine saw the light of day in 1907 and carried construction number 32222.

Below — No. 9 (Rogers 2-6-0) at Clearfield. This machine had two former owners and had two stints with the Southern Iron & Equipment Company. It was scrapped by the M&NF in 1939.   S. P. Guthrie

Bottom—No. 6 (Pittsburgh 4-4-0) with No. 8's tender at Clearfield. In addition to the coach, No. 200, the M&NF owned two combines, Numbers 100 and 101.   S. P. Guthrie

For a short line railroad, the Morehead & North Fork was constructed to above-average standards as to grades, alignments, and quality of materials. Laid to standard gauge of 4'8½" with 65' rail originally, heavier rail was substituted from time to time until the entire line was steeled with rail ranging from 75' to 100'. The entire main line was ballasted with limestone or with local creek gravel and rock.

Dispatching was done from Clearfield over a pair of telephone wires that paralleled the entire railroad. Wyes were located at Clearfield and Wrigley (later moved to Redwine). There were eleven passing tracks in addition to numerous industry spurs.

Above—Builder's photo of No. 3, one of the few locomotives purchased new by the M&NF.
George Yater

At left—No. 12 at Clearfield, September, 1955.   John B. Allen

Below—M&NF's No. 11 (Baldwin 2-6-2).   John B. Allen

Bottom—Caboose No. 3.
S. P. Guthrie

The Morehead & North Fork was not suffering for freight rolling stock, owning at one time or another Cabooses 1-3; Log Cars 1-32; Ditcher Flat Car 1; Flat Cars 50-53, 108-110, 300; Steel Hoppers 101-104; Gondolas 113-118, 140-141; Box Cars 130-136; and a Ford Touring Car with flanged wheels used for inspection service. The cabooses were built in the M&NF shops.

While the services varied from year to year, the more prosperous period of the M&NF saw a daily round trip of a merchandise train, two daily log trains, one or more coal trains, and two passenger round trips. On Sundays the schedules were usually limited to a single passenger round trip. In addition, there were numerous freight movements of refractory products, finished lumber, and coal, between Clearfield and Morehead.

The Morehead & North Fork Railroad had three tunnels —Clack Mountain, a 1334 timber lined bore; Poppin Rock, 725' through solid rock; and Twin Tunnel(s) which consisted of two short bores side by side, one for the railroad and one to provide a shorter route for the North Fork.

The Morehead & North Fork Railroad returned reasonably good profits until 1920, and meanwhile served well the purpose for which it was constructed, namely to bring out the timber and coal from the holdings of the Clearfield Lumber Company. The forest resources of the region were gradually worked out, however, and in 1922 the lumber company ceased operations and the big mill at Clearfield closed down.

The coal resources of the region were also diminishing. By 1932 the bituminous tonnage had been reduced to 77 and the forest products to 515 tons, a far cry from the huge coal and timber movements of earlier years. During the middle of May, 1927, a flash flood caused great damage to the M&NFRR in undermined and destroyed right-of-way and washed out bridges. It cost around $100,000 to repair

At left — Locomotive No. 10 (Cooke 2-8-0) at Clearfield. S. P. Guthrie

Below — No. 3 (Baldwin 2-6-2) with Excursion Train at Lime Kiln en route to Wrigley, circa 1920.

S. P. Guthrie

the damage and it was sometime in August before the railroad was open end to end.

As the lumber and coal business died, and the influx of the automobile and highway truck virtually killed the passenger and LCL freight business, the railroad was faced with the need of drastic adjustment. Request for abandonment of the line with the exception of the first four miles immediately south of Morehead was filed with the ICC on September 12, 1933. The requisite permission was granted October 21, effective one month later.

Today, the four-mile Morehead & North Fork is based largely on the operations of the Lee Clay Products Company which established its refractory plant at Clearfield in 1925. Its chief source of clay is a stripping operation on Clack Mountain, and this is moved to the plant in the cars of the railroad. Lumber interests are located alongside the line. The present-day diversified traffic of the railroad includes pipe, flue lining, wall coping, brick, lumber, pallets, cross ties, switch ties, and coal.

The Lenox Railroad found its origin in the narrow gauge trackage of the Roper-Reese Lumber Company which eventually connected with the M&NF at Redwine. By slow stages the 36" line crept up Straight Creek and Big Mandy. Here construction halted as the Roper-Reese Company became financially embarrassed. It sold its timber land, sawmill, and incompleted railroad to the American Lumber & Manufacturing Company of Pittsburgh, which, through its subsidiary, the Lenox Saw Mill Company, pushed the line by means of a switchback and tunnel through the ridge. Meanwhile there was a renewed development of the cannel coal deposits of Kentucky, and prospecting along the line of the narrow gauge indicated possible sites for future mining operations.

Partly because of this stimulus, the Lenox Railroad Company was incorporated July 3, 1918. During the same year the railroad was changed to standard gauge and was extended 1.7 miles to the mine of the Clearfield Cannel Coal Company on Rush Branch, completing the railroad with a total mileage of 7.7.

The combination of exhausted resources plus a precarious financial situation and other complications caused the railroad to file for abandonment October 16, 1926. This permission was forthcoming March 5, 1927, and the rails were removed shortly thereafter.

Passenger traffic on the Lenox Railroad was taken care of by a nine passenger Buda motor coach. Early each morning this vehicle would leave Lenox for the terminus on Rush Branch. From there it ran straight thru to Redwine in time to meet the passenger train on the M&NF RR, transferring its human load, returning to Rush Branch, and then back to Lenox for the night.

The freight train seldom made more than one round trip a day. The usual consist was a merchandise car and one or more cars of coal and lumber. The train would leave Lenox early enough in the morning to arrive in Redwine by the time the M&NF freight had arrived. The loaded coal and lumber cars were passed on to that carrier, empties were obtained, merchandise freight transferred, and the little train was ready to embark on the return trip. At Lenox the merchandise car and the lumber flats were dropped, but coal empties were brought back to Rush Branch in preparation for the next morning's trip. On those rare occasions when more traffic justified it, additional freight trains were run, as the railroad's Shay locomotive would have had difficulty in propelling more than five loaded cars up to the tunnel from either side of the ridge.

During its lifetime, the largest feeder of business to the Lenox Railroad was the cannel coal mine of the Clearfield Company on Rush Branch, this operation contributing sixty-six carloads between July 1, 1925, and July 1, 1926. However, several smaller lines sprung up along the track and added their respective quotas to the total tonnage.

GEOGRAPHICAL LIST OF STATIONS

DISTANCES FROM REDWINE, KY.

Redwine, Ky.	0.0 Miles	*McClain, Ky.	5.0 Miles
*Bituminous Mine, Ky.	1.6 "	Lenox, Ky.	6.0 "
*Fannin Crossing, Ky.	3.0 "	*Rush Branch, Ky.	7.7 "
*Trimble, Ky.	4.0 "		

Motive power included two narrow gauge Heislers purchased by the Lenox Saw Mill Company, and a standard gauge Shay. One of the Heislers is pictured below with a typical log train.   S. P. Guthrie

M&NF No. 14 at Clearfield, August 29, 1960.
—John B. Allen

Above—The "ten-spot" of the Portsmouth & Tygert Valley Railroad at Lawton Junction. Maxine Perrine

The Portsmouth & Tygert Valley Railroad was constructed by the Portsmouth (Ohio) Firebrick Company to gain access to the company-owned clay mines at Brinegar, three miles southeast of Haldeman on the Chesapeake & Ohio Railway. However, to maintain a water-level route it was necessary to make a connection with the C&O at Lawton Junction, a fraction of a mile west of Lawton, and to ascend the south fork of Tygert Creek and Mocabee Branch for 6.25 miles to reach the clay deposits.

Construction started the summer of 1892, and the road was opened May 25, 1893. A year or so later, a short spur, .33 miles long was built at Gee, making the total mileage 6.58. The track was standard gauge and laid with 50' rail. No. 10 was the sole locomotive owned by the P&TV.

The railroad lasted until the latter part of 1908 when the operation was discontinued and the track dismantled.

The Kentucky Northern Railroad was a narrow gauge lumber road that started at Rodburn on the C&O, followed Perry Creek north to its headwaters, ascended the ridge by a series of switchbacks, descended the opposite side by the same method, and came to a halt in the valley of the North Fork of Triplett Creek in the vicinity of Pine Springs. Before the close of 1896, nine miles had been constructed. Rolling stock included three locomotives, one or more of which were Climaxes, 15 freight cars, 7 other cars, and combine No. 4 from the narrow gauge Kentucky & South Atlantic (See Chapter 7).

With the exhaustion of the forest resources of the area the Kentucky Northern was abandoned in 1900.

The Triplett & Big Sandy Railroad was another short line constructed to bring the timber out. It served the interests of the Rodburn Lumber Company. Starting at Rodburn it ran up Christy Creek for a matter of five miles. Its life span was approximately 1890 to 1894. It was narrow (36") gauge and owned one geared locomotive.

Above—Second No. 1 of the "Christy Creek Railroad." This 2-8-0 remained in service until 1937 when it was replaced with Baldwin No. 2.   C. L. Collom
Left—No. 2 of the "Christy Creek Railroad" on its last run.   Claude Kessler

Approximately 25 years after the demise of the Triplett & Big Sandy, another railroad was built up Christy Creek from Rodburn. This was the 7.2 mile standard gauge line of the General Refractories Company, built to reach clay deposits at Old House Creek and Switman Branch mines.

Construction started in 1919, and on December 20, 1920, the first car of clay was hauled out. The line was discontinued and track abandoned the latter part of April, 1948, due to mounting operational costs. The road owned three locomotives—No. 1, a flat top boiler type in use for the first seven years; second No. 1, a small 2-8-0 which remained in service until 1937; and No. 2, a Baldwin.

The 4.75 mile Panther Gap Railroad, which operated around 1890, was owned by the S. T. Berry Lumber Company of Limestone and ran from that point south into the Berry Company's timber holdings. It was used to bring timber to the stave and nail keg works operated by that company. Two miniature wood burning geared locomotives powered the log cars.

At right — Cowles Swivel Truck Locomotive of the Panther Gap Railroad (0-4-0-0-4-OT). Hugh Boutell

CHAPTER 14
"In the Pennyrile"
Russellville to Adairville
(Louisville & Nashville Railroad)
Gracey to Princeton Junction
(Louisville & Nashville Railroad)
Elkton to Guthrie
(Elkton & Guthrie Railroad)

On February 27, 1867, a charter was granted the Owensboro & Russellville Railroad Company, and by amendment in 1868 the company was authorized to extend its road from Owensboro to the Tennessee state line near Adairville. After passing through a number of reorganizations the Louisville & Nashville Railroad became the owner of the greater part of the line's stock in March, 1880. Through the L&N's subsidiary, the Owensboro & Nashville Railway Company, the track was completed to Russellville in 1883. On January 1, 1884, it reached Adairville, the final terminus.

The 12 mile Russellville-Adairville line traversed the heart of Kentucky's black tobacco belt, a section of the Bluegrass State that abounded in the sense of tradition and well-being so typical of anti-bellum southern Kentucky.

The railroad was constructed to the then prevailing gauge of 5' but on Sunday, May 30, 1886, it was reduced to the new L&N standard of 4'9". When first laid, rail weighing 58¼' per yard was used but this was later replaced with 70' rail for the first six miles out of Russellville, and 65' rail for the remainder of the distance.

During most of the prosperous life of the Russellville-Adairville line, the pattern of operation consisted of a round trip of a mixed train in the morning and a round trip of a passenger train in the afternoon, all of these trains originating and terminating at Adairville. Mail, baggage, and Southern Express were carried on both the mixed and straight passenger runs.

The late twenties showed progressive losses in the operation of the segment, the depression years were even more hopeless, and abandonment became inevitable. Permission to discontinue the line was given October 25, 1938, and the final train puffed into Russellville on November 30. Dismantling started January 16, 1939, and was completed March 27. About three-quarters of a mile of the Branch was allowed to remain at Russellville, to be used as a storage track.

Service to Adairville in the Eighties.   L&NRR
Service to Adairville as of January 5, 1903.   L&NRR

Logan County
Todd County
Simpson County
Russellville
Orndorff
Red Oak
(Oakville)
Red River
(Mortimer)
Adairville
Edwards
Homer
Cooperstown
Gasper
Epley Station
Halo
Danby
Shakertown
Auburn
Gordonsville
Corinth
Ferguson
Olmstead
Lickskillet
Schochoh
Mosley Pond
Dot
Keysburg
Spa
L&N.
To Owensboro
To Louisville
To Memphis
Kentucky
Tennessee

Orndorff
Red Oak
Adairville
Russellville
Red River
Elevation
Miles
Abandoned from here to Adairville
675
650
625
600
575
550
525
500
144
145
146
147
148
149
150
151
152
153
154
155
156

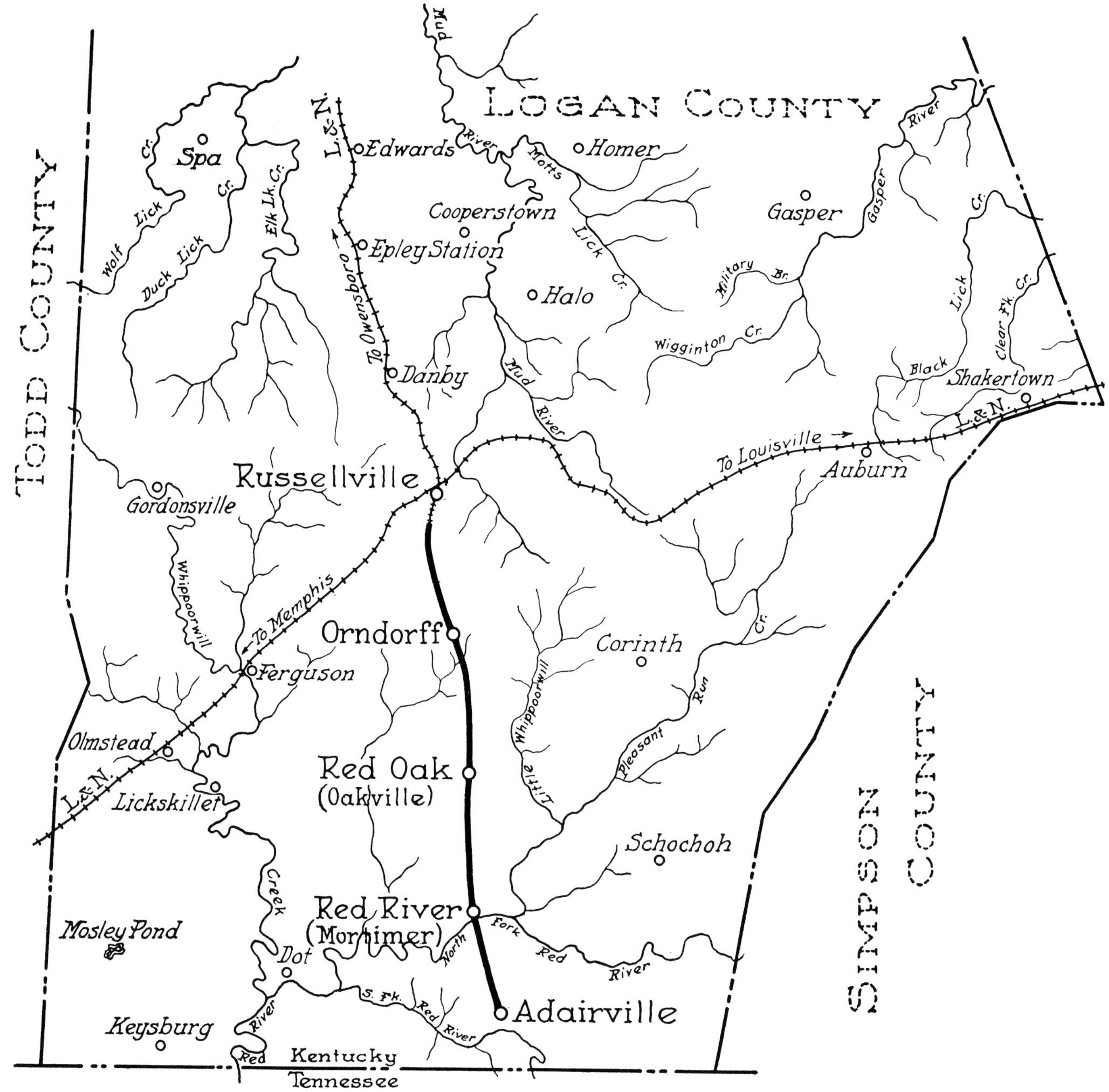

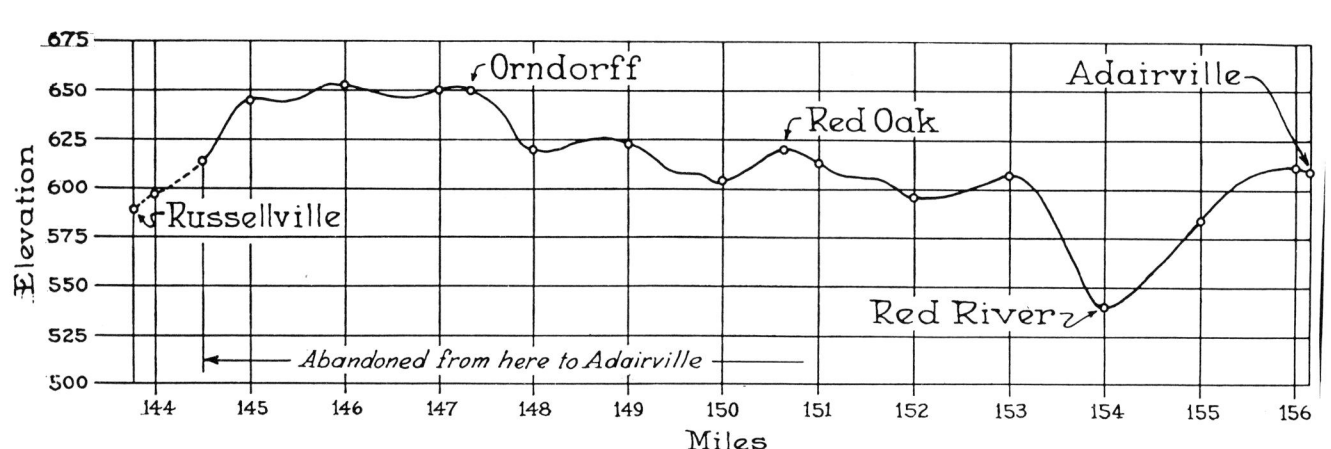

Adairville was the only train order office on the Branch. The terminal boasted of a 60' turntable, and a 1282' sidetrack.

The depot building at Adairville after abandonment. L&NRR

Track view on the Russellville-Adairville Branch prior to abandonment. L&NRR

There were comparatively few curves on the 12 mile line, and three tangents of 4½, 3, and 1¾ miles respectively.

Depot and Platform at Red Oak following abandonment. L&NRR

Besides the station building there was a stock pen and a 1235' passing track. Other stations on the Branch were Orndorff, 3.1 miles from Russellville; and Red River (Mortimer), 9.6 miles from the same point.

Above—Bridge No. 3 over the West Fork of Red River on the C&P Branch. This entire structure consisted of a 730' pile trestle, a 153' deck truss bridge, and a 95' pile trestle. L&NRR

At Right—Bridge No. 1, C&P Branch, built on a 1.65% grade approaching the West Fork of Red River. It was the deterioration of this and other similar structures that precipitated the abandonment of the C&P Branch. L&NRR

The Clarksville & Princeton Branch found its inception in the ambitiously named Indiana, Alabama & Texas Railroad Company, incorporated in 1882. It was constructed as a narrow gauge (36") line. In December, 1885, it had been completed from Clarksville, Tennessee, to Newstead, some six miles south of Gracey, and grading had been completed to Princeton, 22 miles further north.

On April 9, 1887, the rapidly expanding L&NRR acquired the stocks and later the bonds of the IA&TRR. The line was widened to the L&N's standard gauge (4'9") and extended north to Princeton. In the revamping process, six miles of trackage in Tennessee between Clarksville and Elliott's Pond (in the vicinity of Glen Ellen) were abandoned, and a new route was built from a junction (Princeton Junction) with the main line of the L&N three miles northeast of Clarksville, to Elliott's Pond. The line as rebuilt was 52.74 miles long.

The L&NRR on June 26, 1892, agreed to lease to the Ohio Valley Railway (now the Illinois Central Railroad) for 99 years the portion of its route between Gracey and Princeton. In keeping with the financial dilemma that plagued country lines, abandonment of the 32 miles of track between Gracey and Princeton Junction was indicated in the early thirties. The last runs of the mixed trains on the Branch were made May 13, 1933, removal of the light rails and well-worn ties from their dirt ballast started in October, of the same year, and was completed in February, 1934.

At Right—Looking south at Mile 182, one and one-half miles south of the state line. This was part of a 2½ mile tangent. L&NRR

Below—Rocky Cut on the C&P Branch. L&NRR

CHRISTIAN COUNTY
To Henderson
Buffalo
Gracey
Cadiz
R.R.
Montgomery
I.C.
L.&N.
To Evansville
Hopkinsville
Clardy
Gordonsville
Julien
Sinking
Little
Fork
River
Fairview
Casky
Newstead
Little
River
Rich
Tenn. Central
Masonville
Pembroke
Durham
Peedee
Binns
L.&N.
Red
River
To Nashville
Trenton
Herndon
Fidelia
Casey
Cr.
Roaring Springs
Bennettstown
Howel
W. Fk. Red
River
of Red
TRIGG
Co.
Douglas
TODD
Co.
Fork
Big West
Spring Cr.
Garrettsburg
Thompsonville
LaFayette
Oak Grove
Kennedy
Camp Campbell Area
Kentucky
Tennessee
Glen Ellen
Little West Fork Cr.
Ringgold
Crowder Cr.
Ringgold
Needmore
L.&N.
To Guthrie, Ky.
Relocated Line
Kenwood
Original Location
Princeton Junction
New Providence
Red
River
Cumberland River
Briarwood
Clarksville, Tenn.
To Memphis
To Nashville

Elevation
600
580
560
540
520
500
480
460
440
420
400
Clarksville, Tenn.
Princeton Junction
Needmore
Glen Ellen
Tenn.
Ky.
Kennedy
Oak Grove
Douglas
Howel
Herndon
Durham
Rich
Newstead
Julien
Clardy
Gracey
175 176 177 178 179 180 181 182 183 184 185 186 187 188 189 190 191 192 193 194 195 196 197 198 199 200 201 202 203 204 205 206 207
Miles

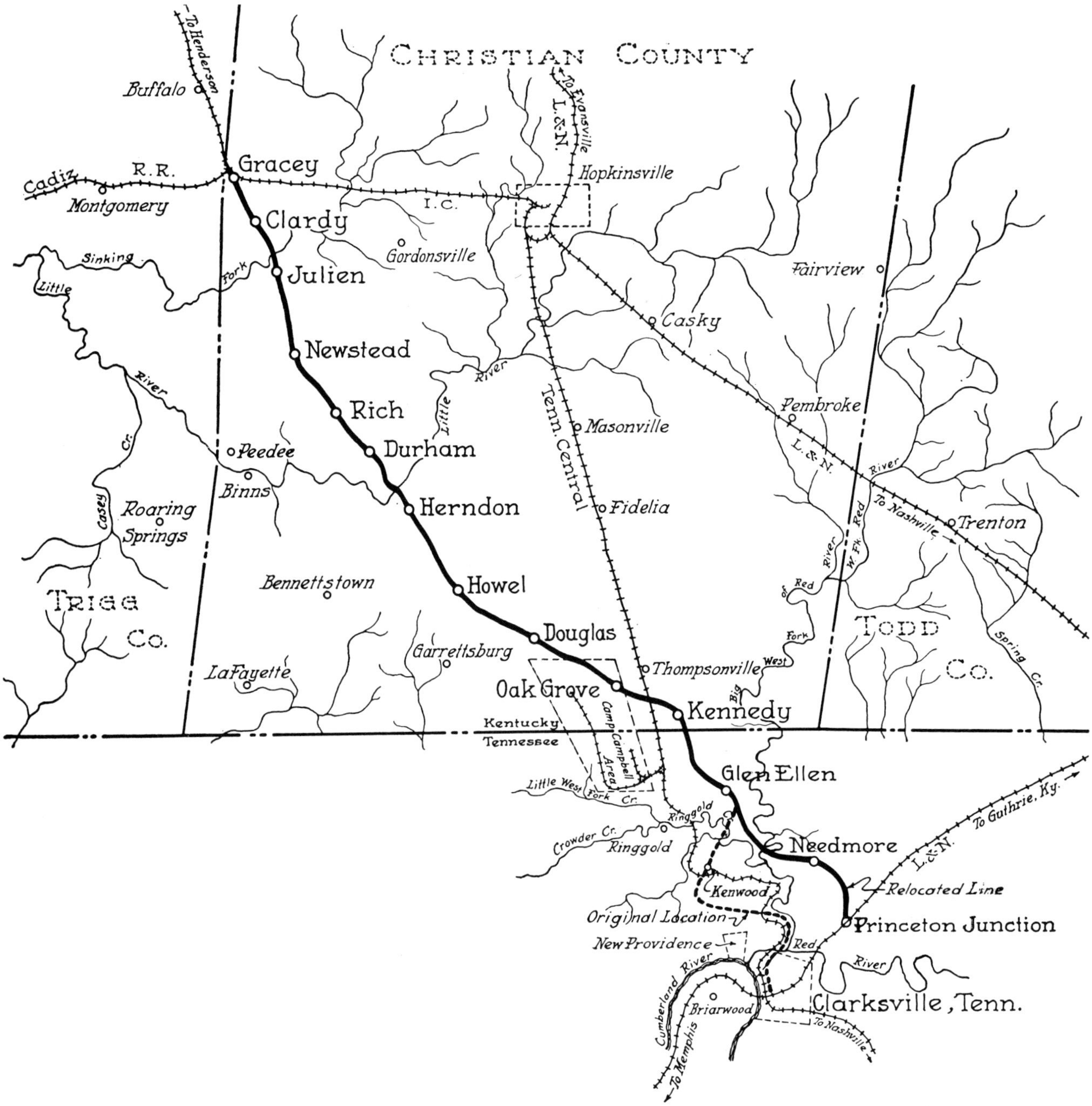

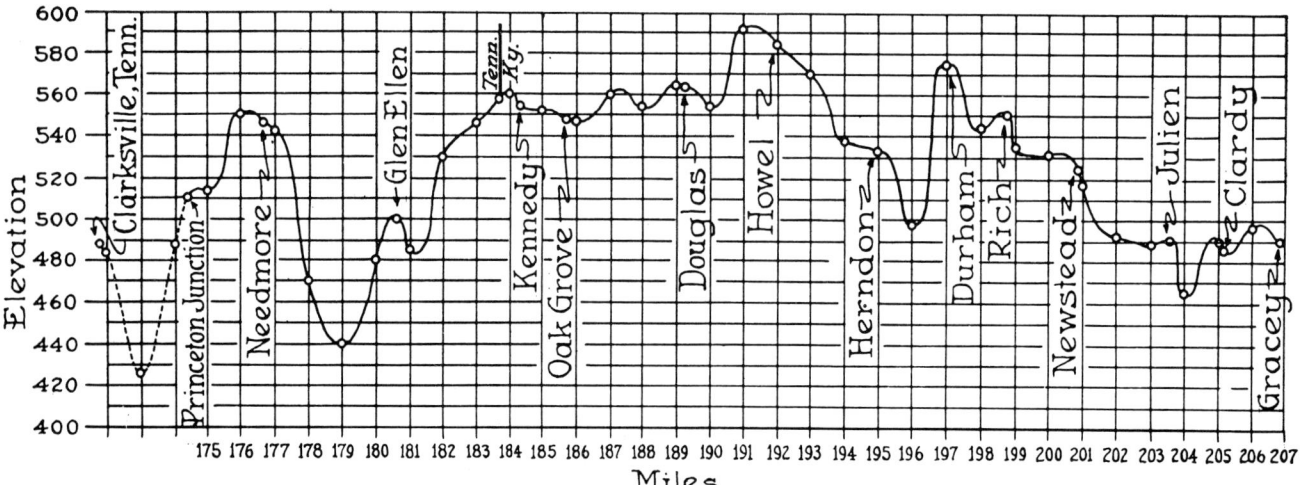

Above—Crossing of the Clarksville & Princeton Branch and the Tennessee Central Railway between Oak Grove and Kennedy. Gate is in its normal position, against traffic on the C&P Branch.   L&NRR

Below Left—Schedule of the C&P Branch in the eighties. L&NRR

Below Right—Service on the C&P Branch, and on the Elkton & Guthrie Railroad as of January 5, 1903. L&NRR

GRACEY TO POND.

No. 3. EX. SUN.	No. 1. EX. SUN.	Dis- tance.	Trains do not stop at Stations where no time is shown.	No. 2. EX. SUN.	No. 4. EX. SUN.
....	7 00 am	.0	Lv .. Gracey .. D Ar	6 50 pm	....
....	7 30 "	5.8	... Newstead ...	6 13 "	....
....	8 00 "	11.6	... Herndon .. D	5 46 "	....
....	8 14 "	14.7	... Howell ...	5 31 "	....
....	8 28 "	17.4	... Douglass ...	5 18 "	....
....	8 46 "	20.8	... Oak Grove ...	5 02 "	....
....	8 55 "	22.4	... Kennedy ...	4 55 "	....
....	9 14 "	26.0	... Glenellen ...	4 38 "	....
....	9 50 "	31.9	.. Princeton Junct D	4 10 "	....
....	10 00 am	34.2	Ar .. Clarksville. D Lv	4 00 pm	....
....	3 30 pm	34.2	Lv .. Clarksville. D Ar	12 51 n'n	....
....	4 01 "	41.0	... Steeles ...	12 20 "	....
....	4 12 "	43.3	... Hematite .. D	12 10 "	....
....	4 21 "	46.4	... Eisen ...	12 00 n'n	....
....	4 36 "	49.2	... Lone Oak ...	11 49 am	....
....	5 13 "	51.7	... Louise ...	11 37 "	....
....	5 25 "	55.8	... Marion ...	11 00 "	....
....	5 42 "	59.1	... Slayden ...	10 48 "	....
....	6 01 "	64.0	... Van Leer ...	10 39 "	....
....	6 20 "	68.9	... Sylvia ...	9 25 "	....
....	6 40 pm	73.9	Ar ... Pond ... Lv.	8 45 am	....

D Day Telegraph Station.   N Day and Night Telegraph Station.   ‖ Meal Station.

ELKTON AND GUTHRIE.

No. 87 EX SUN	No. 85 EX SUN	No. 83 DAILY	Dis- tance.	Trains do not stop at Stations where no time is shown.	No. 84 DAILY	No. 86 EX SUN	No. 88 EX SUN
5-15 PM	9 20 AM	5 40 AM	.0	Lv.... Elkton ....Ar.	9 05 AM	5 05 PM	8 50 PM
F 5 22 PM	F 9 27 AM	F 5 47 AM	2.0	........Bradshaw.........	F 8 58 AM	F 4 58 PM	F 8 42 PM
F 5 30 PM	F 9 35 AM	F 5 55 AM	4.6	........Hermon.........	F 8 50 AM	F 4 50 PM	F 8 34 PM
F 5 40 PM	F 9 45 AM	F 6 05 AM	7.7	........Anderson.........	F 8 40 AM	F 4 42 PM	F 8 24 PM
5 55 PM	10 05 AM	6 19 AM	11.5	Ar..... Guthrie ....Lv.	8 25 AM	4 20 PM	8 10 PM

GRACEY AND POND.

	No. 41 EX SUN	No. 21 EX SUN	Dis- tance.	Trains do not stop at Stations where no time is shown.	No. 20 EX SUN	No. 40 EX SUN	
		7 15 AM	.0	Lv.... Gracey ......Ar.	5 45 PM		
		7 40 AM	5.8	......Newstead......	5 15 PM		
		8 05 AM	11.6	......Herndon......	4 50 PM		
		8 16 AM	14.7	......Howell......	4 39 PM		
		F 8 28 AM	17.4	......Douglass......	F 4 27 PM		
		F 8 42 AM	20.8	......Oak Grove......	4 15 PM		
		F 8 51 AM	22.4	......Kennedy......	F 4 02 PM		
		F 9 08 AM	26.0	......Glenellen......	3 47 PM		
		10 00 AM	34.2	Ar... Clarksville ...Lv.	3 00 PM		
	2 45 PM		34.2	Lv... Clarksville ...Ar.		12 15 NN	
			41.0	......Steeles......			
	3 20 PM		43.3	......Hematite......		11 45 AM	
	3 44 PM		51.7	......Louise......		11 03 AM	
	F 3 59 PM		55.8	......Marion......		F 10 49 AM	
	5 28 PM		64.0	......Van Leer......		10 18 AM	
	7 00 PM		73.9	Ar..... Pond ......Lv.		8 45 AM	

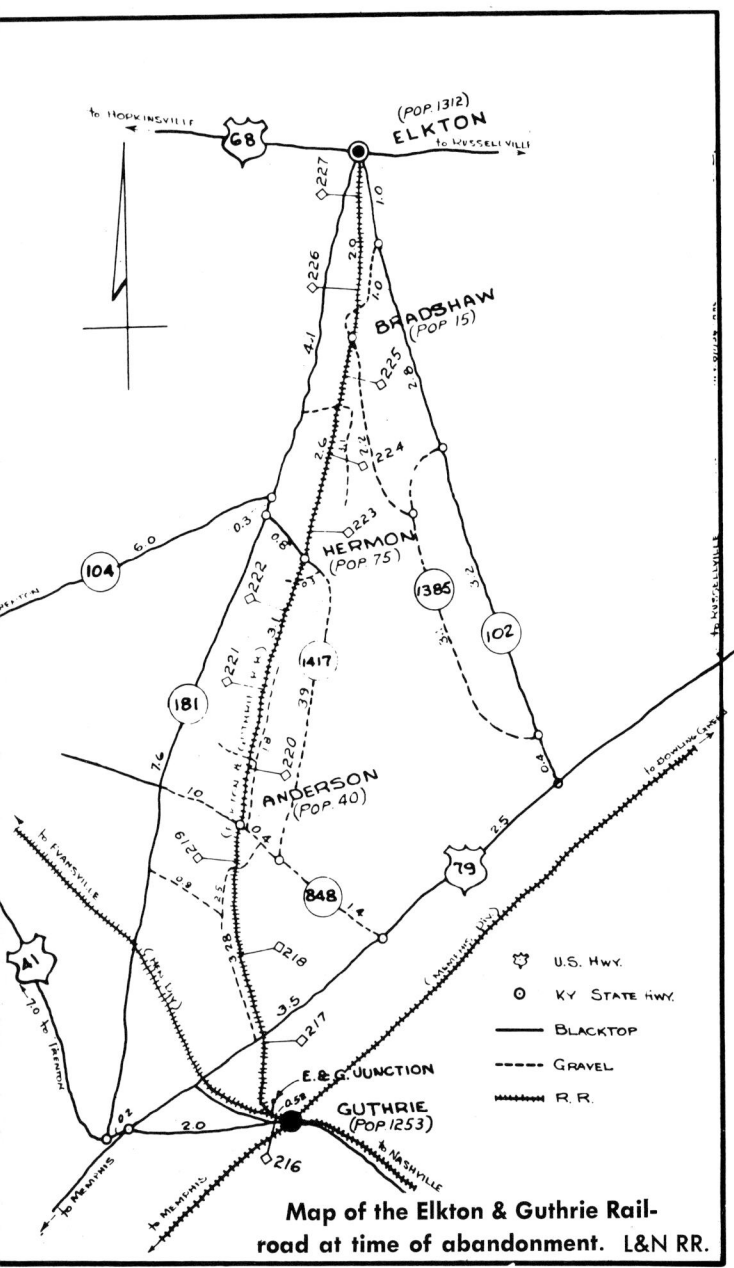

Map of the Elkton & Guthrie Railroad at time of abandonment. L&N RR.

On February 10, 1871, the Elkton Railroad Company was incorporated by the citizens of that community. The sum of $25,000 was raised by public subscription to finance the 11 mile line south to a junction with the Louisville & Nashville Railroad at Guthrie. During the ensuing 13 years the right-of way was procured and the grading completed. But at this point the coffers were exhausted.

The problem was presented to Milton H. Smith who had just assumed the presidency of the L&N. His reaction was sympathetic, his company advanced $25,000, and signed a contract to complete the railroad and lease it for 25 years. The line was completed February 1, 1885, and trains started to run. Preliminary to Mr. Smith's action, the railroad's name was changed to Elkton & Guthrie Railroad, and this company issued bonds covering the $25,000 loan.

During its entire life, the L&N furnished all rolling stock for the E&G. When the original 25 year lease ran out it was renewed for another 25 years. Subsequently it was not renewed, but the operation was continued on a year-to-year basis.

The early years of the Elkton & Guthrie were comparatively prosperous; the last decade paralleled that of other short lines built for the convenience of a local area of limited population and no large industries. Losses mounted in the early fifties, and application was made to the ICC to abandon the railroad. Permission was granted May 12, 1957, effective 40 days later.

The 11 mile railroad was sold to the Mid-West Steel Corporation and the Hyman Michaels Company. The L&N Railroad retained the Elkton depot and salvaged 16 crossing signs, four concrete whistle posts, and eleven concrete mileposts.

The presence of the Elkton & Guthrie must have been a source of minor irritation to the main line engineers since they were required by time table rules to reduce speed to eight miles per hour approaching E&G Junction until it was seen that no trains were passing to or from the E&G. Train registers were maintained at Elkton and Guthrie, and yard limits at Guthrie. Clearances and movement orders were not required at Elkton but were required at Guthrie.

A maximum speed of 25 miles per hour for passenger, mixed, freight, and work trains was prescribed for the Elkton & Guthrie Railroad. Because of the availability of wyes at both Elkton and Guthrie, locomotives on all trains operated in forward direction.

Employees' Timetable No. 242 of the E&GRR in effect December 18, 1927, showing schedules of three daily round trips of passenger service between Elkton & Guthrie. Numbers 10 and 11 ran through to Evansville from Guthrie. A single crew with one set of equipment, based in Elkton, took care of Numbers 9, 12, 89 and 88, in that order, spending the time between runs 89 and 88 in switching chores in Guthrie.   L&NRR

SOUTH BOUND.				BETWEEN ELKTON AND GUTHRIE.				NORTH BOUND.	
SECOND CLASS		FIRST CLASS		(E. AND G. RAILROAD) TIME TABLE No. 242 In Effect Sunday, Dec. 18, 1927 at 12:01 A. M.			FIRST CLASS	SECOND CLASS	
89 Accom.	9 Accom.	11 EVANSVILLE & ELKTON ACCOM.	Distance From St. Louis	STATIONS	Car Capacity / Siding Based on 43 ft. per car	Distance Between Stations	10 EVANSVILLE & ELKTON ACCOM.	12 Accom.	88 Accom.
Daily ex. Sunday	Daily ex. Sunday	Daily					Daily	Daily ex. Sunday	Daily ex. Sunday
....	8.27AM 12	6.45AM		L....ELKTON....A	17		1.25PM	....	8.22AM 89	6.50PM
....	8.34	6.52	279.50	BRADSHAW	5	2.00	1.15	....	8.15	6.43
....	8.42	7.00	276.90	HERMON	5	2.60	1.08	....	8.08	6.36
....	8.51	7.09	273.80	ANDERSON	5	3.10	1.01	....	7.59	6.27
....	8.59	7.17	270.52	E. & G. JUNCTION		3.28	12.53	....	7.50	6.18
....	9.02AM 97	7.20AM 121	271.04	A....GUTHRIE....N.L.	100	0.52	12.50PM	....	7.47AM	6.15PM 61
	Daily ex. Sunday 89	Daily ex. Sunday 9		Daily 11			Daily 10	Daily ex. Sunday 12	Daily ex. Sunday 88

Mechanized Spike Pulling in the process of dismantling the Elkton & Guthrie Railroad. Edison H. Thomas

E&G Depot and Terminus at Elkton. Edison H. Thomas

At Right — L&N crossing at Guthrie. Train No. 198 leaving Guthrie on Louisville-Memphis main at left. Elkton accommodation being pulled by L&N 4-4-0 No. 145 at right. The antique machine was built by Danforth in 1872, rebuilt by L&N in 1908, exL&N 2103, scrapped 1946. Photograph taken in September, 1932.
John W. Slusser, Jr.

Below—South end of the Elkton & Guthrie Railroad showing connection with Evansville main at E&G Junction, .12 mile northwest of Guthrie.
Edison H. Thomas

CHAPTER 15

"Phantom Rails of Southeastern Kentucky"
Altamont and East Bernstadt to Viva (Louisville & Nashville Railroad)
Viva to McKee (Rockcastle River Railway, and Bond-Foley Lumber Co. Railroad)
Burnside Junction to Burnside Landing (Cincinnati, Burnside & Cumberland River Railway)
"Honorable Mentions"

The Altamont & Manchester Railroad Company, chartered May 24, 1890, was a 3½ mile line, built during 1892 and 1893, from Altamont on the Cincinnati-Knoxville track of the L&NRR, east to coal mining developments on Little Raccoon Creek. The railroad was acquired in 1898 by the L&N in consideration of a $10,000 judgment obtained for steel it had furnished. Late in 1899 the L&N made a new junction with its main track at East Bernstadt and built a revised line into Little Raccoon Creek, abandoning the old route of the A&M.

The Rockcastle Railway Company was organized in 1912 in the interest of the Bond-Foley Lumber Company which had acquired rights to 24,500 acres of timber in Jackson County. Before any track was built, the name was changed September 13, 1913, to the Rockcastle River Railway Company. Construction began December 30 of the same year, starting at the termination of the L&N's line from East Bernstadt to the coal developments on Little Raccoon at a point known as Viva. On September 14, 1914, the road was completed to Bond, 13 miles from Viva. The RRRY secured trackage rights on the L&N for the 3 miles between Viva and East Bernstadt, resulting in a 16-mile operating route.

Diamond Mine on the A&MRR.
S. A. Mory, Sr.

Tipple at Bomar Mine on the Altamont & Manchester Railroad.
S. A. Mory, Sr.

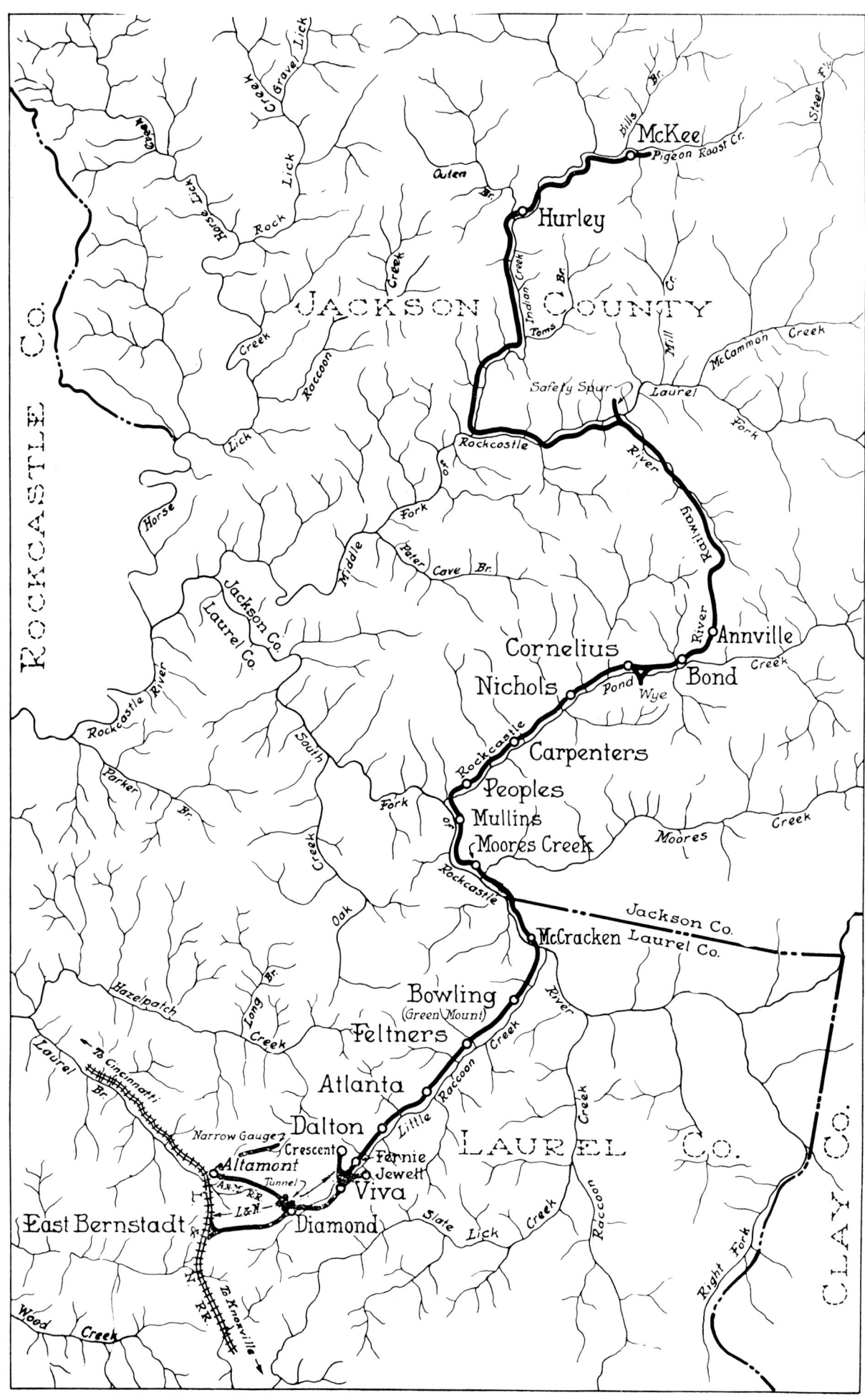

Track scene on the Rockcastle River Railway at Mile 6. Most of the rail was Bessemer 58¼ 'relay rolled between 1886 and 1891 and leased from the L&NRR. Ties were sawed, untreated white oak.
Ernest L. Andes

The daily passenger train out of Bond in the morning was timed to make connections with main line L&N trains at East Bernstadt. The afternoon return trip left East Bernstadt after the arrival of L&N trains from Cincinnati, Knoxville, and way points. The Rockcastle River passenger trains were actually mixed runs, with one of the three combines owned at one time or another by the RRRY hooked on the rear.

Below—Many of the RR locomotives bore names as well as numbers. The Heisler, resting at Feltner during the Kentucky summer of 1920, was named "Jane" and numbered 1. It was purchased new by the railroad in May, 1914.
William Black

When the Rockcastle River Railway reached Bond, that location became the focal point of the Bond-Foley Lumber Company. A huge lumber mill was established here as well as the headquarters of the railroad. The Bond-Foley Company, during 1914 and 1915, extended the tracks a matter of 10½ miles to McKee, and along the route sent numerous spur lines into the adjacent coves and valleys to tap the timber resources. Formal passenger services were never maintained between Bond and McKee, but a spirit of accommodation on the part of the Bond-Foley Company provided many rides for the local residents desiring to travel out of the hills.

RRRY No. 2 (Lima 2-6-2) with the first combine (No. 6).   Jerry York

The third combine at East Bernstadt depot, 1931.   Paul Wobus

No. 5, a Class C Shay locomotive, working between Bond and McKee.   Jerry York

The Bond-Foley Company completed the removal of timber from its holdings in March, 1930, and discontinued its mill at Bond in May of that year. By the last of February, 1931, the tracks of the Bond-McKee segment had been removed. Abandonment of the Rockcastle River Railway was authorized July 20, 1931, all tariffs were cancelled August 1, 1932, and by the middle of September the dismantlement of the railroad was completed. Shortly after this, the Louisville & Nashville Railroad abandoned its three mile line between East Bernstadt and Viva.

Rockcastle River Railway's 7 spot (ALCo 2-6-0) with mixed train near Bond, sometime between 1923 and 1926. Combine is the second one owned by the RRRY. Ernest L. Andes

No. 7 at East Bernstadt on L&N siding, at time of abandonment. Locomotive is in storage and shelter is being erected to protect the locomotive until it is sold or scrapped. Ernest L. Andes

THE WRECKS

Only two wrecks occurred to mar the otherwise perfect record of the Rockcastle River Railway's passenger service. On Monday, October 2, 1922, the passenger coach jumped the track and turned over down a ten foot embankment at Carpenters. J. M. Hurst, Winchester, suffering broken ribs, and Mrs. H. Lee Grimm of Chattanooga, Tennessee, suffering a broken collar bone, were the most seriously injured, and were taken to the hospital at London. Some ten others were bruised and shaken. All damage claims against the railroad due to this accident were settled out of court for a total of $2200.

One of the male passengers was in the wash room of the coach at the time. When he was pulled out of the overturned car his trousers happened to be on backwards. The anxious rescuers asked him the usual question under such circumstances—"Are you hurt?"

"No," replied the passenger who happened to glance down at his trousers at that precise instant, "but I shore am badly twisted."

The other accident occurred at East Bernstadt. Generally the engine made a flying switch of the coach after the passengers had unloaded, but on this particular day the maneuver was carried out with the coach full of passengers. It seems that the engineer was a little slow in accelerating the locomotive after cutting loose from the coach with the result that the vehicle hit the engine with a bang, bringing down parcels and baggage in delightful confusion. The only casualty was a lady who had been traveling with a carnival outfit. She was hit on the neck and shoulders by a dislodged parcel and sent to the hospital for observation. Her injuries did not prove serious and she was dismissed in a day or two.

After the wreck at Carpenters, the railroad's only coach was taken into the shop for repairs and during the interval the work train caboose had to serve as accommodation for passengers.

THE ROLLING STOCK

The Rockcastle River Railway owned none of its rolling stock but leased it from the lumber company. No written contract was made, but an oral agreement required that a stated charge per year would be made for all equipment leased by the R. R. Ry., such amount to cover heavy repairs, obsolescence, and interest on investment. The railroad was to assume the cost of all running repairs. When heavy repairs were needed, the locomotives were sent to the L&N shops at Corbin, Kentucky, and the lumber company footed the bill for both the repairs and the moving of the engines.

New rental rates were established as new units were placed in service, and as actual experience indicated that a rate was out of line it would be adjusted accordingly. Thus the original charge of $2,990 per year was reduced to $2,340 in the fall of 1920. On June 1, 1923, it was increased to $5,400, and in 1926, to $6,440. A reduction in 1926 brought the figure to $5,400 where it stayed until the railroad was abandoned. Allocation of this charge was made at $3,600 for locomotive rental, $1,080 for cars, and $720 for the coach.

Mention has been made of the railroad's first locomotive, "Jane", the Heisler acquired in 1914. In February, 1915,

ROCKCASTLE RIVER RAILWAY.

N. U. BOND, President, Bond, Ky.
F. P. DABOLT, General Manager, "
R. E. RADER, General Freight and Passenger Agent, "
C. M. KENNEDY, Secretary and Treasurer, "
J. L. ATKINS, Master Mechanic, "
H. H. CATCHING, Chief Engineer, London, Ky.
General Offices—Bond, Ky.

	No. 1	Mls	January 1, 1916.	Mls	No. 2	
			LEAVE] [ARRIVE			†Daily, except Sunday. STANDARD—Central time. Connection.—At East Bernstadt—With Louisville & Nashville R.R.
	†9 00 A M	0	Bond	16	3 55 P M	
	9 10 "	1	Cornelius	15	3 55 "	
	9 15 "	2	Nichols	14	3 30 "	
	9 20 "	3	Carpenter	13	3 25 "	
	9 25 "	4	Peoples	12	3 20 "	
	9 40 "	6	Moores	10	3 10 "	
	9 50 "	8	Bowling	8	2 50 "	
	10 10 "	9	Feltners	7	2 40 "	
	10 15 "	10	Atlanta	6	2 35 "	
	10 20 "	11	Dalton	5	2 30 "	
	10 30 "	13	Viva	3	2 25 "	
	10 35 "	14	Diamond	2	2 20 "	
	10 50 A M	16	East Bernstadt	0	†2 10 P M	
			ARRIVE] [LEAVE			

Passenger schedule of the Rockcastle River Railway as of January 1, 1916. Ernest L. Andes

the road received its second locomotive and the first of three passenger coaches. The locomotive, No. 2 was a Prairie type (2-6-2) with 16" x 20" cylinders, light weight 40,000 pounds, built by the American Locomotive Company in 1906, and purchased from the Southern Iron and Equipment Company of Atlanta, Georgia, by the lumber company at a cost of $4,900.

The coach, designated as No. 6, was a fifty foot combination with wooden body and underframes, and four wheel wooden trucks. Built by Jackson and Sharp, Wilmington, Delaware, it was bought second-hand for $875.

Two box cars, Nos. 300 and 301, and a flat car, No. 100, all having wood bodies and underframes and with capacities of 60,000 pounds each, were purchased second-hand. The cost was $442 each for the box cars and $200 for the flat car. The box cars were retired in 1931, and the flat car was placed in storage in 1920 where it remained until it deteriorated and was junked in 1932.

In 1914, the road purchased a Fairbanks-Morse hand car and push car, and later acquired another of each from the lumber company. A gasoline motor car, owned by an official of the lumber company, was occasionally loaned to the railroad for use in making special trips where it was not practical to prepare and use the train, such as those occasions on Sundays when the train did not run, and it was necessary to take important personages or those on urgent business to East Bernstadt to catch L&N trains from that point.

Despite having been rebuilt by the Southern Iron and Equipment Company just prior to sale to the lumber company, locomotive No. 2 had to be removed from service during the latter part of May, 1915, for repairs. Since the other locomotive, "Jane" was needed for lumber service in Jackson county, the L&N RR loaned its locomotive No. 2132 for temporary use between East Bernstadt and Bond until July 6 when No. 2 was again restored to service.

Later on the same summer, the lumber company acquired another locomotive, a Climax geared machine which was used exclusively in logging service. The fourth locomotive, a Heisler built in 1914, was purchased in 1918. Named "Sam", this one replaced "Jane" in emergency road service,

View of old Burnside. Upper railroad track is old main line of the Southern Railway. Lower track is connecting lead to the now-flooded Cincinnati, Burnside & Cumberland River Railway. Southern Railway System

thus permitting the latter to perform exclusively in logging work. A Shay, and another Heisler named "Joe", were the fifth and sixth locomotives obtained by the lumber company. Both were used on the logging road and never operated into East Bernstadt.

The Burnside & Cumberland River Railway Company was incorporated May 10, 1890, to build a connection from a junction with the Cincinnati, New Orleans & Texas Pacific Railway (Southern Railway System) to the Cumberland River landing, all in the village of Burnside. It was to serve as a short bridge line between the CNO&TP and the then-heavy river traffic on the Cumberland; as well as various industries, principally of a lumbering and wood-working type in Burnside.

On July 17, 1905, the B&CR sold its line to the Burnside & Cincinnati Railway Company which had been incorporated July 23, 1903. Less than a month later, August 10, 1905, the B&C was sold to the Cincinnati, Burnside & Cumberland River, the entire capital stock of which was secured by the CNO&TPRY, thus making the CB&CR a component of the Southern Railway System.

For many years the little railroad carried on an extensive switching business. One locomotive was assigned exclusively to duties on the CB&CR. The construction of the Wolf Creek dam and the consequent flooding of old Burnside made it necessary to relocate the CB&CR and abandon the old trackage. On October 10, 1950, the Interstate Commerce Commission granted permission to remove the old line and, at the same time, to purchase approximately 2.2 miles of railroad sidings, spurs, and industry tracks to be constructed by the CNO&TP adjacent to its relocated depot at Burnside, and to lease them back to the CNO&TP.

By this action, the CB&CR was enabled to still carry on as an active corporation although not as an operating railroad.

A close view of the old main track of the Southern Railway at the former Burnside Depot. Lower track is the connecting lead to the Cincinnati, Burnside & Cumberland River Railway.   Southern Railway System

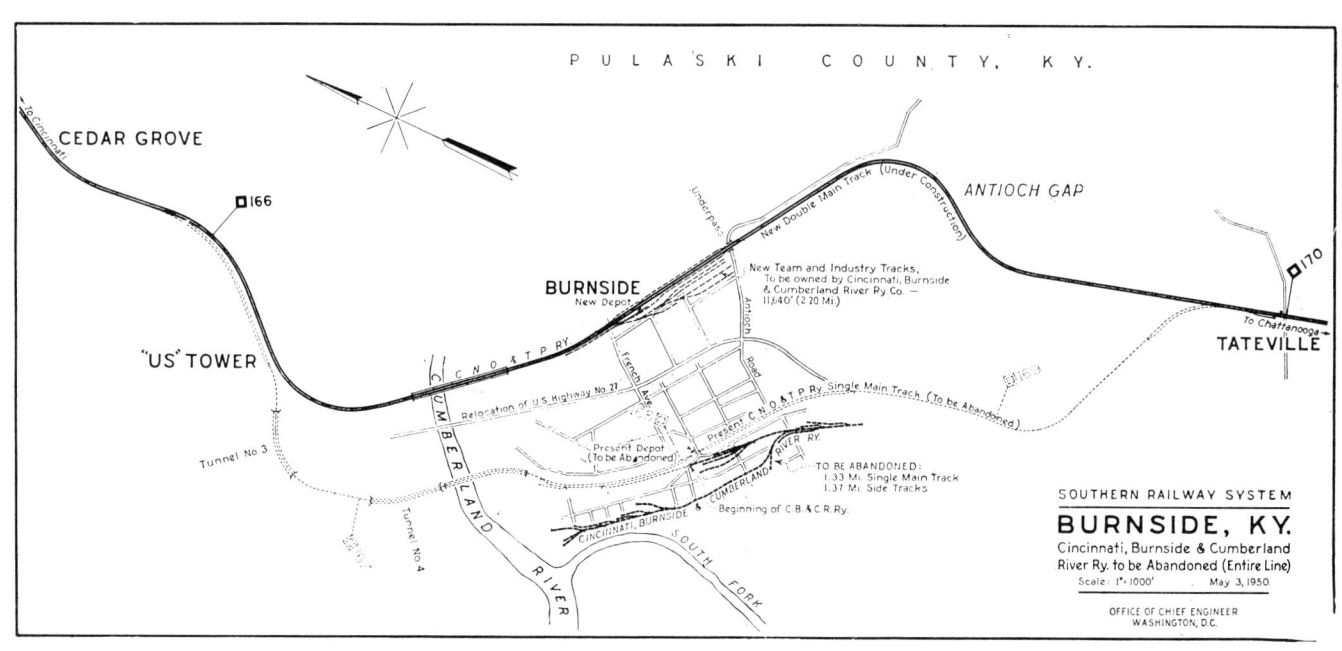

Above—Jellico, Birdeye & Northern Railway Car No. 100. This vehicle served the purposes of Caboose, Way Car, and Passenger Coach.   Richard Hardin

"HONORABLE MENTIONS"

The Jellico, Birdeye & Northern Railway Company was incorporated June 20, 1893, for the purpose of providing an outlet for the mines of the Jellico and Birdeye Coal Company. Construction started at a junction with the L&NRR near Jellico on the Kentucky-Tennessee state line, and proceeded northeastward, reaching Halsey, the seat of the mines and 7.4 miles from Jellico in September of the same year. Loads of "Birdeye" coal flowed forth from the railroad, and a rudimentary sort of passenger service was established. The JB&N acquired one locomotive, a passenger car (No. 100) a baggage car, and three flat cars. Coal and other types of cars were borrowed from the L&N.

The JB&NRR conveyed its railroad to the L&N on July 16, 1902. Henceforth, the line became known as the Halsey Branch. In 1905 the L&N constructed its new line south from Saxton, and for the one-half mile south of Keswick the right-of-way of the old JB&N was followed. The portion of the JB&N from Elk Fork bridge, one-quarter of a mile north of Jellico to a point 1½ miles further east, was retained, which with the addition of a short section of new track, made a junction with the new line at Lot.

In 1914, the extreme east 4.34 miles of the Halsey Branch were abandoned; in 1929, 1.39 more miles were cut back; and in 1942 the quarter-mile section between Jellico Yard and Elk Fork bridge was removed. Today, the only remnants of the JB&N are (a) the 1½ miles of track from the Elk Fork bridge to the east, and (b) the one-half mile section from Keswick south which is on the location of the L&N's relocated main line.

The Beaver Creek & Cumberland River Railroad was constructed around 1885 from Greenwood, a station on the CNO&TP (Southern) Railway in McCreary County, to the Beaver (coal) mine on Lick Fork of Beaver Creek, 6.5 miles to the northeast. The name of the line was changed in 1891 to Greenwood Railway & Coal Company. During its lifetime the railroad owned one locomotive, a 55 ton machine of Pittsburgh parentage.

The Wilton Branch of the L&NRR was opened about December 1, 1901, to serve the North Jellico Coal Company. The 3.97 line ran from Woodbine (near the south end of Corbin) to Wilton. A daily except Sunday round trip of a passenger train was maintained until April 12, 1927. The Branch was retired in 1931.

Pine Hill Railroad. A three mile line constructed in 1878 to serve the owners—The Pine Hill Coal and Iron Company. Narrow gauge (36"). Retired about 1893.

Middlesborough Belt Railroad (L&NRR). Constructed in 1890 and 1891 to serve coal mines and other industries around Middlesboro. In 1897 were retired 6.24 miles comprising the east and west belts, and 5.84 miles comprising the original Stony Fork Branch. Suburban passenger trains were scheduled over the belt, circa 1893.

Red River & Beattyville Southern Railroad. A seven mile, narrow gauge (36") line constructed in 1899 to serve timber interests. Ran from Torrent to timber.

Saxton-Jellico (L&NRR) — Constructed in 1883 as part of the original main line. Retired in 1937. 2.8 miles.

Kensee Coal Road. A 1.75 mile branch built by the Jellico Coal Company in 1886 to serve its mines. Later acquired by the L&N. Retired in 1932.

Nevisdale-Packard (L&NRR). A 2.49 mile branch built in 1908 to serve coal mines. Retired in 1947.

Proctor Coal Company's Road. A 3.75 mile line built in 1888 to serve coal mines of the parent company. Later acquired by the L&N.

Brush Creek-Johnetta (L&NRR). Constructed in 1903 to serve coal mines. 4.85 miles. Retired in 1916.

Chenoa - Grenada (L&NRR). A 3.89 mile segment built in 1907 to serve coal mines. Retired in 1933.

Chenoa-Olcott (L&NRR). A one mile segment built in 1893 to serve coal mines. Retired in 1944.

Glidden - Kawood (L&NRR). A 2.72 mile line built to serve coal mines. Retired in 1929.

Barren Fork Mining and Coal Company. Constructed around 1884, from Flat Rock to Barren Fork to serve coal mines.

Above—Collapsed bridge of the Kentucky Lumber & Veneer Railroad over the North Fork of the Kentucky River, a short distance west of Jackson.   S. P. Guthrie

Below—Locomotive on the narrow gauge track of the Kentucky Lumber & Veneer line on the Pan Bowl, west of Jackson.   S. P. Guthrie

K & P Lumber Company Railroad. A 30 mile, narrow gauge (36") road from Tallega south into Owsley County, built to serve timber interests. In existence before and after 1906.

Kentucky Lumber & Veneer Railroad. A 10-12 mile, narrow gauge (36") road, in existence before and after 1906. Made a junction with the L&NRR one-half mile west of Jackson, and ran north to Robbins (Camp Christy) on Frozen Creek where a large lumber camp was located.

Mowbray and Robinson Lumber Company's Railroad. A timber railroad, eventually totalling 40 miles, built north and east of Quicksand to bring logs into the owner's mill at Quicksand. Construction was started about 1910. Railroad dismantled about 1922 or 1923. Railroad had unusual gauge of 42".

Dumont - Quicksand (L&NRR). Constructed in 1910-11 by the Lexington & Eastern Railway to serve the Mobray & Robinson Lumber Company's mill at Quicksand. Jackson to Quicksand, 3.03 miles. Portion from Dumont to Quicksand, 1.03 miles dismantled upon abandonment of mill. Section between Jackson and Dumont became main line of L&N.

CHAPTER 16
"In Breckinridge, Ohio and Hancock"
Irvington to Hartford
(Louisville & Nashville Railroad)
Cloverport to Victoria
(Breckinridge Coal Road)

Special Train with "Texas" Locomotive No. 11 at Falls of Rough. Jennie S. Green

The building of the "Texas" (Louisville, St. Louis & Texas Railway) along the Ohio River from Henderson east to West Point (with trackage rights from that point into Louisville) was the inspiration for the construction of a number of lines running into the interior of the state. One of these was the Louisville, Hardinsburg & Western Railway, chartered February 24, 1888. Construction started at Fordsville and during 1890, 17 miles were constructed from that point to Jolly (later known as McQuady) as well as the five mile Falls of Rough Branch.

On July 6, 1891, the road was completed to Irvington and a junction with the "Texas." The LH&W consisted, then of a 41 mile main line from Fordsville to Irvington, the five mile Falls of Rough Branch, and a 1.7 mile branch

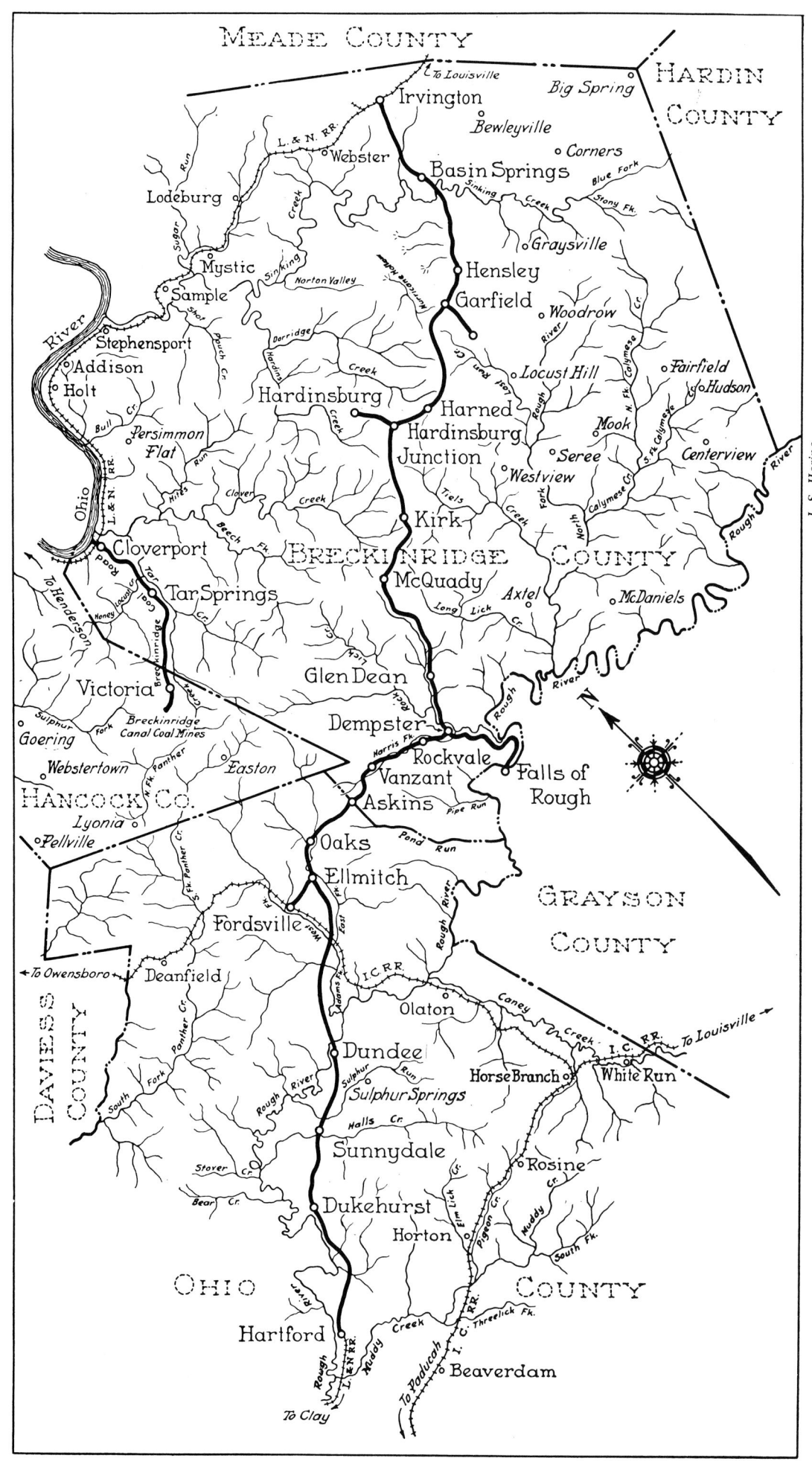

Louisville, Hardinsburg, & Western R'y

PASSENGER TARIFF,

Taking Effect May 1, 1891.

S. A. WIKEL, Gen. Pass. Agent.

STATIONS.	Station Number.	Distance from Irvington.	Irvington.	Garfield.	Harned.	Hardinsburg.	Kirk.	Jolly.	Glendeane.	Dempster.	Rockvale.	Ruth.	Askins.	Oaks.	Mitchell.	Fordsville.	Falls of Rough.
Irvington	47	0.0															
Garfield	159	8.9	.30														
Harned	163	13.0	.40	.15													
Hardinsburg	166	16.2	.50	.25	.10												
Kirk	172	21.5	.65	.40	.25	.15											
Jolly	174	24.2	.75	.45	.35	.25	.10										
Glendeane	179	28.7	.90	.60	.50	.40	.25	.15									
Dempster	180	30.7	.95	.65	.55	.45	.25	.20	.10								
Rockvale	182	32.2	1.25	.95	.85	.75	.55	.50	.25	.10							
Ruth	184	34.2	1.30	1.05	.90	.85	.65	.60	.45	.10	.10						
Askins	186	35.5	1.35	1.10	.95	.90	.70	.65	.50	.15	.10	.10					
Oaks	189	38.5	1.45	1.15	1.05	.95	.80	.70	.60	.25	.20	.15	.10				
Mitchell	190	40.1	1.50	1.20	1.10	1.00	.85	.75	.65	.30	.25	.20	.15	.10			
Fordsville	191	41.1	1.50	1.25	1.15	1.05	.85	.80	.65	.35	.30	.25	.20	.10	.10		
Falls of Rough	204	35.2	1.10	.80	.70	.60	.40	.35	.25	.15	.20	.25	.30	.40	.45	.45	

Passengers paying fare from Dempster will not be carried via Falls of Rough to other stations.

L&N RR

FORDSVILLE BRANCH.

5	3	MI.	*April 5, 1903*		2	4	
PM	AM		LEAVE	ARRIVE	AM	PM	
*6 55	†10 40	0	Irvington δ		8 40	5 45	
7 22	11 15	8.9	Garfield		7 30	5 18	
7 34	11 36	13.0	Harned		7 12	5 06	
7 38	11 42	14.5	Junction		7 07	5 01	
7 53	11 51	16.2	Hardinsburg δ		6 57	4 56	
8 08	12 19	21.5	Kirk		6 32	4 40	
8 15	12 33	24.2	Jolly		6 20	4 32	
8 28	12 57	28.7	Glendeane δ		6 00	4 18	
8 33	1 07	30.7	Dempster		5 50	—	
8 47	1 30	35.2	Falls of Rough δ		5 35	—	
9 01	1 55	30.7	Dempster		5 14	4 12	
9 05	2 02	32.2	Rockvale		5 08	4 07	
9 10	2 10	34.2	Ruth		5 02	4 01	
9 14	2 17	35.5	Askins		4 55	3 57	
9 23	2 32	38.5	Oaks		4 40	3 48	
9 35	2 45	41.1	Fordsville δ		*4 30	†3 40	
PM	PM		ARRIVE	LEAVE	AM	PM	

All orders drawn on St. Louis, for tickets to points on or via this line, should be drawn on the Louisville, Henderson & St. Louis Railway, "HENDERSON ROUTE," as the Louisville & Nashville Railroad does not ticket such Eastbound business out of St. Louis, all such traffic being handled on Louisville, Henderson & St. Louis issue of tickets.

Eldon M. Neff

from a junction to Hardinsburg, the county seat of Breckinridge County. As each portion of the road was finished, the operation was assumed by the "Texas." On August 6, 1892, the Louisville, St. Louis & Texas purchased the Louisville, Hardinsburg & Western.

FORDSVILLE BRANCH.

WEST-BOUND TRAINS.		Distance from Irvington.	Station Numbers.	Telegraph Stations.	STATIONS.	Distance from Fordsville.	EAST-BOUND TRAINS.	
Second Class	First Class						First Class	Second Class
	Mixed, Daily ex. Sun. No. 1.						Mixed, Daily ex. Sun. No. 2.	
	11.00 am	0.0	47	N	Lv Irvington Arr	41.1	9.20 am	
					8.9			
s	11.40 am	8.9	159		Garfield	32.2	s 8.10 "	
					4.1			
s	11.55 "	13.0	163		Harned	28.1	s 7.50 "	
					1.5			
s	12.02 pm	14.5	165		Junction		s 7.40 "	
					1.7			
s	12.12 "	16.2	166	D	Hardinsburg	24.9	s 7.30 "	
					1.7			
s	12.25 "				Junction	23.2	s 7.15 "	
					3.6			
s	12.48 "	21.5	172		Kirk	19.6	s 7.00 "	
					2.7			
s	1.00 "	24.2	174		Jolly	16.9	s 6.50 "	
					4.5			
s	1.18 "	28.7	179	D	Glendeane	12.4	s 6.30 "	
					2.0			
s	1.25 "	30.7	180		Dempster	10.4	s 6.20 "	
					4.5			
s	1.45 "	35.2	185	D	Arr } Falls of Rough { Lv	14.9	s 6.00 "	
					Lv } 4.5 { Arr			
s	2.10 "				Dempster		s 5.37 "	
					1.5			
s	2.20 "	32.2	182		Rockvale	8.9	s 5.27 "	
					2.0			
s	2.32 "	34.2	184		Ruth	6.9	s 5.16 "	
					1.3			
s	2.44 "	35.5	186		Askins	5.6	s 5.08 "	
					3.0			
s	2.59 "	38.5	189		Oaks	2.6	s 4.50 "	
					1.6			
f	3.10 "	40.1	190		Mitchell	1.0	s 4.41 "	
					1.0			
	3.20 pm	41.1	191	D	Arr Fordsville Lv	0.0	4.35 am	

Employees' Timetable No. 3, effective December 27, 1896. E. S. McAfee

The Louisville, St. Louis & Texas Railway went into receivership, August 7, 1893. A foreclosure sale followed and on June 1, 1896, the properties began operation as the Louisville, Henderson & St. Louis Railway. On April 1, 1905, the LH&StL completed its own track from near West Point into Louisville, and later in the same year the L&N purchased a majority of the stock of the company. Thus the Louisville, Hardinsburg & Western came into the L&N fold.

On July 1, 1905, the L&N incorporated the Madisonville, Hartford & Eastern. On January 4, 1910, the 55½ mile line from Como, in the heart of the western Kentucky coal field, east to a junction with the LH&W trackage at Ellmitch, was completed. It was the intention of the L&N to provide a more direct route from the coal field to Louisville than the circuitous ones via Owensboro or Henderson. Unfortunately, this plan proved impractical, largely due to the poor engineering evident in the construction of the section of the old LH&W between Ellmitch and Irvington.

First train of the Louisville, Hardinsburg & Western in Fordsville. Locomotive is "Texas" No. 1.
                                             Mrs. Paul C. Snyder

With the failure of "short cut" plan of the L&N to materialize, the route became relegated to local traffic that became less and less as the gasoline age extended its sway. On June 15, 1941, the last train ran. The track was removed between Irvington and Fordsville (37.73 miles), Dempster to Falls of Rough (4.45 miles), Junction to Hardinsburg (1.73 miles), and Ellmitch to Hartford (19.22 miles). The dismantling was completed in July, 1942, added impetus being given this activity by the nation's then pressing need for scrap metal.

"Texas" 8-Wheeler No. 3 at Cloverport roundhouse.
                                             Hugh G. Boutell-Thomas Norrell

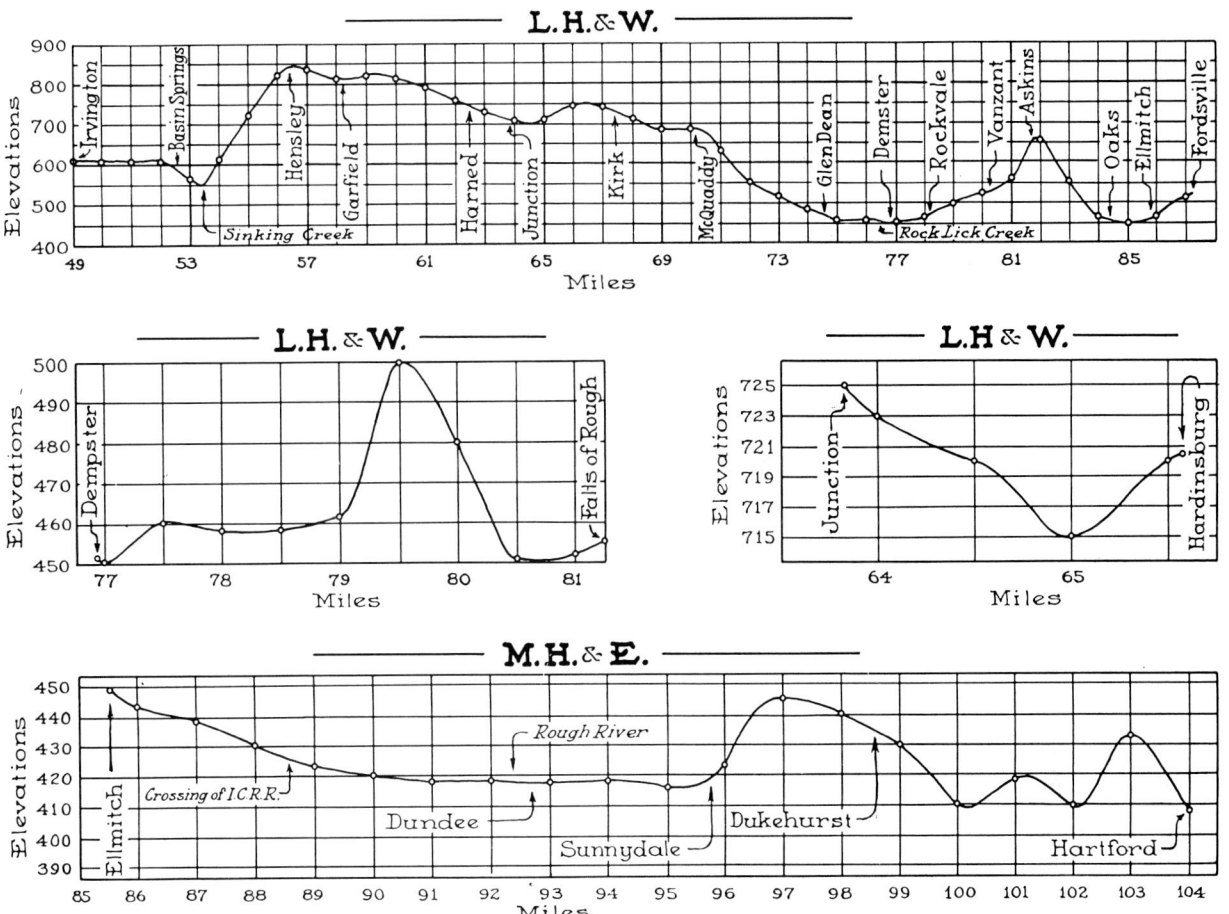

Employee's Timetable No. 90, effective January 20, 1929.

Breckinridge Coal Train on Ohio River tipple, 1899.
R. A. May

In the early 1850's, the Breckenridge Coal and Oil Company, an English firm, purchased and leased several thousand acres of land underlain by cannel coal, centering around Keg Branch of Tar Creek in southeastern Hancock County. Sixteen adits were driven into the hill and the resulting mining community was given the name of Bennettsville.

A broad gauge (4'11") tram railway, seven miles long, was built to bring the coal from Bennettsville to a point near the west end of Cloverport where the coal was to be loaded into flatboats for shipment to New Orleans and transhipped to England.

Business boomed for a time but a combination of events including the Civil War caused a cessation of the industry. The mine, the railroad, and other appurtenances of the company laid dormant for almost 15 years. Finally a new organization was effected and in 1875 plans were made to establish a colliery at the old workings and rehabilitate the railroad.

The rebuilding of the line was completed December 6, 1885. The length was 8.5 miles, and this time the rails were laid to standard gauge. The weight of the steel, however, was 56', and there were 14 wooden trestles along the line. A wooden pile trestle pier carried the railroad out over the river, and on the pier below the track was a tipple into which the cars dumped the coal.

Initially, the Breckinridge Coal Road had no railroad connections, but in 1889, the Louisville, St. Louis & Texas Railway completed its line from Henderson to West Point and established its principal shops in Cloverport. A track connection was made where the lines crossed. About 1891, the English market for the coal failed, the tipple was discontinued and the entire output henceforth went out by rail.

Passengers were carried in a home-made vehicle that resembled a LCL way car.

The Breckinridge Coal Road was never formally abandoned. Apparently the last trains ran in 1893, but it was not until 1898 that the Breckinridge mines were permanently closed and the railroad dismantled.

Locomotive No. 1 and the improvised passenger car of the Breckinridge Coal Road. Note how the lanky employee standing in the car door has to stoop to clear the top sill. Charles E. Fisher

CHAPTER 17
"Memory Routes of Eastern Kentucky"
Riverton to Webbville
(Eastern Kentucky Railway)
Walbridge to Richardson via Peach Orchard
(Chesapeake & Ohio Railway)
"Streaks of Rust"

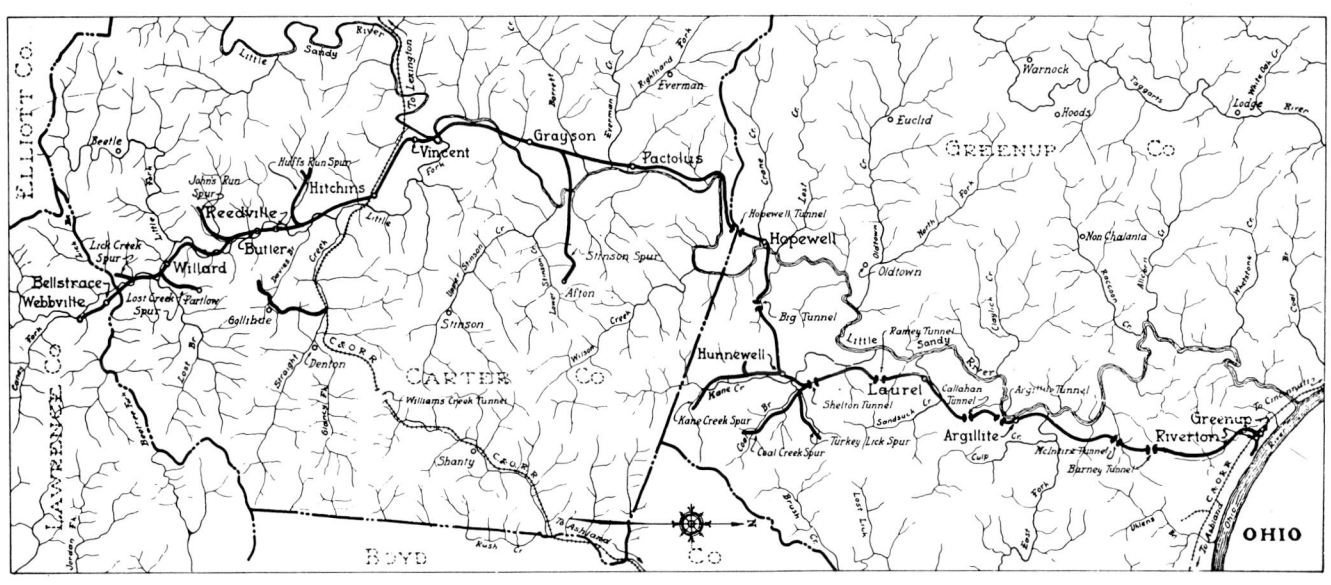

The Eastern Kentucky Railway had its origin in the year 1865, just about at the close of the War Between the States. John and Nathaniel Thayer, Boston bankers, together with George Hunnewell, a merchant from the same city, obtained a charter from the Kentucky legislature on March 4 of that year under the name of "Argillite Mining and Manufacturing Company." Among other features of the charter was a provision carrying with it the power to lock and dam the Little Sandy River. By an act approved December 14, 1865, the name was changed to "Kentucky Improvement Company."

The Thayers and Hunnewell purchased some 25,000 acres of land south of Riverton on the Little Sandy, which was supposedly rich in coal, iron and timber. In 1866-67 the company constructed 6½ miles of railroad from the Ohio River south to a point known as Argillite. Development of the territory's resources was under way.

In 1868 the railroad was extended several miles further south and a station was established at the railhead and named Hunnewell. Nearby were some cannel coal deposits in which the company set great store. However, these proved a disappointment and were practically exhausted by 1869. Two blast furnaces were acquired but they were almost immediately handicapped by lack of sufficient iron ore and coal.

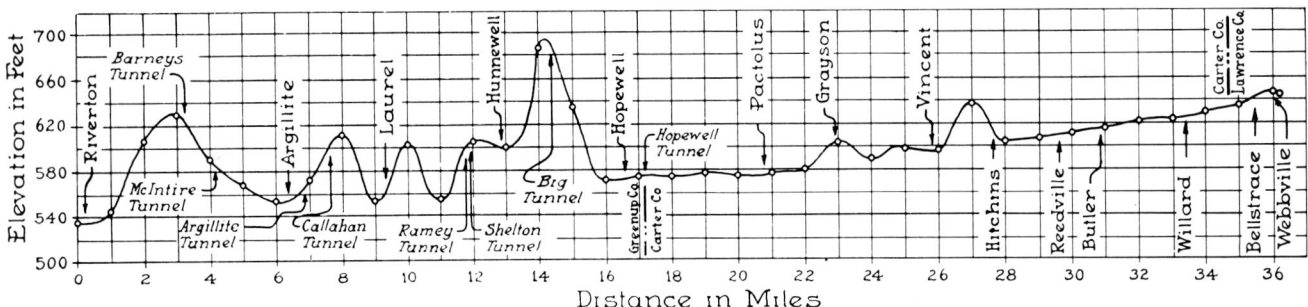

The 12.64 mile line was built to a gauge of 5' with rail of 50' weight. There was a 5.5 mile spur track from Hunnewell to the mines. Rolling stock of the little line included three locomotives, a combine, 44 coal cars, and 36 other freight cars. Shops were maintained at Hunnewell.

A reorganization took place in 1870 and on February 28 the Kentucky Improvement Company deeded to the newly organized Eastern Kentucky Railway its railroad, the two blast furnaces, and about 25,000 acres of ore, coal and timber land.

The original intention of the Thayers was to extend their railroad to a junction with the Southern Atlantic & Ohio at the breaks of the Big Sandy River in Pike County; and to bridge the Ohio River at Riverton to connect with the Scioto Valley Railroad, then abuilding from the north bank of the Ohio to Lake Erie. Such a route would have provided a direct line from the southern coal fields to the Great Lakes and would have caused a much earlier development of the coal resources of the region.

Nathaniel Thayer, who had acquired the major portion of stock in the Eastern Kentucky Railway, became the line's first president and held the office until his death. Colonel H. W. Bates of Cincinnati was the road's first Vice-President and General Manager. Upon his death he was succeeded in the same position by his son, Sturgis G. Bates.

To obtain additional supplies of ore and wood and to create what additional business the region might offer, the EKRY during 1870 and 1871 was extended 10.37 miles. On June 10 of the latter year the line was opened for traffic into Grayson, the county seat of Carter County. Now real estate values began to climb, new investment capital was attracted to the opened areas of virgin timber, coal fields, and iron ore deposits, new blast furnaces were built, sawmills installed, coal mines opened, and the region bid fair to become a thriving industrial area. The general offices of the railroad remained at Riverton, but the shops were moved from Hunnewell to Grayson and substantially enlarged.

Combine No. 13 (later changed to 213), another Ohio Falls product. Richard Hardin

During 1873 and 1874, the Eastern Kentucky Railway was extended 11.30 miles from Grayson to Willard to accommodate the owners of two blast furnaces in Ironton, Ohio, who had acquired large tracts of coal and iron ore lands near Willard, and promised certain shipments of coal and ore in return for building the extension. The proferred shipments were made for a matter of two years and then terminated, the claim being made that the Willard ore was too lean and the coal of a quality unsuitable for blast furnaces. This was only the beginning of the troubles that plagued the EK up to the time of its abandonment.

Old coaches and depot at Grayson shortly after abandonment.
C. L. Collom

During the seventies, passenger service consisted of a daily round trip of the mail train between Riverton and Willard, and a daily round trip of a mixed train between Riverton and Grayson. Grayson was the terminal for the trains with a crew leaving that town on the mixed run at 7 a.m., and returning for the night on the companion schedule at 5:20 p.m.

Around 1874, the gauge of the railroad was changed from 5' to 4'9", presumably to permit interchange of cars with the Scioto Valley at Ironton, Ohio, via the car ferry over the river.

EKRY pass of 1913. S. P. Guthrie

Second No. 5 on turntable at Grayson. This 4-6-0 was a January, 1892, product of Schenectady. It was obtained from the C&ORY April, 1912, ex C&O No. 121, Class F-10. Lad G. Arend

141

Interior of later-type EKRY coach, a product of the Ohio Falls Car Manufacturing Company. George Yater

EK's second No. 4 was a 4-6-0 built by the Pennsylvania Railroad. It was sold in September, 1912, to the Southern Iron & Equipment Company. It is shown at the Willard water tank. Fred Duncan

The Eastern Kentucky Railway is known to have owned seven items of passenger rolling stock—two coaches Nos. 201 and 202; four combines Nos. 19, 211, 212, and 213; and baggage car No. 214.

M1 and M2, known collectively as the "Blue Goose." The vehicles were obtained after the abandonment of the north end of the EKRY, to provide a passenger service over the remaining trackage. Fred Duncan

The East Kentucky Southern Railway, successor to the Eastern Kentucky, obtained this second-hand Mack gasoline-powered rail car, No. 215, more popularly known to its customers as "Queen." It was built 6/10/21 under construction No. 70005 and was secured from the Sewell Valley in 1929. It was scrapped in 1933. Baggage and light express were transported in the homemade product pictured to the rear of "Queen." Fred Duncan

Prior to 1881, the Eastern Kentucky had no physical connection with any other railroad. However, in December of that year, the Elizabethtown, Lexington & Big Sandy Railroad (now the C&ORY) completed its line between Lexington and Ashland, crossing the EK at a point that became known as Hitchens. In 1889, the Maysville & Big Sandy Railroad (also now the C&ORY) was opened between Ashland and Cincinnati, making a junction with the EK at Riverton. In the same year, the Eastern Kentucky Railway extended its track south for 1.77 miles, reaching Webbville, the final limit of its main track which now totalled 36 miles plus about 2½ miles of sidings.

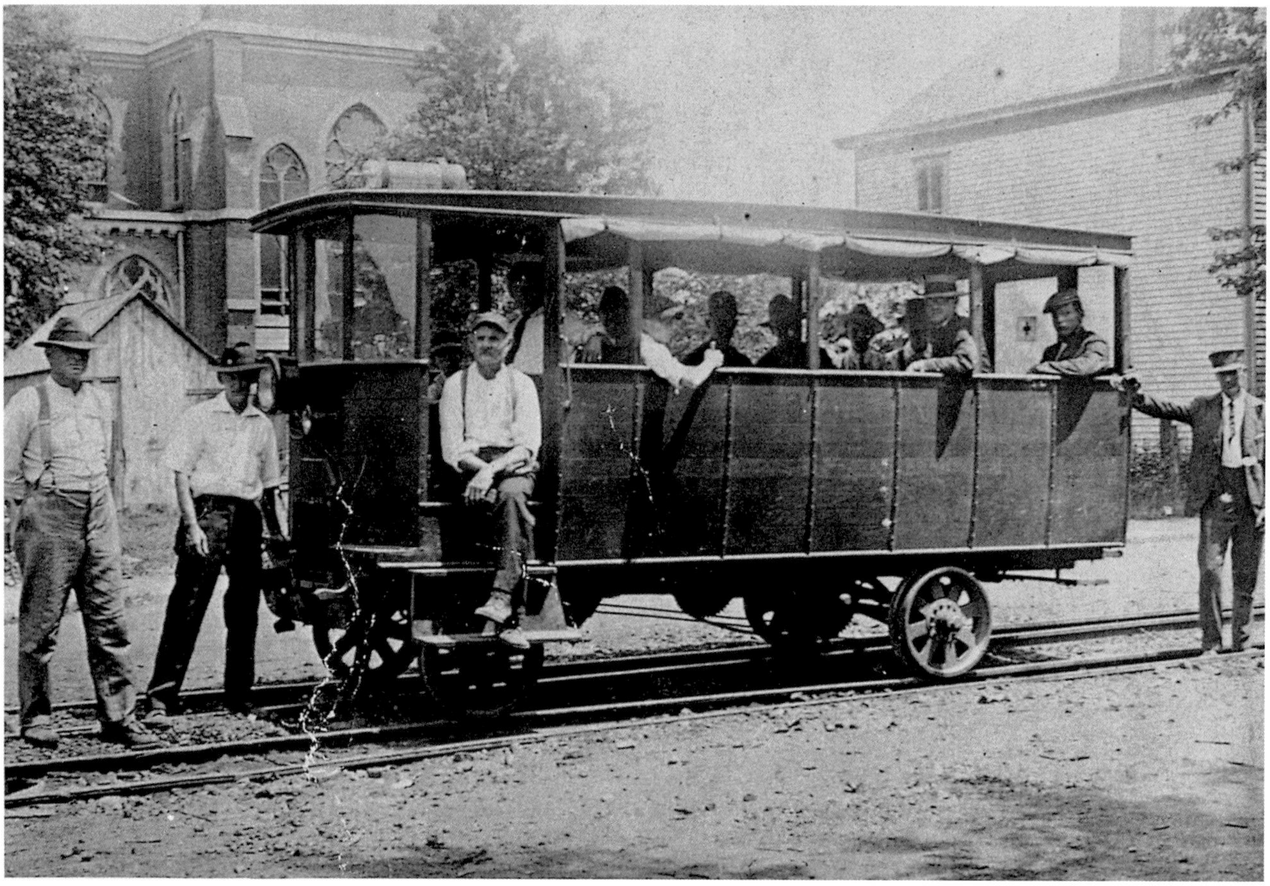

Above — Another "Blue Goose" poses for posterity in a Grayson street.

Right—Last EKRY trip out of Grayson.   Mrs. John W. Kitchen

Below—The general store at Laurel also doubled as the depot.

Lower right—Imagine riding 500 miles on the EKRY. This 500 mile ticket was issued in 1909 to the school-marm, Miss Belva Green.
Fred Duncan

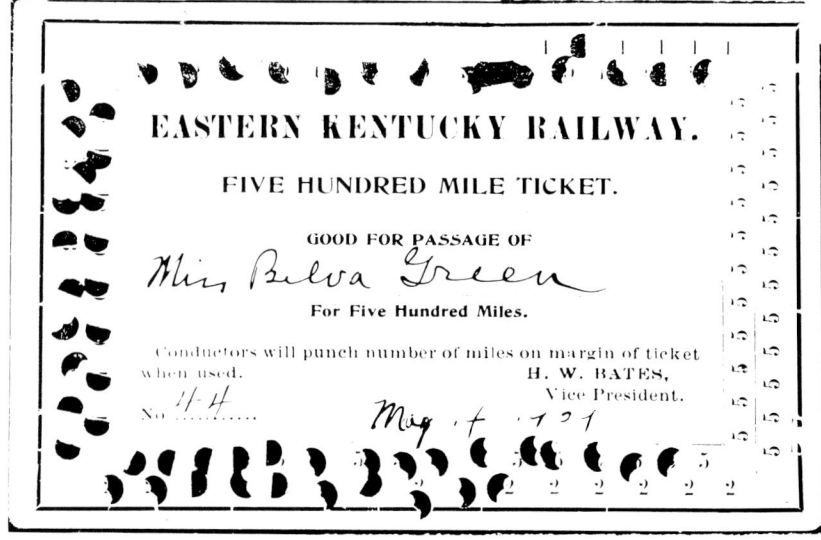

144

Argillite Tunnel. This 610′ bore was one of eight on the Eastern Kentucky. Hazel Boyd

As early as 1845, companies had been formed to mine and ship the bituminous coal of the Big Sandy (Chatterawah) river valley. One of these companies, to become eventually the Great Western Mining and Manufacturing Company developed a mining settlement at Peach Orchard in Lawrence County. Barges were built and as they were completed the Peach Orchard coal was tipped into them, ready to be sent to market when the waters of the Big Sandy rose sufficiently to float them. But the erratic river stages served to frustrate the plans, and this, coupled with the Civil War, put an end to activities for a time.

At the end of the war the Great Western Mining and Manufacturing Company revived its interest in the development of the Peach Orchard mines, and steps were taken to provide rail transportation between Peach Orchard and Ashland. At that time, no railroad entered Ashland with the exception of 13 miles of track from Ashland to Rush, constructed in 1856 and succeeding years by the Lexington & Big Sandy Railroad Company and others.

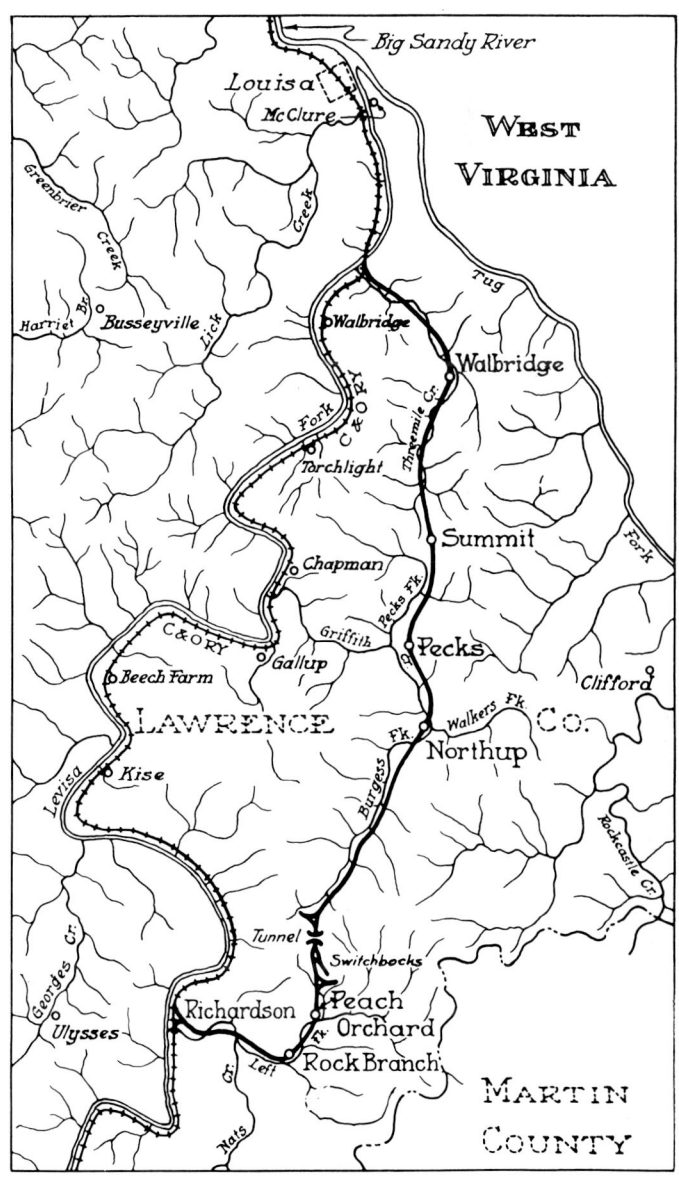

The depletion of the resources of the region and the familiar competition of the motor car and truck progressively deteriorated the economic status of the Eastern Kentucky. On July 10, 1926, the ICC permitted the EKRY to abandon the 22.61 segment between Grayson and Riverton. Losses continued and in 1928 the EK attempted to abandon the remaining portion of the line.

Local citizens on November 22, 1928, organized the East Kentucky Southern Railway Company, purchased the Grayson-Webbsville segment from the owners of the EK and attempted to operate it. In spite of these good efforts it proved impossible to make the venture pay out. Permission to abandon the 13.41 miles of main track and 3.6 miles of siding was forthcoming December 19, 1932. Service on the line terminated near the end of the following January, and the work of dismantling started shortly thereafter.

Locomotive ready to unload freight cars from the Ohio River transfer boat at Coal Grove, Ohio, opposite Ashland. James Wallen

Bottom of Page—Cut of cars being ferried across the Ohio River at Ashland by the steamer, "Bob Ballard." James Wallen

The Chattaroi Railway Company was incorporated March 11, 1873, and shortly thereafter a narrow gauge railroad was constructed for several miles out of Ashland in the direction of Peach Orchard. Construction halted for a number of years. Then, sometime before 1880, plans were changed so that the Chattaroi would be constructed as a standard gauge railroad.

Construction started on April 1, 1880, and Peach Orchard was reached in the winter of 1882. In the spring the railroad was extended from Peach Orchard down Nats Creek to the Big Sandy, reaching that point, May 1, 1883. This terminus was named Richardson after the Vice-President and erstwhile general manager of the road and mining company.

BIG SANDY DIVISION.

WESTWARD.   **EASTWARD.**

SECOND CLASS. No. 39. Mixed. Daily ex. Sunday. A.M. Leave.	Telegraph Offices. Full-face, D. & N. Light, day only.	Distance from Peach Orchard.	STATIONS.	Distance from Ashland.	Side Track Capacity in cars 36 feet long.	SECOND CLASS. No. 38. Mixed. Daily ex. Sunday. P.M. Arrive.
6 00	PO	0.0	PEACH ORCH'D	51.5	130	8 00
			1.8			
f 6 08		1.8	Forbes	49.7		f 7 52
			1.2			
{6 15 / 6 25}	RJ	3.0	W RICHARDSON	48.5	11	{7 45 / 7 35}
			3.8			
f 6 37		6.8	George's Creek	44.7		f 7 23
			1.1			
f 6 42		7.9	Kise	43.6	26	f 7 18
			4.0			
f 6 55		11.9	Gallup	39.6	7	f 7 05
			1.0			
f 7 00		12.9	Chapman	38.6	30	f 7 00
			2.3			
f 7 08		15.2	Torchlight	36.3	28	f 6 50
			3.2			
f 7 18		18.4	Walbridge	33.1	55	f 6 38
			0.9			
f 7 23		19.3	W Camp Ground	32.2		f 6 32
			1.9			
{7 30 / 7 45}	UX	21.2	Louisa	30.3	48	{6 25 / 6 10}
			2.8			
f 7 55		24.0	Whitt's	27.5		f 5 58
			0.8			
f 8 00		24.8	Potter's	26.7	23	f 5 53
			0.8			
s 8 05		25.6	Fuller's	25.9		s 5 48
			2.0			
f 8 13		27.6	Catalpa	23.9		f 5 38
			1.5			
f 8 20		29.1	Curnutt's	22.4	27	f 5 30
			3.5			
s 8 35	BN	32.6	W Buchanan	18.9	28	s 5 15
			1.6			
f 8 42		34.2	Wright's	17.3	19	f 5 08
			1.9			
f 8 50		36.1	Burgess	15.4	20	f 5 02
			2.1			
s 9 00		38.2	Lockwood	13.3	31	s 4 55
			2.6			
f 9 10		40.8	Savage Branch	10.7	19	f 4 47
			4.5			
f 9 25		45.3	Hampton	6.2	13	f 4 35
			0.9			
9 35	CG	46.2	Catlettsburg	5.3		4 25
			5.2			
9 55	AK	51.5	Ashland	0.0		4 05
A.M. Arrive Daily except Sunday.						P.M. Leave Daily except Sunday.

s—regular stop.   f—stop on signal.   W—water tank.
Heavy type in telegraph calls indicate day and night offices. Light type day offices.

RULE 84.—East-bound trains will have absolute right of track over West-bound trains of same class. (See Rules 83, 107, 523.)

RULE 84 (a).—On double track, all trains will run on the right-hand track, and never on the left hand, except to cross over to do work at stations when protected, as per Rule 100. (See Rules 101, 209, and 210.)

Big Sandy Division trains will be governed by Huntington Division schedule between Hampton and Ashland Junction.

Special Instructions.

A.—Standard Clock is located at Dispatcher's office, Ashland; Register Books at Ashland Richardson, and Peach Orchard; Bulletin Book at Ashland.

B.—A train that is passed at an open Telegraph Station by a passenger train going in the same direction will not leave that station until notified by the operator that the passenger train has passed the next telegraph station. If the wire is not working they will wait twenty minutes. A train will not leave a closed or non-Telegraph Station to follow a passenger train until twenty minutes after departure of the passenger train. Conductors and Enginemen will examine Register Books and register departure (conforming to Rule 17 and 18), and will, before going on duty each day, sign for any new bulletins. Conductors will register arrival.

D.—Maximum speed, twenty miles per hour.

E.—Nos. 38 and 39 will stop on signal at Hatfields, Zelda, and Hygeia Springs and will stop on signal to do work at stations not shown on face of Time-Table.

F.—All regular trains will carry passengers.

L. S. STEWART, Train Master and Chief Dispatcher.
H. C. BOUGHTON, Assistant Superintendent.

Above — C&ORY Timetable No. 52, effective Sunday, May 19, 1895.   C&ORY

CHATTAROI RAILWAY.   367

G. T. STEDMAN, Prest., Cincinnati, O.   CHAS. H. ROCKWELL, Gen. Manager, Ashland, Ky.
GEO. S. RICHARDSON, Vice-Prest., Ashland, Ky.   H. B. BUTLER, Auditor,

No. 22.	No. 20.	Mls	July 17, 1882.	Mls	No. 21.	No. 19.
2 00 P.M.	8 00 A.M.	0	lve....Ashland¹....arr.	43	5 15 P.M.	11 20 A.M.
2 20	8 13	3	.......Normal........	40	5 00	11 01
2 33	8 20	5	.....Catlettsburg.....	38	4 53	10 49
2 50	8 40	8	.......Oakland........	35	4 42	10 35
3 40	9 07	14	......Lockwoods......	29	4 15	9 59
4 05	9 22	16	.......Burgess'.......	27	4 03	9 44
4 15	9 32	18	.......Wright's.......	25	3 53	9 32
4 30	9 39	19	.......Rockville......	24	3 45	9 13
4 50	10 03	24	........Catalpa.......	18	3 20	8 37
5 04	10 10	26	........Fuller's.......	17	3 14	8 27
5 22	10 33	31	arr. {Louisa} lve. / lve. { } arr.	12	2 50	7 55
5 37	11 55				2 30	7 25
6 05	11 13	35	.......Walbridge......	8	2 12	6 52
6 23	11 23	37	........Summit........	6	2 03	6 40
6 43	11 40	40	.......Northrup.......	3	1 45	6 18
7 15 P.M.	11 55 A.M.	43	arr. Peach Orchard² lve.	0	1 30 P.M.	6 00 A.M.

CONNECTIONS.—¹ With Chesapeake & Ohio Ry.; Scioto Valley Ry.; Ashland Coal & Iron Ry.; with fast line of steamers on Ohio River. ² Conveyance can be secured going to Eden, Warfield, Paintsville, Prestonsburg, Pikeston and points south.   *Washington time.*

The length of the completed Chattaroi Railway was 49.72 miles. It was later characterized by a C&O engineer as "The Stump-Dodgin' Line," a designation not without some merit. The entire railroad was laid with 60' rail of which 12 miles were steel. The maximum curvature was 15 degrees and the maximum grade in feet per mile was 80.

Near the west end of Ashland, a river transfer permitted an interchange of the Chattaroi, Ashland Coal & Iron, Newport News & Mississippi Valley, and Elizabethtown, Lexington & Big Sandy cars on the south side of the river with those of the Scioto Valley Railway on the Ohio side.

The Chattaroi, approaching Peach Orchard from the north passed through a tunnel, seven-eighths of a mile long. Just south of the south portal of this tunnel the railroad descended the hill by means of two switchbacks. These switchbacks were later by-passed by an optional route that included a 5% grade in contrast to the 1.8% of the remainder of the descent. It is highly probable that the by-pass was not used by ascending trains to any great extent.

The Chattaroi Railway was operated by its own organization from its completion until June 30, 1885. The following day it was turned over to a receiver. After going through several stages of financial "wringing out," its property, rights, and franchise were transferred to the Ohio & Big Sandy Railroad Company on August 24, 1889. The O&BS ran its property until July 1, 1892, at which time the Chesapeake & Ohio Railway assumed operation of the railroad by virtue of ownership of the entire stock of the O&BS.

However, the C&O, even before assuming control of the O&BS, had plans for the extensive development of the coal fields of the Big Sandy. These plans involved not only a major track extension up the Big Sandy from Richardson, but also a considerable revision and rebuilding of the existing line. It was decided to build an entirely new track up the river from a point approximately three miles south of Louisa to Richardson, thus making it possible to abandon the tortuous Chattaroi between these locations.

On May 28, 1892, the new line, 15.7 miles in length, was completed, and the old route, 12.3 miles long, was abandoned. The three miles of the old Chattaroi between Peach Orchard and Richardson remained in service for a number of years. But in February, 1939, operation of this segment was suspended because of extensive damage by flood. Since the coal and timber resources of the region, formerly served by the Branch, had been practically worked out, permission to abandon the section was obtained December 25, 1939, and the major part of the track was removed shortly after.

At left—Tank locomotive on the five mile log track (pole) line. This was used to bring timber to the Eastern Kentucky Railway's railhead at Webbville.   William Conway

Bottom of Page—Passenger train at Peach Orchard in 1892, shortly before the abandonment of the old Chattaroi route.   C&ORY

"Streaks of Rust"

Lexington & Carter County Mining Company's Railroad: From Music to "Bituminous Mine," 3½ miles, with a 3½ mile spur to Stinson Cannel Mine, 5 miles from Music. Total Mileage 7. Built around 1888 and abandoned around 1893. Gauge 44". Several miles of 25' steel. Had one H. K. Porter locomotive, 0-4-0, Const. No. 929, 5/88. Cylinders 9x14."

Bull's Eye Spring Narrow Gauge Railroad: Also known as Brown's Carter County Lumber Company's Railroad. Owned by Andrew Brown, Buffalo, N.Y. Total mileage, 5. Built somewhat earlier than 1889 and abandoned around 1893. Gauge 3'6½". 25' steel rail. Owned 2 locomotives and 16 cars. This railroad, plus the Buffalo Branch and Cave Branch roads were built to serve a big saw mill at Bull's Eye.

Fisher Pole Road: Five mile log track line for transporting timber to railhead at Webbville on the EK. In existence in the eighties.

Stafford Fork Tram Road: Lumber road terminating at mill at Whitehouse, Lawrence County. Owned by Colonel Jay H. Northup. Total mileage, 8. Gauge 3'. Owned three locomotives and 25 cars.

Indian Run Railway: From Mingo Creek, Greenup County, to Firebrick, Lewis County. Mileage, 4½. Built 1899. Mule tramway.

Duane-Pioneer: 1.04 mile L&N RR coal branch. Retired 1942.

Lowndes-McRoberts: 1.63 miles. Constructed 1912 as southeasternmost end of the Lexington & Eastern Railway. Conveyed to the L&N RR in 1915. Abandoned in 1950.

Wheelright-Wheelright Junction: C&ORY Branch approx. 1½ miles long. Built 1917-18. Retired 1952.

Junction-Adalia: 2.16 mile segment known as the Four Mile Branch, Bell County. Constructed 1900-04. Acquired by L&N RR 1911. Abandoned 1954.

Levisa Branch: 19.5 miles of the C&O's Levisa Subdivision, MP 1.6-MP 21.1 (near Nigh). Abandoned 1964 due to construction of Fishtrap Reservoir which flooded right-of-way. Built 1943-44 by Levisa River Railroad Company, a proprietary company of the C&O at estimated cost of $4,800,000. Put in operation December, 1944. Followed Levisa Fork of Big Sandy River from Millard to mining operations at Nigh and Dunlap.

CHAPTER 18
"Western Coal Field Lines of the Past"
Clay to Morganfield
(Louisville & Nashville Railroad)
Clay to Dixon
(Illinois Central Railroad)
Henderson to McClain
(Illinois Central Railroad)
"Work Extras"

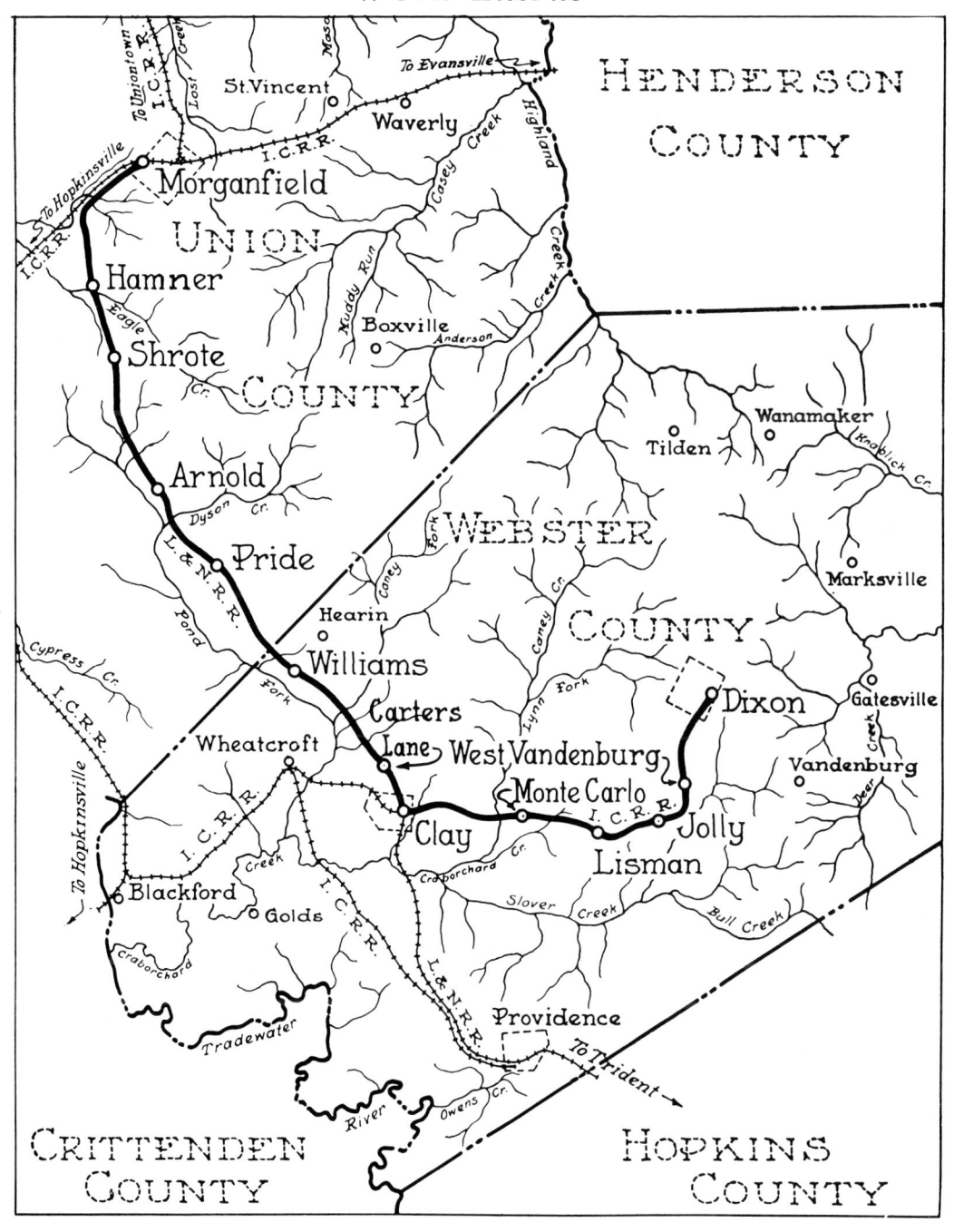

Waiting at the Morganfield depot for the first passenger train on the M&A, April 30, 1907.

Kathryn A. Cromwell

The first train arrived.   Kathryn A. Cromwell

The second section pulls in to the Morganfield station. The two sections were pulled by 10-wheelers Nos. 257 and 259, respectively.   Kathryn A. Cromwell

Shortly after the turn of the century there was a resurgence of interest in the development of certain portions of the Western coal field of Kentucky. A number of operations were projected in the neighborhood of Clay in Webster County. In 1902, the Morganfield Coal & Coke Company was organized to develop mining near Morganfield.

Business and civic leaders of the latter community envisaged a rail line from the prosperous coal mining town of Providence through Morganfield to Shawneetown, Illinois. Overtures were made to the management of the L&N RR and finally, with the blessing of that organization, the Morganfield & Atlanta Railroad was incorporated May 8, 1905. The M&A was operated by the L&N as a proprietary company until July 16, 1921, when it was merged into the parent company.

Work on the Providence-Morganfield route began in May, 1905, and on April 1, 1906, the 25.3 mile segment was opened. The first passenger train came into Morganfield April 30, and for this event the president of the L&N RR gave free transportation to many prominent men along the route. One of the biggest crowds that ever congregated in Morganfield turned out for the occasion.

With the completion of the line, passenger schedules were set up that provided a daily round trip between Morganfield and Earlington, and a daily except Sunday round trip between Morganfield and Madisonville. At Morganfield there was a coal mine operated by the Thomas Coal Company. This shaft operation gave most of its business to the Illinois Central Railroad although a small amount went to the M&A Branch. Around 1930, the Hercules Coal Company at Morganfield added a small tonnage to the Branch. No coal operations developed between Morganfield and Clay.

The village of Pride was literally created by the coming of the M&A, right-of-way through the area having been granted only on condition that a station be established at that point. Real estate developers were active,

Table 42 — MADISONVILLE AND MORGANFIELD

46 Ex.Su. AM	110 Daily PM	Distance		103 Ex.Su. AM	47 Ex.Su. PM	105 Sun. AM	
7 50	5 08	.0	Lv..Madisonville..Ar	6 24	2 15	11 15	All trains stop on signal at Upland, Schmetzer, Lurock and Carter's Lane.
f 8 09	f 5 20	6.3	"....Manitou....Lv	6 11	f 1 45	f10 50	
8 20	5 28	10.0	"....Nebo...... "	6 03	1 25	10 42	
8 50	5 45	17.0	"...Providence... "	5 45	12 50	10 28	
9 32	6 03	24.4	"....Clay...... "	5 30	12 15	10 13	
f 9 50	f 6 12	28.7	"...Williams... "	f 5 20	f12 01	f10 04	
f10 02	f 6 19	31.7	"....Pride..... "	5 14	f11 51	f 9 58	
f10 10	f 6 24	33.9	"....Arnold.... "	f 5 10	f11 44	f 9 53	
f10 23	f 6 31	37.3	"....Shrote.... "	f 5 02	f11 33	f 9 46	
f10 31	f 6 36	39.1	Lv....Hamner.... "	f 4 58	f11 26	f 9 42	
10 45	6 44	42.7	Ar...Morganfield...Lv	4 50	11 15	9 35	
AM	PM			AM	PM	AM	

At left—L&N Public Timetable No. 277 showing service on its Morganfield line as of December 16, 1917. L&NRR

Below—Last employees' timetable covering the Morganfield-Clay segment. This is No. 30, effective April 10, 1939. L&NRR

Bottom of page—Employees' timetable covering the line between Dixon and Clay, 1921. ICRR

lots were sold, and the town of Pride began to exist in fact.

But the town prospered only as long as dependence was placed on the railroad. When in the late twenties highway trucks made their appearance and began to move the region's produce directly to market, the importance of Pride as a trading center decreased almost to the vanishing point.

Depot structures were located at Williams, Pride, Arnold, and Morganfield. Stockpens were built at Williams, Pride, Arnold, and Hammer.

For approximately 20 years the M&A quietly pursued the even tenor of its ways. Then, as highways developed, the familiar branch-line attrition took place. Passenger runs were replaced with slow schedules of mixed trains. The expected coal development along the line failed to materialize. Deficits began to mount.

Permission to abandon the 17.91 miles of trackage between Morganfield and Clay was secured from the ICC November 8, 1939. The rails were removed in the summer of 1940.

Closely paralleling the history of the M&A was the 10.4 mile line between Clay and Dixon. The Kentucky Western Railway Company was incorporated September 7, 1899, to build a railroad from Blackford on the ICRR to Dixon, the county seat of Webster County, a distance of 18.37 miles. The track was completed and the road opened in January, 1901. On September 29, 1902, it was conveyed to a proprietary company of the Illinois Central Railroad.

MORGANFIELD AND TRIDENT (MORGANFIELD BRANCH)

SOUTHWARD / NORTHWARD

TIME TABLE No. 30 — Takes effect Monday, April 10, 1939, at 11:59 P.M.

SECOND CLASS 41 Mixed Daily ex. Sunday P.M.	Distance from St. Louis	STATIONS		Car Capacity of Passing Sidings, based on 42 feet per car	SECOND CLASS 40 Mixed Daily ex. Sunday P.M.
12.50	251.96	L MORGANFIELD	D A	wye	12.40
	8.81				
f 1.09	243.15	ARNOLD		32	f12.20
	2.21				
f 1.15	240.94	PRIDE		16	f12.15
	2.95				
f 1.21	237.99	WILLIAMS		28	f12.05
	4.35				
s 1.31	233.64	CLAY	E	44	s11.55
	4.01				
f 1.50	229.63	UPLAND	E	34 35	f11.40
	3.30				
s 2.10	226.33	PROVIDENCE	D E	43	s11.20
	6.90				
f 2.41	219.33	NEBO		19	f10.53
	6.53				
2.58	212.80	COMO	E	Branch	10.38
	2.37				
3.04	210.43	A TRIDENT	E L	52	10.33

Regular southward trains are superior to trains of the same class moving in the opposite direction.

DIXON and PROVIDENCE BRANCHES—Southward.

Sidings, Standing Room, Cars.	Miles from Blackford.	STATIONS	FIRST CLASS						SECOND CLASS	
			701 Local Passenger	703 Local Passenger	705 Local Passenger	707 Local Passenger	709 Local Passenger	711 Local Passenger	791 Mixed	793 Mixed
		EVANSVILLE	L 12 50PM	L 5 05PM			5 05PM			
			Except Sunday	Sunday Only	Except Sunday	Except Sunday	Sunday Only	Sunday Only	Except Sunday	Except Sunday
		N...BLACKFORD	L 3 35PM	L 7 40PM					L 9 30AM	
	5.31	D...WHEATCROFT	A 3 48PM	A 7 55PM					A 9 50AM	
		D...WHEATCROFT			L 7 07AM	L 3 48PM	L 7 52AM	L 7 55PM	L 9 50AM	
	4.55	MONTEZUMA			7 22	3 59	8 07	8 10	10 10	
	4.67	PROVIDENCE			A 7 35AM 706	A 4 20PM 708	A 8 20AM 710	A 8 25PM 712	A 10 30AM	
		D...WHEATCROFT	L 4 55PM	L 9 00PM					L 11 25AM	
	2.77	OLAY	s 5 02	s 9 10					s 11 55	
8.08	5.14	LISMAN	s 5 15	s 9 25					s 12 15PM	
13.22	5.15	D...DIXON	A 5 30PM	A 9 40PM					A 12 50PM	
18.37			Except Sunday	Sunday Only	Except Sunday	Sunday Only	Sunday Only	Sunday Only	Except Sunday	Except Sunday

D—Day train order office.   N—Day and night train order office.

DIXON and PROVIDENCE BRANCHES—Northward.

Sidings, Standing Room, Cars.	Miles from Blackford.	STATIONS	FIRST CLASS						SECOND CLASS	
			702 Local Passenger	704 Local Passenger	706 Local Passenger	708 Local Passenger	710 Local Passenger	712 Local Passenger	792 Mixed	794 Mixed
		EVANSVILLE	A 11 00AM	A 12 10PM					A 6 05PM	
			Except Sunday	Sunday Only	Except Sunday	Except Sunday	Sunday Only	Sunday Only	Except Sunday	Except Sunday
		N...BLACKFORD	A 8 20AM	A 9 05AM					A 2 30PM	
	5.31	D...WHEATCROFT	L 8 05AM	L 8 50AM					L 2 05	
		D...WHEATCROFT			A 8 05AM	A 4 55PM	A 8 50AM	A 9 00PM	A 11 25AM	
	4.55	MONTEZUMA			7 52	4 40	8 37	8 45	11 05	
	4.67	PROVIDENCE			L 7 40AM 705	L 4 25PM 707	L 8 25AM 709	L 8 30PM 711	L 10 50AM	
		D...WHEATCROFT	A 7 07AM	A 7 52AM					A 2 05	
8.08	2.77	OLAY		A 7 45					s 1 45	
13.22	5.14	LISMAN	s 7 00	A 7 30					s 1 25	
18.37	5.15	D...DIXON	L 6 30AM	L 7 15AM					L 1 05PM	
			Except Sunday	Sunday Only	Except Sunday	Sunday Only	Sunday Only	Sunday Only	Except Sunday	Except Sunday

D—Day train order office.   N—Day and night train order office.

Ten-wheeler 309, formerly 259, used in passenger service to Morganfield during the early days of the Morganfield & Atlantic Railroad. This machine, a 1901 product of Rhode Island, was classified by the L&N as a G-11. It was retired in September, 1937. L&NRR

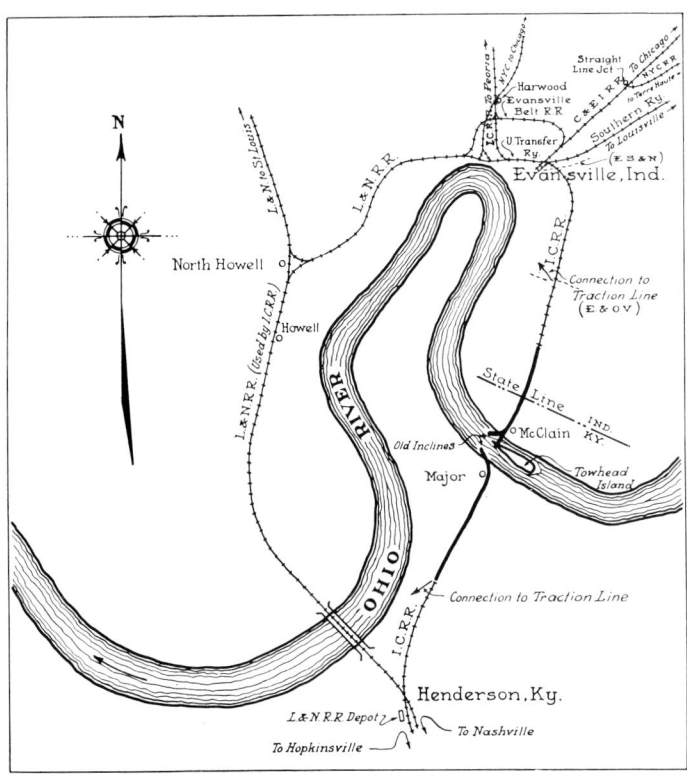

Map showing location of Illinois Central abandonments on each side of the Ohio River in the vicinity of Henderson and Evansville.
J. S. Horine

By November, 1887, the main line of the Ohio Valley Railroad had been completed from Henderson, south, to Princeton. Plans were being made for extending the railroad further south, and it seemed vital that the road gain access to Evansville, Indiana, where a number of important rail connections could be made. The L&N RR had completed its bridge over the Ohio River at Henderson on July 13, 1885, and it was loath to lend its facilities to a potential rival.

Accordingly, the Ohio Valley decided to establish a car ferry across the Ohio River at Green River Island, five miles up river from Evansville. Construction started in 1888 and was completed the same year. The track work consisted of about six and a quarter miles of line north of the river of which one mile was in Kentucky and the remainder in Indiana; and slightly over five miles of track south of the Ohio into Henderson.

At the point of crossing, the Indiana-Kentucky state line was (and is) located about one mile north of the river, owing to an historic quirk of the river which left what was formerly Green River Island rather firmly cemented to the Indiana mainland. On June 1, 1889, the car ferry boat was secured and the line put into operation. The north and south river bank points were named McClain and Major, respectively.

On June 7, 1898, the Ohio Valley Railway was acquired by a proprietary company of the Illinois Central Railroad. Then in 1904, the ICRR obtained trackage rights over the L&N tracks and bridge between Henderson and Evansville. At once, the car ferry was discontinued, and the segments north and south of the Ohio river became relegated to switching trackage.

While other portions of the old Kentucky Western proved profitable to the Illinois Central, the Clay-Dixon segment showed little future. No permanent industries had settled on the line, and by the thirties private and public highway carriers had absorbed practically all of the traffic that formerly went to the railroad.

On March 17, 1937, the Interstate Commerce Commission granted the request to abandon the Clay-Dixon section and shortly thereafter the line was dismantled.

Car No. 127 in original paint job. Nos. 126, 127, and 128 were originally cars of the Evansville, Henderson & Owensboro Railway.

153

READ DOWN — EVANSVILLE TO HENDERSON — SOUTH BOUND — READ DOWN

STATIONS AND SIDINGS	Miles	Train 77	Train 75	Train 73	Train 71	Train 69	Train 67	Train 65	Train 63	Train 61	Train 59	Train 57	Train 55	Train 53	Train 51		STATIONS AND SIDINGS
		PM	PM	PM	PM	PM	PM	PM	PM	PM	AM	AM	AM	AM	AM		
Evansville	0.00	11.15	9.15	7.30	6.30	5.30	4.30	3.30	2.30	1.10	11.30	10.30	9.30	8.30	7.10		Evansville
1.95																	1.95
Kentucky Avenue	1.95	11.25	9.25	7.40	6.40	5.40	4.40	3.40	2.40	1.20	11.40	10.40	9.40	8.40	7.20		Kentucky Avenue
.30																	.30
Maley	2.25	11.26	9.26	7.41	6.41	5.41	4.41	3.41	2.41	1.21	11.41	10.41	9.41	8.41	7.21		Maley
.80																	.80
Clay	3.05	11.28	9.28	7.43	6.43	5.43	4.43	3.43	2.43	1.23	11.43	10.43	9.43	8.43	7.23		Clay
1.05																	1.05
State Line	4.10	11.30	9.30	7.45	6.45	5.45	4.45	3.45	2.45	1.25	11.45	10.45	9.45	8.45	7.25		State Line
1.00				74	72	70	68	66	64	62	60	58	56	54	52		1.00
McClain	5.10	11.32	9.32	**7.47**	**6.47**	**5.47**	**4.47**	**3.47**	**2.47**	**1.27**	**11.47**	**10.47**	**9.47**	**8.47**	**7.27**		McClain
.96																	.96
Major	6.06	11.43	9.43	7.58	6.58	5.58	4.58	3.58	2.58	1.38	11.58	10.58	9.58	8.58	7.38		Major
1.81																	1.81
Midway	7.87	11.47	9.47	8.02	7.02	6.02	5.02	4.02	3.02	1.42	12.02	11.02	10.02	9.02	7.42		Midway
1.30																	1.30
Hassett	9.17	11.50	9.50	8.05	7.05	6.05	5.05	4.05	3.05	1.45	12.05	11.05	10.05	9.05	7.45		Hassett
.22																	.22
Atkinson Park	9.39	11.51	9.51	8.06	7.06	6.06	5.06	4.06	3.06	1.46	12.06	11.06	10.06	9.06	7.46		Atkinson Park
1.51																	1.51
Henderson	10.90	11.58	9.58	8.13	7.13	6.13	5.13	4.13	3.13	1.53	12.13	11.13	10.13	9.13	7.53		Henderson

All trains must register at Maley between 8:30 P.M. and 6:00 A.M.   Dark Faced Type Denotes Regular Meeting Points.

With the coming of the electric interurban, The Evansville, Henderson & Owensboro Railway Company was organized to construct a line between the cities named. Pending a determination as to whether or not to bridge the Ohio, it was decided to lease from the Illinois Central Railroad and its proprietary company the trackage on both sides of the river leading to the car ferry. The railroad reserved the right to operate freight service subject to the electric road's dispatching.

Employees' Timetable No. 4, effective July 16, 1925, showing operations between Evansville and Henderson. The car ferry operated between the two river bank points —McClain and Major.

About three miles of the Henderson-Major segment were electrified. Only 800' of new trackage was needed at the south end to connect with the tracks of the Henderson street railway properties. The car ferry "Henderson," possibly the first interurban ferry ever to be built, was constructed by the Dubuque Boat and Boiler Works of Dubuque, Iowa. It had an all-steel hull and could carry two heavy 50' interurban cars.

On August 1, 1912, the Evansville-Henderson service was inaugurated with nine daily round trips.

READ UP — HENDERSON TO EVANSVILLE — NORTH BOUND — READ UP

STATIONS AND SIDINGS	Train 52	Train 54	Train 56	Train 58	Train 60	Train 62	Train 64	Train 66	Train 68	Train 70	Train 72	Train 74	Train 76	Train 78	Miles	STATIONS AND SIDINGS
	AM	AM	AM	AM	AM	PM	PM	PM	PM	PM	PM	PM	PM	PM		
Evansville	7.44	9.04	10.04	11.04	12.04	1.44	3.04	4.04	5.04	6.04	7.04	8.04	9.08	11.08	10.90	Evansville
1.95																1.95
Kentucky Avenue	7.34	8.54	9.54	10.54	11.54	1.34	2.54	3.54	4.54	5.54	6.54	7.54	8.57	10.57	8.95	Kentucky Avenue
.30																.30
Maley	7.33	8.53	9.53	10.53	11.53	1.33	2.53	3.53	4.53	5.53	6.53	7.53	8.56	10.56	8.65	Maley
.80																.80
Clay	7.31	8.51	9.51	10.51	11.51	1.31	2.51	3.51	4.51	5.51	6.51	7.51	8.54	10.54	7.85	Clay
1.05																1.05
State Line	7.29	8.49	9.49	10.49	11.49	1.29	2.49	3.49	4.49	5.49	6.49	7.49	8.52	10.52	6.80	State Line
1.00	51	53	55	57	59	61	63	65	67	69	71	73				1.00
McClain	**7.27**	**8.47**	**9.47**	**10.47**	**11.47**	**1.27**	**2.47**	**3.47**	**4.47**	**5.47**	**6.47**	**7.47**	8.50	10.50	5.80	McClain
.96																.96
Major	7.15	8.35	9.35	10.35	11.35	1.15	2.35	3.35	4.35	5.35	6.35	7.35	8.39	10.39	4.84	Major
1.81																1.81
Midway	7.11	8.31	9.31	10.31	11.31	1.11	2.31	3.31	4.31	5.31	6.31	7.31	8.36	10.36	3.03	Midway
1.30																1.30
Hassett	7.08	8.28	9.28	10.28	11.28	1.08	2.28	3.28	4.28	5.28	6.28	7.28	8.33	10.33	1.73	Hassett
.22																.22
Atkinson Park	7.07	8.27	9.27	10.27	11.27	1.07	2.27	3.27	4.27	5.27	6.27	7.27	8.32	10.32	1.51	Atkinson Park
1.51																1.51
Henderson	7.00	8.20	9.20	10.20	11.20	1.00	2.20	3.20	4.20	5.20	6.20	7.20	8.25	10.25	0.00	Henderson

All trains must register at Maley between 8:30 P.M. and 6:00 A.M.   Dark Faced Type Denotes Regular Meeting Points.

No. 128 in the Evansville & Ohio Valley garb. Blt. 1912 by American Car Co. for the EH&O.   William A. Steventon

Side view of the car ferry "Henderson."   Robert F. Wolff

Car ferry, approaches, and cradle on the south side of the river.   Earl W. Clark

Car ferry locked in cradle.   Charles Vernon Hess

On December 18, 1918, the Evansville Railways Company was reorganized, and under the name of Evansville & Ohio Valley Railway Company took control of its proprietary lines including the Evansville, Henderson & Owensboro. Late in 1927, largely because of a wreck on September 7 of the same year and the resulting suits, the E&OV was placed in the hands of a receiver. The electric operation to Henderson was replaced with buses and the last interurban car operated out of Henderson the night of April 4, 1928.

Again most of the ICRR-controlled trackage on both sides of the river fell into neglect and disuse. On October 4, 1934, permission was given for the abandonment of 3.9 miles of the branch on the south side of the river from the river bank at Major to a point near Henderson. Actual abandonment took place one month later.

On the north side of the river, the south two miles between Evansville and McClain were severely damaged by the Ohio Valley flood in January, 1937. Permission to abandon this section, precisely 2.21 miles, was granted February 16, 1938, and with the removal of this trackage the last vestige of the old car ferry route disappeared.

"Work Extras"

DeKoven to the Ohio River (DeKoven Coal Road)

This 1.75 mile line, built to the odd gauge of three feet, eight and one-half inches, was constructed in the 1870's by the Ohio Valley Coal & Mining Company, to move coal from the Shotwell mine near DeKoven to the Ohio River for shipment by barge to points along the river but principally Memphis, Tennessee.

At the mine tipple the coal was loaded into funnel-shaped coal cars of 50 bushel capacity and moved to the riverside tipple. Mules were the original motive power, but in 1881 a steam locomotive started chuffing along the narrow gauge tracks. Named "Arthur Kelsey" after a resident director of the company, the little six ton locomotive was built at Pittsburgh and had cylinders of 10-16" dimensions.

The railroad was laid largely with 56' iron rails although steel was used near the river. The line crossed the river bottom land on a half-mile long fill of eight or more feet in height. The railroad was changed to standard gauge, probably around 1903, for late in 1902 a second-hand standard gauge locomotive formerly used on the Manhattan elevated lines was purchased. This machine, displaced by the electrification of the elevated lines, was built by Grant in 1878 and carried road number 225 on the Manhattan line. It had 39" drivers, 10x16" cylinders, and tipped the scales at 16 tons.

The DeKoven Coal Road became a part of the Ohio Valley Railway and later a branch of the Illinois Central Railroad. The riverside tipple was demolished by an ice gorge in the early spring of 1918 and the line was abandoned shortly thereafter.

Penrod to Mud River Mines (L&N RR)

A 4.49 mile branch to a coal development. Completed July 1, 1886. Abandoned 1910 and removed by March 10 of the same year.

Como to Madisonville (L&N RR)

Completed in 1882 as part of the original main line between Madisonville and Providence. The 1.85 mile segment was abandoned in 1943.

Indian Creek and Black Gold Quarries to Kyrock (Kentucky Rock Asphalt Company)

A narrow gauge (36") line approximately 12 miles long, completed in 1921 to move rock asphalt from the quarries to the plant at Kyrock on Nolin River where it was loaded in barges and transported to Bowling Green. There were 16 locomotives ranging in weight from 14 to 22 tons, plus 16 side dump cars of 8-yard capacity, and 75 side dump cars of 4-yard capacity. A number of the locomotives were 0-4-0T's manufactured by Porter. Some were secured new and others from previous owners.

Kentucky Rock Asphalt Company #219 and #220, taken on flat car at the transfer table of the BR&L Shops. The Porter machines, c/n 6691 and 6692, originally served the Wayne Coal Co. Thomas Lawson, Jr.

CHAPTER 19

"Three Jackson Purchase Odyssies"
Mississippi Odyssey
(Railroads of Columbus)
Obion Odyssey – Hickman to Union City
(Nashville, Chattanooga & St. Louis Railway)
Bayou Odyssey – Barlow to East Cairo
(Illinois Central Railroad)

Old Columbus, Kentucky, the part in the valley of the mighty Mississippi, has all but disappeared, gobbled up literally by the meanderings of the "Father of Waters." Yet in the years 1870-1873 it was a busy railroad terminal for four important lines. The Mobile & Ohio Railroad stretched from its southern terminus at Mobile north to Columbus where it connected via a car ferry with the St. Louis & Iron Mountain Railroad. The increasingly aggressive Nashville & Chattanooga Railroad moved its freight cars over the M&O into Columbus from Union City, Tennessee, and, in partnership with the Iron Mountain, developed an interchange of such proportions that the N&C on May 30, 1873, changed its name to the more impressive Nashville, Chattanooga & St. Louis Railway. Finally, the Illinois Central Railroad, then terminating at Cairo and fearing that the car ferry interchange at Columbus would divert to the Iron Mountain much of the traffic it previously enjoyed, purchased the sidewheel steamer, *Dan Able,* and set up a schedule of passenger and freight connections with the Mobile & Ohio, the boat making the run between Cairo and Columbus in a little more than one hour.

But first on the scene at Columbus was the pioneer Mobile & Ohio Railroad, planned in 1847 by a group of Mobile business men who hoped to build a railroad to a point near

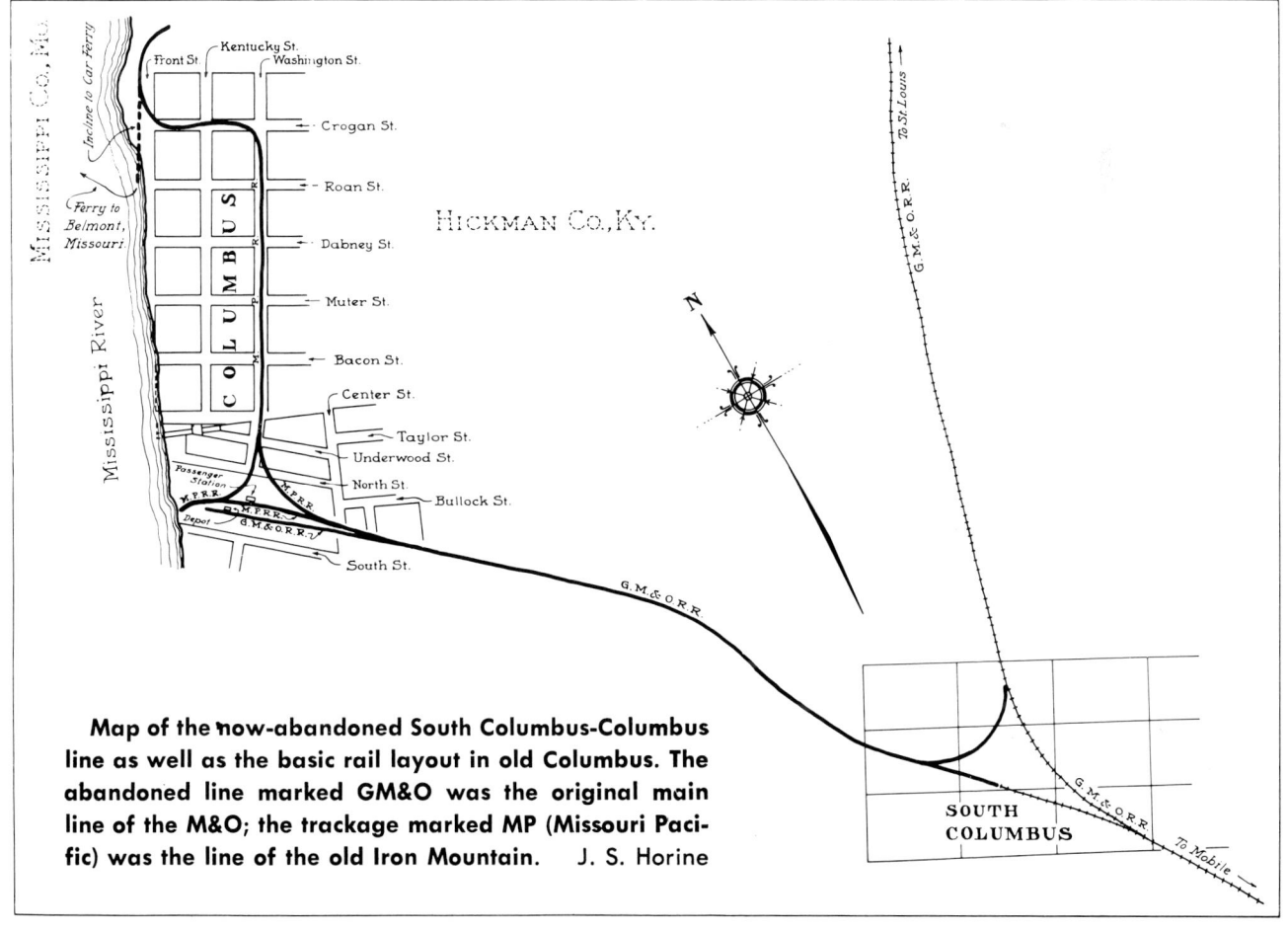

Map of the now-abandoned South Columbus-Columbus line as well as the basic rail layout in old Columbus. The abandoned line marked GM&O was the original main line of the M&O; the trackage marked MP (Missouri Pacific) was the line of the old Iron Mountain.   J. S. Horine

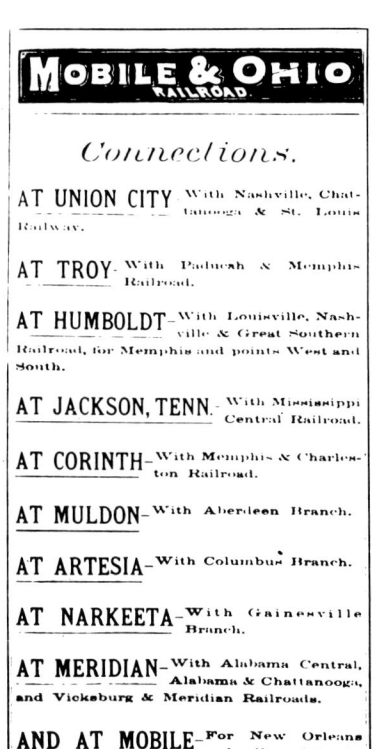
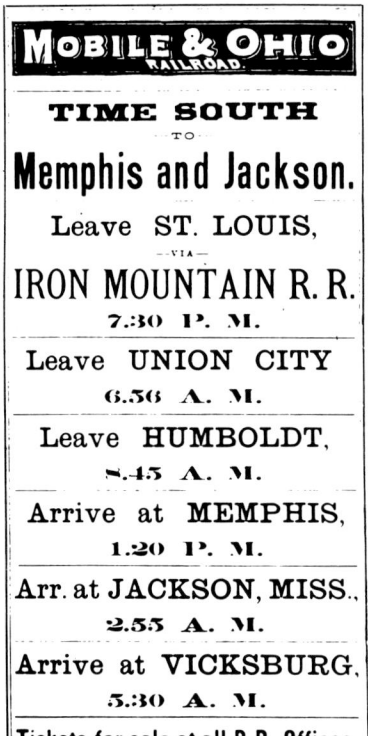
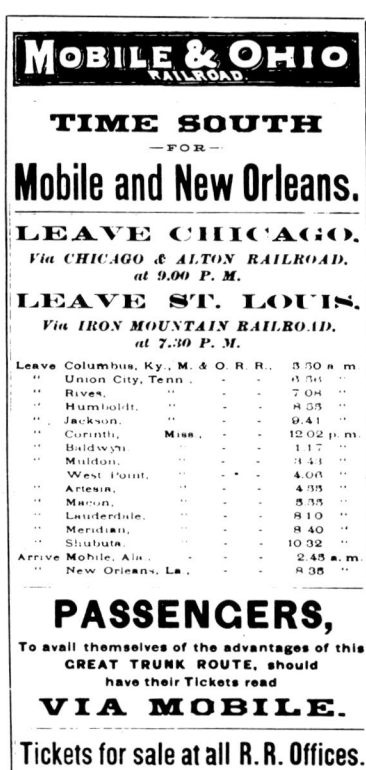

Pages from a rare Mobile & Ohio Railroad folder of 1877, advertising through passenger service between Chicago/St. Louis and Mobile, via the Columbus-Belmont car ferry. Note that through Pullmans were scheduled between St. Louis and Mobile/New Orleans. (Folder continues at top of opposite page).

Missouri Pacific Railroad

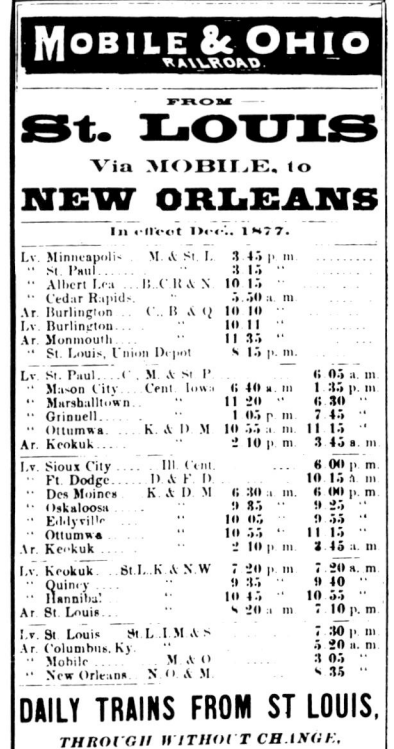
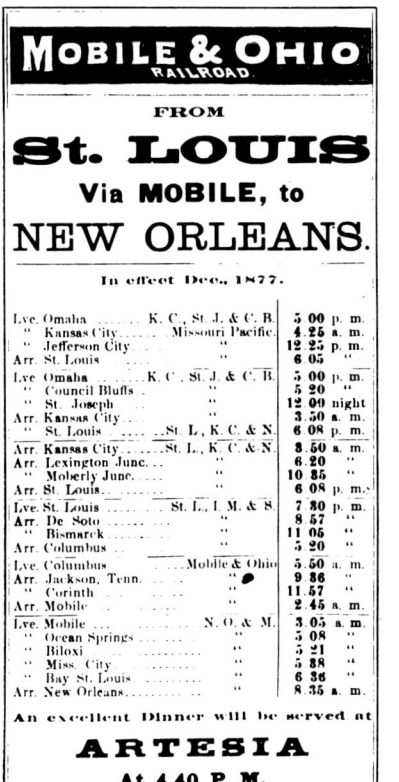

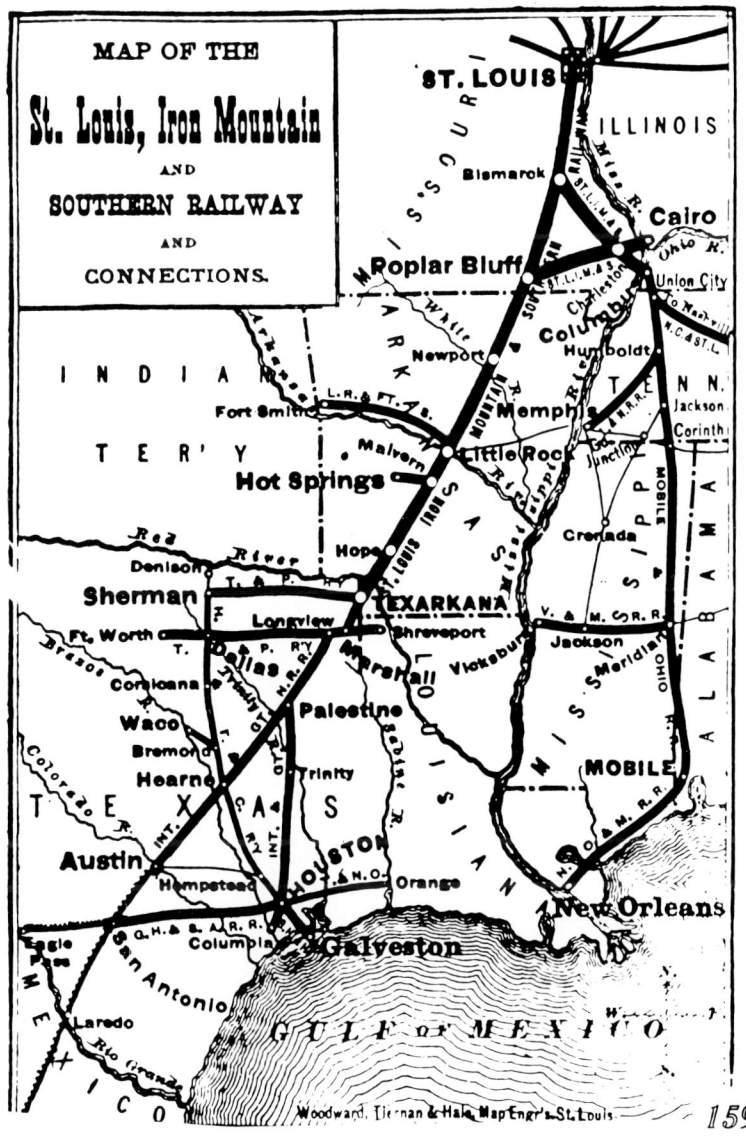

Map of the St. Louis, Iron Mountain & Southern Railway, showing the Columbus gateway.
Missouri Pacific Railroad

Cairo, Illinois, tap the Mississippi, Ohio, and Missouri river traffic, and divert it to the port of Mobile. Because of the interest (generous stock subscriptions) shown by the citizens of Columbus and vicinity, that town was to become the M&O's northern terminal. In November, 1858, the M&O was opened to traffic between Columbus and Jackson, Tennessee, but it was not until April 22, 1861, that the entire line to Mobile was completed.

Previous to 1869, all freight arriving at Columbus from the south and bound for western and northern destinations had to be transferred to river steamboats. But on August 14, 1869, the Iron Mountain's line into Belmont, across the river from Columbus, was completed and put into operation.

Meanwhile, the Mobile & Ohio had scarcely reached Columbus when it was faced with the vissisitudes of the War Between the States. Sabotage of the railroad resulted in the wrecking of the line from Union City, Tennessee, down to Okolona, Mississippi, the destruction taking place in trestles, bridges, stations, and rails. Even the shops at Mobile were gutted. When peace came, the M&O owned little more than its right-of-way and the few items of rolling stock that escaped the enemy.

Above—The "St. Louis," the single track car ferry that operated across the Mississippi River between Columbus, Kentucky, and Belmont, Missouri. The boat was built at Freedom, Pennsylvania, at a cost of $34,436. The entire ferry service as well as both inclines were owned by the Iron Mountain. The wood-burning "Yard Goat" pictured was the property of the St. Louis, Iron Mountain & Southern.   Harry Lee Waterfield

Below—Mobile & Ohio Railroad wharf, and steamboat "General Anderson." The latter made connections at Columbus with two daily trains leaving for the south. Scene is probably at Cairo, Illinois.   Harry Lee Waterfield

The Mobile & Ohio track between Columbus and South Columbus during the 1927 flood.   GM&ORR

It had been expected that the Mobile & Ohio would share in the cost of the Columbus-Belmont car ferry as well as provide the incline on the east bank of the Mississippi. Upon its failure to do so, the Iron Mountain built both inclines at a cost of $25,782 and constructed two and one-half miles of track in Columbus to effect a junction with the M&O.

A steam car ferry, the "St. Louis," was delivered in December, 1869. This was operated by the Iron Mountain without help from the M&O, and remained in service until January 1, 1912, when the car ferry service was discontinued. The "St. Louis" was a single track boat and thus could carry only five or six freight cars, or three passenger coaches at one time.

Details of the car ferry incline and cradle at Columbus.
Harry Lee Waterfield

In 1879, the gauge of the Iron Mountain was changed from 5' to 4'8½" to freely accommodate freight interchange at St. Louis. This meant the installation of a Nutter Car Hoist at Columbus to interchange with the 5' M&O. Then in 1880, when Jay Gould acquired the Iron Mountain and Missouri Pacific, routes to New Orleans were established on the west side of the Mississippi, by-passing Columbus.

The third blow to the Columbus terminal occurred December 1, 1881, when the Mobile & Ohio opened its extension to East Cairo, making a junction with the main line at South Columbus, thus placing Columbus and the car ferry at the end of a spur. But for a time, freight service hummed, due largely to the Nashville, Chattanooga & St. Louis Railway, which about 1887 gained traffic rights over the M&O

Profile of the Hickman-Union City line.

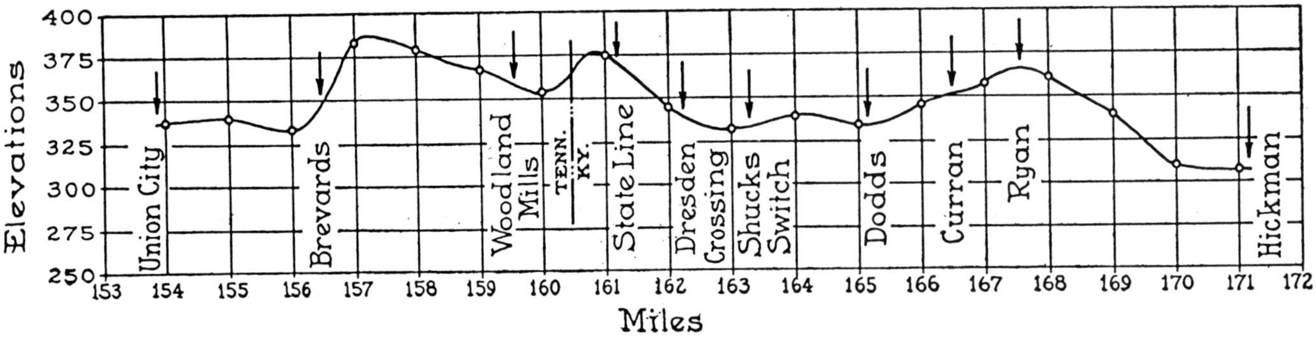

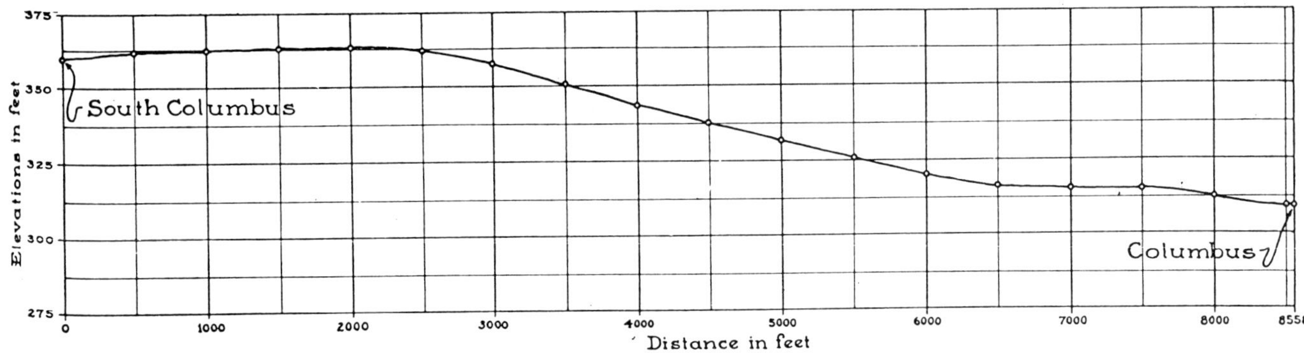

Profile of the Columbus-South Columbus line.

and was running its "Green Line" trains through to Columbus, for further movement via the car ferry. The NC&StL operation terminated in 1911, when the Iron Mountain abandoned the ferry due to the severe damage suffered by one of the inclines at time of high water.

Old Man River dealt the final blow to the railroad aspirations of Columbus in 1927, when that stream at flood level washed away much of the old town and buried the Columbus depot to a depth of eight feet. On March 19, 1928, the Interstate Commerce Commission gave the M&O permission to abandon its 1.6 miles of track between the South Columbus Junction and Columbus. The track in the lower part of town was retired in November of the same year, and the remainder in March, 1929.

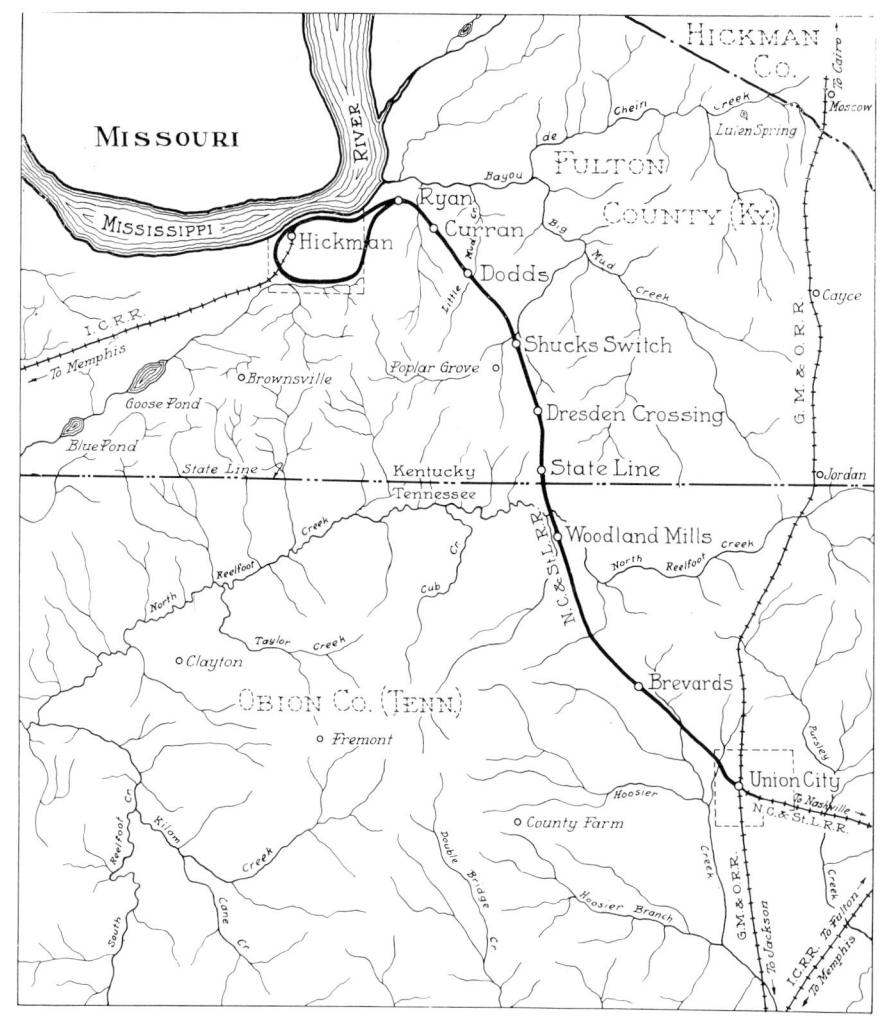

BETWEEN HICKMAN AND BRUCETON
SOUTH BOUND—READ DOWN

Distances from Hickman	Station Numbers	THIRD CLASS			TIME-TABLE NO. 325 Taking effect Sunday, June 30, 1946, at 12:01 A.M.	FIRST CLASS		HOURS TRAIN ORDER OFFICES ARE OPEN
		59	**51**	**23**		**5**	**3**	
		Fast Freight	Fast Freight	Local Freight		Passenger	Passenger	
		Daily	Daily	Daily Ex. Sun.	STATIONS	Daily	Daily	
				A.M.		A.M.	P.M.	
	X 172			7.40	Lv. HICKMAN	7.30	1.00	7:00 A.M. to 4:00 P.M. Except Sundays
3.68	X 168			7.50	RYAN 3.68	D 7.40	D 1.09	
10.00	X 162			8.02	STATE LINE 6.32	F 7.52	F 1.23	
11.53	X 160			8.07	WOODLAND MILLS 1.53	s 7.57	s 1.28	
17.29	X 154			8.55	UNION CITY 5.76	s 8.15 22	s 1.45	CONTINUOUS
20.49	X 151			9.16	GIBBS 3.20	s 8.25	s 1.55 4	8:00 A.M. to 11:59 P.M.
24.10	X 147			9.24	TERRELL 3.61	F 8.33	s 2.03	
27.31	X 144	P.M.	A.M.	9.35	GARDNER 3.21	F 8.40	s 2.11	
30.13	X 141	1.35	9.05	10.00	MARTIN 2.82	s 8.55	s 2.25	CONTINUOUS
33.16	X 138	1.42	9.20	10.15	RALSTON 3.03	s 9.10	s 2.35	
39.29	X 132	1.55	9.35	10.44 51	DRESDEN 6.13	s 9.25	s 2.50	9:00 A.M. to 6:00 P.M. Except Sundays
46.68	X 125	2.10	9.50	11.00	GLEASON 7.39	s 9.40	s 3.07	8:00 A.M. to 5:00 P.M. Except Sundays
54.45	X 117	2.28	10.06 51	11.20	McKENZIE 7.77	s 9.56 54	s 3.27	CONTINUOUS
59.12	X 112	2.38	10.20	11.30	HICO 4.67	F 10.10	F 3.36	
66.13	X 105	2.52	10.40	11.48 44	HUNTINGDON 7.01	s 10.30	s 3.55	9:00 A.M. to 6:00 P.M. Except Sundays
70.32	X 101	3.00	10.50	11.58	ROSSER 4.19	D 10.40	D 4.05	
74.95	X 97	3.09	11.00	12.08 PM	HOLLOW ROCK 4.63	s 10.50	s 4.15	
76.63	X 95	3.15	11.10	12.15	Ar. BRUCETON 1.68	11.00	4.25	CONTINUOUS
		P.M.	A.M.	P.M.		A.M.	P.M.	
		Daily	Daily	Daily Ex. Sun.		Daily	Daily	
		Fast Freight	Fast Freight	Local Freight		Passenger	Passenger	
		59	**51**	**23**		**5**	**3**	

Hickman, Kentucky, located about 15 miles down the Mississippi from Columbus, also wanted a railroad. Hence, the Hickman & Obion was incorporated, 1853-54, to build a line from Hickman to some point in Tennessee to connect the then-building M&O, or the Nashville & Northwestern. After the grading between Hickman and Union City, Tennessee, was essentially complete, the property was sold to the Nashville & Northwestern Railroad, which railed the line and opened it to traffic before 1860. It was not until 1887 that the entire route from Nashville to Hickman was finished. On November 10, 1871, the Nashville & Northwestern was sold to the Nashville & Chattanooga. As mentioned in the previous portion of this chapter, the N&C changed its name to the Nashville, Chattanooga & St. Louis Railway, legally effective May 30, 1873, with a major portion of its traffic channeled over the Mobile & Ohio between Union City and Columbus. As a result the Union City-Hickman segment became relegated to the status of a local branch, a category from which it never emerged.

Nevertheless, a schedule of two daily passenger round trips between Hickman and Paducah via Bruceton, remained in effect for many years. A daily except Sunday local freight between Hickman and Martin, Tennessee, also added traffic to the 56' and 68' rails. For a time in the twenties, the local freight also carried passengers, giving Hickman citizens considerable latitude in their choice of schedules.

NC&StL consolidation No. 372, typical of the 2-8-0's used on the Hickman line. Baldwin, c/n 19637, 11/01. 23x28",56"   NC&StL RY

Consolidation No. 406, NC&StL Class H7c, was used for both passenger and freight service into Hickman. Baldwin, 1906, 23x28", 56". NC&StL RY

As originally built, the line entered Hickman from the east, running along and descending the river bluff. High water frequently got over the tracks and into the one business street under the bluff, and often trains would come into Hickman axle deep in water. Furthermore, after the floods went down, the bluff just above the town and the steep slope occupied by the railroad would slip.

It was decided in 1911 to make a new entrance into Hickman. This route left the old line at Ryan, circled the town on the east, south, and west, thus gaining the name "Belt Line." Then on April 22, 1926, the Mississippi River invaded the levee at West Hickman, and the main track of the railroad was broken again. It was necessary to relocate and rebuild the tracks around the loop created by the levee, involving the installing of 1498' of new track, and 705' of new north leg wye track.

With the coming of the gasoline competition, the only substantial business on the Hickman-Union City segment remaining was that of the Mengel Company's Hickman plant, and when that burned in October 1942, business on the Branch took a decided nose-dive. After a number of postponements, permission to abandon the line was granted October 3, 1951, as of 12:01 a.m., Monday, October 15. The line was abandoned on that date with the arrival of trains 5 and 23 at Union City.

The 34 mile Paducah-East Cairo line was built in 1902 and 1903 by the Chicago, St. Louis & New Orleans Railroad Company, a subsidiary of the Illinois Central Railroad. At the time of construction, the IC operated two north-south lines which converged at Fulton, Kentucky, forming a rough "V". One of these lines passed through Cairo, Illinois, the other through Paducah.

The new construction thus connected the points of the "V" and enabled traffic from Paducah and points east, and Cairo and points west, to flow east and west without necessity of the longer route through Fulton.

A schedule of two daily round trip passenger runs was instituted between Paducah and Cairo. One of these, No. 801, which departed from Paducah at 6:20 p.m. and arrived at Cairo at 8:00 p.m. gained a special distinction through the years. Paducah was a dry town and Cairo was wet. This led to a colorful passenger clientele for No. 801 on Saturday nights, and the train gained the designation of "Whiskey Dick."

As the Paducah-Cairo trackage was essentially that of a local segment, business began to shrink in the early thirties. Passenger service was reduced to a mixed train and this was discontinued November 6, 1937. The desire to abandon the western portion of the route was precipitated by the burning of a 1,172' long trestle about three miles east of East Cairo on August 2, 1942.

Permission to abandon the 7.13 miles of the line between East Cairo and Barlow was granted on July 29, 1943. It was necessary to retain the section between Paducah and Kevil to serve the Kentucky Ordnance Works.

An interesting feature of the abandoned section was the fact that with the exception of the one and one-half miles of line immediately west of Barlow, the entire segment was constructed to zero grade.

Table 17 — CHICAGO, ST. LOUIS, CAIRO AND PADUCAH.

836	822	Mls	February 15, 1920.	801	835
A M	P M		LEAVE] [ARRIVE	A M	P M
*8 45	8 15		Chicago	*8 45	*9 45
*1 00	*9 56		lve...St. Louis...arr.	7 00	4 45
P M	A M			P M	A M
*5 55	*7 00	0	lve.....Cairo.....arr.	9 45	10 50
6 50	7 20	8.1	East Cairo	9 22	10 20
7 04	7 34	15.3	Barlow	9 08	10 05
7 13	7 42	19.7	La Center	9 00	9 53
7 23	7 51	24.7	Kevil	8 50	9 43
7 32	8 01	29.9	Heath	8 40	9 33
7 36	8 05	32.3	Maxon	8 35	9 23
7 42	8 11	35.4	Futrell	8 30	9 15
8 05	8 35	42.0	arr...Paducah...lve.	*8 15	*8 55
2 33	10 23		arr..Princeton..lve.	5 15	*6 55
7 50	5 50		arr..Louisville..lve.	12 01	8 45
6 00	2 45		lve..Princeton..arr.	12 10	6 45
7 10	3 55		arr..Hopkinsville..lve.	*11 00	*5 35
			(Tenn. Cent. R.R.)	A M	
8 23	5 15		arr..Clarksville..lve.	9 45	
10 30	7 40		Nashville	*7 30	
A M	P M		ARRIVE] [LEAVE	A M	

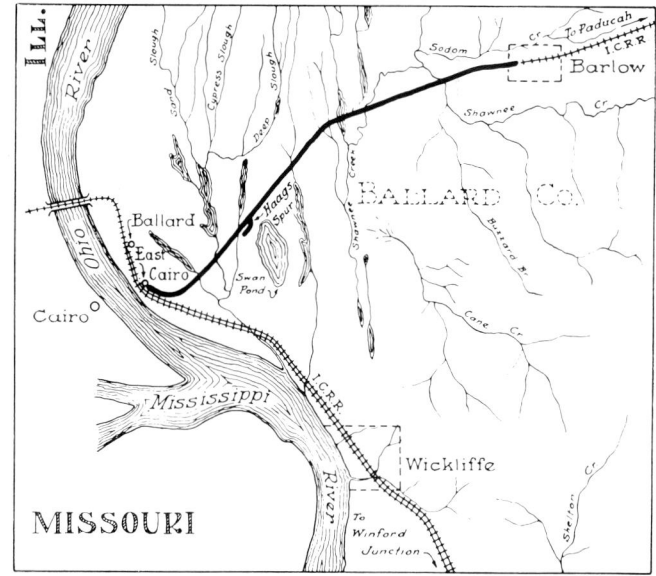

Southward — EAST CAIRO DISTRICT — Northward   5

SECOND CLASS			Miles from Paducah	TIME TABLE No. 4 Taking Effect February 20, 1938 STATIONS	Siding Capacity in Cars with Engine	THIRD CLASS		
		373 Freight				374 Freight		
		Mon. Wed. Fri.						
		L 8 00AM	0.0	NORTH YARD		A 1 45PM		
		8 10AM	0.8 / .8	PADUCAH	8 / 6	1 30PM		
		L 8 20AM	3.9 / 1.5	C. R. JUNCTION		A 1 20PM		
		8 25	6.2	FUTRELL	100	1 10		
		8 35	9.6 D / 3.4	MAXON		1 01		
		8 40	11.9 / 2.3	HEATH		12 50		
		8 55	17.2 / 5.3	KEVIL	45	12 35		
		9 10	22.2 D / 5.0	LA CENTER	4	12 20		
		9 25	26.6 D / 4.4	BARLOW	100	12 05PM		
		A 9 55AM	33.8 / 7.2	EAST CAIRO	52	L 11 40AM		
		A 10 01AM		BALLARD		L 11 35AM		
		A 10 20AM		NORTH CAIRO		L 11 20AM		
						Mon. Wed. Fri.		

Schedules shown in Cairo District time table are in effect between East Cairo and Ballard.

Bridge on the Illinois Central Railroad between Kevil and LaCenter, typical of bridge and trestle construction on the Barlow-East Cairo segment.
Illinois Central Railroad

CHAPTER 20
"A Thoroughbred, A Workhorse, Two Old Sires, and a Patriarch"
Chicle to Paris
(Louisville & Nashville Railroad)
Shelbyville to Bloomfield
(Louisville & Nashville Railroad)
Mention of Two Old Sires
LaGrange to Eminence
(Louisville & Nashville Railroad)

THE THOROUGHBRED—

The location was the beautiful bluegrass country of Kentucky. Green carpeted fields, gently rolling away in the distance were populated by thoroughbreds plus their children—colts and fillies—born to a life of equine aristocracy.

This was the sight that greeted travelers riding the trains of the Kentucky Central enroute to Lexington or those departing the Bluegrass for the north. And so, a railroad, physically no different from those in less endowed parts of the country, acquired an aura and association that characterized it as the *Bluegrass Route*. Sadly enough, the most picturesque part of this trackage is no more; but the story of this abandoned line is worth this brief mention if only to preserve that portion of the romance and tradition of which at one time it was an integral part.

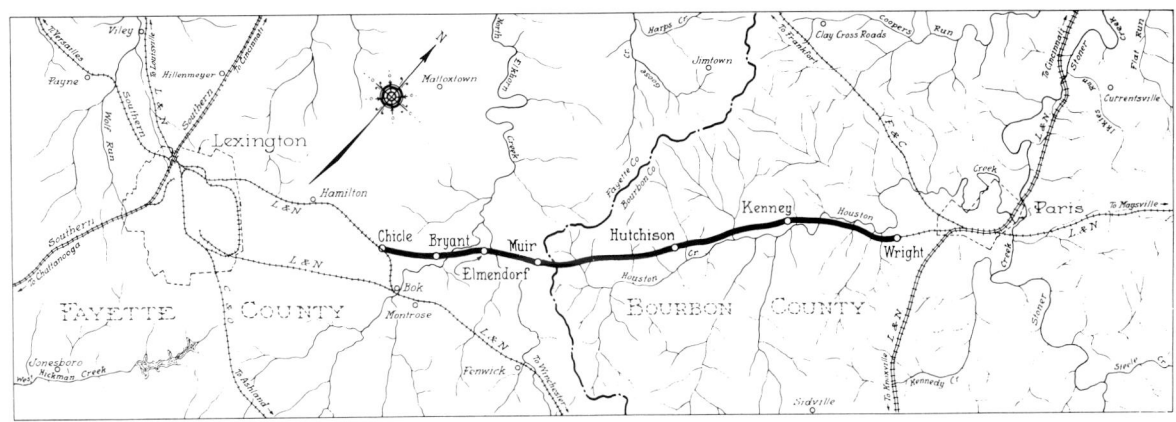

J. S. Horine

The Lexington-Paris line found its inception in the Maysville & Lexington Railroad, chartered March 4, 1850. By December 19, 1854, the 18 mile stretch between Lexington and Paris was completed and this was promptly leased to the Covington & Lexington Railroad which had been incorporated in 1849. On January 21, 1868, the Maysville & Lexington Railroad was split into two parts—the M&L Southern Division which included the Lexington-Paris line; and the M&L Northern Division which was to complete the trackage between Paris and Maysville. Actual operation of the Lexington-Paris route, however, remained in the hands of the Covington & Lexington.

On January 1, 1861, a joint stock association, known as the Kentucky Central Railroad Association was formed for the purpose of acquiring the property previously operated by the Covington & Lexington Railroad, and the new company operated the line until July 7, 1875, when the Kentucky Central Railroad took over the properties of the association.

The KCRR went into the hands of a receiver on January 28, 1886, and emerged as the Kentucky Central *Railway* June 7, 1887. On September 22, 1891, the KCRY was acquired by the Louisville & Nashville Railroad, which ownership continued until the abandonment of the Chicle-Paris line.

Top of page — Mixed train between Lexington and Paris on the Lexington-Maysville run, circa the thirties.   David M. Young

Middle — Junction at Chicle, 5.9 miles from Lexington. Line to Paris at left, Winchester to right.
   J. Winston Coleman, Jr.

Bottom of page — Same location, Ravenna-South Louisville freight is heading into the junction, Summer, 1952.   J. Winston Coleman, Jr.

The Lexington-Paris line indeed deserved the designation of "thoroughbred." Running closely adjacent to some of the finest horse farms of the inner bluegrass, the railroad on many occasions moved famous horses to their homes, or, conversely, to race tracks, horse sales, or new owners. Many persons whose names are legendary in the annals of horse racing, industry, and the amusement world, traveled on the railroad to attend the Lexington races, or visit nearby thoroughbred establishments.

The Kentucky Central Railroad designated the Covington-Lexington line as the *Bluegrass Route,* and advertised "Free Parlor Cars on Afternoon Trains." As of May 20, 1881, three daily round-trips were scheduled over the Lexington-Paris line, two to Covington, and one to Maysville. A freight train was scheduled to leave Lexington on Tuesdays, Thursdays, and Saturdays, at 5:20 a.m.

But like many other lines, the Lexington-Paris trackage was affected by extensions, connections, and changed facilities at points many miles away. On Christmas Day, 1888, the road gained access to Cincinnati by completion of the Ohio River bridge at Covington. On the other end of the line certain extensions in conjunction with the L&N RR plus trackage rights on that railroad opened a route to Jellico, Tennessee, with a connection to Knoxville. Thus, a through service was in process of development from Cincinnati to the southeast which was destined to eventually by-pass the Lexington-Paris line.

Upper — Typical overhead highway bridge spanning the Chicle-Paris segment.
J. Winston Coleman, Jr.
Center—North end of abandonment at Wright, just south of Paris. View is looking towards Lexington.
J. Winston Coleman, Jr.
Lower—Depot at Muir.
J. Winston Coleman, Jr.

"BLUE GRASS ROUTE."
Kentucky Central Railroad.
Local Time Table.

TRAINS NORTH.   In Effect May 20, 1881.

MAIN LINE.

STATIONS	No. 2. Expr'ss	No. 4. Mail.	No. 18. Expr'ss.
	P. M.	A. M.	P. M.
Lve. LEXINGTON	2 15	7 30	4 35
" Muirs	2 37	7 52	4 58
" Hutchinson	2 43	7 59	5 05
" Paris Junction	3 00	8 15	
" PARIS	3 05	8 20	5 25
" Kiser	3 20	8 35	P. M.
" Shawhan	3 24	8 39	
" Lair	3 32	8 47	
" CYNTHIANA	3 40	8 55	
" Poindexter			
" Garnett	3 56	9 11	
" Robinson	4 02	9 16	No. 6.
" BERRY	4 11	9 25	Falm'h Accom.
" Boyd	4 17	9 30	A. M.
" Morgan	4 28	9 42	6 30
" Livingood	4 36	9 50	6 36
" FALMOUTH	4 46	10 00	6 42
" Catawba	5 00	10 13	6 51
" Irving	5 08	10 21	6 58
" Boston	5 12	10 25	7 04
" BUTLER	5 18	10 31	7 14
" Demossville	5 27	10 40	7 25
" Morning View	5 37	10 50	7 32
" Benton	5 43	10 56	7 42
" VISALIA	5 52	11 05	7 49
" Ryland	5 57	11 10	
" Grant			
" Culbertson	6 11	11 25	8 06
" DeCoursey			
" S. Covington	6 22	11 37	8 22
Arr. COVINGTON	6 30	11 45	8 30
	P. M.	A. M.	A. M.

Free Parlor Cars on Afternoon Trains Between Cincinnati and Lexington.

Maysville Division.

STATIONS	No. 14 Expr'ss	No. 16 Accom.
	A. M.	P. M.
Lve. MAYSVILLE	5 45	12 30
" Summit	5 59	12 44
" Clark's	6 08	12 53
" Marshall	6 13	12 58
" Helena	6 25	1 10
" JOHNSON	6 34	1 19
" Elizaville	6 42	1 27
" Ewing	6 47	1 32
" Cowan	6 58	1 38
" Pleasant Valley	7 03	1 48
" Meyers	7 10	1 55
" CARLISLE	7 25	2 10
" Millers		
" MILLERSBURG	7 49	2 34
" Paris Junction	8 15	3 00
Arr. PARIS	8 25	3 10
	A. M.	P. M.

Close connections at Lexington with Louisville, Cincinnati & Lexington R'y, and Cincinnati Southern R'y, for all points South and Southwest.

The Figures in **Heavy Type** indicate meeting and passing points.

T. A. HASLETT, Gen'l Trav. Pass. Agt.

LIVINGSTON, LEXINGTON AND CINCINNATI.

Distance.	Trains do not stop at Stations where no time is shown.	No. 2 EX SUN	No. 4 DAILY	No. 6 DAILY	No. 12 EX SUN	No. 18 DAILY
.0	Lv. Livingston		2 25 AM	10 37 AM		
2.9	Sinks		2 33 AM	10 48 AM		
3.8	Mullins		F 2 35 AM	F 10 50 AM		
7.4	Brush Creek		F 2 47 AM	F 11 01 AM		
10.0	Wards		F 2 55 AM	F 11 10 AM		
11.8	Wildie		3 00 AM	11 15 AM		
15.9	Conway		F 3 08 AM	F 11 23 AM		
17.6	Sniders		F 3 13 AM	F 11 27 AM		
22.8	Berea		3 24 AM	11 39 AM		
25.8	Mayde		F 3 29 AM	F 11 47 AM		
27.0	Whites		F 3 32 AM	F 11 50 AM		
33.2	Ft. Estill		F 3 45 AM	12 04 NN		
35.7	Ar. Richmond		3 52 AM	‖12 10 NN		
35.7	Lv. Richmond	6 22 AM	3 52 AM	1 55 PM		
42.5	Red House	F 6 35 AM		F 2 10 PM		
46.3	Shearer	F 6 43 AM		F 2 17 PM		
47.6	Ford	F 6 47 AM	F 4 13 AM	F 2 21 PM		
48.6	Riverside	F 6 49 AM		F 2 24 PM		
51.2	Elkin	F 6 55 AM		F 2 30 PM		
52.9	Flanagan	F 6 59 AM		F 2 34 PM		
57.9	Ar. Winchester	7 10 AM	4 35 AM	2 45 PM		
57.9	Lv. Winchester	7 10 AM	4 35 AM	2 45 PM		
63.0	Renick	F 7 20 AM		F 2 55 PM		
65.2	Austerlitz	F 7 24 AM	F 4 48 AM	F 2 59 PM		
67.7	Escondida	F 7 30 AM		F 3 05 PM		
74.1	Ar. Paris	7 43 AM	5 05 AM	3 18 PM		
.0	Lv. Lexington	7 05 AM	4 40 AM	2 50 PM	5 25 PM	
4.0	Hamilton	F 7 15 AM			F 5 35 PM	
7.1	Bryant	F 7 21 AM			F 5 41 PM	
9.1	Muir	7 25 AM			5 45 PM	
12.2	Hutchinson	F 7 32 AM			F 5 54 PM	
15.1	Kenney	F 7 38 AM			F 6 01 PM	
16.6	Wrights				F 6 04 PM	
19.1	Ar. Paris	7 45 AM	5 11 AM	3 23 PM	6 10 PM	
74.1	Lv. Paris	7 55 AM	5 15 AM	3 30 PM		
79.8	Kiserton	8 06 AM		3 41 PM		
81.4	Shawhan	8 10 AM		3 45 PM		
84.9	Lair	8 17 AM		3 52 PM		
88.4	Cynthiana	8 24 AM	5 37 AM	4 00 PM		
92.5	Poindexter	F 8 33 AM		F 4 09 PM		
94.6	Garnett	F 8 36 AM		F 4 13 PM		
97.2	Robinson	8 41 AM		F 4 18 PM		
100.4	Berry	8 47 AM		4 25 PM		
102.7	Boyd	8 52 AM		4 30 PM		
106.9	Morgan	9 03 AM		4 37 PM		
108.9	Uma	F 9 07 AM				
110.1	Levingood	F 9 09 AM				
114.3	Falmouth	9 16 AM	6 20 AM	4 50 PM		3 42 PM
118.4	Catawba	F 9 26 AM			No. 8 EX SUN	F 3 57 PM
121.3	Menzies	F 9 31 AM				F 4 05 PM
122.7	Lynns	F 9 33 AM				4 08 PM
125.1	Butler	9 38 AM			6 43 AM	4 14 PM
128.8	DeMossville				6 52 AM	4 23 PM
132.6	Morning View				7 00 AM	4 32 PM
135.3	Kenton				7 07 AM	4 39 PM
138.3	Bethel Grove				F 7 14 AM	F 4 47 PM
138.8	Visalia				7 15 AM	4 48 PM
140.7	Ryland				F 7 21 AM	F 4 53 PM
146.2	Spring Lake				7 36 AM	5 08 PM
150.4	Latonia	10 16 AM	7 13 AM	5 43 PM	7 48 AM	5 20 PM
152.8	Covington	10 23 AM	7 20 AM	5 50 PM	7 55 AM	5 28 PM
154.4	Fourth St. Station				8 02 AM	5 35 PM
154.4	Ar. Cincinnati (C. U. Sta.)	10 30 AM	7 30 AM	6 00 PM		

1903
Ray Alford

LEXINGTON AND NORTH CABIN—PARIS—SOUTHWARD

THIRD CLASS		2nd CLASS	FIRST CLASS											Distance from Lexington	TIME TABLE No. 86. Takes effect Monday, April 10, 1939, at 11:59 p. m.
47	45	481	15	63	323	321	19	1	31	1401	3	7	341		
South Lou. Ravenna Freight	South Lou. Ravenna Freight	Cincinnati Division Freight	Western Express	Louisville Passenger	C. & O. Passenger	C. & O. Passenger	Louisville Express	Passenger	Cincinnati Division Passenger	Cincinnati Division Mixed	Passenger	Passenger	Cincinnati Division Passenger		STATIONS
Daily	Daily	Daily	Daily ex. Sunday	Sunday only	Daily	Daily	Daily	Daily	Daily	Daily	Daily	Daily	Daily		
P. M.	A. M.	P. M.	P. M.	P. M.	P. M.	P. M.	A. M.	P. M.	P. M.	P. M.	P. M.	A. M.	A. M.		
			4.55	4.00	2.28	7.35	4.10	11.30	9.10	12.28	12.45	8.05	7.00		L LEXINGTON N C
														0.6	
5.00	1.25	8.00	4.58	4.03	2.31	7.38	4.13	11.34	9.14	12.32	12.49	8.09	7.04	0.6	WEST LEXINGTON N
														0.5	
5.05	1.40	8.10				11.38		9.17	12.36	12.55	8.14	7.06	1.1	DODGE STREET	
5.17	1.52	8.30				11.48		9.25	12.46	1.02	8.24	7.15	5.9	CHICLE N C	
														3.2	
		8.44							/12.52			7.21	9.1	MUIR E	
		8.56							/12.57			7.26	12.2	HUTCHISON E	
		9.15							1.10			7.37	19.2	PARIS N	
														7.0	
5.20	1.55					11.50		9.27		1.04	8.26		6.8	BON E	
5.21	1.56					11.51		9.28		1.05	f 8.27		7.6	MONTROSE E	
														2.4	
5.27	2.02					11.55		9.32		1.08	f 8.31		10.0	FENWICK E	
														2.0	
5.33	2.07					11.59		9.36		f 1.11	f 8.35		12.0	AVON E	
														3.6	
5.40	2.15					12.04		9.41		1.15	f 8.39		15.6	WYANDOTTE E	
														5.6	
5.55	2.25					12.12		9.50		1.23	8.47		21.2	A NORTH CABIN E	
P. M.	A. M.	P. M.	P. M.	P. M.	P. M.	P. M.	A. M.	P. M.	P. M.	P. M.	P. M.	A. M.	A. M.		
Daily	Daily	Daily	Daily ex. Sunday	Sunday only	Daily	Daily	Daily	Daily	Daily	Daily	Daily	Daily	Daily		
47	45	481	15	63	323	321	19	1	31	1401	3	7	341		

The railroad did not attempt to match the hourly service. Instead it developed a schedule of six round-trips daily (two daily except Sundays) between Lexington and Paris, and extended one of the turn-arounds 14 miles further to Cynthiana. Shortly after the close of World War I, the "Lexington Special," Nos. 39 and 40 were added to the schedule. This provided a morning run to Cincinnati and a late afternoon return to Lexington, and featured both coach and chair car equipment.

Shortly after the turn of the century, an interloper arose to challenge the Blue Grass Route's supremacy in the transportation field. This was the electric interurban. From Lexington in the heart of the Blue Grass, four radiating lines were constructed. One of these, the line to Paris, was built by the Bluegrass Traction Company, and its cars started running in 1903. Soon an hourly service was set up and a tough competitive situation between the railroad and the electric line developed.

Top — Deck girder bridge over Houston Creek between Chicle and Paris.   J. Winston Coleman, Jr.
  Middle—Depot and general store at Hutchison station.
   J. Winston Coleman, Jr.
  Bottom—Horse loading platform at Elmendorf farm.
   J. Winston Coleman, Jr.

Lexington-Maysville passenger local at Paris, 1908. No. 42 (ex No. 437) was an 1883 Baldwin, 17″x24″, 64″. L&N RR

Around 1914, the Louisville & Nashville Railroad built a cut-off track connecting its Lexington-Winchester line at a point 6.8 miles from Lexington with a point on its Lexington-Paris trackage 5.9 miles from Lexington. The former junction was named *Bok* after Edward W. Bok, the famous editor, and the latter junction was named *Chicle* after a famous racehorse. With the completion of the cut-off track, practically all of the L&N traffic between Lexington and points east and south was routed over this connection.

In fact, it became practicable to route some of the Lexington-Cincinnati passenger and freight trains via Chicle, Bok, and Winchester. Hence, as local service on the Lexington-Paris line dwindled, the use of the slightly longer route for through service and the abandonment of the Paris route became a matter of practical economics. Permission to abandon the 12.68 mile segment between Chicle and Wright was received from the ICC on June 8, 1951. Thus *finis* was written to the famous thoroughbred line of the L&N. The autopsy was commenced around September 1, 1951, and by December 1 of the same year, the last of the corpse was buried.

Contrary to the physical condition of many railroads at time of abandonment, the Chicle-Wright segment was in good condition. Two or three weeks prior to dismantlement, the services of a Sperry rail car were employed to run over the segment to detect the few sections of the 100' rail that were unfit for relay purposes.

THE WORKHORSE—

The early history of the Louisville & Nashville's Bloomfield Branch is quite involved, and starts with the Cumberland & Ohio Railroad, incorporated by a special act of the Kentucky General Assembly approved February 24, 1869. Skipping over a myriad of corporate detail, on July 28, 1879, unfinished roadbed, right-of-way, and other improvements owned by the Cumberland & Ohio, Northern Division, and extending from Eminence to Bloomfield, were leased for 30 years to the Louisville, Cincinnati & Lexington Railway Company. In January, 1880, the lease was modified so as to provide for the immediate construction of the road between Shelbyville and Bloomfield by the LC&LRY. During the same year this segment was completed at a cost to the lessee of $395,524. The section between Eminence and Shelbyville was never finished.

From the time of its completion until November 1, 1881, the Bloomfield Branch was operated by the LC&L. On the latter date that railroad was acquired by the Louisville & Nashville Railroad. As a consequence, the branch was operated from the date of purchase until January 25, 1896, by the L&N.

Since the branch had been built to the LC&LRY's prevailing gauge of 4'9", it did not share in the L&N's wholesale gauge change that took place on May 30, 1886. However, the gauge was about the only favorable thing concerning its construction, the Railroad Commission of Kentucky reporting in 1889—

"The Northern Division of the Cumberland & Ohio is not in first-class condition. It was not originally well built. Was laid with light weight iron rails, not well ballasted, and having of number of trestles now old which have not been well maintained . . ."

Things looked better to the Commissioners two years later, as they remarked in 1891—

"The repairs so badly needed on the Cumberland and Ohio (N.D.), in the way of new trestles, have been largely made."

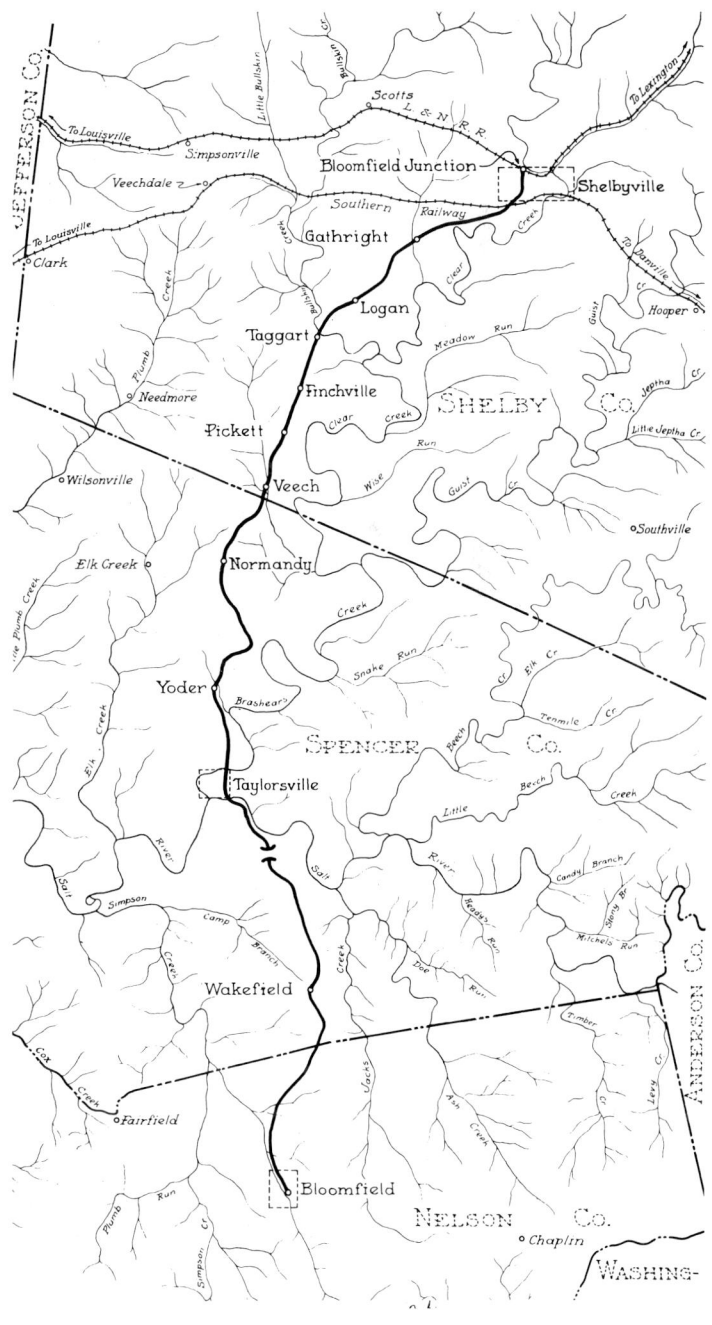

173

Consolidation No. 940, frequently used on the Bloomfield Branch during its latter years. This Cooke product of 1902 has 21x26" cylinders, 52" drivers, and was classified by the L&N as an H-20. L&N RR

Crossing of the Bloomfield Branch and the Southern Railway at the south limits of Shelbyville. Gate is across the L&N track looking towards Shelbyville.   L&N RR

Track Scene near Normandy, looking north. Note the light ballast of screenings. John B. Fravert

Picturesque Rock Cuts south of Finchville. L&N RR

Finchville Depot.   L&N RR

Taylorsville station looking north. The Diesel-powered mixed train symbolized the final type of service on the Bloomfield Branch. L&N RR

South end of Taylorsville yard showing bridge over Salt River. L&N RR

North portal of the one tunnel on the line, a 356' bore located on an ascending grade 1½ miles south of Taylorsville.   L&N RR

South portal of same tunnel as previous picture. The tunnel was a favorite place for the children of the neighborhood in playing hide and seek, not to mention a facility for cooling off in extremely hot weather. L&N RR

Looking south in the Bloomfield yards and the end of the branch.   L&N RR

View of the trestlework that dominated the branch south of Taylorsville. L&N RR

Trestlework, still further south. Maintenance of the many feet of such structures on the branch plagued the L&N's auditors for many years. L&N RR

Depot at Bloomfield.   L&N RR

Wakefield Depot and General Store.   L&N RR

The last train to run on the Bloomfield Branch. Shelbyville, Friday, October 10, 1952.   L&N RR

A period of legalities involved the Bloomfield Branch when, in August, 1892, the L&N instituted suit against the Northern Division of the Cumberland & Ohio to recover monies paid on its account. On January 31, 1895, a judgment was rendered in the L&N's favor for $419,803, and for a sale of the property. The L&N continued to operate the branch during a following receivership, and then on December 17, 1897, the property was sold to Samuel Spencer, then president of the Southern Railway System. The L&N operated the line as agent for Spencer until February 5, 1898, and Spencer, himself, operated the road to June, 1900, using it as a feeder to the line of the Louisville Southern from Louisville through Shelbyville to Danville, which had been completed in 1888.

Skipping over a few details of interest only to corporate buffs, the road was sold again on March 2, 1900, to certain bondholders who organized the Shelbyville, Bloomfield & Ohio Railroad Company to operate the 26.72 mile line. Finally, the sale of the Bloomfield Branch to the Louisville & Nashville Railroad Company was consummated, the L&N gaining possession of the trackage by deed dated September 28, 1901.

For a number of years following the L&N's purchase of the line, the quantity of the traffic had its moments and profits were shown every year or so. Several freight and passenger trains were operated daily in each direction, and the railroad serving Bloomfield became a very necessary community institution.

Traversing a prosperous agricultural region of the type dominating the outer bluegrass, most of the freight hauled reflected this economy. Principal commodities moved were tobacco, fertilizers, feeds, coal, dairy products, agricultural machinery, lumber, hay, grain, sand, gravel, and the like.

There were no railroad telephone lines paralleling the tracks, a situation which led to unusual operating conditions at times. For example, when the station agent needed a stock car he would put a note in the waybill box and flag the local freight. On one occasion the agent at Finchville needed such a car the following Saturday, and to play it safe he left the message in the waybill box on Thursday. He was home at lunch as the local went by but he heard it stop and naturally assumed that his message had been received.

Friday came, but when the local arrived there was no stock car for Finchville. The agent asked the conductor if he had received the note but the "brains" replied that all the box contained was a birds nest. An examination verified the truth of the statement, plus evidence to the effect that the all-important note had been carried off by the wren.

In the severe winter of 1917, the agent at Finchville went home late at night before the passenger train, due at 11 p.m. had arrived. The next morning, hearing a train blowing, the agent hurried into his clothes in his rush to get down to the station and meet the early morning local. You can imagine his surprise when he was greeted by the preceding night's train—just arriving after having been stuck in a snowdrift.

The Bloomfield Branch, in common with many other "country short routes" suffered the usual traffic attrition

Trestlework on curve as Bloomfield Branch ascends hill south of Taylorsville.   John B. Fravert

starting in the late thirties. The initial proposed abandonment of 1942 aroused considerable opposition from residents along the line. In view of the patrons' promises to supply greater traffic volume, plus an actual temporary increase in business, the application to the ICC for permission to abandon the segment was withdrawn.

However, the anticipated traffic-shot-in-the-arm failed to materialize on a permanent basis. A second application for abandonment was filed with the ICC on October 1, 1951. In spite of another round of protests, the Washington body gave the requested permission on September 3, 1952. The last trains were run over the branch on Friday, October 10, with the abandonment becoming officially effective October 13. Shortly thereafter, forces were at work removing the track, trestles, bridges, and other structures.

MENTION OF TWO OLD SIRES—
   Jett to Frankfort (Lexington & Frankfort Railroad)

The original line of the Lexington & Ohio Rail Road between Lexington and Frankfort was completed from Lexington to the top of the hill at Frankfort on January 31, 1834. Entrance into Frankfort was had by means of an incline-plane operation, descending into Frankfort from the hilltop terminus. The plane was 2,200' long with an inclination of 40 degrees, and the cars of the L&O were let down under the control of a stationary engine.

Although this operation was usually safe enough, occasionally the cars would get out of control and careen wildly down the plane and onto Broadway, greatly frightening the citizens, and passengers, but doing no great damage. However, one wreck of more serious proportions caused several deaths and had the effect of building up a considerable reluctance on the part of the passengers to ride the plane.

Left—Service on the Bloomfield Branch in 1917. L&N RR
Bottom Left—Service on the branch in 1903. Ray Alford
Below — The last employees' timecard covering the Bloomfield Branch. L&N RR

LOUISVILLE, SHELBYVILLE AND BLOOMFIELD.

No. 52 DAILY	No. 54 EX SUN	Distance.	Trains do not stop at Stations where no time is shown.	No. 51 EX SUN	No. 53 EX SUN	No. 65 SUNDAY
5 00 PM	7 30 AM	.0	Lv.. Louisville, 1st St...Ar.	8 20 AM	6 00 PM	9 00 AM
F 5 07 PM	F 7 37 AM	1.7	East Louisville	F 8 13 AM	F 5 50 PM	F 8 53 AM
		3.8	Crescent Hill			
		5.4	St. Matthews	F 8 05 AM		F 8 45 AM
		8.2	Lyndon	F 7 59 AM		F 8 39 AM
		11.1	Lakeland	F 7 52 AM		F 8 32 AM
5 25 PM	8 05 AM	12.0	Anchorage	7 50 AM	5 25 PM	8 30 AM
F 5 32 PM	F 8 12 AM	14.4	Avoca	F 7 41 AM	F 5 05 PM	F 8 22 AM
F 5 39 PM	F 8 21 AM	17.4	Eastwood	F 7 34 AM	F 4 50 PM	F 8 16 AM
F 5 43 PM	F 8 27 AM	19.1	Long Run	F 7 29 AM	F 4 45 PM	F 8 12 AM
5 53 PM	8 40 AM	23.2	Simpsonville	7 18 AM	4 30 PM	8 02 AM
F 6 01 PM	F 9 00 AM	27.2	Scotts	F 7 08 AM	F 4 15 PM	F 7 53 AM
6 10 PM	9 27 AM	31.1	Shelbyville	7 00 AM	4 00 PM	7 45 AM
6 15 PM	10 00 AM	31.6	Bloomfield Jct.	6 55 AM	3 07 PM	7 40 AM
F 6 28 PM	F 10 18 AM	36.7	Logan	F 6 37 AM	F 2 48 PM	F 7 22 AM
F 6 33 PM	F 10 29 AM	38.9	Finchville	F 6 30 AM	F 2 40 PM	F 7 15 AM
F 6 40 PM	F 10 38 AM	41.2	Veech	F 6 24 AM	F 2 34 PM	F 7 08 AM
F 6 45 PM	F 10 49 AM	43.1	Normandy	F 6 19 AM	F 2 28 PM	F 7 03 AM
F 6 54 PM	F 11 02 AM	46.0	Yoder	F 6 10 AM	F 2 15 PM	F 6 53 AM
6 59 PM	11 11 AM	48.2	Taylorsville	6 05 AM	2 05 PM	6 48 AM
F 7 16 PM	F 11 36 AM	53.4	Wakefield	F 5 52 AM	F 1 45 PM	F 6 33 AM
7 30 PM	11 59 AM	58.2	Ar.. Bloomfield ...Lv.	5 40 AM	1 30 PM	6 20 AM

LOUISVILLE & NASHVILLE

Table 19 — LOUISVILLE, SHELBYVILLE AND BLOOMFIELD

18 Ex.Su.	52 Daily	56 Ex.Su.	Distance	Trains 55 and 56 run via Lagrange.	51 Daily	55 Ex.Su.	15
AM	PM	AM			AM	PM	PM
	8 05	5 10	.0	Lv...Louisville....Ar	8 05	6 45	6 20
	8 13	5 17		" ..Fourth Street.. "	7 56	6 37	6 11
	8 20	5 25	4.5	" ..Baxter Avenue..Ar	7 48	6 28	6 03
f 8 25	f 5 32	f 7 41	7.1	" ..Crescent Hill..Lv	f 7 42	f 6 22	f 5 57
	. f .	f 7 44	8.8	" ..St. Matthews.. "	f 7 38	f 6 19	(152)
	. f .	f 7 48	11.6	" ....Lyndon..... "	f 7 32	f 6 15	(152)
(151)	f 5 45	f 7 52	14.5	" ....Lakeland.... "	f 7 26	f 6 11	(152)
8 36	5 46	7 53	15.3	" ....Anchorage.... "	7 24	6 09	5 43
f 8 42	f 5 51		17.7	" .....Avoca..... "	f 7 17		f 5 38
f 8 48	f 5 57		20.8	" .....Eastwood.... "	f 7 09		f 5 32
f 8 51	f 6 00		22.4	" ....Long Run.... "	f 7 04		f 5 28
9 00	6 10		26.4	" ..Simpsonville.. "	6 50		5 19
f 9 07	f 6 20		30.4	Lv.....Scotts..... "	f 6 39		f 5 09
9 15	6 33		34.3	Ar...Shelbyville..Lv	6 25		5 00
		7 53	15.3	Lv...Anchorage...Ar		6 09	
		f 7 58	17.7	" ...O'Bannon...Lv		f 6 05	
		f 8 02	19.9	" ..Pewee Valley... "		f 6 01	
		f 8 04	21.3	" ...Crestwood... "		f 5 58	
		f .	22.7	" ....Camden.... "		f .	
		f 8 08	23.7	" ...Glenarm..... "		f 5 54	
		f 8 14	26.4	" ....Buckner.... "		f 5 49	
		8 25	30.3	" ....Lagrange.... "		5 35	
		f 8 35	35.8	" ....Jericho...... "		f 5 20	
		f 8 40	38.6	" ...Smithfield... "		f 5 14	
		8 50	43.3	" ....Eminence.... "		5 05	
		f 8 55	45.6	" ...Hill Spring... "		f 5 01	
		8 58	47.3	" ..Pleasureville... "		4 57	
		f 9 03	49.7	Lv ....Cropper.... "		4 50	
		9 08	52.7	Ar ..Christiansburg.. "		4 45	
		9 55	61.2	Ar ...Shelbyville..Lv		3 02	
9 55	6 33	9 55	34.3	Lv ..Shelbyville..Lv	6 25	3 02	3 02
f 10 26	f 6 55	f 10 26	39.7	" ....Logan...Lv	f 6 05	f 2 47	f 2 47
f 10 33	f 7 02	f 10 33	42.1	" ...Finchville... "	f 5 58	f 2 40	f 2 40
f 10 40	f 7 09	f 10 40	44.5	" .....Veech..... "	f 5 52	f 2 33	f 2 33
f 10 46	f 7 15	f 10 46	46.1	" ...Normandy... "	f 5 47	f 2 28	f 2 28
f 10 56	f 7 25	f 10 56	49.4	" ....Yoder..... "	f 5 39	f 2 19	f 2 19
11 02	f 7 32	11 02	51.2	" ...Taylorsville... "	5 33	2 13	2 13
f 11 18	f 7 50	f 11 18	56.3	Lv ...Wakefield.... "	f 5 19	f 1 57	f 1 57
11 30	8 05	11 30	61.4	Ar ...Bloomfield...Lv	5 05	1 45	1 45
AM	PM	AM			AM	PM	PM

Nos. 15, 18, 51 and 52 stop on signal at Lincoln Ridge.
Nos. 15, 18 and 52 stop at all platforms north of Anchorage.
Trains 51 and 52 stop at all stations south of Anchorage to let off passengers.
(151) Stops at Lakeland to pick up passengers for north of Anchorage. (152) No.15 stops at all stations north of Anchorage.

LOUISVILLE & NASHVILLE RAILROAD COMPANY

Form 31 — TRAIN ORDER No. 26   May 31, 27

To C. and E. Extra 935 South at Bloomfield Ky.

No. 66 Eng 932 Meet Extra 935 South at Wakefield No. 66 take Siding.

Conductor: J. A. Rude   Train: Extra 935 South   Made: Conp   At: 10:57 am

---

BLOOMFIELD BRANCH

Southward 2nd CLASS 167 Mixed Tuesday Friday A.M.	Distance from Bloomfield	TIME TABLE No. 111 Takes effect Sunday, April 27, 1952 at 12:01 A. M. STATIONS	Car Capacity of Passing Sidings based on 41 feet per car	Northward 2nd CLASS 166 Mixed Tuesday Friday A.M.
10.10		BLOOMFIELD	32	9.40
	4.8			
f 10.22	4.8	WAKEFIELD	13	f 9.15
	5.2			
f 10.34	10.0	TAYLORSVILLE	24	f 8.50
	1.9			
f 10.49	11.9	YODER		f 8.43
	3.2			
f 10.55	15.1	NORMANDY	10	f 8.32
	1.9			
f 11.00	17.0	VEECH		f 8.25
	2.3			
f 11.07	19.3	FINCHVILLE	16	f 8.17
	2.2			
f 11.12	21.5	LOGAN		f 8.10
	4.6			
f 11.34	26.1	MAIN STREET		f 7.50
	0.5			
11.39	26.6	BLOOMFIELD JCT. E		7.45
A.M.				A.M.
Tuesday Friday				Tuesday Friday
167				166

The Lexington & Ohio Rail Road operated the Lexington-Frankfort line from January 31, 1834, until June, 1842, after which it was operated by the State of Kentucky, it having obtained ownership by purchase following foreclosure proceedings. In March, 1843, the road was leased to Phillip Swigert and William R. McKee, who operated the line until February 29, 1848, when the Lexington & Frankfort Railroad acquired possession.

During the Swigert-McKee period, the railroad was completely rehabilitated. A new entrance into Frankfort was planned, which would leave the old trackage at Jett, descend convenient stream courses to the Kentucky River, and follow it into Frankfort. A 500' tunnel had to be dug without the use of dynamite or any other present-day, high-powered explosive. Nevertheless, sometime in 1848, the new route was opened and the old trackage (approximately six miles long) from near Jett to the Frankfort hill-top, as well as the inclined plane, was abandoned.

Louisville to Portland (Lexington & Ohio Rail Road)

In Louisville, a dislocated fragment of the Lexington & Ohio Rail Road was built in 1838, this being known locally as the Portland Railroad. It was to serve the western terminus of the L&O, if and when that road ever reached Louisville.

Approximately three miles in length, it originally started at Sixth and Main Streets, proceeded west on Main to Thirteenth, to Rowan, to Bank and on to the heart of Portland, coming to a terminus on the levee at the foot of Grove Street, about two blocks below the westerly tip of Sand Island.

Prolonged lamentation greeted the building of the railroad, it being held that city streets were no place for a railroad and especially the locomotives thereof. Most vocal were the drayage and transfer interests who had been reaping a rich harvest hauling freight between the communities of Louisville and Portland.

Protests were so violent that an injunction, issued by the Chancellor of Louisville, stayed operation between Sixth and Seventh Streets. Later the eastern terminus was cut back to Twelfth. For some reason not obvious at this date, the railroad to Portland was turned over to the Blind Asylum for operation. Business did not justify the continuance of the line and some time after 1855, the railroad was abandoned.

AND A PATRIARCH BREATHES ITS LAST—

The severing of a railroad artery more than a century old was authorized December 7, 1959, when the Interstate Commerce Commission approved the request of the Louisville & Nashville Railroad to abandon the 11.85 mile segment between the county seats of LaGrange and Eminence.

In 1869, the Louisville & Frankfort consolidated with the Lexington & Frankfort to form the Louisville, Cincinnati & Lexington Railroad Company. Receivership took place in 1874, largely due to the expense of constructing the "Short Line" between LaGrange and Covington. Three years later the LC&L emerged from the hands of the receiver, with the *Railroad* in its former name changed to *Railway* as the result of the reorganization. And on November 1, 1881, it was formally sold to the Louisville & Nashville Railroad.

All this detail by way of tracing the corporate history of the LaGrange-Eminence trackage!

For many, many years all main line traffic over the L&N from the Bluegrass Region to the west funnelled through Eminence and LaGrange. Then on April 1, 1896, the 8.51 mile cut-off was completed between Christiansburg and Shelbyville, thereby shortening the Louisville-Lexington route by a matter of ten miles. Henceforth the cut-off was utilized by some of the L&N trains and all of the C&O passenger and freight runs.

Still for a number of years the older line carried considerable traffic.

By 1913, the local from Frankfort to Louisville was gone, but the two round trips between Lexington and Louisville via LaGrange were extended to include Sundays, with a slightly different schedule on the Sabbath. Both round trips carried parlor cars.

During the late thirties one of the Sunday round trips was dropped, leaving two weekday and one Sunday round trip over the segment. However, something additional had been added—a curious mixed run that originated at LaGrange at 8:00 a.m., then proceeded over the track through Eminence to Lewis (Christiansburg), then to Shelbyville, down the Bloomfield Branch to Bloomfield, and an afternoon return over the same route. Two through freights between Lexington and Louisville were also scheduled through Eminence-LaGrange during this period.

Ten years later (1948), these same through freights were still on the timecard, but one of the Lexington-Louisville passengers trains via LaGrange was gone. The mixed train on this branch was also among the missing.

Around the middle or latter part of 1952 the through Lexington-Louisville freights discontinued the use of the LaGrange route, leaving the daily passenger train and a daily except Sunday one-way local freight run as the only occupants of the track. Then in 1955 the daily round trip of the passenger run became a thing of the past. The daily except Sunday local plugged along on the following schedule:

6:50 a.m.—lv. Lewis; 7:05, Pleasureville; 7:30 Eminence; 7:50, Smithfield; 8:10 a.m.—ar. LaGrange.

Eventually this run was confined to Lewis-Eminence and return. The section between Eminence and LaGrange became used for the storing of bad order and obsolete freight cars. On August 20, 1959, the L&N RR made application to the Interstate Commerce Commission for permission to abandon the 11.25 miles between LaGrange and Eminence. The permission was forthcoming December 7 of the same year effective 30 days later. Work on dismantling the trackage commenced March 21, 1960 and was completed May 3. No portion of the track was left in at LaGrange, but at Eminence about 600 feet beyond the station in the direction of LaGrange was undisturbed.

Since the complete line of the Louisville & Frankfort between those points was not finally completed for operations until 1851, it is rather doubtful if the construction entailed the use of flat bar rail as was the case between Lexington and Frankfort. In any event, light rail of "pear" profile was unquestionably in use before too long. Standards were gradually improved under LC&L, and L&N ownership, and by 1920 the rail between LaGrange and Eminence consisted of a mixture of 80' and 90', but mostly 90', steel of surprisingly recent vintage. A few years later six miles of 100' rail was substituted.

Grades on the route were light, scarcely more than .6 percent at the most, and this obtained for extremely short distances. Outside of modest culverts there were no bridge structures.

Speed on the segment was set for a top limit of 50 miles per hour for passenger trains, and 35 for freights. This latter figure was elevated to 40 with the coming of the diesels. The line between LaGrange and Eminence was quite crooked in places, continuous sections of two miles of curves occurring at two points. About one-half of the curves were spiralled, the others, simple.

The "Scott" of the Louisville & Frankfort Railroad, taken at Eminence about 1860. L&N RR

Several years before abandonment of the Eminence-LaGrange segment, the track was used for the storage of bad order hopper cars. L&N RR

Another view of the bad order hoppers, parked on the unused Eminence-LaGrange trackage.   L&N RR

CHAPTER 21
"Gay Nineties Rendezvous"
Glasgow Junction to Mammoth Cave
(Mammoth Cave Railroad)

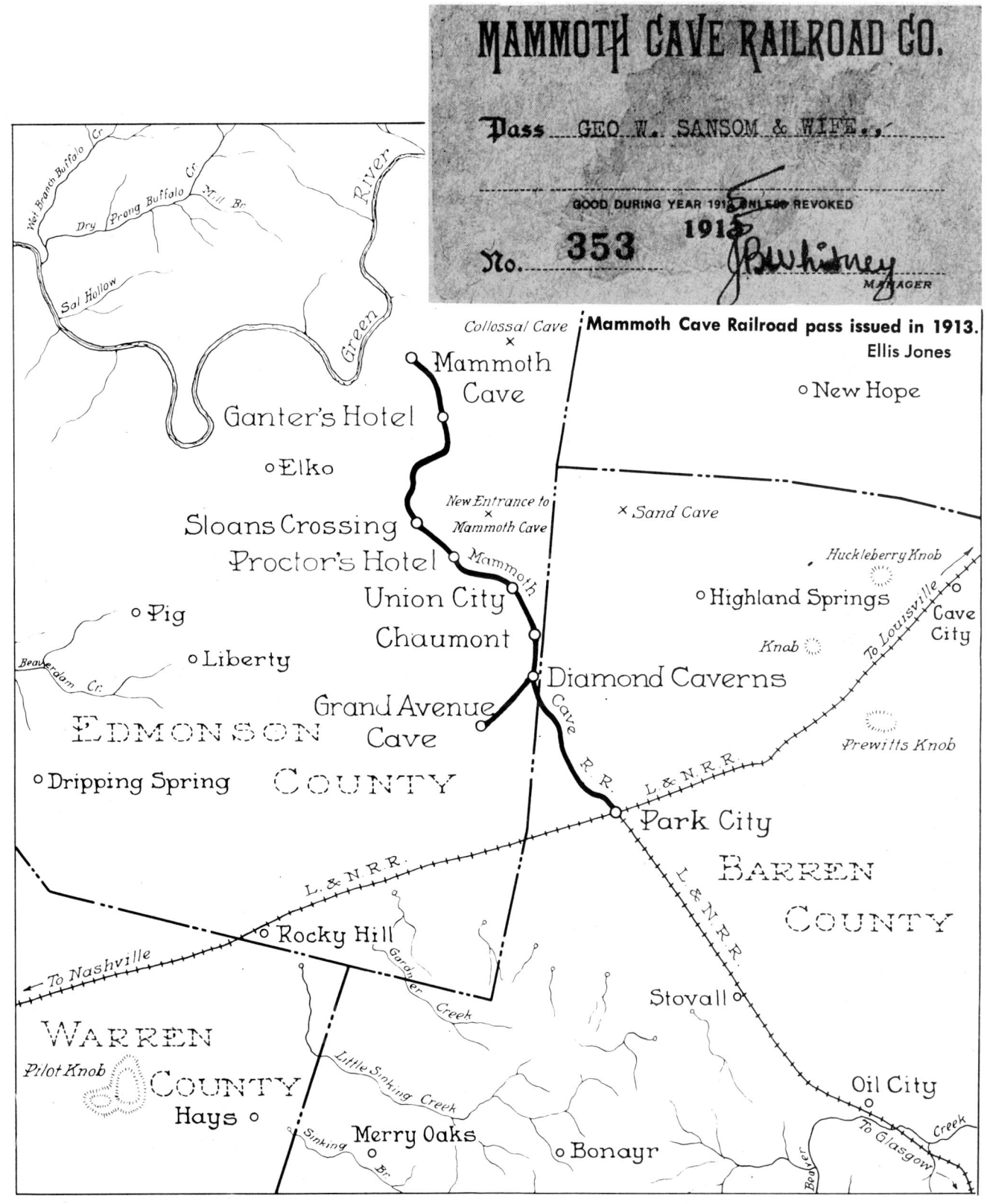

Mammoth Cave Railroad pass issued in 1913.
Ellis Jones

When Houchins, the hunter, allegedly chased a wounded bear into a chasm of the earth and inadvertently discovered Mammoth Cave in 1799, little did he know that he was setting in motion a chain of events that would result in the development and popularization of what was to be one of the nation's foremost natural wonders. Nevertheless, as the word spread and as hardy explorers started to chart the ramifications of the cave (a chore that is still going on), the popularity of Mammoth Cave as a scenic and recreation spot increased mightily and, by 1837, it was well established.

The Mammoth Cave Railroad was incorporated in 1874, but it was not until July 7, 1886, that an agreement for its building was entered into with the Mammoth Cave Construction Company. Work on the 8.7 mile line proceeded rather rapidly and on November 8 of the same year, the first paying passenger—one W. F. Richardson—rode the line.

Prior to the construction of the MCRR, a contract was made with the L&N RR whereby the latter railroad would lease the MC for 25 years. On September 25, 1886, the lease was made effective. By terms of the agreement the L&N was to furnish the needed rolling stock without rental charges, stop-over privileges at Glasgow Junction were to be given L&N's patrons, and the net earnings of the line were to be paid to the MCRR. On November 17, 1886, the road was formally opened for business.

Shortly after completion of the Glasgow Junction-Mammoth Cave trackage, a branch line, approximately one and one-half miles long, was built to the Grand Avenue Cave in the southeastern part of Edmonson County. It was believed at the time that this cave might eventually rival Mammoth as an attraction.

Above—Pass on the Mammoth Cave Railroad issued in 1893.   L&N RR

Below—"Ticket to the Cave."   L&N RR

GLASGOW JUNCTION AND MAMMOTH CAVE.

No. 5 DAILY	No. 3 DAILY	No. 1 DAILY	Distance.	MAMMOTH CAVE R. R.	No. 2 DAILY	No. 4 DAILY	No. 6 DAILY
5 35 PM	11 35 AM	7 45 AM	.0	Lv.... Glasgow Junc ...Ar.	9 35 AM	3 40 PM	6 50 PM
5 50 PM	11 50 AM	7 58 AM	3.0	.... Proctor's Cave	9 15 AM	3 20 PM	6 35 PM
6 10 PM	12 10 NN	8 20 AM	8.5	Ar....Mammoth Cave...Lv.	9 00 AM	3 00 PM	6 15 PM

Above—Schedule of the MCRR as of January 5, 1903.
L&N RR

Below—Typical Track Scene on the Mammoth Cave.

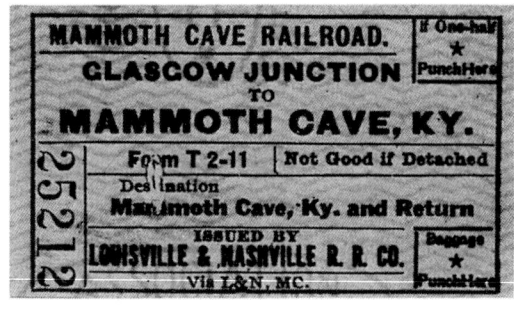

Above—All in all, the Mammoth Cave Railroad purchased four second-hand dummy-type Baldwin locomotives for use on its line. (See Appendix No. 1) No. 3, The "Hercules," annexed the greatest fame among these machines, perhaps because of its rather ambiguous name.
George Yater

Below—No. 4 with Combine No. 2 at Glasgow Junction. The MCRR owned two combines, Nos. 1 and 2, a short coach, No. 3, and a longer one, No. 4, obtained from the L&N RR. All were wooden, had open platforms, painted red, and heated by coach stoves. Robert Hatcher

Continued decreases in gross income with relatively inflexible expenses led the Mammoth Cave Railroad into insolvency, and a receiver was appointed for the little road August 12, 1895. On March 17, 1898, the line was sold under foreclosure. It was reorganized April 1, 1900.

With the incorporation of the "new" Mammoth Cave Railroad, the direct operation by the L&N RR ceased although the latter road continued to maintain a sort of benevolent protectorate over the MC, a condition that proved favorable to both, and one that endured until the demise of the Mammoth Cave line.

As the twenties rolled on and the American public became more automobile-conscious, deficits started mounting. To operate the railroad more economically, the old dummy locomotives and coaches made their last creaking run February 28, 1929, and in their place was substituted a rail car—a Ford chassis with a bus body mounted on flanged wheels. Two miniscule turntables were installed at each end of the line to reverse the vehicle.

For a number of years, the creation of a national park embracing the Mammoth Cave area had been in the making. Since no railroad is allowed to operate in a national park, the Mammoth Cave National Park Association on March 31, 1931, acquired the MCRR for the upset price of $5,000, which included all stocks, bonds, and property. On June 8, the formal decision to abandon the line was made. On August 1, the gasoline car made its final run, carrying its passengers and the United States mail to the end.

This story would be incomplete without recording the fact that success crowned the efforts of the MCNPA and others who had boosted for the park. On March 22, 1936, the Mammoth Cave National Park became a reality, although, due to World War II and other events, the park was not formally dedicated until September 18, 1946.

Below—Rail Bus used by the MCRR as a replacement for the Dummy Locomotives and Coaches. Note the Tiny Turntable. L&N RR

When the Mammoth Cave Railroad was abandoned, "Hercules" (No. 3) was too decrepit to make a deadhead trip to Mammoth Cave. In its place, No. 4 made the last journey and as its reward now bears the erroneous label 'Hercules' for those who visit the park.
S. P. Guthrie

Probably MC No. 1, 0-4-2T, location unknown. Picture taken before 1900.   S. P. Guthrie

"Hercules" (No. 3) and coach at the Mammoth Cave terminal, 1926. This was the L&N coach which apparently took over the road number of a former combine.
Geo. McKinney

Spring comes to the rolling cave region of Southern Kentucky, and in a perfect blending of budding greenery, venerable Hercules and its coach merrily jog along between Mammoth Cave and Glasgow Junction over primeval ribbons of rail and earth-surfaced ties.
Painting by Norman C. Miller, Jr.

Scene on the Mammoth Cave Railroad at Mammoth Cave, around 1900. Water tank in background. Locomotive is probably No. 2. L&N RR

CHAPTER 22
"Black Diamond Routes in Knox and McCreary"
Artemus to Wheeler and Anchor
(Artemus-Jellico Railroad)
White Oak Junction to Bell Farm,
and Oz to Co-Operative
(Kentucky & Tennessee Railway)

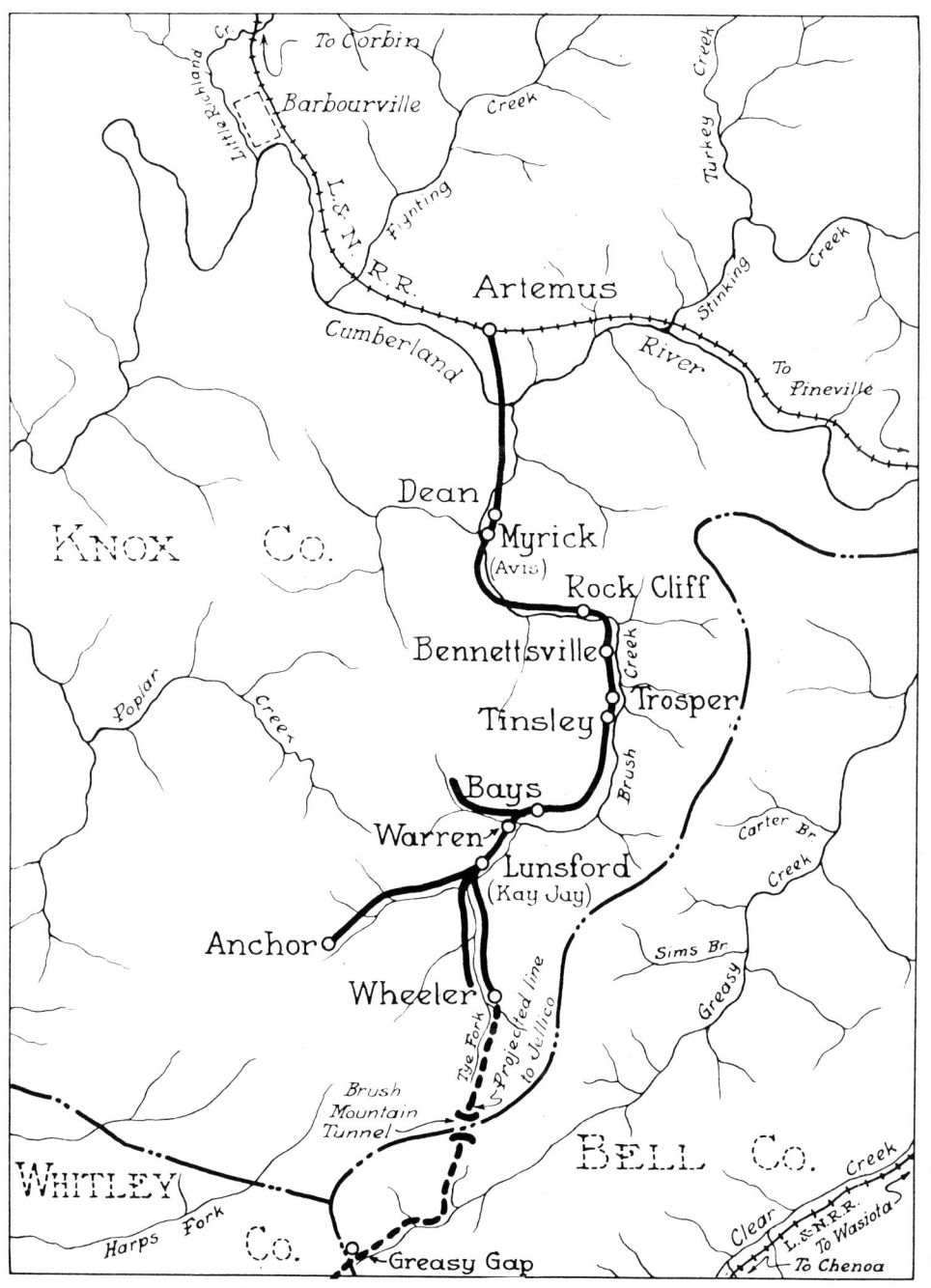

In the early part of the century, a syndicate from Warren, Pennsylvania, purchased a large section of undeveloped coal land in Knox County and incorporated as the Cumberland Coal Company. The organization's engineers found that the most logical place for the principal openings of their mines would be about nine miles from Artemus, a station on the Cumberland Valley division of the Louisville & Nashville Railroad. Artemus was already the junction of the three-mile line built by the East Jellico Coal Company in 1894 to serve its mine up on Owens Branch.

Recognizing that under Kentucky law railroads could usually obtain rights-of-way easier than coal companies, the syndicate on July 15, 1902, organized the Cumberland Railroad Company to build the eight miles of track from Artemus to its mining center which was subsequently named Warren after the Pennsylvania town. The Artemus-Warren trackage was completed about December, 1905, and a little work was also done on some branches and extensions. The first two miles out of Artemus up Brush Creek paralleled the Coalport Railroad including parallel bridges over the Cumberland River.

Subsequently, the company found itself in rather pinched financial straits, the purchase of the coal lands and the construction of the railroad leaving very little ready cash to operate the mines. The solution was to sell the railroad. Officials of the

Southern Railway System evidenced interest in the proposal, and during the latter part of 1905 or early part of 1906 the stock of the Cumberland Railroad was acquired by the Southern.

Plans were immediately formulated for an extension from Warren to Jellico, a distance of 26.4 miles, a point already reached by the Southern. However, at the same time the L&N RR was also making plans to invade the untapped area by a branch which would leave its Corbin-Knoxville line at Savoy. Both surveys involved the use of a narrow, high level, defile in southeastern Bell County known as Greasy Gap, through which there was space for a single railroad.

Much litigation ensued, all of which became moot. The L&N, under the name of *Pine Mountain Railroad —West* built a line from Savoy to Gatliff and Packard, and that is as close as the "Old Reliable" ever got to Greasy Gap. The Cumberland Railroad started work on its Jellico extension in earnest and much work was accomplished on the tunnels, grading and bridge abutments. But with the death of Samuel Spencer, president of the Southern and prime mover in the project, coupled with a general business recession, the project of the Jellico extension languished into a permanent suspension.

The first full year's operation of the Cumberland Railroad—1906— was rather unprofitable, resulting in a deficit of $1,156, but effective July 1, 1908, and continuing until June 30, 1912, the sum of $357.81 a year was set aside by the Post Office Department as the compensation to the CRR for carrying the mails, a modest sum that was nevertheless welcomed by the little line.

In 1909, two round trips of the passenger train were scheduled daily, one in the morning and one in the afternoon. Consist of the train included the locomotive; a combine that carried bulk mail, packages, and colored passengers; and a full coach. During the same year a local freight train made a daily round trip during daylight hours and a mine train made a round trip each night.

On August 10, 1911, a two-mile extension from Warren to Wheeler was completed, and on August 15 services started on the 2.7 mile branch from Lunsford to Anchor.

As time went on, the railroad became more prosperous. Spurs were thrust up tributary creeks in increasing numbers to tap new mining operations. Moving passengers and supplies to and from these camps became an expanding business, and, by 1916, we find a passenger schedule embracing three daily round trips (two on Sundays). All of these trains served both Wheeler and Anchor with the exception of a single daily round trip which included Anchor but excluded Wheeler.

During all the years that the Cumberland Railroad was owned by the Southern Railway, the CRR was operated as a separate entity, although 100% controlled through stock ownership. At times, the little road was revitalized by cash advances made by the parent organization. Even-

Timetable of the Cumberland Railroad, June 4, 1916.
Official Guide

Cumberland Railroad trip pass, 1916. S. P. Guthrie

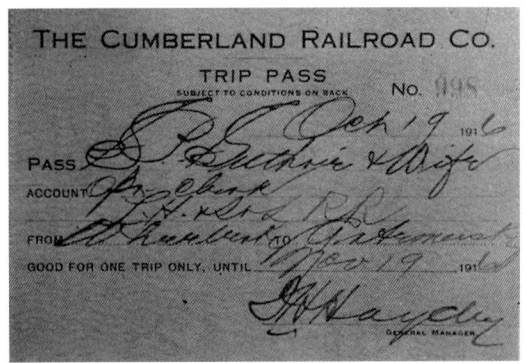

Cumberland Railroad, and Artemus-Jellico Railroad switch keys.
Philipp Fox

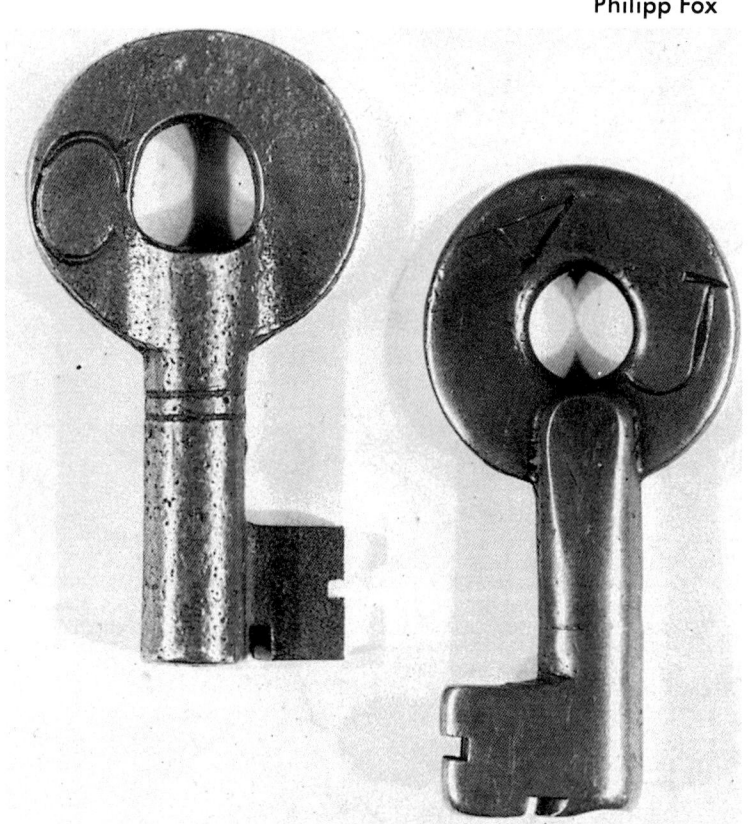

tually, however, the Cumberland Railroad was allowed to go into receivership, then bankruptcy.

A public auction was held on June 19, 1924, by order of the United States District Court, and the Cumberland Railroad was purchased by James A. McDermott of Barbourville. He promptly changed its name to the Artemus-Jellico Railroad, reminiscent, no doubt, of the unfulfilled ambitions of the previous owner.

Engine House and Office Building at Artemus.   S. P. Guthrie

Typical mountain scene on the Artemus - Jellico Railroad, looking south from Artemus.   S. P. Guthrie

Track of the Artemus-Jellico at Warren during flood.   Philipp Fox

During Southern Railway ownership, the passenger equipment included one coach and one combine, both of wooden construction and having open platforms. After the sale of the line to McDermott, these were returned to the Southern, and in their place were substituted two Ford A-model buses adapted for running on rails, and seating 15 passengers each. Also purchased were two trailer coaches of the "hog car" variety from the Knoxville, Tennessee, street railway system.

Looking north across Cumberland River bridge, showing water tank.   S. P. Guthrie

This 14x16' cypress tank was kept filled by the simple process of having the night engine watchman back a locomotive down to the south end of the river bridge and pump the water from the river into the tank. The other tank on the railroad, a 8x10' cedar facility at Warren, was kept filled by a gasoline pump.

Artemus - Jellico Railroad bridge over Cumberland River looking south. Pier on right belonged to the old Coalport Railroad built before the A-J.   S. P. Guthrie

The Artemus-Jellico bridge consisted of a 210' span, a through pin-connected Pratt truss on two masonry piers. There was an 89' approach trestle on one end. The A-J had 20 other open-deck frame trestles totaling 1998'.

Cumberland River bridge at time of flood.   Philipp Fox

On bridge is the road's one caboose, No. 99, and locomotive No. 33, a 2-8-0. ALco. The latter was scrapped by the A-J at time of abandonment. The Artemus-Jellico did not own a "big hook," and when bad derailments occurred, an S.O.S. went out for the L&N RR's wreck equipment at Corbin.

The route of the railroad was completely a water-level one, following the meanderings of a single stream and one tributary. There were no tunnels. When built, the line used mostly 60' and 70' rail. However, at time of abandonment, all of the main line was railed with 90', with 60', 70', and 80' steel in the various sidetracks and spurs.

Coal was the life-blood of the Artemus-Jellico Railroad. The operation at Kay Jay was owned by the Kentucky-Jellico Coal Company. Other mines at the south end of the line were the Anchor Block Coal Company at Anchor; the Wheeler Coal Company, Richland Coal Company, and Congleton Coal Company at Wheeler; the Fayette-Jellico Coal Company and the Carter Coal Company at Warren; the Jones Coal Company at Bays; and the Trosper Coal Company at Trosper.

Besides the mines and other operations at Artemus, facilities on the north end of the railroad included those of the Dean Coal Company, Dean; R. Dean Collieries Company, and Slick Lizzard Coal Company, Myrick; Southwestern Fuel Company, and Franklin Coal Company, Rock Cliff; and Bennettsville Coal Company, Bennettsville.

The beginning of the Artemus-Jellico Railroad at low switchstand on right, Artemus. L&N RR main tracks are on left. A-J office building is in distance. S. P. Guthrie

Tipple and Tracks at Kay Jay. S. P. Guthrie

On right the tipple of the Jellico Coal Company, and on left the stocker plant of the Coal Facilities Company, Artemus. Scene is one-half mile south of the Cumberland River bridge. S. P. Guthrie

207

In 1928, Murat H. Davidson bought controlling interest in the A-J from McDermott. During the thirties the passenger business waxed exceedingly prosperous, and in its best year, about $14,000 was taken in from this source. Contributing to this income were revenues derived from transporting miners, school children, and special passenger movements, which included occasional excursion trains run to Kay-Jay to carry baseball teams and their supporters.

In spite of this comparative lush period of operation there were some somber undertones. Sometime during 1929, the one and one-half mile segment between Lunsford and Wheeler was abandoned due to the closing of coal mines formerly served by that trackage. Then, in the late thirties, a flash flood due to a cloudburst near the head of Brush Creek knocked out almost every bridge on the line as well as about one mile of track near Bennettsville. In spite of these setbacks, the railroad was back in full operation in four days.

One of the two hoppers, and the single box car owned by the Artemus-Jellico Railroad. These were all junked at time of abandonment.
S. P. Guthrie

Artemus-Jellico Railroad's one caboose, No. 99, at Artemus, October 1947. George Yater

208

Alco 2-8-0, Artemus-Jellico road number 33, at Artemus. George Yater

A-J No. 16. This Baldwin machine, builder's number 40944, of 1913 vintage, was a 2-8-0 with 21x28" cylinders, purchased second-hand from the BR&L Company for $5,475. It was scrapped at time of abandonment.
S. P. Guthrie

Brooks 2-8-0, Artemus-Jellico road number 33, at Artemus. George Yater

Three fatal events, occurring within a span of 12 years, spelled the doom of the Artemus-Jellico Railroad. The completion of a hard-surfaced highway in 1939, paralleling the line, had the usual impact on passenger service which was discontinued in 1941. In July, 1949, the Fayette-Jellico Coal Company, the railroad's largest shipper decided to abandon its mine. Then on April 1, 1952, the Kentucky-Jellico Coal Company, the largest remaining shipper notified the railroad's management of its intention to discontinue operations.

Time Table

Artemus-Jellico Railroad Company

Effective Aug. 1, 1935

5 P. M.	3 *A. M.	1 A. M.	STATIONS	2 A. M.	4 *P. M.	6 P. M.
3:30	11:00	5:50	Lv. ARTEMUS Ar.	7:17	12:18	4:50
3:35	11:05	5:55	MYRICK	7:12	12:13	4:45
3:40	11:10	6:00	ROCK CLIFF	7:07	12:08	4:40
3:42	11:12	6:02	BENNETTSVILLE	7:05	12:05	4:37
3:45	11:15	6:05	TINSLEY	7:03	12:02	4:35
3:48	11:17	6:08	BAYS	6:58	11:58	4:30
3:52	11:22	6:12	WARREN	6:53	11:53	4:25
3:55	11:25	6:15	KAYJAY	6:50	11:50	4:22
4:05	11:35	6:30	Ar. ANCHOR Lv.	6:40	11:40	4:10

This Brill-Mack Rail Bus was purchased from the Pennsylvania Railroad for $2,000, and replaced the two Ford A model buses and their diminutive trailers. It went into service in 1930 and continued until 1941 when it was sold to the Buffalo Creek & Gauley Railroad in West Virginia.   Philipp Fox

Left without any substantial traffic, the Artemus-Jellico had no alternative than to abandon its railroad.

Operations stopped as of November 1, 1952, and dismantlement was completed about March 31, 1953.

Profile of the Artemus-Jellico Railroad. John S. Horine

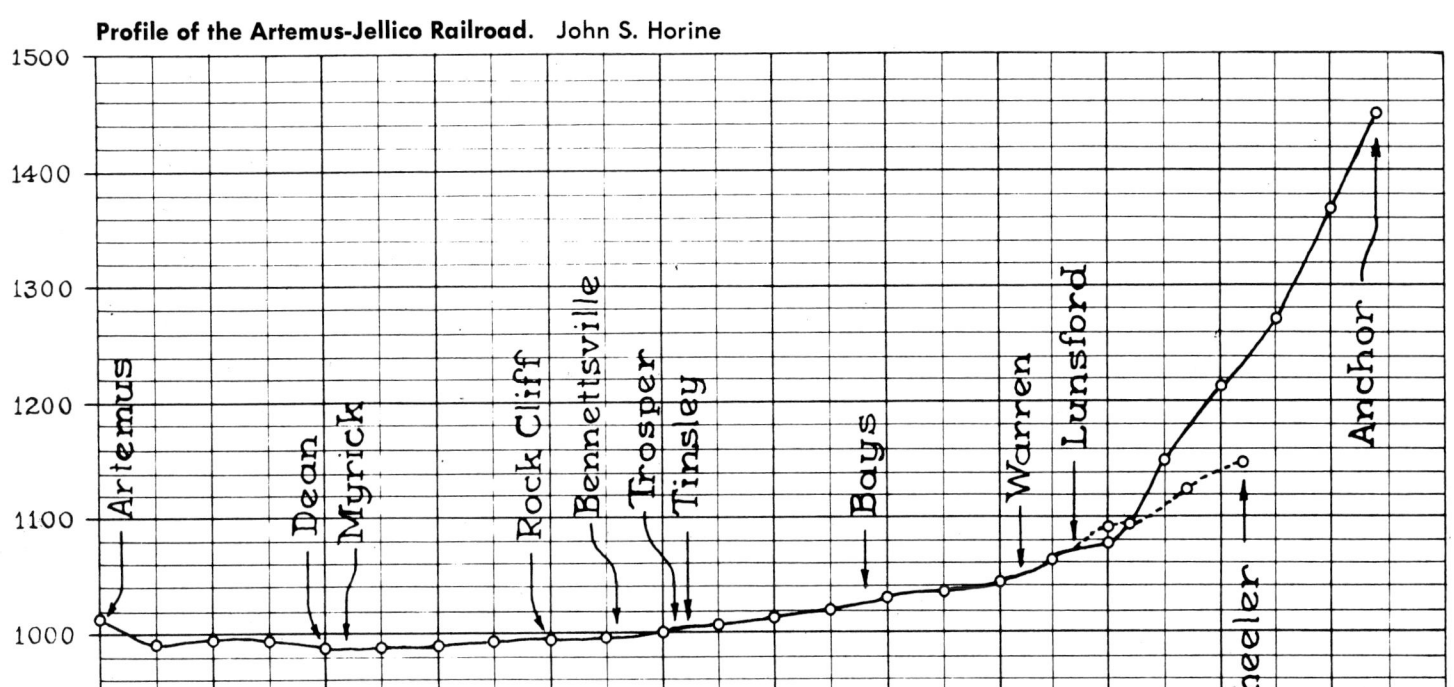

Coal Tipple and Loading Ramp, Ardean Collieries, Myrick. S. P. Guthrie

Now-Abandoned Mining Operation at Worley on the South Fork.
Aerial Surveys of Pittsburgh, Inc.

The history of the Kentucky & Tennessee Railway is inseparable from the story of Justus S. Stearns of Ludington, Michigan. Through his energies was founded the Stearns Coal and Lumber Company in 1902. To an original purchase of 30,000 acres of timber and coal land were added subsequent acquisitions until the company controlled some two hundred square miles of area, most of it in McCreary County, Kentucky, but also extending into Scott, Fentress, and Pickett Counties, Tennessee.

Lumber mills and coal mines were established, and the town of Stearns was created as the center of this activity. The need of a railroad was obvious and on May 22, 1902, the Kentucky & Tennessee *Railroad* was incorporated. By May 15, 1903, the 3.5 miles from Stearns to Barthell had been completed and opened to traffic.

When it became apparent that the K&TRR through its articles of incorporation was not authorized to issue sufficient bonds to provide for the proper expansion of the road, the Kentucky & Tennessee *Railway* was incorporated February 8, 1904, with the same incorporators as the previous company. Conveyance of the K&TRR properties to the K&TRY took place by deed dated March 28 of the same year.

Activity on the construction of the railroad was resumed. By 1906, the line to Yamacraw, 7.5 miles from Stearns had been completed, and only the building of the bridge across the South Fork held up further work. The bridge, the present concrete arch structure, was finished in 1907, and by the middle of 1908 the track had reached the crossing of Rock Creek beyond Oz. By 1909, White Oak Creek had been tapped, and here the terminus of the K&TRY remained for a number of years.

As the road progressed, new mines were opened, mining towns were established, homes built, and traffic developed

Tracks and Tipple at Co-Operative, looking west. S. P. Guthrie

West Portal of Tunnel east of Barthell. This, the only tunnel on the railroad, was an unlined bore, 265' long. S. P. Guthrie

for the railroad. Passenger service was now being maintained between Stearns and Yamacraw. The railroad was receiving annually from the Government $331.32 for carrying the mail between these two points. At first, coal was the big traffic item as lumbering had not yet developed appreciably.

During the years 1913-14, the tracks of the K&T RY were extended to a point somewhat over 16 miles from Stearns to a location, originally named *Difficulty*, but later changed to *Exodus*. By May, 1918, two daily except Sunday round trips of passenger trains were scheduled between Stearns and Yamacraw, and one daily round trip covered the entire Stearns-Exodus segment.

More important than this passenger service, however, was the increased freight business developed by the extension. By now, immense areas of virgin forest had been tapped and the hauling of logs became a vital factor in the railway's economy. Additionally, new coal mines were opened in the vicinity of Trace Branch and Fidelity, and now scores of gondolas and hoppers loaded with the "black diamonds" began to go out over the tracks.

In 1921, two important additions were made to the K&T. The main line was extended about three and one-half miles from Exodus to Bell Farm, the latter point marking the final terminus of the road. Here it connected with the 25 mile logging road of the Stearns Coal and Lumber Company that extended from Bell Farm south into Tennessee to a point northeast of Jamestown. Operated by the SC&LCO as a private carrier, it poured hundreds of loaded log cars into Bell Farm or White Oak Junction, to be hauled by the K&T to the Company's big lumber mill at Stearns.

The other addition was a branch, slightly more than a mile long, from White Oak (which now became White Oak Junction) to Co-Operative, the site of what was to become the second largest coal operation on the railroad and the source of from 25 to 40 loaded cars a day while the mine was in full swing.

Coal train passing over the South Fork.
    Thompsons, Knoxville

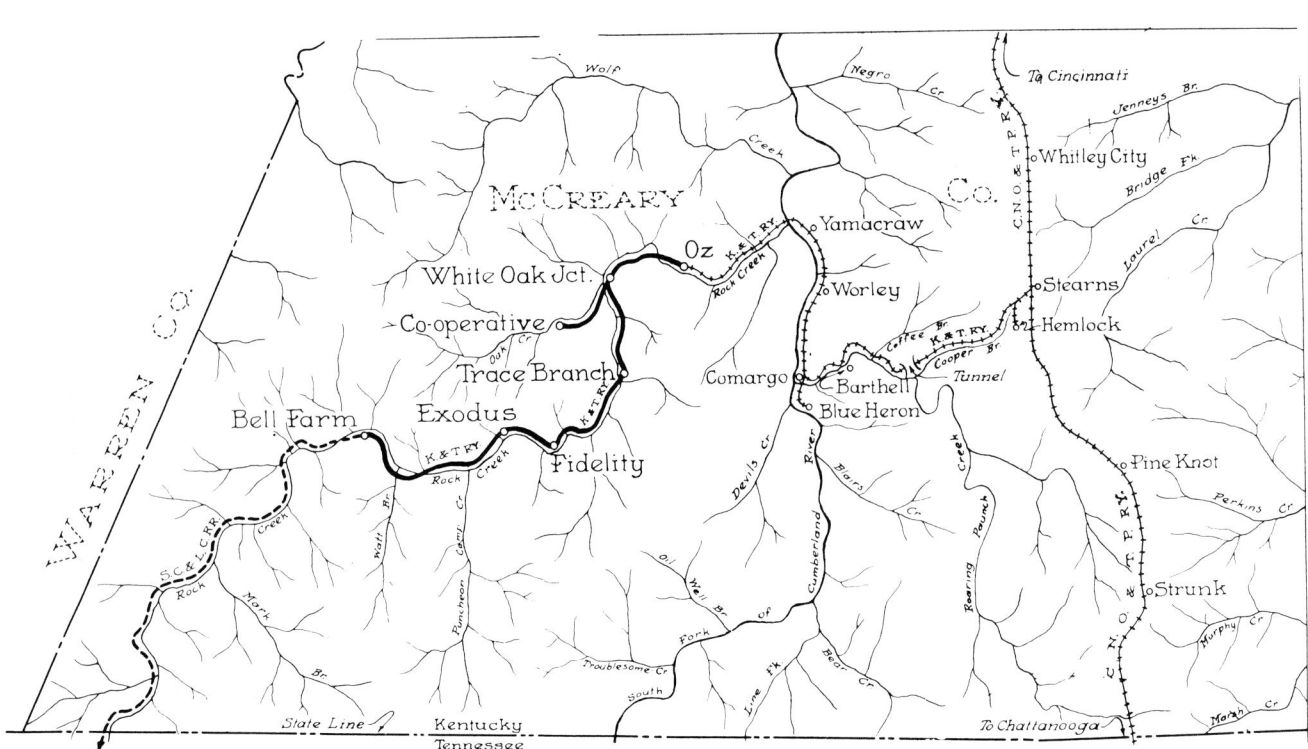

The middle and late twenties were perhaps the heyday of the K&TRY. But as all good things must come to an end so did the boom for the 20 mile railroad. As areas were "timbered out" and coal mines closed, corresponding sources of traffic were eliminated. In 1935, passenger service between Bell Farm and Exodus was discontinued. Around the first of 1939, all scheduled passenger trains between White Oak Junction and Exodus were cancelled.

In 1937, the mine at Fidelity closed and by 1938, practically all coal traffic between White Oak Junction and Bell Farm had ceased with the exception of Mine 15, just south of the Junction. And symbolic of the declining timber resources was the fact that, in 1937, the Stearns Company deeded 47,000 acres of land to the Cumberland National Forest.

Of a positive nature, however, was the opening of the coal mine, No. 18, at Blue Heron, and the building of one mile of track from the junction at Comargo, to the new operation. This development occurred in 1937-38 and resulted in the most modern and up-to-date mine on the K&T.

Loading Tipple and Mine Car Tracks at Co-Operative. L. C. Bruce

Station and Post Office at White Oak Junction. Boyce Whitcomb

Concrete arch bridge of the Kentucky & Tennessee Railway over the South Fork.
Louisville Courier-Journal and Times

As the areas of merchantable timber become worked out, the log trains became fewer and fewer. Finally, in 1948, the 25 mile logging road of the Stearns Coal and Lumber Company between Stearns and a point near Jamestown, Tennessee, was abandoned. As a result the log traffic from the vicinity of Bell Farm ceased practically overnight. At about the same time, a highway was completed to Bell Farm which further served to diminish the importance of the railroad.

Permission to abandon the 8.32 miles of main track between White Oak Junction and Bell Farm was received from the Interstate Commerce Commission March 3, 1949. While operations on the segment were promptly discontinued, the track and other appurtenances were allowed to remain in place until March, 1953.

On the Bell Farm Branch, looking east across bridge to White Oak Junction. S. P. Guthrie

White Oak Junction. Track to left led to Bell Farm; straight ahead to Co-Operative. Structure on left is Depot. S. P. Guthrie

Water Tank between Yamacraw and Oz. Other water tanks were located at Hemlock (the shops), west of Worley, Bell Farm, and at Exodus. S. P. Guthrie

A major blow was dealt the K&T in 1950, when the huge mining operation at Co-Operative closed, due to a gradual sickening coal industry and the inability to maintain the mine on a paying basis. As a result, traffic practically evaporated on the Oz-Co-Operative section of the railroad. Passenger service was cut back to Worley and operated daily except Saturdays and Sundays.

On January 1, 1952, all passenger service on the Kentucky & Tennessee Railway was discontinued. Meanwhile, the difficulties in respect to the coal business multiplied. In 1951, the Blue Heron mine went on a standby basis; late in 1953, mines at Worley and Yamacraw closed; and in December, 1953, the mine at Oz was shut down by a strike.

End of Track at Bell Farm. The line of the Stearns Coal and Lumber Company started at the bridge and continued south for 25 miles into Tennessee.   S. P. Guthrie

Loaded Log Cars on Bell Farm Branch.   S. P. Guthrie

As many of these cars as the locomotive could handle were incorporated into the scheduled mixed trains at Bell Farm or White Oak Junction. At one time, all passenger cars were handled at the rear of westbound mixed trains, and immediately behind the engine on eastbound trains. Later this requirement was dropped.

In 1950 the mine at Co-Operative ceased production, and in 1953 the decision was made to close the operation permanently. Hence the K&T-RY requested the ICC for permission to abandon the 2.41 miles of track between Oz and Co-Operative. The request was granted Nobember 23, 1953, but the physical retirement of the Oz-Co-Operative segment was deferred by K&T officials until it was definitely determined that no more coal would be mined in the region.

The K&TRY owned at least 55 flat cars of the type pictured, numbered 25-26, 28-29, 31-34, 39-41, 43-53, 56-61, 63-66, 68-75, 77, and 79-80. Other freight rolling stock, including their road numbers, were water car 54, cap board cars (used in mines) 35 and 55, Gondolas, 4, 6, 8, 14, 201-202, 204-205, 207, 209-211, oil tank flat (used on log road) 0, hoppers 213-215, ash cars 216-217, box cars 304-311, dump cars 450-451, 453-457, and a spreader 452.

Water Tank at Bell Farm, Looking North.   S. P. Guthrie

KENTUCKY & TENNESSEE RAILWAY

TIME TABLE NO. 96

EFFECTIVE MONDAY, DECEMBER 20th, 1942 AT 5:00 A.M.

PREVIOUS TIME TABLES ARE VOID AND MUST NOT BE USED. THIS TIME TABLE IS FOR THE GOVERNMENT AND INFORMATION OF EMPLOYEES. THE MANAGEMENT RESERVES THE RIGHT TO VARY FROM IT AT PLEASURE.

WESTBOUND TRAINS				EASTBOUND TRAINS	
@ No. 3	@ No. 1	STATIONS		@ No. 2	@ No. 4
10:30 AM	6:00 AM	Lv Stearns	Ar	8:04 AM	5:19 PM
-	-	Lv Hemlock	Lv	-	-
f 10:45 AM	6:15 AM	Lv Barthell	Lv	f 7:49 AM	5:04 PM
f 10:49 AM	6:19 AM	Lv Comargo	Lv	f 7:43 AM	4:58 PM
For Freight Service Only		Lv Blue Heron		For Freight Service Only	
# 10:50 AM	# 6:20 AM	Lv East Bridge]	Lv	# 7:42 AM	# 4:57 PM
10:55 AM	6:25 AM	Lv Worley	Lv	7:35 AM	4:55 PM
11:01 AM	6:31 AM	Lv Yamacraw	Lv	7:29 AM	4:50 PM
f 11:11 AM	6:39 AM	Lv Oz	Lv	f 7:15 AM	4:41 PM
-	6:41 AM	Lv Mine 17	Lv	-	4:39 PM
11:17 AM	6:46 AM	Lv White Oak Jct.	Lv	7:10 AM	4:35 PM
11:27 AM	6:51 AM	Lv Co-operative	Lv	7:05 AM	4:30 PM
# 11:45 AM	# 6:57 AM	Ar Mine 15	Lv	# 7:08 AM	# 12:01 PM
For Freight Service Only		Bell Farm		For Freight Service Only	

\# - No stop to be made. Shown as information only.
f - Flag stop only.
@ - Daily except Sunday.

No. 1 has right over No. 2
No. 2 has right over No. 3
No. 3 has right over No. 4

Extra trains must clear the time of opposing regular trains not less than five minutes unless authorized by train order.

EDW. WINCHESTER,
Chief Dispatcher.

APPROVED:
   L. C. BRUCE,
     Traffic Manager.

Employees' Timetables on the K&TRY were neatly mimeographed. Timetable No. 96, effective December 20, 1942, shows two daily round trips of mixed trains between Stearns and Mine 15.   K&T RY

Coach 108 at Co-Operative.
S. P. Guthrie

The K&T's passenger equipment included Coaches 108-110, and Combine No. 104.

The Combine, No. 104, at Co-Operative. S. P. Guthrie

This vehicle and the three coaches, were wooden, heated with stoves, and painted a dark green.

Box Car N. 309. S. P. Guthrie

Most of the K&T Box Cars had wooden sides, steel ends and underframes.

Car No. 80
S. P. Guthrie

Photo taken at the site of the Stearns Coal and Lumber Company's mill at Hemlock, one-half mile from Stearns.

Baldwin 2-6-2, No. 8.
John B. Allen
This machine, born 1911, with birth certificate No. 37269, was purchased new by the K&TRY.

Schenectady 2-8-0, No. 1.
S. P. Guthrie
The one spot of the K&T was built in 1903 under c/n 27409. Technically, this engine was originally the property of the Stearns Coal and Lumber Company and was that company's FIRST No. 1.

Baldwin 2-8-2 No. 7. This 91 ton locomotive was built in April, 1908, c/n 32763.
John B. Allen

Depot at Stearns. Louisville Courier-Journal and Times The Stearns Depot was owned by the Southern (CNO&TP) Railway but jointly used with the K&T. Here Conductor Robert Foster hands engineer Clyde Bales the orders for a run of the K&T from Stearns to the Blue Heron coal mines. Several box cars of freight are to be distributed to company stores along the way.

At Hemlock, a half mile from the depot at Stearns, the Kentucky & Tennessee Railway had a large machine shop in which heavy repairs were made on the locomotives and other rolling stock, as well as on mine machinery and mine cars. Also located here were the railroad's store room, rip tracks, yards, and other usual facilities of a railroad terminal.

Locomotive No. 12 at Hemlock Shops. S. P. Guthrie This ex-Southern Railway (No. 4501) machine, while no longer pulling loaded hoppers for the K&T, is still in a very active service of propelling fan trips of railway enthusiasts all over the south and midwest.

No. 10 (Baldwin 2-8-2) undergoing repairs in the K&TRY shops at Hemlock. Louisville Courier-Journal & Times

K&T No. 10. This machine is now at the Tennessee Valley Railway Museum and marked "Southern 6910."

KENTUCKY & TENNESSEE RAILWAY

1946-1947   No. SX 120

PASS — Mr. Sam Snicklehopper – –
ACCOUNT   NEWS BUTCH – K&TRy.
          Stearns and Bell Farm, Ky.

BETWEEN ALL STATIONS

UNTIL DECEMBER 31ST, 1947 { UNLESS OTHERWISE ORDERED AND SUBJECT TO CONDITIONS ON BACK }

VALID ONLY WHEN COUNTERSIGNED BY MYSELF OR L. C. BRUCE

COUNTERSIGNED BY

L C Bruce

J F Binkler
Pres. & Gen'l Mgr.

Pass Form used on the K&T. It is doubtful if either Sam Snicklehopper, or a news butch on the K&T ever existed.
L. C. Bruce

CHAPTER 23
"The Whiskey Route"
Georgetown to Paris
(Frankfort & Cincinnati Railroad)

The short-line Frankfort & Cincinnati Railroad, running through the heart of Kentucky's Bluegrass for 40.8 miles to connect Frankfort with Paris, via Georgetown appropriately gained its nickname by its services to distillers of the corn located in Frankfort, Stamping Ground, and other points. Today, 90% of its business is based on that single industry.

But this service is a far cry from the glowing words of former state geologist John R. Proctor who predicted in a rare publication of the State Geological Survey that its predecessor line, the Paris, Georgetown and Frankfort Rail Road Company would be "the great mineral road of the country." And the prediction might have come true had the PG&F realized its ambitions to build from Louisville through Frankfort, Georgetown, Paris, Winchester, and Jackson, to a point in Harlan County where it would be connected with railroads (also to be built) running to tidewater in Virginia, and Johnson City and Elizabethton in Tennessee.

Unfortunately, the Paris, Georgetown and Frankfort, incorporated under a special act of Kentucky approved March 23, 1871, built nothing. But on February 24, 1888, the name was changed to the Kentucky Midland Railway Company, and construction started. The section between Frankfort and Georgetown was built during the years 1888-1889, and that between Georgetown and Paris 1889-1890. The work was begun by Mason, Gooch, and Hoge, independent contractors, and was completed by the Home Construction Company which was composed of the officers and directors of the Kentucky Midland.

Important financial help was received from the communities the building railroad intended to serve. In 1888 Frankfort subscribed $100,000 and Paris took $50,000 in preferred stock of the railway. Franklin and Scott Counties subscribed to the common stock of the company in amounts of $150,000 and $100,000, respectively, which the railroad would receive upon reaching Paris. Bourbon and Bath Counties subscribed $250,000 and $150,000, respectively.

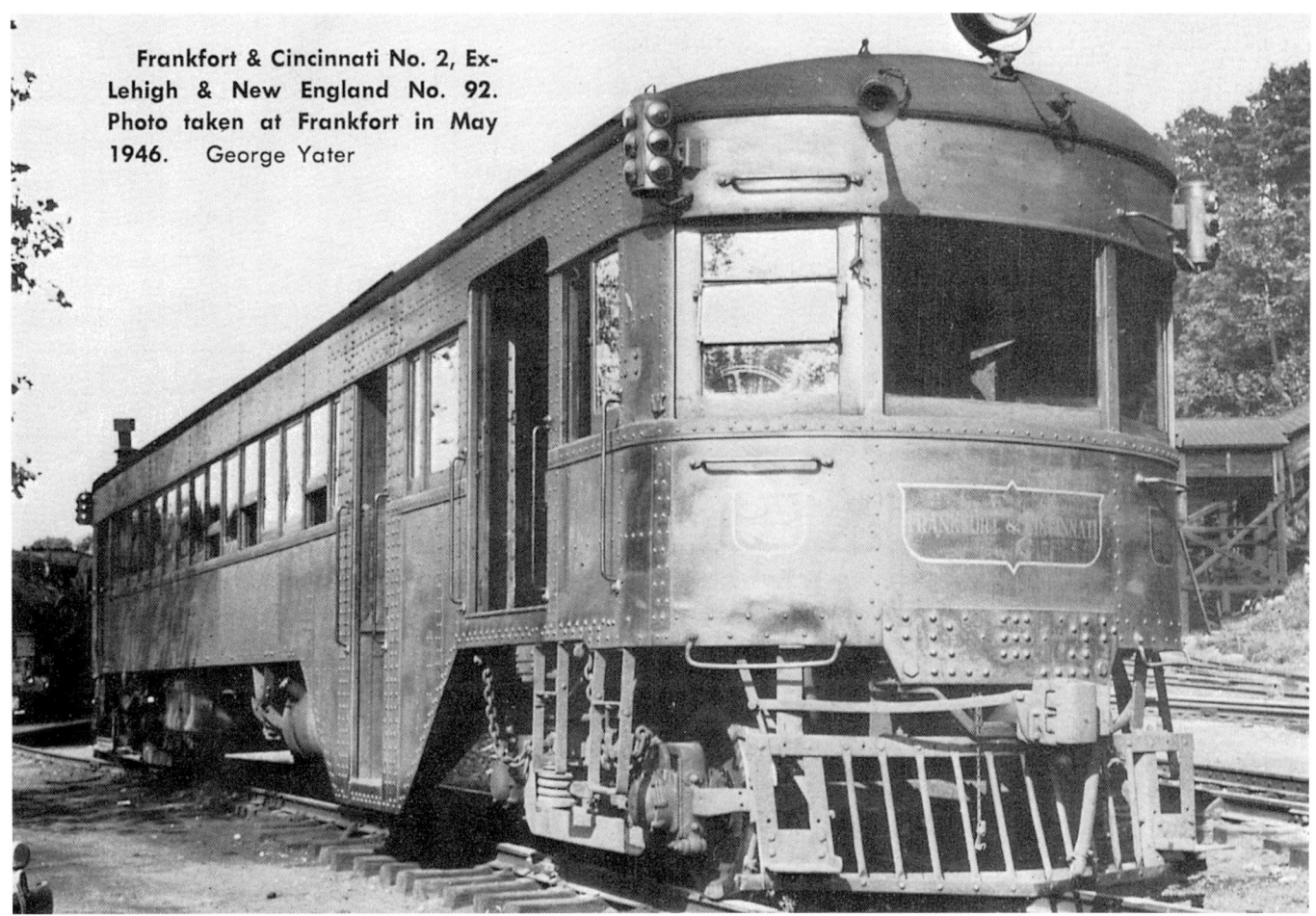

Frankfort & Cincinnati No. 2, Ex-Lehigh & New England No. 92. Photo taken at Frankfort in May 1946. George Yater

FRANKFORT AND CINCINNATI RAILROAD COMPANY

30   TIME TABLE   30

TAKES EFFECT

MONDAY, APRIL 30, 1956, AT 12:01 A. M.

For the Government and information of employees only. The Company reserves the right to vary from it at pleasure. Destroy all the Time Tables of previous dates. Study carefully all regulations and rules and note all changes.

NORTH BOUND   Daily Except Sunday Between Paris and Frankfort   SOUTH BOUND

2nd Class Freight			Car Capacity Based on 42 Ft. Per Car	Distance from Frankfort	STATIONS		2nd Class Freight		
42	**40**						**41**	**43**	
READ DOWN	DAILY EXCEPT SUNDAY						DAILY EXCEPT SUNDAY		READ UP
P.M.	A.M.						A.M.	P.M.	
4:00	4:30		......	......	Lv. FRANKFORT, KY. E Ar.		9:45	7:18	......
4:13	4:43		8	2.0	TOPLAND, KY. E		9:38	7:12	......
......	......		......	3.4	STEDMANTOWN, KY.		......	......	......
4:23	4:51		24	5.0	ELSINORE, KY. E		9:30	7:04	......
4:33	5:01		2	8.6	SWITZER, KY. E		9:20	6:51	......
......	......		......	9.8	KISSENGER, KY.		......	......	......
4:43	5:10		25	13.5	STAMPING GROUND, KY. E		9:11	6:38	......
......	......		......	16.8	DUVALL, KY.		......	......	......
......	......		......	19.9	SCHIFF, KY.		......	......	......
5:08	5:33		50	22.8	Ar. GEORGETOWN E Lv.		8:48	6:08	......
5:13	5:39		......	23.2	Ar. C. S. STATION E Lv.		8:43	6:05	......
......	6:00		......	......	Lv. C. S. STATION E Ar.		8:10	......	......
......	6:15		24	28.5	NEWTON, KY. E		7:55	......	......
......	......		......	30.4	SPRINGVALE, KY.		......	......	......
......	6:25		23	32.7	CENTERVILLE, KY. E		7:45	......	......
......	6:30		8	34.7	ELIZABETH, KY.		7:40	......	......
......	6:45		40	40.1	Ar. PARIS, JCT., KY. E		7:25	......	......
......	......		......	40.8	Ar. PARIS, KY. E Lv.		......	......	......
P.M.	P.M.						A.M.	P.M.	

(When necessary No. 42 and No. 43 will run as EXTRA between Georgetown and Paris)

Regular South bound trains are superior to trains of the same class moving in the opposite direction when running in accordance with Rule No. 72.

E—Telephone

GEO. L. FOWLER, President

A. E. PARKER, Supt. of Transportation

F&C Employees' Timetable - No. 30, dated April 30, 1956. (last one issued)

Maintenance of way car No. 42309 still carries its MW number from its former L&N ownership, in Frankfort, May 1939. George Yater

The promoters who raised $750,000 from communities adjacent to the line had contributed only $70,000 of their own money, and this was in preferred stock which had priority over the common stock.

The Kentucky Midland was authorized to issue $25,000 in mortgage bonds for each mile of line. As a result of this and other financial "arrangements" the little railroad was required to meet fixed charges of $57,720 per year. This it failed to do, and the Kentucky Midland went into receivership in 1894.

In connection with the community subscriptions it should be mentioned that part of the route of the Kentucky Midland was dictated by stipulations of the counties involved. Franklin County required the railroad to build as near to Forks of Elkhorn as possible, and Scott County required a route through Stamping Ground.

The Kentucky Midland Railroad was sold at foreclosure January 4, 1897, and conveyed by deed dated January 24, 1899, to the Frankfort & Cincinnati Railway Company. The F&C had been incorporated February 27, 1897.

The "Kentucky Cardinal" was the name given to F&C's M-55-1, shown here on the turntable at Frankfort on June 16, 1940. This car has been preserved by the Kentucky Railroad Museum in Louisville. George Yater

Subsequently, the Louisville & Nashville Railroad acquired the entire outstanding capital stock and bonds of the F&C and on October 28, 1909, the F&C conveyed its property to the L&N. This action was strongly protested by the Kentucky Railroad Commission and others, principally due to the single ownership of parallel lines. The transaction was adjudged null and void by the courts and by deed dated April 22, 1912, the property was transferred back to the Frankfort & Cincinnati Railway.

Insolvency struck the Frankfort & Cincinnati *Railway*. The line was sold at public auction in January, 1927, and reorganized as the Frankfort & Cincinnati *Railroad*. The F&C Railroad was incorporated February 7, 1927, and was composed largely of local citizens of Frankfort and Lexington. This situation obtained until the early part of 1961 when the F&C was acquired by Samuel M. Pinsley.

While most of the railroad's traffic was always concentrated over the Frankfort-Georgetown segment, for many years two round trips of a passenger train plus a scheduled round trip of a freight covered the entire line. When diminished passenger patronage dictated the change, the steam "varnish" was replaced in 1927 by the "Cardinals," a pair of self-powered passenger and express cars that were painted red (naturally). But the flight to auto transportation spelled the doom of these cars. All passenger service on the F&C was scheduled to end December 31, 1952.

But on Christmas Eve, seven days before the official abandonment, the last remaining Cardinal broke an axle on the Southern Railway crossing at Georgetown. To maintain passenger service to the last, Superintendent A. E. Parker kept the schedules by running the few passengers back and forth between Frankfort and Paris in his own sedan. This Cardinal, incidentally, is now the property of the Kentucky Railway Museum and on display in Louisville with the other acquisitions of the Museum.

On October 6, 1966, the Frankfort & Cincinnati Railroad Co. filed an application with Interstate Commerce Commission to abandon its Georgetown-Paris segment, a distance of 18 miles. It was proposed to sell to the Louisville & Nashville Railroad approximately 1.3 miles of the F&C's main line, sidings, and spur tracks at Paris, the main line acquisition extending west from Paris for 6,634 feet, thus serving an industrial section of the city and continuing for about a mile through undeveloped territory.

In recent years traffic on the Georgetown-Paris section had steadily diminished. During 1964 and 1965, there were 231 and 163 carloads of freight, respectively, which moved from and to points on the line which originated or terminated at points beyond the line. Service became reduced to the "as needed" status, and track maintenance was correspondingly reduced.

On May 16, 1967, the hearing examiner recommended approval of the application subject to exceptions which had to be filed within 30 days. No such exceptions were filed and thus the recommendation became the order of the Commission. The E.M.S. Associates of Boston, Mass., were

F&C No. 11 has just been checked over, and is ready to steam out of Frankfort prior to World War II.
George Yater

Locomotive No. 12 was ready to run, in 1939, at Frankfort.
George Yater

Locomotive No. 8 was originally from L&N. This photo was taken in Frankfort in 1940, and she was scrapped in 1946. George Yater

F&C No. 14 gets a drink of water and a little squirt of oil as she poses for this pre-war photo at Paris, Ky. George Yater

Locomotive No. 10, in the scrap pile in Frankfort in 1939. George Yater

given the contract for removing the track. Work started about July 20 and was completed about November 1.

The Georgetown-Paris line was a remarkably straight piece of track, crossing as it did the northern edge of the inner Bluegrass Region with its gently rolling topography. Bridge structures were few and unremarkable.

Stations and track facilities were as follows:

Miles from Frankfort	Stations	Facilities
24.8	Halley	
28.5	Newtown	Depot, 24 car siding
30.4	Springvale	
32.7	Centerville	23 car siding, stock pen
34.7	Elizabeth	Depot, 8 car spur
39.2	West Paris	
39.9	Paris	Yard

At Georgetown there was a manually operated interlocking at the crossing of the Southern Railway, normally set for movements on the latter line. Approaching Georgetown, all trains were required to come to a full stop at the crossing of the Paris pike.

During the operation of the passenger cars, their speed was limited to 45 miles per hour. A limit of 30 miles per hour obtained for freight trains.

August, 1951 timetable from Official Guide showing the two daily passenger round trips.

Top.—F&C No. 14 at Frankfort, June, 1941.   J. B. Allen
Bottom—F&C's No. 10, a consol built by Baldwin in 1923.   J. B. Allen

F&C Locomotive No. 16.
Si Herring

"Kentucky's Modern Railroads for the Future"

Information given in following order:

Name of Line

( ) Controlling line by lease, stock control, or ownership)

Mainline mileage in Kentucky

LH(line-haul) or T(terminal)

P(passenger service over all or part of Kentucky mileage)

BALTIMORE & OHIO (C&O RY)—O—LH—Operates into Louisville over bridge and tracks of K&IT RR.

CADIZ RR—10—LH—from Cadiz to junction with IC RR at Gracey.

CARROLLTON RR (L&N RR)—10—LH—from Carrollton to junction with LN RR at Worthville.

CHESAPEAKE & OHIO RY—approx. 700—LH—P—from Louisville and Cincinnati to eastern border of state, plus the Big Sandy River valley. Trackage rights over L&N RR between Louisville and Lexington.

CHICAGO, BURLINGTON & QUINCY RR—O—LH—operates into Paducah over bridge and tracks of P&I RR.

CINCINNATI, BURNSIDE & CUMBERLAND RIVER RR (CNO&TP RY)—2.11—T—switching trackage at Burnside.

CINCINNATI, NEW ORLEANS & TEXAS PACIFIC RY (S RY)—approx. 200—LH—P—route from Cincinnati to Chattanooga, Tenn.

CLINCHFIELD RR (L&N RR and SCL RR)—2.79—LH—from junction with C&O RY at Elkhorn City to Spartanburg, S.C.

COVINGTON & CINCINNATI ELEVATED RR TRANSFER & BRIDGE (C&O RY)—6.91—T—Ohio River bridge between Covington and Cincinnati and trackage in Covington, used by C&O RY and L&N RR.

FRANKFORT & CINCINNATI RR — 24.8 — LH — between Frankfort and Georgetown.

GULF, MOBILE & OHIO RR—42.80—LH—route between St. Louis, Mo. and Mobile, Ala. through extreme western Kentucky. Trackage over IC RR's Ohio River bridge at Cairo.

ILLINOIS CENTRAL RR—approx. 640—LH—P—from Louisville to Paducah, and three north-south routes in Jackson Purchase region.

KENTUCKY & INDIANA TERMINAL RR—124.63—T—jointly owned and operated by B&O RR, Monon RR, and S RY. Owns Ohio River bridge between Louisville and New Albany, Ind.

KENTUCKY & TENNESSEE RAILWAY—10.5—LH—from Oz to junction with CNO&TP RY at Stearns.

LOUISVILLE & NASHVILLE RR — approx. 1,800—LH—P—has mainline trackage in virtually all parts of Kentucky.

LOUISVILLE BRIDGE & TERMINAL RR (PRR)—4.28—T—owns Ohio River bridge and terminal trackage in Louisville.

MONON RR—O—LH—operates into Louisville over bridge and tracks of K&IT RR.

MOREHEAD & NORTH FORK RR—4—LH—from Clearfield to junction with C&O RY at Morehead.

NEW YORK CENTRAL RR—10.75—LH—operates into Louisville over own Ohio River bridge (Big Four).

NORFOLK & WESTERN RY—approx. 36—LH—coal branches in extreme eastern part of state.

PADUCAH & ILLINOIS RR—18.77—T—from Metropolis over its own Ohio River bridge to Paducah. Furnishes facilities for CB&Q RR, IC RR, and L&N RR.

PENNSYLVANIA RR—O—LH—P—operates into Louisville over bridge and tracks of LB&T RR.

SOUTHERN RY — 138.50 — LH — Louisville to Danville, Lawrenceburg to Lexington, and Louisville to St. Louis, Mo., over K&IT RR bridge. (Also see CNO&TP RY.)

TENNESSEE CENTRAL RAILWAY—16.29—LH—from Hopkinsville to Harriman, Tenn.

Constant change keeps a railroad up to date, to provide the service demanded by new products and methods. The "Dixie Jet" at Anchorage, just outside of Louisville.

—Louisville & Nashville Railroad

Train-front view of the reconstructed railroad bridge across the Ohio River from Kentucky to Cairo, Ill. Anchoring this new span in place marked the completion of a 3-year $6,300,000 reconstruction job, aimed at facilitating rail service throughout the area.

—Illinois Central Railroad

A Chesapeake & Ohio coal train winds its way through the hills of eastern Kentucky. The Road of Progress was built with rolling wheels.

—Chesapeake & Ohio Rwy.

Curving beyond Deep Hollow fill near Tateville, a southbound freight, with five "Big John" cars on the head end, approaches the cut at Deep Hollow Road. Another example of continuing modernization.
—Southern Railway System

A heavy-tonnage freight train rolls north out of the new Kings Mountain cut. The grey scar on the grass at right is the old roadbed angling away toward the north portal of the old Kings Mountain tunnel. The deepest part of the cut—142 feet—is at the point where the train curves.

—Southern Railway System

BIBLIOGRAPHY

Information for this volume was obtained from two primary sources, the printed page and the personal interview. The most authoritative printed information has come from the railroads, themselves, taking the form of—

    Location Maps
    Line Profiles
    Track Diagrams
    Old Employees' Timetables
    Old Public Timetables
    Railroad Annual Reports
    Company Magazines
    Station Lists
    Direct Correspondence

Exceedingly fine cooperation was obtained from the following railroads:

    Artemus-Jellico Railroad
    Chesapeake & Ohio Railway
    Flemingsburg & Northern Railroad
    Gulf, Mobile & Ohio Railroad
    Illinois Central Railroad
    Kentucky & Tennessee Railway
    Louisville & Nashville Railroad
    Missouri Pacific Railroad
    Morehead & North Fork Railroad
    Nashville, Chattanooga & St. Louis Railway
    Southern Railway System

A secondary source of printed information has come from contemporary newspaper accounts, souvenir issues of newspapers, and county histories. Some of Kentucky's early lines issued stock promotion pamphlets which have proven valuable.

Following is a bibliography of the principal book and pamphlet material used as sources:

ASSOCIATION OF AMERICAN RAILROADS, **Chronology of American Railroads**: Washington. (various editions)
ASSOCIATION OF AMERICAN RAILROADS, **Railroads in this Century**: Washington. March, 1944.
BASTIN, S. L. and MORY, S. A., Sr., **History of Coal Mining in Laurel County, Kentucky—1750-1944**: London. 1944.
CLARK, THOMAS D., **Beginning of the L&N, The**: Louisville. 1933.
CLARK, THOMAS D., **History of Kentucky, A**: New York. 1937.
CLARK, THOMAS D., **Pioneer Southern Railroad, A**: Chapel Hill. 1936.
CORLISS, CARLTON J., **Main Line of Mid-America—The Story of the Illinois Central**: New York. 1950.
DeBOW, J. D. B., **Legal History of the Nashville, Chattanooga & St. Louis Railway and Possessions**: Nashville. no date.
DUKE, BASIL W., **Commercial and Railroad Development of Kentucky, The**: Frankfort. 1887.
EASTERN RAILROAD PRESIDENTS' CONFERENCE, **A Yearbook of Railroad Information**: New York. (various years)
FERGUSON, E. A., **Founding of the Cincinnati Southern Railway**: Cincinnati. 1905.
FRAZIER, HARRY, **Recollections**: Huntington. 1938.
HACKWORTH, W. S., **Over a Century of Railroad Service**: Nashville. 1953.
HERR, KINKAID, **Louisville & Nashville Railroad, The**: Louisville. Printings April, 1943; August, 1943; October, 1959; December, 1960. March, 1964
HERINGTON, EDWARD R., **Regulation of Railroad Abandonments**: Cambridge. 1948.
HINES, EDWARD W., **Corporate History of the Louisville & Nashville Railroad Company and Roads in its System**: Louisville. 1905.
HUNGERFORD, EDWARD, **History of the Monon Railroad**: unpublished manuscript.
INTERSTATE COMMERCE COMMISSION. **Abandonment Reports**. (Finance Dockets printed since 1925)
INTERSTATE COMMERCE COMMISSION. **Railroad Abandonments 1920-1943**: Washington. 1945.
INTERSTATE COMMERCE COMMISSION. Valuation Reports listed below. Numbers are those of the respective Valuation Dockets.
    Ashland Coal & Iron Railway Company. 258.
    Brooksville Railroad Company. 682.
    Chesapeake & Ohio Railway Company et al. 457.
    Cincinnati, Burnside & Cumberland River Railway. 917.
    Cincinnati, Flemingsburg & Southeastern Railroad. 253.
    Cumberland Railroad. 289.
    Eastern Kentucky Railway. 513.
    Illinois Central Railroad Company et al. 387
    Kentucky & Tennessee Railway. 860.
    Kentucky, Rockcastle & Cumberland Railroad. 1127.
    Louisville & Nashville Railroad Company et al. 456.
    Louisville, Henderson & St. Louis Railway. 892.
    Mammoth Cave Railroad. 337.
    Mobile & Ohio Railroad Company et al. 149.
    Morehead & North Fork Railroad. 657.
    Mountain Central Railway. 278.
    Nashville, Chattanooga & St. Louis Railway et al. 367.
    Ohio & Kentucky Railway Company et al. 375.
    Rockcastle River Railway. 780.
    Southern Railway Company et al. 556.
KENTUCKY, STATE OF, **Geological Surveys**, various reports.
KENTUCKY, STATE OF, **Department of Mines**, annual reports.
KENTUCKY, STATE OF, **Railroad Commission**, annual reports and state railroad maps.
KERR, JOHN LEEDS, **Louisville & Nashville, The, An Outline History**: New York. 1933.
KERR, JOSEPH G., **Historical Development of the Louisville and Nashville Railroad System**: Louisville. 1926.
KULP, RANDOLPH L. (editor), **History of Mack Rail Motor Cars and Locomotives**: Allentown. 1959.
LEMLY, JAMES H., **Gulf, Mobile & Ohio, The**: Homewood. 1953.
MOODY, JOHN, **Steam Railroads**: New York. (various years)
Official Time Tables of Railways: New York. 1877.
Official Guide, The: New York. (various issues)
Official Equipment Register, The: New York. (various issues)
POOR, N. V. and H. W., **Manual of the Railroads of the United States**: New York. (various years)
PRINCE, RICHARD E., **Louisville & Nashville Steam Locomotives**: Green River. 1959.
PROCTER, JOHN R., **Resources Adjacent to the Kentucky Union Railway Company**: Frankfort, 1881.
RIEBEL, R. C., **Louisville Panorama**: Louisville. 1954.
SULZER, ELMER G., **Kentucky's Abandoned Railroads**, a series of preliminary chapters appearing in issues of THE KENTUCKY ENGINEER for May, Aug. 1945; Feb., Aug. 1946; Feb., Aug. 1947; Feb., Aug. 1948; Feb., Aug 1949; Feb., Aug. 1950; Feb. Aug. 1951; Feb., May, Aug. 1952; Aug. 1953; Aug., Nov. 1954; Aug. 1955; Feb., May 1956.
SULZER, ELMER G., **Mammoth Cave Railroad, The**, R&LHS Bull. 99: Boston. 1958. Also in Register, Ky. Hist. Soc., Vol. 57, No. 2: Frankfort. April, 1959.
SULZER, ELMER G., **Kentucky Thoroughbred, A Workhorse and Two Old Sires, A**, R&LHS Bull. 102: Boston. 1960.
SULZER, ELMER G., **Another Kentucky Railroad**, R&LHS Bull. 105: Boston, 1961.
SULZER, ELMER G., **An Abandoned Kentucky Railroad. The Artemus-Jellico RR.** R&LHS Bull. 108: Boston, 1963.
TABER, THOMAS T. and CASLER, WALTER, **Climax—An Unusual Steam Locomotive**: Rahway, 1960.
TAYLOR, GEORGE ROGERS and NEU, IRENE D., **American Railroad Network, 1861-1890, The**: Cambridge. 1856.
TURNER, CHARLES W., **Chessie's Road**: Richmond. 1956.
VAN SCOYOC, L. S., **Men, Bonds and the Monon**, Register, Ky. Hist. Soc. Vol. 59, No. 3: Frankfort. June, 1961.

Appendix 1

Locomotive Rosters of the Ghost Lines

Chapter 1

During L&N operation of the North Winchester-Maloney segment, the heaviest power permitted were classes G13 and H18 between North Winchester and Glencairn, and H23 and K24 between Glencairn and Maloney.

KENTUCKY UNION RAILWAY Locomotive Roster

Number	Type	Builder	C/N	Date	Cylinders	DD	Remarks	Scrapped
1	4-4-0	Pittsburgh	781	1885		62"	Work Train Service	?
2	4-4-0					62"		?
3	4-4-0	Baldwin		1888	17x24"	62"	To L&E #3; L&N #64.	1925
4	4-4-0	Baldwin	10704	1889	17x24"	62"	To L&E #4; L&N #65.	1925
10	2-6-0	Baldwin	10410	1889	19x24"	54"	To L&E #10; L&N #459*.	1926
11	2-6-0	Baldwin	10409	1889	19x24"	54"	To L&E #11; L&N #460*; C&W #460	1931
12	2-6-0	Baldwin	10418	1889	19x24"	54"	To L&E #12; L&A #5; L&N #551	1927

*L&N numbers 459 and 460, for a number of years were used in passenger transfer service between Latonia, Ky. and the old Central Union Depot in Cincinnati, O. For this use they were painted a rich brown with yellow trim, inside of cab and boiler heads were painted aluminum; and brass boiler fittings were kept highly polished.

LEXINGTON & EASTERN RAILWAY Locomotive Roster

Number	Type	Builder	C/N	Date	Cylinders	DD	Remarks	Scrapped
3	4-4-0	Baldwin		1888	17x24"	62"	ex-KU #3; To L&N #64.	1925
4	4-4-0	Baldwin	10704	1889	17x24"	62"	ex-KU #4; To L&N #65.	1925
5	4-4-0	Baldwin	9710	1888	17x24"	62"	To L&N #66.	1925
9	4-6-0	Baldwin	12726	1892	19x24"	60"	To L&N #365.	1933
10	2-6-0	Baldwin	10410	1889	19x24"	54"	ex-KU #10; To L&N #459.	1926
11	2-6-0	Baldwin	10409	1889	19x24"	54"	ex-KU #11; To L&N #460; C&W #460.	1931
12	2-6-0	Baldwin	10418	1889	19x24"	54"	ex-KU #12; To L&A #5; L&N #551.	1927
20	2-8-0	Baldwin	17680	1900	20x24"	50"	To L&N #659.	
21	2-8-0	Baldwin	18751	1901	20x24"	50"	To L&N #660.	
22	2-8-0	Baldwin	18818	1901	20x24"	50"	To L&N #661	
23	2-8-0	Baldwin	20014	1902	20x24"	50"	To L&N #662.	
24	2-8-0	Baldwin	20015	1902	20x24"	50"	To L&N #663.	
25	2-8-0	Baldwin	22966	1903	20x24"	50"	To L&N #664.	
26	2-8-0	Baldwin	22967	1903	20x24"	50"	To L&N #665.	
27	2-8-0	Baldwin	23402	1903	20x24"	50"	To L&N #666.	

Chapter 2

MOUNTAIN CENTRAL RAILWAY Locomotive Roster

Number	Type	Builder	Date	Remarks
1	A	Climax	1904	Nickname "Betsy"
2 (first)	A	Climax	1904	
2 (second)	B	Climax		ex-Ridgewood Lumber Co.
3	B	Climax		ex-BWRR&L #2; Simcoe Land Co.
4	Shay	Lima		ex-Simcoe Land Co.

Chapter 3

When the Louisville & Nashville Railroad acquired the Beattyville & Cumberland Gap Railroad, it received the latter line's one locomotive, a 4-4-0 bearing road No. 1, and generally known as "Old Betsey".

Likewise, the Kentucky Highlands Railroad, when acquired by the L&N, owned one locomotive, a 4-4-0 carrying road No. 3. It was renumbered 63 by the L&N and assigned D-0 class. Built in 1891. 17x24" cylinders and a DD of 63".

Permissable L&N classes were H27's and K4's between Cliffside and Nicholasville, and F9's and K4's between Nicholasville and Irvine.

RICHMOND, NICHOLASVILLE, IRVINE & BEATTYVILLE RAILROAD Locomotive Roster

Number	Type	Builder	C/N	Date	Cylinders	DD	Remarks	Scrapped
1	4-4-0	Pittsburgh						
2	4-4-0	Rogers						
3	4-6-0	Baldwin	12514	1892	18x24"	57"	To L&N #147, #366.	
4	4-6-0	Baldwin	13623	1894				

LOUISVILLE & ATLANTIC RAILROAD Locomotive Roster

Number	Type	Builder	C/N	Date	Cylinders	DD	Remarks	Scrapped
3	4-6-0	Baldwin	12514	1892	18x24"	57"	ex-RNI&B #3; To L&N #147, #366.	
4	2-6-0	Baldwin	32269	1907	19x24"	52"	To L&N #550.	1937
5	2-6-0	Baldwin	10419	1889	19x24"	54"	ex-KU #12, L&E #12. To L&N #551.	1927
6	4-4-0	Taunton		1871	17x24"	57"	To L&N #67.	1924
7	2-6-0	Baldwin	20240	1902	19x24"	52"	To L&N #552.	1932
8	2-6-0	Baldwin	20341	1902	19x24"	52"	To L&N #553.	1930
9	4-4-0	Pittsburgh			17x24"	64"	To L&N #68.	1925
10	2-6-0	Baldwin	31073	1907	19x24"	52"	To L&N #554.	1930
11	2-6-0	Baldwin	24845	1904	19x24"	52"	To L&N #555; F&C #9	
12	2-6-0	Baldwin	26092	1905	19x24"	52"	To L&N #556; F&C #8	

Chapter 4

The Caney & West Liberty Railroad's motive power included a Shay registered in the name of its parent, The White Oak Cannel Coal Company. Bearing road No. 3, the Lima, b/n 959; 11/04, had 12x12" cylinders, 36" drivers, wighed in at 55 tons, and was a two truck model. Following its stint in Kentucky, the Shay went west, sucessively serving lumber and timber lines in Nevada, Washington, Oregon and California.

OHIO & KENTUCKY RAILROAD Locomotive Roster

Number	Type	Builder	C/N	Date	Cylinders	DD	Remarks
14	2-6-0	Pittsburgh	30123	1904	19x24"	50"	Nos. 14 & 15 purchased shortly before O&K undertook operation of its road, July 1, 1904. Middle sets of drivers converted to blind drivers because of frequent derailments.
15	2-6-0	Pittsburgh	30124	1904	19x24"	50"	
18	4-4-0	Rogers		1870	15x24"	61"	ex-GARR #37 "L.M.Hill". To O&K in 1910, and converted from wood to coal burning. To LNA&C
8	4-4-0	Rogers			17x?		ex-LNA&C. Swapped for #18, as #18's small cylinders were inadequate for the O&K hills.
16	2-6-0	Pittsburgh	53819	1913	19x24"	50"	

Chapter 5

KENTUCKY, ROCKCASTLE & CUMBERLAND RAILROAD Locomotive Roster

Number		Type	Builder	C/N	Date	Cylinders	DD	Remarks
1 "Jeanne"		B	Climax					Purchased new. To Emory River Lbr. #1, 1941.
2		B	Climax					Purchased new.
3		2-6-2	Vulcan		1915	17x24"	44"	Middle drivers blind. Sold to a Texas Lbr. Co.
4 "Edwin"		Shay	Lima	2827	1916	12x13"	26"	To Bond-Foley Lbr. #5; Little River Lbr. #27; Grey Knox Marble.
5		B	Climax					From a W.Va. Lumber Co.

NOTE: Numbers 1, 2 and 5 belonged to the Turkey Foot Lumber Co., and Nos. 3 and 4 to KR&C RR.

Chapter 6

Unfortunately, we have only scraps of information on the Versailles & Midway locomotives. We do know that 4-4-0 No. 2 was built by Pittsburgh in 1885, c/n 783. This machine sucessively became Louisville Southern No. 10, Southern Railway No. 1001, 1791 and finally 3791. It was scrapped in Birmingham, Ala. in January 1922. It is said that another Pittsburgh 4-4-0 was purchased new and numbered 10. It was a coal burner equipped with air brakes, oil headlight, and link and pin couplers. Its drivers were about 5' in diameter, and the cylinders 18x24".

The Southwestern Railway owned one locomotive, a 4-4-0 Baldwin, road No. 1. After the Louisville Southern acquired the Southwestern, LS 4-4-0's 2, 4, 6, 8 and 10 were used for passenger service, the 10 spot being the former Versailles & Midway No. 2. Moguls 3, 5, 7, 9, 11 and 13 were used for freight. Later, under the control of the Southern Railway System, 8-wheelers Nos. 158 and 2300 were used on the Branch.

Chapter 7

While a narrow gauge line, the Mt. Sterling-Rothwell segment had a total of three locomotives. No. 1, a 4-4-0 was possibly a McQueen. No. 2 was a 2-6-0 Brooks of 1876 vintage, with 36" drivers and 11x16" cylinders. No. 7 was a Baldwin.

Locomotives used on the segment after its acquisition by the Chesapeake & Ohio Railway, included 4-4-0 No. 817, 4-6-0 No. 115 (from the C&O of Indiana), 2-6-0's nos. 265, 427 and 428, and 2-8-0's Nos. 653 and 658.

Chapter 8

L&N power used on the Fort Estill-Rowland segment included 2-8-0's Nos. 23, 24, 25 and 26; and 4-6-0's Nos. 14, 15, 16, 17, 337 and 338.

Chapter 9

LICKING RIVER RAILROAD and LICKING VALLEY RAILWAY Locomotive Roster

Number	Type	Builder	C/N	Date	Cylinders	DD	Remarks	Scrapped
1 (1st)	0-4-0	Baldwin						
1 (2nd)	B	Climax			9x12"	28"	20 ton. Bought new. Original number: 6	
2 (1st)	Heisler	Dunkirk						
2 (2nd)	B	Climax			9x12"	28"	20 ton. Bought new. Original number: 7	
3 (1st)	A	Climax					from West Virginia	
3 (2nd)	Shay	Lima	1650				Bought new.	
4	0-4-0	Porter	1752	1897	8x14"		10 ton saddle tank.	
5	0-4-0	Porter	1753	1897	8x14"		10 ton saddle tank.	
6	B	Climax (see second No. 1)						
7 (1st)	B	Climax (see second No. 2)						
7 (2nd)	2-6-0						Brought from south as a diamond stack woodburner. Converted to coal. To O&O on abandonment of LR.	
8	4-4-0	Baldwin					Purchased from Cincinnati Eqpt. Co. Ex-CG&P	
9	4-4-0	Baldwin					Same as No. 8	

Chapter 10

BROOKSVILLE RAILROAD and BROOKSVILLE & OHIO RIVER RAILROAD Locomotive Roster

1	4-4-0	Baldwin						
2	4-4-0	Baldwin					from C&O Ry.	
3	4-4-0	Baldwin						
62	4-6-0	Baldwin					from SI&E. Equipped with air pumps.	
195	4-4-0	Danforth	1180	1897		62"	From C&O Ry 7/7/23. Equipped with air pumps.	
12	4-6-0						From Joe Joseph, Cincinnati. Middle drivers blind. Equipped with air pumps. Only locomotive with electric headlights. At abandonment, run to Wellsburg and scrapped.	

FLEMINGSBURG & NORTHERN RAILROAD and predecessors Locomotive Roster

1	2-6-0-ng	Baldwin		1877	16x24"	36"	Named "W.J.Hendricks". Damaged in 1907 wreck.	
2	2-6-0-ng	Baldwin			16x24"	48"		
10	2-6-0	Baldwin					From Georgia Locomotive Co. 1909. Scrapped	
9	4-6-0	Baldwin	40009	1913	15x24"	48"	Retired 1937. Scrapped	
547	2-6-0	Rogers	37555	1906	20x24"	51"	Leased from L&N 1937. Scrapped by L&N 1948	
549	2-6-0	Rogers	37557	1906	20x24"	51"	Leased from L&N 1937. Purchased from L&N 1949. Scrapped 1956.	

Chapter 12

LOUISVILLE, HARRODS CREEK & WESTPORT RAILWAY (Narrow Gauge) Locomotive Roster

Number	Type	Builder	C/N	Date	Cylinders	DD	Remarks	Scrapped
1	4-4-0			1872			Sold 1885. Named "James Callahan"	
2	4-4-0	Webster & Marks (Chattanooga)		1874			Sold 1892 to J.Joseph & Bro. for $166.91 for scrap. Named "Glenview"	
3	4-4-0			1875			Sold 1892 to Pittsburg Coal Co. for $2000. Named "Alex Duerson"	

All of these locomotives were equipped with link and pin couplers. They had no air brakes, depending entirely on the hand brakes on locomotives and cars.

Chapter 13

MOREHEAD & NORTH FORK RAILROAD Locomotive Roster

Number	Type	Builder	C/N	Date	Cylinders	DD	Remarks	Scrapped
1	0-4-2 (Forney)	Porter					From Snyder Const. Co. 1904. Sold.	
2	Shay	Lima	1946	1907	11x12"	32"	New. Sold to Clyde Eqpt.; Wheeler-Olmstead Lbr.; F. Hunter Hill; Braymill White Pine; Shaw-Bertram; Anderson & Middleton Lbr. #7; Siskiyou Lbr.; Walker Hovey Lbr.	
3	2-6-2	Baldwin		1907	17x24"	50"		
4	4-6-0	Baldwin		1890			ex- N&W.	1919
5	4-6-0	Pittsburgh		1891			ex- N&W. to Canasauga River Lbr. 1923.	
6	4-4-0	Pittsburgh	841	1888	17x24"		ex-LStL&T #3	1923
7	2-4-2 T	Porter	2001	1899			ex-Vinton Lbr. #777	1918
8	4-4-0	Rogers					ex-NC& StL	1926
9	2-6-0	Rogers	6252	1904			ex-DU #4; SI&E #1802; C&NE; SI&E #2005	1939
10	2-6-2	Cooke	65191	1926	19x26"	48"	ex-Cuban Sugar, W.P.Brown & Son Lbr., Mobile & Gulf #10; BR&L; to M&NF #10, 1939	1954
11	2-6-2	Baldwin	33333	1909	19x24"	48"	ex-McKell Coal & Coke #200, SI&E, KGJ&E; to Everett #11.	
12	0-6-0	Pittsburgh	37672	1908	20x26"	51"	ex-SRy #1643	
14	0-6-0	ALCo.	71323	1944	22x28"	51"	ex- URR #77	
M-200	Rail-car	Edwards		1926			New. Combine, seats 36. Green. To CWR&N, 1934.	

LENOX RAILROAD and LENOX SAW MILL COMPANY Locomotive Roster

Number	Type	Builder	C/N	Date	Remarks
?	Heisler	Heisler	1002	1895	Saw Mill Co. Narrow Gauge. 17 ton, 2 truck
?	Heisler	Heisler	1220	1911	Saw Mill Co. Narrow Gauge. 20 ton, 2 truck ex-Garysburg Mfg. Co.
1	Shay	Lima	2992	1918	New. LRR Standard Gauge. To Lee Coal Co.; to Dents Run Coal Co. #1.
?	Rail-car	Buda			New. To M.C.Crosley; James Rigsby; Jess Williams. Scrapped.

Chapter 14

LOUISVILLE & NASHVILLE RAILROAD Locomotive Roster*

*Used on Russellville-Adairville line, and Clarksville-Princeton Branch.

Number	Type	Builder	C/N	Date	Cylinders	DD	Remarks	Scrapped
9	4-4-0	Rogers	4134	1882	17x24"	64"	Ex-L&E #3; L&N #64	1925
10	4-4-0	Rogers		1882	17x24"	64"	ex-L&N #939	1916
11	4-4-0	Rogers		1882	17x24"	64"	ex-L&N #940	1924
16	4-4-0	Danforth & Cooke		1881	17x24"	64"	ex-L&N #457	1916
24	4-4-0	Baldwin	2212	1870	17x24"	64"	ex-L&N #83	1924
32	4-4-0	Baldwin		1870	17x24"	64"	ex-L&N #309	1929
37 (old)	4-4-0	L&N RR		1871	17x24"	59"	ex-L&N #82	1899
264	4-6-0	Baldwin	23479	1904	20x26"	67"	ex-L&N #275; to L&N #314	
320	4-6-0	Rome		1884	18x24"	55"	ex-L&N #226	1916
364	4-6-0	Baldwin		1890	19x24"	55"	ex-AK&N #18	1926
611	2-8-0	Rogers		1890	21x24"	51"	ex-BMRR	
1192	2-8-0	Rogers		1907	21x28"	57"	ex-S&NARR	
2121	4-4-0	Rogers		1875	16x24"	54"	ex- L&N #1121; #426.	1907

Number	Type	Builder	C/N	Date	Cylinders	DD	Remarks	Scrapped

Chapter 15

The original locomotive on the Jellico, Birdeye & Northern Railway was an 0-6-0, Baldwin, 1891, 18x24", 51" bearing the name "Uncle Joe", but no road number. In 1898, it was traded to the L&N for that road's No. 414, a 2-6-0 Rogers, 1872, which could better negotiate the mountain curves than "Uncle Joe" which had no pony truck. No. 414 returned to the L&N fold in 1902 when that road acquired the JB&N. It was scrapped in 1908.

At the time the L&N acquired the Middlesboro Belt Railroad it received two locomotives in the deal--No. 53 an 0-6-0 which became L&N 1022, later 2022; and No. 54, a 2-6-0, which became L&N 1033, later 2033, and still later 457.

Serving the Mowbray and Robinson Lumber Company's 42" gauge railroad were seven Climaxes, and two 53 ton, 2 truck Heislers with builder's numbers 1340 and 1400. No. 1340 to SI&E #1940 in 1916, to Williams Bros. Const. Co. No. 1400 went to SI&E #1944 in 1919, to Cross Country Gravel, Cherry Valley, Ark.

ROCKCASTLE RIVER RAILWAY and BOND-FOLEY LUMBER COMPANY Locomotive Roster

Number	Type	Builder	C/N	Date	Cylinders	DD	Remarks	Scrapped
1 "Jane"	B	Heisler	1295	1914			54 ton, 2-truck, New. To BR&L, Sunlight Coal 10/30/33	
2	2-6-2	Lima	1036	1906	16x20"		ex-T&NO #2, SI&E #989. To SI&E #1972, C&NE #2, SI&E #2206, Alcolu RR.	
3	B	Climax		1915	13x14"	31"	New. 45ton. Sold to SI&E, 1923	
4 "Sam"	B	Heisler	1320	1916			New. 52 ton, 2-truck. To BR&L, Maumee Collieries, 1933.	
5	Shay C	Lima		1916			ex-KR&C #4; to Little River Lbr. #7, Gray-Knox Marble.	
6 "Joe"	B	Heisler		1916			New.	
7	2-6-0	ALCo-Cooke		1906	19x24"	48"	For Panama RR, but never delivered. To RRRy 1923. Scrapped 1933	

Chapter 16

The Breckinridge Coal Road had one locomotive, bearing road No. 1. This was purchased new from the builder, the Pittsburgh Locomotive Works, c/n 798. Delivery was made by steamboat on July 6, 1885. The machine was an 0-4-0, 14x22" cylinders, and 43" drivers. It was sold 10/4/12 by BR&L to Albert Hansen Lbr. and shipped to Garden City, La.

LOUISVILLE, ST. LOUIS & TEXAS RAILWAY Locomotive Roster

Number	Type	Builder	C/N	Date	Cylinders	DD	Remarks	Scrapped
1	4-4-0						Bought 2nd Hand, 1888.	1897
2	4-4-0						Bought 2nd Hand, 1888.	1897
3	4-4-0	Pittsburgh	841	1888	17x24"	62"	To M&NF #6.	
4	4-4-0	Pittsburgh	842	1888	17x24"	62"		
5	4-4-0	Pittsburgh	863	1888	17x24"	62"		1933
6	4-4-0	Pittsburgh	864	1888	17x24"	62"	Sold	
7	4-4-0	Pittsburgh	895	1888	17x24"	62"		
8	4-4-0	Pittsburgh	839	1888	17x24"	62"	To Cheyenne RR #8, 1913.	
9	4-4-0	Pittsburgh	896	1888	17x24"	62"		
10	4-4-0	Pittsburgh	917	1889	17x24"	62"		
11	4-6-0	Pittsburgh	1102	1890	18x24"	50"	To Hemphill Lumber Co.	
12	4-6-0	Pittsburgh	1103	1890	18x24"	50"	To Alabama Central Rwy. #12	
13	4-6-0	Pittsburgh	1168	1890	18x24"	50"		
14	4-6-0	Pittsburgh	1169	1890	18x24"	50"		
15	4-6-0	Pittsburgh	1170	1890	18x24"	50"		
16	4-6-0	Pittsburgh	1380	1892	18x24"	50"		
17	4-6-0	Pittsburgh	1381	1892	18x24"	50"	To Arcade & Attica RR #5	
18	4-6-0	Pittsburgh	1382	1892	18x24"	50"		

All of these locomotives to LH&StL, 1896. Nos. 5 and 6 to L&N, 1929.

Chapter 17

The Chatteroi Railway owned six light locomotives, four of which were 8-wheel passenger engines, and two (Nos. 6 and 7) were Baldwin moguls. All were equipped with link and pin couplers and Eams' vacuum brakes.

EASTERN KENTUCKY RAILWAY and EAST KENTUCKY SOUTHERN RAILWAY Locomotive Roster

Number	Type	Builder	C/N	Date	Cylinders	DD	Remarks	Scrapped
1 (1st)	0-4-0	Porter						
2 (1st)	4-4-0	PRR					"Argillite"	
3 (1st)	0-4-0	Porter						
4 (1st)	2-6-0	Baldwin		1873			"Carter" New from Builder	
5 (1st)	4-4-0						"Alice"	
1 (2nd)	4-6-0	NJL&M		1867			ex-PRR #418	
2 (2nd)	4-6-0	PRR					Sold 1911 to SI&E	
3 (2nd)	4-4-0	PRR				72"		1911
4 (2nd)	4-6-0	PRR					Sold 1912 to SI&E	
5 (2nd)	4-6-0	Schenectady		1892			ex-C&O #121 Class F-10 (1912)	
6	4-6-0	Schenectady		1892			ex-C&O #123 Class F-10 (1912)	
291	2-8-0	Cooke		1883			ex-C&O #291 Class G-1 (1921) was to be EK #7.	
M-1	rail car				gas motor			
M-2	rail car		trailer		gas motor		"Blue Goose"	
215	rail car	Mack Trucks Brill body	70005	1921	Model AB gas motor		"Queen" ex-Sewell Valley #29 purchased 2nd Hand by EKS Rwy.	1933

Chapter 21

MAMMOTH CAVE RAILROAD Locomotive Roster

Number	Type	Builder	C/N	Date	Cylinders	DD	Remarks
1	0-4-2 T	Baldwin	9539	1888	12x16"	37"	ex-Nashville & West Nashville RR #4 Steam Dummy type
2	0-4-2 T	Baldwin	9142	1888	12x18"	42"	ex-East End Rwy. (Memphis) Steam Dummy type
3	0-4-2 T	Baldwin	9456	1888	12x16"	37"	ex-N&WN RR #3 "Hercules" Steam Dummy type
4	0-4-2 T	Baldwin	9442	1888	12x18"	40"	ex-EE Ry. Steam Dummy type

Chapter 22

CUMBERLAND RAILROAD and ARTEMUS-JELLICO RAILROAD Locomotive Roster

Number	Type	Builder	C/N	Date	Cylinders	DD	Remarks
142	2-8-0	Schenectady	2906	1889	20x24"	50"	ex-ETV&G #454. To A-J #142 (1926); To Dripping Springs RR (1935).
175	2-8-0	Richmond	2676	1897	21x26"	56"	ex-SC&G #57. 85 ton.
176	2-8-0	Richmond	2677	1897	21x26"	56"	ex-SC&G #58. 85 ton.
177	2-8-0	Richmond	2678	1897	21x26"	56"	ex-SC&G #59. 85 ton. To A-J #177 (1926) Scrapped 1933
282	2-8-0	Richmond	2913	1899	21x28"	60"	
361	2-8-0	Baldwin	19685	1901	21x28"	60"	
3384	4-6-0	Cooke	1304	1882	18x24"	60"	ex-ETV&C #77
15	2-8-0	Brooks	55416	1915	21x28"	57"	ex-DT&I #95, BR&L; to A-J 4/23/35. To BR&L (traded in on A-J #33), to Lancaster & Chester #42.
16	2-8-0	Baldwin	40944	1913	21x28"		Bought from BR&L Co. for $5475. ex-Ligonier Valley #16. 86 ton. Scrapped 1952
33	2-8-0	Brooks	45723	1908			ex-Birm.-Sou. #33, BR&L; to A-J, 10/27/38; Scrapped 1952
1	Rail car	Mack Trucks Brill body	60005	1921	Model AC gas motor		ex-Lewisburg, Milton & Watstown Passenger Rwy. #20; ex-PRR #4738: To A-J #1 (1931); to BC&G # "A" (1941)

KENTUCKY & TENNESSEE RAILWAY and STEARNS COAL & LUMBER CO. Locomotive Roster

Number	Type	Builder	C/N	Date	Cylinders	DD	Remarks	Scrapped
1	2-8-0	Schenectady	27409	1903	22x26"	51"	New.	1953
2	Shay	Lima	874	1904	10x12"	29½"	New. To Ga. Car & Loco.; Grasse River #6	
3	Shay	Lima	1530	1905	10x12"	29½"	New. To Raleigh Lbr.Co.,1909; SI&E #720 Smokey Mtn.#1, Ritter Lbr. #5.	1942
4	Shay	Lima	1675	1906	10x12"	29½"	New. To Millstead Mfg., 1909	
5	0-4-0T	Porter	406	1881			ex-Lucy Furnace #3; to SI&E #1211, Pittsburgh Constr. #5, 1917	
6	0-6-0T	Baldwin	4202	1877			ex-Memphis & Little Rock #16, Cincinnati Equip.	1920
7	2-8-2	Baldwin	32763	1908	21x24"	44"	New.	1951
8	2-6-2	Baldwin	37269	1911	20x24"	51"	New.	1951
9	2-6-0	Pittsburgh	44416	1907			ex-Atlantic Eqpt. & Const. #1, SA&N #1	1940
10	2-8-2	Baldwin	53182	1920	24x30"	56"	New. To Tennessee Valley Railway Museum, 1964	
11	2-8-2	Schenectady	63271	1922	25x30"	56"	New. To Aberdeen Proving Grounds, 1963	1966
12	2-8-2	Baldwin	37085	1911	27x30"	63"	ex-Sou $4501. To Paul H. Merriman 1964	
2	B-B	ALCo.	69925	1942	Diesel-Electric		ex-NYC&St.L. Acquired 1964.	

Chapter 23

FRANKFORT & CINCINNATI RAILROAD and predecessor Locomotive Roster

Number	Type	Builder	C/N	Date	Cylinders	DD	Remarks	Scrapped
1	4-4-0	Pittsburgh		1889	17x24"	62"	Ky. Midland #1; Sold 1897	
1 (2nd)	4-4-0	Pittsburgh	751	1885	17x24"	68"	ex-C&IC #1, C&EI #201, #111	
2	4-4-0	Pittsburgh		1889	17x24"	62"	Ky. Midland #2	
3	4-4-0	Pittsburgh	750	1885	17x24"	62"	ex-C&IC #2, C&EI #202, #112	
4	4-4-0	Pittsburgh	787	1885	17x24"	62"	ex-C&IC #3, C&EI #203, #113	
5	4-4-0	Baldwin					ex-N&W	
6	4-4-0	Rogers					ex-C&NW	
7	4-6-0	Baldwin	12726	1889	19x24"	60"	ex-L&E #9; L&N #365.	
8	2-6-0	Baldwin	26092	1905	19x24"	52"	ex-L&A #12; L&N #556.	
9	2-6-0	Baldwin	24845	1904	19x24"	52"	ex-L&A #11; L&N #555.	
10	2-8-2	Baldwin	57071	1923	18x24"	44"	ex-Maryland & Delaware Coast #201, SI&E. to F&C 1933	
11	2-8-0	Schenectady	65199	1923	18x24"	44"	Rebuilt 1934 by Schenectady for F&C.	
12	2-8-0	Schenectady	65197	1923	18x24"	44"	Purchased from Ferguson Co. Sold 1947 to Jeffersonville Boat & Machine Co.	
14	2-8-0	Schenectady	65198	1923	18x24"	44"	ex- West River (Vt.)#1 Sold to St. Regis Paper Co.	
15	2-8-0	Lima	5929	1920		45½"	ex-AT&N #202; acquired March 1945	
16	2-8-0	Lima	6958	1925		45½"	ex-AT&N #205; acquired March 1945	
M-55-1	rail car	Brill		1927	gas motor			
2	rail car	Brill		1927	gas motor		ex-L&NE #90	
100	B-B	Alco-GE		1946	Diesel-Electric		New.	
101	B-B	Alco-GE		1947	Diesel-Electric		New.	
102	B-B	Alco-GE		1947	Diesel-Electric		New.	

Appendix 2

Chronology and Mileage Table of Abandonments

Year Abandoned	Trackage and Owner at Time of Abandonment	Mileage	Discussed in Chapter
1848(?)	Jett-Frankfort (Lexington & Frankfort RR)	6.00	20
1856(?)	Louisville-Portland (Louisville & Frankfort RR)	3.00	20
1890(?)	Flat Rock-Barren Fork (Barren Fork Mining & Coal Co.)	2.00	15
1891(?)	Limestone to timber (Panther Gap RR)	4.75	13
1892	Walbridge-Peach Orchard (C&O Ry)	12.30	17
1893	Music-Bituminous Mine and Stinson Cannel Mine (Lexington & Carter County Mining Company's RR)	7.00	17
1893(?)	Pine Hill to tunnel (Pine Hill RR)	3.00	15
1893	Bull's Eye Spring Narrow Gauge Railroad (Brown's Carter County Lumber Company's RR)	8.00	17
1893(?)	Greenwood to Beaver coal mine (Greenwood RY & Coal Co.)	6.50	15
1894(?)	Rodburn to timber (Triplett & Big Sandy RR)	5.00	13
1895(?)	Whitehouse to timber (Stafford Fork Tram RR)	8.00	17
1896	Yosemite-Kings Mountain (Cincinnati & Green River RY)	13.00	5
1897	Middlesboro east and west belts (L&N RR)	6.24	15
1897	Middlesboro-Stony Fork (L&N RR)	5.84	15
1898	Cloverport-Victoria (Breckinridge Coal Road)	8.50	16
1899	Altamont-Diamond (L&N RR)	2.50	15
1900	Rodburn-Pine Springs (Kentucky Northern RR)	9.00	13
1901(?)	Mingo Creek-Firebrick (Indian Run RY)	4.50	17
1907	Caney-Piedmont (Caney, Piedmont & Morehead RR)	3.50	4
1907	Flemingsburg-Hillsboro (Cincinnati, Flemingsburg & Southeastern RR)	11.00	10
1908	Amos-Apperson (Red River Valley RR)	5.00	7
1908(?)	Jackson-Robbins (Kentucky Lumber & Veneer RR)	12.00	15
1908	Lawton Jct.-Brinegar (Portsmouth & Tygert Valley RR)	6.25	13
1909	Artemus-Coalport (Coalport RR)	3.00	22
1909	Jellico-Red Ash (L&N RR)	3.75	15
1909	KN Jct.-Simcoe (Kentucky Northern RR)	8.00	5
1909(?)	Lombard to timber (Big Woods, Red River & Lombard RR)	10.00	5
1909(?)	Torrent to timber (Red River & Beattyville Southern RR)	7.00	15
1909(?)	Tallega to timber (K&F Lumber Co. RR)	30.00	15
1910	Penrod-Mud River Mine (L&N RR)	4.49	18
1911	Rothwell-McCausey (Red River Valley RR)	14.00	9
1911	Trackage in Columbus (St. Louis, Iron Mountain & Southern RR)	1.00	19
1912	Salt Lick-Blackwater (Licking River RR)	32.30	9
1914	Halsey-Myrlin (L&N RR)	4.34	15
1916	Ida May to timber (English Narrow Gauge)	10.00	5
1916	Brush Creek-Johnetta (L&N RR)	4.85	15
1918	DeKoven to Ohio River (IC RR)	1.75	18
1918	Olympia-Owingsville (Owingsville & Olympia RR)	6.00	9
1923	Dumont-Quicksand (L&N RR)	1.03	15
1923	Quicksand to timber (Mowbray & Robinson Lumber Co.)	65.00	15
1923	Wild Dog-Turkey Foot (Kentucky, Rockcastle & Cumberland RR)	7.10	5
1926	Riverton-Grayson (Eastern Kentucky RY)	23.01	17
1927	Redwine-Rush Branch (Lenox RR)	7.70	13
1928	Campton Jct.-Campton (Mountain Central RY)	12.31	2

Year	Line	Miles	Ref
1928(?)	Lunsford (Kay Jay)-Wheeler (Artemus-Jellico RR)	1.50	22
1928	Columbus-South Columbus (GM&O RR)	1.60	19
1929	Myrlin-Keswick (L&N RR)	1.39	15
1929	Glidden-Kawood (L&N RR)	2.72	15
1930	Wild Dog-Banford (Kentucky, Rockcastle & Cumberland RR)	3.00	5
1931	Bond-Mckee (Bond-Foley Lumber Co.)	10.63	15
1931	Brooksville-Wellsburg (Brooksville & Ohio River RR)	9.89	10
1931	Mt. Sterling-Rothwell (C&O RY)	19.70	7
1931	Park City-Mammoth Cave (Mammoth Cave RR)	8.70	21
1931	Wilton-Wilton Jct. (L&N RR)	3.97	15
1932	East Bernstadt-Viva (L&N RR)	2.91	15
1932	Maxie-Kensee (L&N RR)	1.75	15
1932	Millville-Irvine (L&N RR)	70.20	3
1932	Viva-Bond (Rockcastle River RY)	12.72	15
1933	Chenoa-Grenada (L&N RR)	3.89	15
1933	Clack Mountain Tunnel-Redwine (Morehead & North Fork RR)	21.00	13
1933	Gracey-Princeton Jct. ...(in Ky.) (L&N RR)	23.00	14
1933	Grayson-Webbville (East Kentucky Southern RY)	13.06	17
1933	O&K Jct.-Licking River (Ohio & Kentucky RY, and Caney Valley RY)	38.58	4
1934	Lancaster-Fort Estill (L&N RR)	22.89	8
1934	Major-Henderson (IC RR)	3.92	18
1934	Poplar-Gesling (C&O RY)	4.14	11
1935	Banford-Caryton (Kentucky, Rockcastle & Cumberland RR)	8.00	5
1935	Heidelberg-Ida May (L&N RR)	2.98	3-5
1935	Water Works-Prospect (Louisville & Interurban RR)	7.70	12
1936	Clay-Dixon (IC RR)	10.40	18
1937	Saxton-Jellico (L&N RR)	2.08	15
1938	Burgin-Burgin Jct. (Southern RY)	3.80	6
1938	McClain-milepost 4 ...(in Ky.) (IC RR)	1.00	18
1938	Russellville-Adairville (L&N RR)	11.77	14
1939	Clay-Morganfield (L&N RR)	17.91	18
1939	Peach Orchard-Richardson (C&O RY)	2.74	17
1940	Versailles-Georgetown (Southern RY)	16.74	6
1941	Dempster-Falls of Rough (L&N RR)	4.45	16
1941	Ellmitch-Hartford (L&N RR)	19.22	16
1941	Garrison-Poplar (C&O RY)	17.40	11
1941	Irvington-Fordsville (L&N RR)	37.73	16
1941	Junction-Hardinsburg (L&N RR)	1.73	16
1942	Duane-Pioneer (L&N RR)	1.04	17
1942	Jellico-Elk Fork Bridge (L&N RR)	.25	15
1942	North Winchester-Fincastle (L&N RR)	46.26	1
1943	Barlow-East Cairo (IC RR)	7.18	19
1943	Como-Madisonville (L&N RR)	1.85	18
1944	Chenoa-Olcott (L&N RR)	1.00	15
1945	Lunsford (Kay Jay)-Anchor (Artemus-Jellico RR)	2.70	22
1946	Indian Creek and Black Gold Quarries to Kyrock (Ky. Rock Asphalt Co.)	12.00	18
1947	Fincastle-Maloney (L&N RR)	6.07	1
1947	Nevisdale-Packard (L&N RR)	2.49	15
1948	Rodburn to clay mines ("Christy Creek RR")	7.20	13
1948	White Oak Jct.-Bell Farm (Kentucky & Tennessee RY)	8.32	22
1950	Burnside Jct.-Burnside Landing (Cincinnati, Burnside & Cumberland River RY)	2.70	15
1950	Lowndes-McRoberts (L&N RR)	1.63	17
1951	Hickman-Union City ....(in Ky.) (NC&StL RY)	10.50	19
1951	Chicle-Paris (L&N RR)	12.68	20
1952	Bloomfield Jct.-Bloomfield (L&N RR)	26.60	20
1952	Artemus-Kay Jay (Artemus-Jellico RR)	8.70	22
1952	Wheelwright-Wheelwright Jct. (C&O RY)	1.50	17
1953	Oz-Co-Operative (Kentucky & Tennessee RY)	2.41	22
1954	Junction-Adalia (L&N RR)	2.16	17
1955	Flemingsburg-Flemingsburg Jct. (F&N RR)	5.60	10
1957	Elkton-Guthrie (E&G RR)	10.95	14
1960	LaGrange-Eminence (L&N RR)	11.85	20
1964	Millard-Nigh (C&O RY)	19.50	17
1967	Georgetown-Paris (Frankfort & Cincinnati RR)	16.7	23

Appendix 3

Abandoned Railroads by Counties

County	Railroad	Described in Chapter
BALLARD	Illinois Central Railroad	19
BARREN	Mammoth Cave Railroad	21
BATH	Licking River Railroad	9
	Owingsville & Olympia Railroad	9
BELL	Louisville & Nashville Railroad	15-17
BOURBON	**Frankfort** & Cincinnati Railroad	23
	Louisville & Nashville Railroad	20
BRACKEN	Brooksville & Ohio River Railroad	10
BREATHITT	Kentucky Lumber & Veneer Railroad	15
	Louisville & Nashville Railroad	15
	Mowbray & Robinson Lumber Co.	15
	Ohio & Kentucky Railway	4
BRECKINRIDGE	Breckinridge Coal Road	16
	Louisville & Nashville Railroad	16
CARTER	Bull's Eye Spring Narrow Gauge Railroad	17
	Chesapeake & Ohio Railway	11
	Eastern Kentucky Railway	17
	East Kentucky Southern Railway	17
	Lexington & Carter Co. Mining Co.'s RR	17
	Panther Gap Railroad	13
	Portsmouth & Tygert Valley Railroad	13
CASEY	Cincinnati & Kentucky Southern Railroad	5
CHRISTIAN	Louisville & Nashville Railroad	14
CLARK	Louisville & Nashville Railroad	1
EDMONSON	Kentucky Rock Asphalt Co.	18
	Mammoth Cave Railroad	21
ESTILL	Kentucky Northern Railroad	5
	Louisville & Nashville Railroad	3
FAYETTE	Louisville & Nashville Railroad	20
FLEMING	Cincinnati, Flemingsburg & Southeast. RR.	10
	Flemingsburg & Northern Railroad	10
FLOYD	Chesapeake & Ohio Railway	17
FRANKLIN	Lexington & Frankfort Railroad	20
FULTON	Nashville, Chattanooga & St. Louis Ry.	19
GARRARD	Louisville & Nashville Railroad	8
GREENUP	Eastern Kentucky Railway	17
	Indian Run Railway	17
HANCOCK	Breckinridge Coal Road	16
HARLAN	Louisville & Nashville Railroad	15
HENRY	Louisville & Nashville Railroad	20
HICKMAN	Gulf, Mobile & Ohio Railroad	19
	St. Louis, Iron Mountain & Southern RR	19
HENDERSON	Illinois Central Railroad	18
HOPKINS	Louisville & Nashville Railroad	18
JACKSON	Bond-Foley Lumber Co.	15
	Kentucky, Rockcastle & Cumberland RR	5
	Rockcastle River Railway	15
	Turkey Foot Lumber Co.	3-5
JEFFERSON	Louisville & Frankfort Railroad	20
	Louisville & Interurban Railroad	12
JESSAMINE	Louisville & Nashville Railroad	3
KNOX	Artemus-Jellico Railroad	22
	Coalport Railroad	22
LAUREL	Louisville & Nashville Railroad	15
	Rockcastle River Railway	15
LAWRENCE	Chesapeake & Ohio Railway	17
	East Kentucky Southern Railway	17
	Stafford Fork Tram Railroad	17
LEE	English Narrow Gauge	5
	K & F Lumber Co.	15
	Kentucky Northern Railroad	5
	Kentucky, Rockcastle & Cumberland RR	3-5
	Louisville & Nashville Railroad	1-3-5
	Red River & Beattyville Southern Railroad	15
LETCHER	Louisville & Nashville Railroad	17
LEWIS	Chesapeake & Ohio Railway	**11**
	Indian Run Railway	17
LINCOLN	Cincinnati & Kentucky Southern Railroad	5
LOGAN	Louisville & Nashville Railroad	14
McCREARY	Barren Fork Mining & Coal Co.	15
	Greenwood Railway & Coal Co.	15
	Kentucky & Tennessee Railway	22
	Stearns Coal & Lumber Co.	22
MADISON	Louisville & Nashville Railroad	3-8
MENIFEE	Big Woods, Red River & Lombard Railroad	5
	Chesapeake & Ohio Railway	7
	Licking River Railroad	9
	Red River Valley Railroad	7
MERCER	Southern Railway	6
MONTGOMERY	Chesapeake & Ohio Railway	7
MORGAN	Caney, Piedmont & Morehead Railroad	4
	Lenox Railroad	13
	Licking River Railroad	9
	Morehead & North Fork Railroad	13
	Ohio & Kentucky Railway	4
MUHLENBERG	Louisville & Nashville Railroad	18
NELSON	Louisville & Nashville Railroad	20
OHIO	Louisville & Nashville Railroad	16
OLDHAM	Louisville & Nashville Railroad	20
OWSLEY	English Narrow Gauge	5
	K & F Lumber Company	15
	Kentucky, Rockcastle & Cumberland RR	5
PERRY	Louisville & Nashville Railroad	17
PIKE	Chesapeake & Ohio Railway	17
POWELL	Big Woods, Red River & Lombard RR	5
	Louisville & Nashville Railroad	1
	Mountain Central Railway	2
PULASKI	Cincinnati, Burnside & Cumb. River Ry	15
ROCKCASTLE	Louisville & Nashville Railroad	15
	Pine Hill Railroad	15
ROWAN	"Christy Creek Railroad"	13
	Kentucky Northern RR (Rowan Co.)	13
	Morehead & North Fork Railroad	13
	Triplett & Big Sandy Railroad	13
SCOTT	Frankfort & Cincinnati Railroad	23
	Southern Railway	6
SHELBY	Louisville & Nashville Railroad	20
SPENCER	Louisville & Nashville Railroad	20
TODD	Elkton & Guthrie Railroad	14
UNION	Illinois Central Railroad	18
	Louisville & Nashville Railroad	18
WEBSTER	Illinois Central Railroad	18
	Louisville & Nashville Railroad	18
WHITLEY	Louisville & Nashville Railroad	15
WOLFE	Louisville & Nashville Railroad	1
	Mountain Central Railway	2
	Ohio & Kentucky Railway	4
WOODFORD	Louisville & Nashville Railroad	3
	Southern Railway	6

Appendix 4

Kentucky's Abandoned Narrow Gauge Railroads

Name	Gauge	Changed to Standard or Wider Gauge	Year Abandoned	Described In Chapter
Big Woods, Red River & Lombard RR	36"	—	1909(?)	5
Bull's Eye Spring Narrow Gauge RR	42½"	—	1893	17
Cincinnati & Green River RY	36"	1884	1896	5
Cincinnati, Flemingsburg & Southeastern RR, and Flemingsburg & Northern RR	36"	1909 (in part)	1907 (in part) 1955 (in part)	10
DeKoven Coal Road	44½"	1903(?)	1918	18
English Narrow Gauge	36"	—	1916	5
Indiana, Alabama & Texas RR	36"	1887	1933 (in part)	14
K & F Lumber Company RR	36"	—	1909(?)	15
Kentucky Lumber & Veneer RR	36"	—	1908(?)	15
Ky. Northern RR (Rowan County)	36"	—	1900	13
Kentucky Rock Asphalt Co.	36"	—	1946	18
Louisville, Harrods Creek & Westport RR	36"	1888	1935 (in part)	12
Lenox RR	36"	1918	1927	13
Lexington & Carter Co. Mining Co's RR	44"	—	1893(?)	17
Lula Road	36"	—	1894(?)	15
Licking River RR	36"	—	1912	9
Miller Creek Logging Co. RR	36"	—	1908(?)	5
Mt. Sterling Coal Road	36"	1895	1931	7
Mountain Central RY	36"	—	1928	2
Mowbray & Robinson Lumber Co.	42"	—	1923	15
Owingsville & Olympia RR	36"	—	1918	9
Pine Hill RR	36"	—	1893(?)	15
Portsmouth & Tygert Valley RR	36"	—	1908	13
Red River & Beattyville Southern RR	36"	—	1909(?)	15
Red River Valley RR	36"	—	1908 & 1911	7
Simcoe Land Co. RR	36"	—	1908(?)	7
Stafford Fork Tram Road	36"	—	1895(?)	17
Triplett & Big Sandy RR	36"	—	1894	13

Appendix 5

Abandoned Mileages by Trunk-Line Systems

Railroad	Mileage Abandoned
Chesapeake & Ohio Railway	77.28
Gulf, Mobile & Ohio Railroad	1.60
Illinois Central Railroad	24.25
Louisville & Nashville Railroad	388.00*
St. Louis, Iron Mountain & Southern Railroad	1.00
Southern Railway System	23.24**

*includes 10.50 miles abandoned by the Nashville, Chattanooga & St. Louis Railway.

**includes 2.70 miles abandoned by the Cincinnati, Burnside & Cumberland River Railway.

Appendix 6

Index and Cross-References of Abandoned Line Names

Note 1: A dash (———) in the "Preceding Name" or "Succeeding Name" column indicates that the railroad had no preceding or succeeding name, respectively.

Note 2: Since the purpose of this compilation is to facilitate the identification of names, the use of the words "railroad" and "railway" in the titles is eliminated. Recourse to the chapters indicated will provide full information on the **exact** names of the railroads involved.

Name	Preceding Name	Succeeding Name	Described in Chapter
ALTAMONT & MANCHESTER	———	Louisville & Nashville	15
ARTEMUS-JELLICO	Cumberland	———	22
BARREN FORK MINING & COAL COMPANY	———	———	15
BEATTYVILLE & CUMBERLAND GAP	Winchester & Beattyville	Louisville & Atlantic	1-3
BEAVER CREEK & CUMBERLAND RIVER	Greenwood Railway & Coal Co.	———	15
BIG WOODS, RED RIVER & LOMBARD	———	———	5
BOND-FOLEY LUMBER CO.	———	———	15
BRECKINRIDGE COAL ROAD	———	———	16
BROOKSVILLE	———	Brooksville & Ohio River	10
BROOKSVILLE & OHIO RIVER	Brooksville	———	10
BULL'S EYE SPRING NARROW GAUGE	———	———	17
BURNSIDE & CINCINNATI	Burnside & Cumberland River	Cincinnati, Burnside & Cumberland River	15
BURNSIDE & CUMBERLAND RIVER	———	Burnside & Cincinnati	15
CANEY & WEST LIBERTY	———	Caney, Piedmont & Morehead	4
CANEY, PIEDMONT & MOREHEAD	Caney & West Liberty	———	4
CANEY VALLEY	———	———	4
CHATTAROI	———	Ohio & Big Sandy	17
CHESAPEAKE & OHIO	Kentucky & South Atlantic	———	7
	Kinniconnick & Freestone	———	11
	Ohio & Big Sandy	———	17
	Levisa River	———	17
CHICAGO, ST. LOUIS & NEW ORLEANS	Kentucky Western	Illinois Central	18
CHRISTY CREEK	———	Illinois Central	19
CINCINNATI & GREEN RIVER	Cincinnati, Green River & Nashville	Cincinnati & Kentucky Southern	5
CINCINNATI & KENTUCKY SOUTHERN	Cincinnati & Green River	———	5
CINCINNATI & SOUTHEASTERN	Covington, Flemingsburg & Southeastern	Covington, Flemingsburg & Ashland	10
CINCINNATI, BURNSIDE & CUMBERLAND RIVER	Burnside & Cincinnati	———	15
CINCINNATI, FLEMINGSBURG & SOUTHEASTERN	Covington, Flemingsburg & Ashland	Flemingsburg & Northern	10
CINCINNATI, GREEN RIVER & NASHVILLE	———	Cincinnati & Green River	5
COALPORT	———	———	22
COVINGTON & LEXINGTON	Maysville & Lexington	Maysville & Lexington	20
COVINGTON, FLEMINGSBURG & ASHLAND	Cincinnati & Southeastern	Cincinnati, Flemingsburg & Southeastern	10
COVINGTON, FLEMINGSBURG & SOUTHEASTERN	Licking Valley	Cincinnati & Southeastern	10
COVINGTON, FLEMINGSBURG & POUND GAP	———	Licking Valley	10
CUMBERLAND	———	Artemus-Jellico	22
CUMBERLAND & OHIO	———	Louisville, Cincinnati & Lexington	20
DeKOVEN COAL ROAD	———	Ohio Valley	18
EASTERN KENTUCKY	Kentucky Improvement Co.	East Kentucky Southern	17
EAST KENTUCKY SOUTHERN	Eastern Kentucky	———	17
ELKTON	———	Elkton & Guthrie	14
ELKTON & GUTHRIE	Elkton	———	14
ENGLISH NARROW GAUGE	———	———	5
EVANSVILLE, OWENSBORO & NASHVILLE	Owensboro & Russellville	Owensboro & Nashville	14
FISHER POLE ROAD	———	———	17
FLEMINGSBURG & NORTHERN	Cincinnati, Flemingsburg & Southeastern	———	10

FRANKFORT & CINCINNATI	Kentucky Midland	—	23
GREENWOOD RAILWAY & COAL CO.	Beaver Creek & Cumberland River	—	15
GULF, MOBILE & OHIO	Mobile & Ohio	—	19
HICKMAN & OBION	—	Nashville & Northwestern	19
ILLINOIS CENTRAL	Chicago, St. Louis & New Orleans	—	18-19
	Ohio Valley	—	18
INDIANA, ALABAMA & TEXAS	—	Louisville & Nashville	14
INDIAN RUN	—	—	17
JELLICO, BIRDEYE & NORTHERN	—	Louisville & Nashville	15
K & F LUMBER CO.	—	—	15
KENSEE COAL ROAD	—	Louisville & Nashville	15
KENTUCKY & SOUTH ATLANTIC	Mt. Sterling Coal Road	Chesapeake & Ohio	7
KENTUCKY & TENNESSEE	—	—	22
KENTUCKY CENTRAL	Louisville & Nashville	Louisville & Nashville	8
	Maysville & Lexington	Louisville & Nashville	20
KENTUCKY COAL DEVELOPMENT CO.	—	Louisville & Atlantic	3-5
KENTUCKY HIGHLANDS	—	Louisville & Nashville	3
KENTUCKY IMPROVEMENT CO.	—	Eastern Kentucky	17
KENTUCKY LUMBER & VENEER	—	—	15
KENTUCKY MIDLAND	Paris, Georgetown & Cincinnati	Frankfort & Cincinnati	23
KENTUCKY NORTHERN (Estill-Lee Counties)	—	—	7
KENTUCKY NORTHERN (Rowan County)	—	—	13
KENTUCKY ROCK ASPHALT CO.	—	—	18
KENTUCKY, ROCKCASTLE & CUMBERLAND	Turkey Foot Lumber Co.	—	5
KENTUCKY UNION	—	Lexington & Eastern	1
KENTUCKY WESTERN	—	Chicago, St. Louis & New Orleans	18
KINNICONNICK & FREESTONE	—	Chesapeake & Ohio	11
LENOX	Roper-Reese Lumber Co.	—	13
LEVISA RIVER	—	Chesapeake & Ohio	17
LEXINGTON & CARTER COUNTY MINING COMPANY'S RR	—	—	17
LEXINGTON & EASTERN	Kentucky Union	Louisville & Nashville	1-15
LEXINGTON & FRANKFORT	Lexington & Ohio	Louisville, Cincinnati & Lexington	20
LEXINGTON & OHIO	—	Lexington & Frankfort	20
LICKING RIVER	Licking Valley	—	9
LICKING VALLEY (Bath County)	—	Licking River	9
LICKING VALLEY (Fleming County)	Covington, Flemingsburg & Pound Gap	Covington, Flemingsburg & Southeastern	10
LOUISVILLE & ATLANTIC	Beattyville & Cumberland Gap	Louisville & Nashville	3
	Richmond, Nicholasville, Irvine & Beattyville	Louisville & Nashville	3
LOUISVILLE & FRANKFORT	Lexington & Ohio	Louisville, Cincinnati & Lexington	20
LOUISVILLE & INTERURBAN	Louisville & Nashville	—	12
LOUISVILLE & NASHVILLE	Altamont & Manchester	—	15
	Indiana, Alabama & Texas	—	14
	Jellico, Birdeye & Northern	—	15
	Kensee Coal Road	—	15
	Kentucky Central	—	8-20
	Lexington & Eastern	—	1-15
	Louisville & Atlantic	—	3
	Louisville, Cincinnati & Lexington	Louisville & Interurban	12
	Louisville, Cincinnati & Lexington	—	20
	Louisville, Henderson & St. Louis	—	16
	Madisonville, Hartford & Eastern	—	16
	Middlesboro Belt	—	15
	Morganfield & Atlanta	—	18
	Owensboro & Nashville	—	14
	Proctor Coal Company's Road	—	15
	—		15-17-18
LOUISVILLE, CINCINNATI & LEXINGTON	Cumberland & Ohio	Louisville & Nashville	16
	Lexington & Frankfort	Louisville & Nashville	20
	Louisville & Frankfort	Louisville & Nashville	20
	Louisville, Harrods Creek & Westport	Louisville & Nashville	12

Railroad	Predecessor	Successor	Chapter
LOUISVILLE, HARDINSBURG & WESTERN	—	Louisville, St. Louis & Texas	16
LOUISVILLE, HARRODS CREEK & WESTPORT	—	Louisville, Cincinnati & Lexington	12
LOUISVILLE, HENDERSON & ST. LOUIS	Louisville, St. Louis & Texas	Louisville & Nashville	16
LOUISVILLE, ST. LOUIS & TEXAS	Louisville, Hardinsburg & Western	Louisville, Henderson & St. Louis	16
LOUISVILLE SOUTHERN	Southwestern	Southern	6
	Versailles & Midway	Southern	6
MADISONVILLE, HARTFORD & EASTERN	—	Louisville & Nashville	16
MAMMOTH CAVE	—	—	21
MAYSVILLE & LEXINGTON	—	Covington & Lexington	20
	Covington & Lexington	Kentucky Central	20
MIDDLESBORO BELT	—	Louisville & Nashville	15
MISSOURI PACIFIC	St. Louis, Iron Mountain & Southern	—	19
MOBILE, CLARKSVILLE & EVANSVILLE	—	Indiana, Alabama & Texas	14
MOREHEAD & NORTH FORK	—	—	13
MOREHEAD & WEST LIBERTY	—	—	13
MOBILE & OHIO	—	Gulf, Mobile & Ohio	19
MORGANFIELD & ATLANTA	—	Louisville & Nashville	18
MOUNTAIN CENTRAL	—	—	2
MT. STERLING COAL ROAD	—	Kentucky & South Atlantic	7
MOWBRAY & ROBINSON LUMBER CO.	—	—	15
NASHVILLE & CHATTANOOGA	Nashville & Northwestern	Nashville, Chattanooga & St. Louis	19
NASHVILLE, CHATTANOOGA & ST. LOUIS	Nashville & Chattanooga	—	19
NASHVILLE & NORTHWESTERN	Hickman & Obion	Nashville & Chattanooga	19
OHIO & BIG SANDY	Chattaroi	Chesapeake & Ohio	17
OHIO & KENTUCKY	—	—	4
OHIO VALLEY	—	Illinois Central	18
	DeKoven Coal Road	Illinois Central	18
OLYMPIA & OWINGSVILLE	Owingsville & Olympia	—	9
OWENSBORO & NASHVILLE	Evansville, Owensboro & Nashville	Louisville & Nashville	14
OWENSBORO & RUSSELLVILLE	—	Evansville, Owensboro & Nashville	14
OWINGSVILLE & OLYMPIA	—	Olympia & Owingsville	9
PANTHER GAP	—	—	13
PARIS, GEORGETOWN & FRANKFORT	—	Kentucky Midland	23
PINE HILL	—	—	15
PORTSMOUTH & TYGERT VALLEY	—	—	13
PRINCETON & OHIO RIVER	—	Indiana, Alabama & Texas	14
PROCTOR COAL COMPANY'S ROAD	—	Louisville & Nashville	15
RED RIVER & BEATTYVILLE SOUTHERN	—	—	15
RED RIVER VALLEY	—	—	7
RICHMOND, NICHOLASVILLE, IRVINE & BEATTYVILLE	—	Louisville & Atlantic	3
ROCKCASTLE RAILWAY	—	Rockcastle River	15
ROCKCASTLE RIVER	Rockcastle Railway	—	15
ROPER-REESE LUMBER CO.	—	Lenox	13
ST. LOUIS, IRON MOUNTAIN & SOUTHERN	—	Missouri Pacific	19
SOUTHERN	Louisville Southern	—	6
SOUTHWESTERN	—	Louisville Southern	6
STAFFORD FORK TRAM	—	—	17
STEARNS COAL & LUMBER CO.	—	—	22
TRIPLETT & BIG SANDY	—	—	13
TURKEY FOOT LUMBER CO.	—	Kentucky, Rockcastle & Cumberland	5
VERSAILLES & MIDWAY	—	Louisville Southern	6
WINCHESTER & BEATTYVILLE	—	Beattyville & Cumberland Gap	1-3

End of Track.

S. P. Guthrie

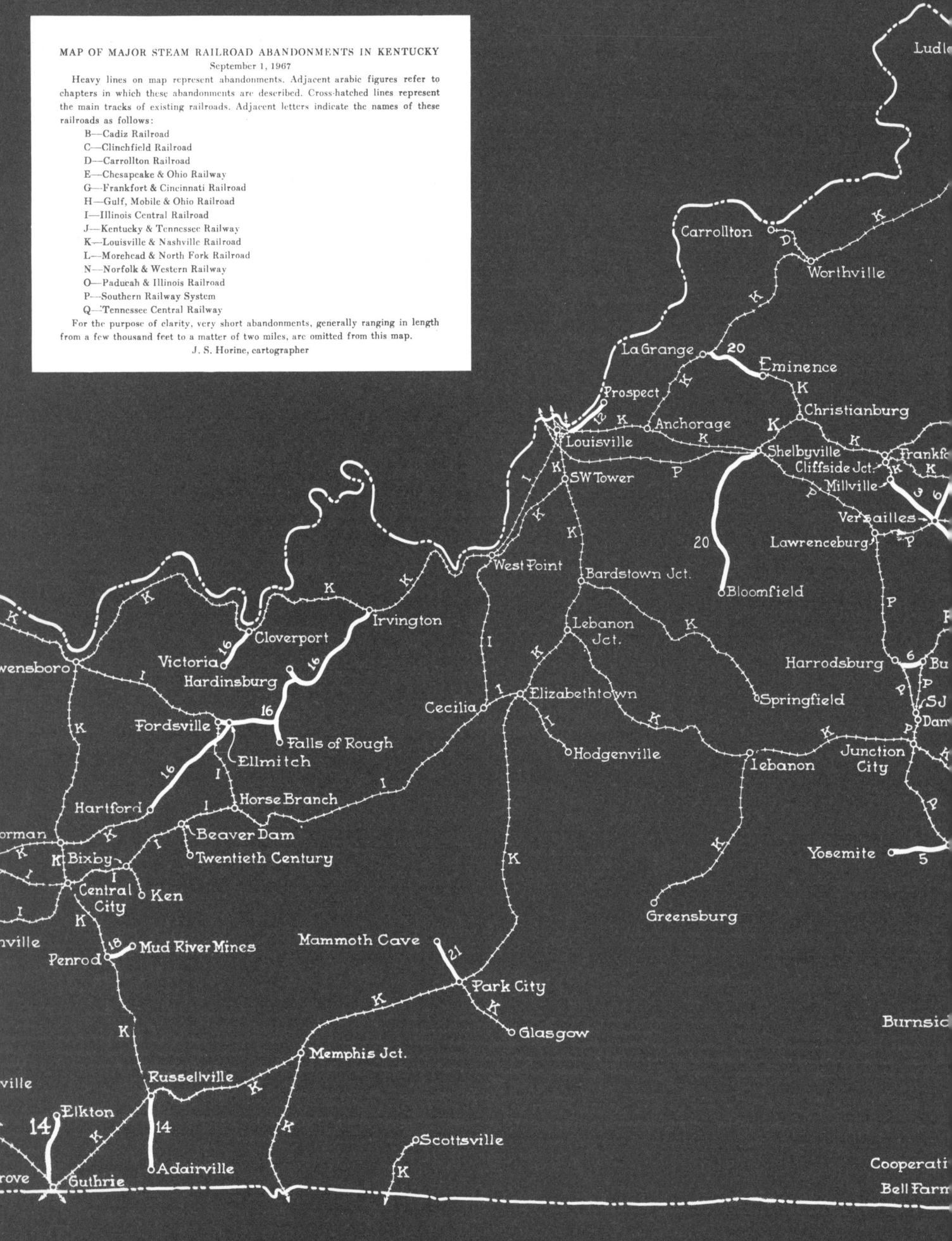